D0222657

# The Hollywood War Machine

Other books by Carl Boggs

*Gramsci's Marxism*

*The Politics of Eurocommunism* (with David Plotke)

*The Impasse of European Communism*

*The Two Revolutions: Antonio Gramsci and the Dilemmas of Western Marxism*

*Social Movements and Political Power*

*Intellectuals and the Crisis of Modernity*

*The Socialist Tradition: From Crisis to Decline*

*The End of Politics: Corporate Power and Decline of the Public Sphere*

*A World in Chaos: Social Crisis and the Rise of Postmodern Cinema* (with Tom Pollard)

*Masters of War*

*Imperial Delusions: American Militarism and Endless War*

# The Hollywood War Machine

## U.S. Militarism and Popular Culture

CARL BOGGS AND TOM POLLARD

*Paradigm Publishers*
Boulder • London

All rights reserved. No part of the publication may be transmitted or reproduced in any media or form, including electronic, mechanical, photocopy, recording, or informational storage and retrieval systems, without the express written consent of the publisher.

Copyright © 2007 Paradigm Publishers

Published in the United States by Paradigm Publishers, 3360 Mitchell Lane, Suite E, Boulder, CO 80305 USA.

Paradigm Publishers is the trade name of Birkenkamp & Company, LLC, Dean Birkenkamp, President and Publisher.

Library of Congress Cataloging-in-Publication Data

Boggs, Carl.
  The Hollywood war machine : U.S. militarism and popular culture / Carl Boggs and Tom Pollard.
     p. cm.
  Filmography: p.
  Includes bibliographical references.
  ISBN-13: 978-1-59451-297-1
  ISBN-10 1-59451-297-3
  ISBN-13: 978-1-59451-298-8 (pbk.)
  ISBN-10: 1-59451-298-1 (pbk.)
1. War films—United States—History and criticism. 2. War and society—United States. 3. Militarism—United States. 4. United States—civilization—21st century. I. Pollard, Tom (Leslie Thomas) II. Title.
  PN1995.9.W3B64 2006
  791.43'658—dc22

                              2006011992

Printed and bound in the United States of America on acid-free paper that meets the standards of the American National Standard for Permanence of Paper for Printed Library Materials.

Designed and Typeset by Cheryl Hoffman

11 10 09 08 07        1 2 3 4 5

*To Iraq Veterans Against the War
and the Goldstar Families for Peace*

# Contents

# Preface

The overriding motif of this book concerns the growing influence of militarism within American popular culture, focusing on the major contribution that mainstream entertainment (notably filmmaking) has made to this corrosive process. What we call the "Hollywood war machine" refers to the production of studio films that depict and glorify the heroic exploits of U.S. military power, either directly or indirectly, across the whole expanse of film history. From its inception, the motion picture industry has been fascinated with warfare not only as entertainment but also as a vital part of the country's deeply patriotic legacy—a phenomenon that has taken on new meaning since the end of the cold war and, more emphatically, since the events of September 11, 2001. From D. W. Griffith through the "good war" films of World War II, cold war hyperdramas, and later action-adventure films starring the likes of Sylvester Stallone, Arnold Schwarzenegger, and Stephen Seagal, Hollywood's addiction to combat films in one form or another has, if anything, deepened. A survey of the Hollywood film tradition reveals that a surprisingly large proportion of movies have dramatized U.S. wartime experiences or have framed combat more broadly along lines of related genres: Westerns, thrillers, horror pictures, sci-fi movies, action-adventure spectacles, and historical dramas.

Following the pattern of great imperial powers throughout history, the United States has produced a culture of militarism in which the themes of warfare, combat, and patriotism have resonated across the entire society. Though the vast majority of Americans may refuse to acknowledge it, perpetual and far-reaching military activity has been an enduring feature of national life, something akin to an addiction consuming the political system, mass media, corporate structure, and even daily life. It would be hard to imagine otherwise, given the ascension of the most powerful war machine the world has ever known. An instrument not merely of national "defense" but of ongoing intervention around the world, the U.S. military provides the American public with spectacular images of patriotic combat against a backdrop of noble crusades against hated demons. As we argue in the following pages, the Hollywood war machine has come to occupy a special cultural and ideological niche within an expanding U.S. imperialism.

The terrorist attacks of 9/11 and their aftermath have given a new dimension to all this. President George W. Bush's pronounced war on terrorism has taken on a character that can only be described as both global and endless, a seemingly religious mission with no finite boundaries of time or space. Indeed the very logic of U.S. militarism—and the multiple forms of blowback it engenders—guarantees precisely this nightmarish future. Insofar as war and preparation for war are endemic to the American grand strategy of global rule, a popular culture that legitimates, even celebrates, that strategy becomes indispensable. And nowhere is the dynamic interaction of culture and politics more visible than in contemporary Hollywood movies that, in one fashion or another, embellish colorful spectacles of violence and warfare. If popular culture helps legitimate domestic power, its role in sustaining the ideological firmaments of U.S. *international* power turns out to be even greater. U.S. efforts to dominate the world economically, politically, and militarily—now brazenly asserted by the elites themselves—thrive upon a labyrinthine network of hegemonic values, attitudes, prejudices, and myths that shape public consciousness. The Hollywood war machine can be located within the main corridors of this ideological fortress. If an ingrained culture of militarism helps generate popular backing for empire, then warfare itself—waged repeatedly by the United States across more than two centuries—depends on intense and widespread patriotic feelings that, in recent years, seem to have morphed into a virulent jingoism. As ultrapatriotism takes hold of the governing system and corporate media, it frames and justifies virtually any Pentagon adventure, obliterating discussion of political alternatives.

One intractable problem with the civic religion of ultrapatriotism is that it corrupts and militarizes those institutions it permeates: corporations, government, universities, the media. As in the Bush administration, much public discourse winds up denatured and twisted by doublespeak in the service of outright imperial ambitions. An obsession with war and warmaking that goes back to the Indian Wars inevitably subverts the universe of collective democratic values—not to mention international rules and laws—allowing the lone superpower in all its mounting hubris to carry out a rogue agenda presided over by a stratum of corporate predators and militarists—an agenda rooted in a pervasive warrior ethos that in the post–cold war milieu seems to recognize few limits to its exercise of power. It reflects the interests of a war economy and security state that have become increasingly self-perpetuating. As Chris Hedges observes in *War Is a Force That Gives Us Meaning,* "the myth of war sells and legitimizes the drug of war. Once we begin to take war's heady narcotic, it creates an addiction that slowly lowers us to the moral depravity of all addicts" (25). One source of this addiction for the American public has been Hollywood cinema, with its decades-long parade of high-tech, ultraviolent, action-filled, hero-driven, patriotic movies, watched by tens of millions of people, which functions as nothing less than propaganda for the warmaking elite.

Ultrapatriotism is one of the great mythologies embedded in American political culture—a product of Manifest Destiny, colonial expansion, growth of the permanent war system, and the continuing legacy of foreign military intervention that has few if any parallels elsewhere. Viewed historically, there is little new about the Bush Doctrine, "preemptive war," unilateralism, or military aggression in violation of international law. Media culture aids and abets this imperial strategy to the fullest extent, with the film industry often in the vanguard. If war is a brutal, dehumanizing experience for those who must endure it, Hollywood cinema performs the function of aestheticizing and romanticizing it in hundreds of movies, as dashing male heroes (military and civilian) take on demonic enemies in defense of every noble cause: democracy, freedom, human rights, civilization itself. Hollywood has done this across its entire history, beginning with early D. W. Griffith pictures and down to the present. Over time the film industry has adeptly transformed the horrors of warfare into vast commodified spectacles that help empower the U.S. war system as it moves along the path of global domination.

To the degree it remains true, as Hedges suggests, that "states at war silence their own authentic humane culture" (63), we might expect the contemporary impact of Hollywood cinema on American public life to confirm the worst. As we argue throughout this book, Hedges's fear is sadly borne out: a large percentage of commercial films tend to be violent, technology-driven extravaganzas largely devoid of historical, social, or dramatic authenticity. Such films—and they are the lifeblood of corporate profit-making—deeply influence other media forms, above all TV and video games. Their greatest influence, moreover, is on youthful mass audiences that are the main targets of increasingly desperate Pentagon recruiters anxious to renovate a crisis-ridden U.S. military. In the meantime, warrior images and symbols have invaded and colonized the public sphere, further eviscerating political dialogue and democratic input on matters of foreign and military policy. This is one reason the Bush administration has had carte blanche in its illegal and immoral move to invade and occupy Iraq.

The United States still operates according to its own time-honored warrior code, no longer that of the lone frontier gunman, local militias, or even the noble grunt of John Wayne lore, but of highly technologized, depersonalized mass killing that is ritual fare in Hollywood movies, which, like the Pentagon, embrace all the glories of technowar. Those few pictures offering antiwar narratives, or dystopic views of combat, frequently succumb to the warrior seductions of the blockbuster spectacle with its fashionable high-tech violence. Probably more than any other medium, film has broken down certain taboos against violence, outlawry, and murder owing to its exciting, digitalized big-screen imagery. Most pictures we explore in the following pages are made by first-rate directors at established studios, with well-known actors and slick cinematography, and costing tens of millions of dollars to produce, advertise, and distribute. They are usually high-tech extravaganzas that reach large audiences in the United States and around the world, reproducing a powerful national mythology shared by liberals and conservatives, Democrats and Republicans alike.

This project is the outgrowth of two earlier works—a book on contemporary film culture that we jointly authored, *A World in Chaos* (2003), and a volume that sets forth a critical analysis of U.S. foreign and military policy, *Imperial Delusions* (2005), written by Carl Boggs. A precursor to these works was Tom Pollard's article "The Hollywood War Machine," published in the anthology edited by Carl Boggs, *Masters of War* (2003), and informed by many themes we develop further in the present book. From the outset our conceptual focus has been on the vital convergence of several discourses: film studies, social theory, cultural criticism, and global concerns related to military power and warfare. Our research and writing has been motivated by a deep revulsion against the ongoing militarization of American society, culture, politics, and foreign policy.

Carl Boggs owes special gratitude to his longtime friend and colleague Ray Pratt, a superb scholar of film, politics, and social theory, for his generous intellectual and personal support spanning nearly four decades. In writing this volume both authors benefited enormously from the many excellent comments and suggestions we received from participants at the "War in Film, TV, and History" conference held in Dallas in November 2004, as well as from reviewers and editors at Paradigm Publishers. We both wish to express our thanks to those at National University who for several years have done everything possible to help sustain our work: Dean Alice Scharper and associate regional deans Maggie Yadegar and Charlene Ashton, vice president for academic affairs Cathleen Greiner, and most of all Jerry C. Lee, longtime president and now chancellor of National University, who has always taken a strong personal interest in our work. Carl Boggs owes a deep personal and intellectual debt to Laurie Nalepa, whose faith in this project has often exceeded his own. Tom Pollard wishes to thank Sue Dickey for her critical feedback as well as constant support, Edna Espanol for her astute advice, and Julie Tsoi for her insightful suggestions.

# Introduction

The steady growth of a militarized society in the United States cannot be understood apart from the expanded role of media culture in its different forms: TV, radio, Internet, publishing, video games, film. An unsurpassed source of information, opinion, and entertainment, the corporate media have become the linchpin of ideological hegemony in the United States, a repository of values, attitudes, and myths that shape public opinion on a daily basis. Transnational media empires like Disney, Time Warner, Viacom, News Corporation, and General Electric, bulwarks of privilege and power, routinely celebrate the blessings of a "free-market" economy, the virtues of personal consumption, the wonders of a political system built on freedom and democracy, a benevolent and peace-loving U.S. foreign policy, the need for a globalized permanent war system to protect against imminent foreign threats, and of course old-fashioned patriotism. A wide panorama of militaristic images and discourses infuses media culture today, probably nowhere more than in Hollywood cinema, helping legitimate record Pentagon budgets and U.S. armed interventions abroad. If elements of the mass media can be viewed as outright propaganda, for the most part we are talking about something entirely different—an extension of already deeply ingrained traditions within the popular and political culture that by the 1990s had come to permeate every corner of American life.

Given the century-long influence of Hollywood movies, and with it the power of related newer media such as TV, video games, and the Internet, it might be useful to adopt Norman Denzin's reference to the United States as something akin to a "cinematic society."[1] Within this conceptual framework we have set out to analyze a cultural phenomenon we identify as the Hollywood war machine, an integral part of the film industry and media culture that produces dozens of motion pictures yearly featuring combat, warfare, and other violent high-tech spectacles. The corporate studios release on average 450 films each year, drawing hundreds of millions of viewers from every class, income, age, ethnic, and gender category—and from every part of the world. Mainstream cinema in general exerts a unique influence on public discourse in great measure owing to its visual power and entertainment appeal. The American culture industry cannot be understood apart from what George Ritzer refers to as "cathedrals of consumption" and Guy Debord long ago identified as the "society of the spectacle."[2] In the following chapters we argue that these dynamic tendencies converge within an increasingly militarized society, both reflecting and feeding into an ensemble of beliefs and attitudes that help sustain U.S. empire and the war system that protects it.

As Denzin observes, "American cinema created a space for a certain kind of communal urban life [just as] Americans entered the public realm," providing a terrain of fantasies, myths, and illusions that would take hold of the popular imagination.[3] Film "became a technology and apparatus of power that would organize and bring meaning to everyday lives."[4] He adds: "Within this birth American society became a cinematic culture, a culture which came to know itself, collectively and individually, through the images and stories that Hollywood produced."[5] This facet of the motion picture industry has grown steadily from the period of its supposed peak popularity in the 1930s and 1940s to an omnipresent cultural force, flexing its power internationally as well as domestically. Today, as Denzin suggests, "the everyday is now defined by the cinematic. The two can no longer be separated. A single epistemological regime governs both fields."[6] As movies have come to simultaneously reflect and shape reality, their trajectory is inseparable from that of the expanding megacorporations, which bind the lives of ordinary citizens to an assortment of fantasies, myths, and illusions churned out by the most far-reaching culture industry ever. The patriotic war experience, embellished and glorified within this culture industry, best captures the essence of the Hollywood war machine. With this in mind, we mention here that our media explorations in this book have been strongly influenced by earlier seminal works on the media/culture industry, including those of the Frankfurt School, Marshall McLuhan, Guy Debord, the Noam Chomsky–Edward Herman work, Jean Beaudrillard, Douglas Kellner, and Robert McChesney.[7] At the same time, we have embarked on some new journeys as our investigations take us into a rapidly changing universe.

By the 1990s the American media had become little more than an extension of gigantic corporate interests, its power increasingly concentrated, global, and, especially after the Telecommunications Act of 1996, far more deregulated and commercialized. Through mergers, acquisitions, worldwide operations, and sheer scope of activity, media culture had grown more pervasive, oligarchical, and profit driven. At the same time, it had become more profoundly *conservative*—a trend evident from even the most superficial glance at the content of TV programs, talk radio, popular magazines and tabloids, and the endless parade of blockbuster movie extravaganzas.[8] The studios had become more commodified as fewer and fewer media empires competed ever more fiercely for consumer markets, which meant that advertising, sales, and marketing took center stage. McChesney writes: "The clear trajectory of our media and communications world tends toward ever-greater corporate concentration, media conglomeration, and hypercommercialism. The notion of public service—that there should be some motive for media other than profit—is in rapid retreat, if not total collapse."[9] Under such circumstances the "public" wound up transformed into a depoliticized mass of atomized, fragmented, and largely passive spectators, while the notion that the media ought to inform, educate, or simply furnish space for open debates appeared more and more archaic, made obsolete by the working of "market forces."

Yet if media culture was now synonymous with corporate power and a crucial pillar of ideological hegemony, then "market forces" surely do not equate with cultural or political neutrality, but rather coincide with the dominant interests and values. The film studios, despite their unwarranted liberal reputation, are an integral part of this structure and its well-planned agendas. As profit-making enterprises first and foremost, the studios favor definite "products"—typically high-tech, fast-paced, violent extravaganzas driven by conventional narratives, heroic deeds, and happy endings. The combat genre itself has been visible in Hollywood since the time of D. W. Griffith, but nowadays this same (though broadened) format extends to other fare including sci-fi, thrillers, horror pictures, and action-adventure movies. It is a format that resonates with the desires of studio executives, producers, and directors attuned to the world of technological wizardry, celebrity actors, and narrative devices (battlefield clashes, car chases, wild shootouts, etc.) appealing to mass audiences already immersed in video games, MTV, and computer technology.[10] The result is a perfect matrix for the familiar convergence of entertainment and propaganda, helping account for both the box-office success and the ideological influence of the Hollywood war machine. Beyond a particular "cycle" or "genre" of films, we refer here to a more general media *commodity* structure that exists also as *spectacle,* reflecting what audiences can expect to see in the *Star Wars* episodes, *Terminator* films, *Batman,* and *War of the Worlds* just as much as in the *Rambo* series, *Top Gun, Saving Private Ryan,* and other easily identified combat pictures.

It is a truism that film audiences today, as in the past, seem little aware of movies as business or political enterprises, oriented as they are to what appears as simple, unmediated entertainment. The average filmgoer does not read *Variety* or other trade periodicals. Of course studios do publicize gross box-office receipts shortly after a picture's release, but they rarely divulge vital information about sources of investment, preproduction budgets, casting, shooting, editing, distribution, and marketing—allocations that can determine success or failure. For many years the film industry was confined to a small group of studios that included Columbia, MGM, Paramount, Twentieth Century Fox, and Warner Bros., where executives wielded nearly absolute control over every aspect of production. By 1988, when Neal Gabler's book *An Empire of Their*

*Own* was published, the old studio system had undergone such radical transformation that Gabler was able to conclude that it had become essentially defunct.[11] At the start of the twenty-first century, just a few of the old studios remain, although even these have been taken over by such conglomerates as Gulf and Western, General Electric, Viacom, Sony, and News Corporation. Controlled mostly by big-time corporate entrepreneurs, investment bankers, and lawyers, the reincarnated studios are more obsessed than ever with profits and marketability, less interested in the quality and originality of what is produced. Today studio executives face entirely new challenges such as competition from TV, the Internet, and cable outlets like HBO and Showtime, and they have responded with new business methods unrecognizable to golden-age executives.

Given the astronomical budgets of many first-run movies, projects soon bring large and risky investments for megacorporations looking furtively at profit-and-loss statements. Production strategies are clearly linked to financial agendas involving some combination of bankers, investment brokers, wealthy entrepreneurs, and celebrity investors, not to mention possible creative profit-sharing with distribution outlets or kindred entertainment firms. The daunting task of bringing motion pictures to the big screen, especially blockbusters, means that "development"—financing, production, distribution, marketing— is bound to consume ever-greater human, material, and technological resources dependent on an army of professionals, technicians, temp workers, agents, and lawyers, not to mention the usual stable of investors. Filmmaking depends on continuous, but always fragile, interaction among studios, banks, talent agencies, unions, insurance companies, lawyers, and consultants, each input presumably leaving some mark on the final product. Delays in filming, unforeseen problems on the set, and cost overruns can prove devastating. Severe difficulties can also arise from code struggles with the Motion Picture Association of America, an industry-run regulatory body responsible for rating film content.

In the "new" Hollywood, limited partnerships, institutional loans, foundation grants, government loans, distribution arrangements, and profit-sharing contracts along with celebrity backing influence filmmaking strategies in ways unheard of in previous decades. Fast-rising production costs, including rich contracts for star actors and technical personnel, account for what are commonly labeled "monster budgets" that by 2004 had reached an *average* of $63.6 million per film. Specific blockbusters can far exceed this budget: *Poseidon* at $175 million, *Pirates of the Caribbean* parts 1 and 2 at $200 million each, *King Kong* at $207 million. By the late 1990s major studios like Fox and Paramount had begun combining their resources to minimize financial risk—for example with the costly ($200 million) production of *Titanic*. "Blockbusters" of an earlier period such as *Gone with the Wind, Cleopatra,* and the early *Star Wars* episodes were made for a tiny fraction of such budgets. Given such bloated costs, investors are predictably less willing to risk their money on innovative, creative, or otherwise outside-the-mainstream projects, especially material that might be regarded as too "political" or "controversial." A studio executive famously lamented this state of affairs when he observed: "Rupert Murdoch isn't looking at the quality of script, I promise you. He's looking at the quality of return."[12] Intense aversion to financial risk can be disastrous for any ambitious Hollywood venture intent on challenging mainstream, formulaic approaches to filmmaking.

This predicament turns out to be even more daunting for producers of combat movies and related fare, which often require special assistance and expertise: access to military bases and equipment, use of warships, airplanes, and vehicles, Pentagon advice, stock footage, and so forth. Cost reductions made possible by this kind of support can be substantial, literally the difference between success and failure. It is difficult to imagine pictures like *Saving Private Ryan, Black Hawk Down,* or *Pearl Harbor,* for example, coming to fruition without Pentagon support. As Lawrence Suid notes, the well-known partnership between Hollywood and the Pentagon, despite its inevitable twists and turns, has solidified over the years, with big-budget combat films depending more and more on provision of troops, equipment, technology, and historical resources.[13] In return for this largesse, of course, the military insists upon special treatment for its all-important operations and personnel—treatment vital to its public image and its ability to secure budgetary requests and meet recruitment quotas. With few exceptions, the Pentagon has supported only those movies depicting courageous American troops fighting (and winning) noble wars against hated enemies—a maxim that applies, though less strictly, to comparable genres. Films departing from this modality—*From Here to Eternity, Apocalypse Now,* Oliver Stone's Vietnam trilogy, *Memphis Belle*—have been deprived of military support, explaining why most filmmakers today, with their swollen budgets, tend to embrace "good war" motifs and shy away from antiwar messages of the sort found in *All Quiet on the Western Front* and *Born on the Fourth of July.* Whether the advent of digital technology can relieve such pressures on producers and directors who want to capture more "realistic" images and narratives of modern warfare remains to be seen.

Given the huge budgets needed to make high-profile mainstream films, the odds against projects with distinctly antiwar themes, or with narratives that focus on Pentagon misconduct, strategic blunders, misuse of funds, or botched war planning—not to mention possible atrocities or war crimes committed by U.S. forces—have risen dramatically. (Such critical motifs are restricted to lower-budget documentaries and small indie movies, viewed by much smaller "art-house" audiences.) After World War I a few Hollywood pictures appeared questioning the warrior mentality and conventional ways of thinking about combat—for example, *The Big Parade* and *All Quiet on the Western Front,* both of which reached mass audiences. A similar cycle followed the intensely unpopular Vietnam War, including *The Deer Hunter, Coming Home, Platoon, Born on the Fourth of July,* and *Full-Metal Jacket.* By the 1990s, however, the situation had profoundly reversed: films with even the most tepid criticisms of the U.S. military were far less likely to receive Pentagon assistance. One recent startling exception is the powerful antiwar documentary *Why We Fight,* which did receive ample Pentagon support; the brass must have believed (no doubt correctly) that the picture would never achieve much box-office success. In the context of 9/11, the Bush presidency, preemptive warfare, and U.S. armed interventions in Afghanistan and Iraq, the political atmosphere shifted rightward, with heightened media emphasis on patriotism, the war on terror, and efforts to rally the population against foreign enemies—hardly an atmosphere conducive to big-budget blockbusters that might challenge any or all of this. Movies like *Black Hawk Down, Behind Enemy Lines, Under Siege, Pearl Harbor,* and *Windtalkers* are certain to be the order of the day for at least the immediate future.

The deepening militarization of American popular and political culture corresponds to the global realities of the current period: U.S. imperial power, measured in economic, political, cultural, and above all military terms, now reaches every corner of the globe, dwarfing all previous empires. Of course ruling elites want the public to believe this power is being wielded for entirely noble ends, for universal principles of freedom, democracy, and human rights, in accordance with the long-held myth of Manifest Destiny—a sense of imperial entitlement—but the historical actuality has always clashed with that convenient self-image. From its beginnings the United States moved inexorably along the path of colonialism, racism, and militarism, first waging the Indian Wars and conquering vast areas of Mexico, and then, following the settlement of North America, pushing outward into Central and South America and Asia at the end of the Spanish-American War. For most of the twentieth century the United States was at war (or preparing for war), across the two world wars, Korea, Vietnam, Central America, the Balkans, Afghanistan, and Iraq, with no end in sight at the start of the twenty-first century. World War II established the permanent war economy, later bringing with it a security state of epic proportions—the kind of military-industrial complex that President Dwight Eisenhower warned about at the end of his presidency.[14] By the 1990s the United States had firmly established itself as an unchallenged superpower backed by the largest war machine ever, with bases in 130 nations, a growing military presence in space, and consumption of more resources than all other major armed forces in the world combined.

Continued expansion of the U.S. war machine, misleadingly labeled a "defense" system, has reconfigured every dimension of American life: economy, politics, culture, social relations, foreign policy. The warnings of Eisenhower and others at the time have been validated many times over. The system is sustained ideologically by the strong tradition of national "exceptionalism" reflected in Manifest Destiny, the Monroe Doctrine, a peculiarly messianic nationalism, and a long series of presidential "doctrines" endowing U.S. leaders with the right to intervene anywhere national interests are considered to be at stake. Bush II's doctrine of preemptive war is therefore no radical departure but follows a long pattern of imperial arrogance and self-righteousness, backed by military force. President Jimmy Carter's State of the Union speech in 1980 contains a passage that will suffice as a typical example: "An attempt by any outside force to gain control of the Persian Gulf region will be regarded as an assault on the vital interests of the United States of America, and such an assault will be repelled by any means necessary, including military force." In 1986 the Christian fundamentalist Pat Robertson announced that the United States was anointed to "rule the world for God," a sentiment widely held today. While politicians and the media routinely frame exceptionalism as proof that the United States is innately democratic and peaceful, in historical reality the country has always been a warrior culture propelled by the same interests as previous empires: resources, markets, cheap labor, national chauvinism, geopolitical advantage. What makes the United States unique today is the distinctly *global* character of its interests and ambitions at a time when leading strategists are increasingly overt and brazen about the blessings of U.S. world domination. While the new grand strategy is typically attributed to the neoconservatives, in fact the events of 9/11 and the war on terror have further legitimated this imperium in the minds of liberals and conservatives, Democrats and Republicans alike. Congress has fully endorsed every step along the road to invasion and occupation of Iraq, with the media and the bulk of academia totally compliant in this brazen exercise of militarism.

Unlimited military power appears to give the majority of Americans a sense of national pride if not grandeur, something dramatically shown at the time of the first Persian Gulf War, which TV and other media outlets glorified as a combat spectacle, mobilizing widespread but ersatz feelings of community and empowerment. Military supremacy, moreover, came to be equated with *moral* and *political* supremacy; armed victory both extirpated the famous "Vietnam syndrome" (public aversion to costly foreign interventions) and reaffirmed the legacy of exceptionalism. Further, the very real threat of terrorism after 9/11 served to reinforce the long-held myth that U.S. power (by definition benevolent) was needed to overcome the chaos and violence of a Hobbesian universe filled with evildoers intent on destroying American freedom and democracy. As the Iraq venture shows, however, U.S. militarism has veered entirely out of control. Reflecting on Iraq, T. D. Allman writes that we are witnessing a "systemic dysfunction in America," a colossus that "struts the world stage . . . on steroids" and now "poses the greatest threat to world peace" among all countries.[15] In Iraq the United States has carried out brazenly illegal military aggression, occupied a sovereign nation, killed an estimated hundred thousand people, tortured prisoners, and wasted untold hundreds of billions of dollars in pursuit of naked resource and geopolitical interests, all with contemptuous disregard for the United Nations and justified by an endless barrage of lies and deceptions.

The Iraq disaster has generated astonishingly little opposition from within the political establishment; until early 2006 the Bush/neocon stratagem was fully endorsed by the Democratic leadership. This is no aberration from long-established patterns. As Floyd Rudmin comments: "There is something wrong at a much deeper level in American political culture. The American malady of militarism extends across decades, across generations, and is so deeply rooted in the American mind that attacking another nation seems to be the natural, spontaneous reaction of choice."[16] Thus recent U.S. violations of the UN Charter outlawing unprovoked attacks on sovereign nations (not only Iraq but Afghanistan, Yugoslavia, and Panama) simply reveal longstanding U.S. contempt for the UN when it refuses to go along with superpower designs. The United States has violated or rejected a long series of international treaties and agreements concerning, for example, the militarization of space, nuclear proliferation, chemical warfare, land-mine bans, and global warming. It has dismissed the International Criminal Court, supported by some 150 nations, fearful that its jurisdiction will intrude on U.S. freedom to pursue its imperial ventures. The United States has opted to set up and finance its own tribunals in The Hague and Baghdad to try designated enemies.

U.S. exceptionalism has always been linked to the idea of "global activism" embedded in the nineteenth-century frontier push westward, Theodore Roosevelt's colonial triumphalism, Woodrow Wilson's plan to "democratize" the world, the Truman Doctrine justifying intervention anywhere on U.S. terms, John F. Kennedy's cold war liberalism, and of course Bush II's strategy of preemptive war. Bush's State of the Union address in January 2006 vigorously restates this heritage: the United States is called upon by God and history to fulfill the imperatives of a global order that "would end tyranny in our world." Citing the great blessings of Providence, Bush said that "we accept the call of history to deliver the oppressed." In his speech the president seemed fixated on purging all lingering sentiments of "isolationism" and defeatism that might impose limits on U.S. efforts to "remap" the Middle East and dominate the globe, although where such sentiments are likely to be found among the elites was never made clear. That a country so stridently interventionist across its entire history—one now wielding unprecedented global power—could possibly embrace isolationism strains credulity, but the fear that public opinion, tired of the risks and costs of a fraudulent war, might turn against the Iraq disaster is surely genuine.

Despite such fears, the idea that the United States has an inalienable right to rule the world by force, to frame its own doctrines, rules, and laws, remains a durable feature of the political culture. The Iraq war is just the latest manifestation of national exceptionalism, bolstered by elevated levels of economic, technological, and military strength. The principle of universality that the United States avowedly upholds is in fact regularly violated and subverted.[17] Invasion and occupation of nations, aerial attacks on civilian populations, support for brutal regimes and death squads, the practice of torture—all this has come to seem acceptable and readily justifiable to elites fully convinced that their mission is one of peace and democracy. According to the neocon Robert Kaplan, writing in *Warrior Politics,* the American public ought to be proud of its military tradition, for that tradition is needed as the weapon of a special nation destined to fight chaos, mob rule, terrorism, and barbarism wherever they surface around the world. In a Hobbesian jungle the United States is obligated to erect a powerful Leviathan that cannot be squeamish about the use of armed force. Kaplan writes: "As Machiavelli cruelly but accurately puts it, progress often comes from hurting others."[18] Dismissing international law as utopian, he adds: "Alas, our prize for winning the Cold War is not merely the opportunity to expand NATO, or to hold democratic elections in places that never had them, but something far broader: *We and nobody else will write the terms for international society.*"[19] It would be difficult to find a bolder contemporary reaffirmation of Manifest Destiny. Elsewhere, after insisting it is time the United States extirpated, Rambo-style, all "pacifist tendencies," Kaplan argues that it is ordinary American troops on the ground who are today's global heroes battling on many fronts the ubiquitous evildoers.[20]

In neocon Donald Kagan's words, "the ambition to play a grand role on the world stage is deeply rooted in the American character."[21] Like Kaplan, he sees a world of unending chaos, violence, and anarchy that U.S. military power is uniquely equipped to counter under the banner of modern civilization. The problem with European nations today, writes Kagan, is their reluctance to use armed force toward this end, preferring instead the security of the "U.S. umbrella" and social over military spending. Thus, "Europeans have stepped out of the Hobbesian world of anarchy into the Kantian world of perpetual peace."[22] In other words, the Europeans have become mired in pure fantasy, quite at odds with the "realistic" outlook of Americans familiar with a long history of imperial expansion and military intervention. With such hubris, unfortunately, there are few psychological or military limits. In his frenzied support of the Iraq war, Christopher Hitchens refers approvingly to Bush's goal of "regime change," which "has come to mean less and less a secondhand involvement in a proxy struggle waged by other people, and more and more a direct and avowed engagement in the enterprise of invading and then remaking someone else's country."[23] This kind of imperialist mentality, made recently fashionable by the neocons, was not invented by Bush or even the neocons but, as we have seen, has the imprimatur of many Bush predecessors. In 1844 President James Polk outrageously instigated war against Mexico, lied about threats to U.S. security, and waged preemptive attacks to steal half of Mexican lands, all in the name of national progress. More than a century later, liberal icon JFK inspired a new wave of U.S. global activism: "Other countries look to their own interests. Only the United States has obligations which stretch 10,000 miles across the Pacific, and 4000 miles across the Atlantic, and thousands of miles to the South. Only the U.S. . . . bears that kind of burden."[24] Precisely who or what endowed the United States with such far-reaching burdens Kennedy never specified. It was JFK, of course, who set in motion the Vietnam War, one of the great catastrophes of modern times.

To the degree war and orientation toward war have become a way of life in the United States, the society can be said to have grown addicted to war, above all economically but also politically and culturally. It takes little effort to see that empire manifests itself domestically as well as internationally, all the more so since 9/11. Bush and the neocons, after all, have promised an endless, protracted war on diabolical enemies spread around the world. As with Rome and later empires, the pursuit of imperial domination has enduring consequences: vast funding for a war machine, staggering human and material costs of intervention, blowback, consolidation of a security state, subversion of democratic values and practices, widespread civic violence, and the decay of public infrastructures, as recently dramatized by the Hurricane Katrina debacle. Meanwhile, an aggressive war system creates more enemies abroad (blowback), *undermining* instead of reinforcing national security. The militarization of society and the political system, moreover, narrows public debate, stalling any popular efforts to counter deteriorating social conditions. Neal Wood refers to the "tyranny of advanced capitalism" in the United States that "imposes its will and discipline initially in the workplace. Then it penetrates and seizes control over the political apparatus. The victim of capitalist tyranny, America is neither substantively nor procedurally a democracy in any very meaningful sense of the term."[25] He adds that the vacuity of national politics means "numerous fundamental questions in domestic and international politics require urgent attention, informed discussion and speedy resolution, but . . . little is being done."[26]

Since at least the late 1970s, American elites have worked strenuously to extend the doctrine of Manifest Destiny across the entire globe, premised on a strategy of first controlling the Middle East in order to secure a resource and geopolitical foothold. This gambit was facilitated by the Soviet exit from the world scene in 1991, an epochal moment that happened to coincide with the first Gulf War. The famous "New World Order" enunciated by President Bush I at that time would be a unipolar globe dominated by the United States, with American power making the world safe for unfettered neoliberal globalization. By the 1990s the United States was indeed the first truly unrivaled imperial power, its every move calculated to negate possible future challengers: Russia, China, Europe, Japan. The goal of world domination was clearly laid out in a series of government and quasi-official documents and statements beginning in the early 1990s, with military action against Iraq a taken-for-granted priority always placed at the top of the agenda. By "remapping" the Middle East, the

United States would gain a stranglehold over oil and other resources at a time of growing demand and declining supply worldwide. This "new imperialism," resting increasingly on *military* power, was taken up not only by the neocon hawks but also by leaders of both major parties. Within this scenario, as the United States arrogantly pursues global hegemony in a cauldron of chaos and violence, the distinction between war and peace, armed engagement and politics as usual, begins to disintegrate, as militarism and "terrorism" now have the impetus to spread to all regions of the planet.

At a time of expanding U.S. imperial power, when the American people are asked to endure burdensome costs and sacrifices, the always-vital mechanisms of legitimation take on new meaning. All power structures need systemic ideological and cultural supports, or "hegemony," along the lines theorized by Antonio Gramsci, but the imperatives of empire serve to ultimately intensify these ordinary requirements. Empire, a bloated war economy, constant armed interventions—all these must be made to appear "natural," routine, and desirable if not noble. Themes of national exceptionalism, superpatriotism, the glories of high-tech war, and the demands of a (global) civilizing mission help satisfy this legitimation function, as does the impenetrable hubris associated with economic, technological, and military supremacy. To translate such an ideological syndrome into popular language, to fully incorporate it into the political culture, is the task not so much of a classical propaganda apparatus as of a developed educational system and media culture appropriate to advanced capitalism. In the United States today, as we have seen, media culture is an extension of megacorporations that comprise the largest and most influential media-entertainment complex the world has ever seen. And the Hollywood war machine, as we argue in the following chapters, has become increasingly central to this complex—a crucial instrument for the legitimation of empire.

The U.S. plan for global domination brings with it a growing concentration of corporate, government, and military power surrounded by a refined law-enforcement and surveillance apparatus that, while in some ways indispensable, cannot by itself possibly furnish *legitimation.* That is the function of media culture. Hollywood filmmaking contributes admirably to this function, despite the release of pictures here and there that run counter to the dominant paradigm. Legitimation occurs not primarily by means of censorship or propaganda (though both exist) but through ordinary canons and formulas of studio production, where "conspiracies" are scarcely necessary to enforce hegemonic codes. The repetitive fantasies, illusions, myths, images, and story lines of Hollywood movies can be expected to influence mass audiences in predictable ways, much in the fashion of advertising. One popular response to the flood of violent combat, action-adventure, sci-fi, and horror films is a stronger readiness to support U.S. military operations, which, in a patriotically charged milieu, will require little justification. (Indeed the popular ethical standards for what constitutes a "rational" armed intervention are scandalously loose.) This aspect of legitimation is unique to the foreign policy of the United States, the only nation with a sprawling network of military bases around the world.

To be sure, complex societies like the United States have many agencies of politicization, but none today rival the power of media culture. As Douglas Kellner points out: "Media culture spectacles demonstrate who has power and who is powerless, who is allowed to exercise force and violence, and who is not. They dramatize and legitimate the power of the forces that be and demonstrate to the powerless that if they fail to conform, they risk incarceration or death."[27] It is a culture overwhelmingly geared toward young people—not only film but also TV, video games, and music—whose social views are in their formative stage and thus highly malleable. That such views might be partial, uneven, and lacking in coherence hardly detracts from their *intensity*, which often achieves its peak around issues of patriotism and use of military force. The corporate media routinely translate U.S. imperial agendas into deeply felt popular beliefs and attitudes about the world and the U.S. role in it, usually validating something akin to the motif of Manifest Destiny. Despite its liberal image, therefore, Hollywood tends to produce expensive, high-tech, entertaining movies that, directly or indirectly, help satisfy the ideological requirements for empire. One might go further: owing to powerful tendencies within the general culture, the once-prevailing liberal tradition itself appears to have lost its significant hold on public opinion as it collapses into the new conservative hegemony.[28]

We concede that it is difficult to measure the precise impact of any media form on the popular consciousness; the available instruments are much too crude and the social mediations too numerous. We can, however, identify with some specificity the particular *content* of films and other media forms, which can be investigated and decoded just as we would literature and other texts or discourses, and that is the task we have set for ourselves in this project. We assume, further, that the societal influence of movies and related forms we subsume under the heading "Hollywood war machine" has been, and probably will continue to be, quite substantial. We are convinced this is true for several reasons: huge audiences; the seductions of modern cinematic technology; the intersection between film content and what is conveyed by other media, including advertising; and the commonsense observation that what people are exposed to as a steady diet will inevitably shape their beliefs and attitudes. At the same time, as mentioned above, insofar as teenage audiences are the main target of blockbuster marketing, they are more likely to psychologically *assimilate* whatever ideological motifs a film conveys than would older audiences. We have abundant indicators—increased levels of violent youth crime, gang membership, gun ownership, and civil clashes, for example—suggesting that the familiar "culture of violence" has intensified over the past two decades, a theme running through Michael Moore's documentary *Bowling for Columbine*, which also looks at the contributing role of the warfare state. We should not be surprised to find a correlation between these indicators and elevated public support for U.S. armed ventures abroad. By late 2005, it is true, public opposition to the Iraq war had galvanized, but most questioning stemmed from the escalating *costs* of a war and occupation viewed as a failure rather than any political or moral revulsion. Such antiwar sentiment, moreover, scarcely made a dent in the armor of the political establishment.

What generalizations, then, might be formulated regarding films that we have identified as part of the Hollywood war machine? Although the images, narratives, and ideological motifs we explore in this book diverge enormously from one picture to another, from one genre to another, several basic themes clearly emerge from our analysis:

1. U.S. military forces are innately driven by noble ends, an assumption so embedded in movie images and narratives that it rarely demands much overt articulation within the script. While this is a distinctly "good war" staple, it applies to *any* combat activity (broadly defined) where it can be shown that evil demons must be vanquished by American troops. Even in those films that convey the "war is hell" theme (*Black Hawk Down, Saving Private Ryan, The Thin Red Line*), we see that larger American objectives create the very *necessity* of war, justifying all the painful costs and sacrifices.

2. Enemy forces are routinely shown as primitive and barbaric—Nazis and Japs in World War II, gooks in Korea and Vietnam, ragheads in the Gulf War—a cinematic portrait often infused with strong elements of racism and national chauvinism. In terrorist-themed pictures Arabs are with few exceptions shown as subhuman agents of destruction lacking any motive or purpose.[29] Like Indians of Western movie lore, opposition to U.S. military power is seen as the work of cartoonish, one-dimensional male warriors whose very mission is to visit evil on the world. In the form of demons, moreover, such figures are easily dehumanized, making them ready fodder for mass extermination, as graphically depicted in such films as *Sands of Iwo Jima* and *Windtalkers*.

3. U.S. military forces inevitably triumph, often against seemingly insurmountable odds, even if a few lesser skirmishes are lost in the meantime. In "good war" scenarios American troops will commonly be outnumbered but manage to prevail owing to superior guile and ability, better technology, perhaps embellished by acts of John Wayne–style heroism, visible for example in *Hamburger Hill*. Even terrible defeats have been transformed by Hollywood into improbable victories—for example, *Pearl Harbor* (shifting the focus to the daring Doolittle raid on Tokyo) and Rambo's Vietnam ("We get to win this time!").

4. In contrast to typically faceless and often disheveled enemy forces, U.S. officers and enlisted men are shown as belonging to a well-organized

national military structure, bound by strong leadership, discipline, order, and dedication—features that lend Americans an aura of efficiency and authority. Chaos and disarray are traits linked to backwardness, while strong organization is tied to "progress" and enlightened values. Even the most heroic actions are mediated through the military command system, as in *Saving Private Ryan* and *U-571*. One rare exception is *Behind Enemy Lines,* where a downed navy pilot is forced to survive on hostile terrain, cut off from his supporting units.

5.  Supreme military technology always prevails over weaker (though possibly more numerous) enemy troops, a maxim carried over from hundreds of combat Westerns designed to show the "primitive" character of Indians in their resistance to white-settler modernity—a motif emphatically repeated when the designated opponent is Arab. Advanced technology is equated not only with elevated moral status but also with an epic victory of "civilization" over barbaric enemies—a trope permeating films about the Pacific theater in World War II and later representations of Asians in Korea and Vietnam.[30] The Gulf War media spectacle referred to above fits this pattern, from the first U.S. aerial blitz in 1991 to the "shock-and-awe" campaign of 2003.

6.  Despite its horrors, war crosses the big screen as an exhilarating human activity, the most noble and even existential of all personal experiences, filtered through larger-than-life visual images made possible by the wonders of modern cinematography, including digital imaging. The more the nightmares of combat are presented as visually graphic and beautified by special effects, the more they seem to appeal to mass audiences. This aesthetic dimension of warfare is realized through several devices: dazzling technology, triumph of good over evil, exotic locales, breathtaking heroism. Here the Hollywood war machine marks a unique culmination of the merger between war and entertainment, combat and art, which turns out to be yet another manifestation of the cinematic society.

7.  It is by now an axiom that Hollywood effortlessly turns warfare into a media spectacle, a tendency shared with TV and video games, all beneficiaries of much the same technology. Violence and bloodshed, the inevitable price of military victory, become the stuff of cinematic overkill, whether in the hands of Tony Scott or Oliver Stone, Edward Zwick or Stanley Kubrick. The war spectacle is best exemplified by the work of Steven Spielberg, the master not only of the combat genre (*Empire of the Sun, Saving Private Ryan*) but also of related fare like *Indiana Jones* and *War of the Worlds*. If scenarios of death and destruction are the inescapable fruits of empire, they are simultaneously the stock-in-trade of Hollywood blockbusters, both mirroring and contributing to the irrepressible culture of militarism.

8. As the war phenomenon becomes a sacralized feature of American society—that is, as violent campaigns attached to "higher" values (democracy, freedom, human rights, etc.) take on a quasi-religious meaning—cinematic heroism too comes to occupy a special niche in the culture. Hundreds of mainstream films depict glamorous, courageous military leaders able to storm the heavens and remake the world, or at least make the world "safe" for all the wonderful "American" virtues to flourish. Examples are not difficult to find: John Wayne, Patton, Rambo, the Terminator, *Top Gun*. Combat heroism, moreover, is often fueled by motives of vengeance as the protagonist sets out to punish wrongdoers for some earlier transgression or atrocity, as in the *Rambo* episodes.

9. Patriotism, most often represented as jingoism or ultrapatriotism, is a defining feature of the Hollywood war machine, above all the good-war cycle long a favorite subgenre of studio filmmakers. If, as Hedges argues, "war is a force that gives us meaning," it does so mainly by virtue of the viewer's psychological attachment to the nation and its ascribed identities or missions.[31] Indeed, the most emotionally compelling images of patriotism usually appear within the war setting. (Think of the billowing American flag that crosses the screen at the end of *Saving Private Ryan* or the planting of the flag on Mount Suribachi in *Sands of Iwo Jima*.) The modern film experience lends itself to the kinds of psychological responses that such scenes are calculated to instill, and few are more cathartic than nationalism. Empire, the security state, the permanent war economy, the warrior mythology—none of these could be sustained in the absence of patriotic legitimation. After all, the twentieth century has shown that both war and patriotism endow otherwise powerless individuals with a sense of being able to achieve something in a difficult and confining world. Hedges refers to the "plague of nationalism" as providing something of a false communal enterprise, and this must be considered one of the signal contributions of the cinematic society.

Among the nearly two hundred films we explore in this book, few will exhibit *all* of these motifs; the vast majority, however, will be seen to contain most of them, with inevitable consequences for how Americans think about U.S. foreign and military policy—and about their own society. The point here is that such a wide panorama of militarized images and narratives, visible across several decades, has contributed deeply to the legitimation of empire. The Hollywood war machine, we argue, remains a dominant feature of the American landscape at the start of the twenty-first century—a logical parallel to the permanent war system, with its frightening prospects for world peace. The blockbuster as larger-than-life media spectacle takes on a special role in all this. We concede that a number of important mainstream films stand apart from the dominant pattern, witness the antiwar pictures that now and then cross the cinematic terrain—for example, *Born on the Fourth of July* and, in a different vein, *The Thin Red Line.* Some embrace the "war is hell" motif. We conclude, however, that the influence of such films is dwarfed by the much larger output of motion pictures that fit the prevailing norm, which usually wind up reproducing elements of the war spectacle, given their embrace of standard cinematic devices for conveying the "realism" of warfare.

Can it be said that the Hollywood war machine, having come to fruition during an age of empire, operates essentially as a *propaganda* apparatus that sends out crude messages to gullible mass audiences on the model of earlier authoritarian regimes? The popular consensus behind U.S. militarism, revealed again during the invasion and occupation of Iraq, might well be viewed as evidence for the propaganda model. David Robb, in his book *Operation Hollywood,* argues for this point of view, suggesting that the film industry has become a full-blown propaganda vehicle, one of the most powerful opinion-forming mechanisms ever. (Robb's work is limited strictly to motion pictures.) We know that "propaganda" is supposed to be alien to the American experience, but Robb convincingly describes a process that is largely unseen by the public in which blatant political messages in support of Pentagon interests are regularly and brazenly transmitted to viewers fully convinced they are getting nothing more than "entertainment." Thus, "the military propaganda that is inserted into our television programs in the form of films and TV shows is done so subtly the American people don't even know it's there."[32] The undeniable fact that the United States has grown more warlike over the past fifty years is cited by Robb as validation of a sophisticated propaganda model.

Robb is surely correct to emphasize the growth of efforts at ideological manipulation in American society over the past few decades, a trend surely accelerated by the events of 9/11, not to mention the expansion of media culture. He is also on the mark when he points to the increased public readiness to endorse U.S. military ventures, again more easily understood with the onset of Bush's war on terror. At the same time, whether the film medium as such can be described as a propaganda outlet is another matter. While some pictures might well fit this model, and many clearly bear the imprint of Pentagon influence, our conclusions in the following pages depart significantly from Robb's: filmmakers, most of them already immersed in the political culture and the canons of patriotism, typically do not require formal government censorship or controls as they look to produce movies that fit the contours of U.S. foreign and military policy—nor do they in fact need or prefer heavy-handed brain-washing techniques that can only run counter to entertainment values (and thus box-office prospects). For producers like Jerry Bruckheimer and directors like Michael Bay, patriotic war spectacles are merely business as usual at the Hollywood studios. The motifs we have identified above simply flow with the cinematic-political terrain. Many filmmakers who are ordinarily inclined toward liberal or progressive scripts on *domestic* issues often suddenly lose that same critical edge once matters reach the water's edge: patriotism nearly always trumps progressivism when it comes to global politics. There is nothing particularly surprising or even novel about this—consider the earlier cases of John Ford, Howard Hawks, and Frank Capra, all strong liberals who would never be outdone in their celebration of patriotic warrior virtues.

The expanded role of propaganda *outside* Hollywood cinema, not to be denied, actually ends up reinforcing the capacity of motion pictures to help ideologically bolster empire and the war system. Movies could be even more effective instruments than outright propaganda. In his provocative book *The War on Truth,* Nafeez Mossadeq Ahmed writes: "A massive external threat is an ideally convenient excuse to consolidate and expand U.S. hegemony, further counter Russian, Chinese, and European rivals, and to drum up the domestic consensus required to legitimate the unrelentingly interventionist character of U.S. foreign policy in the new and unlimited 'war on terror.'"[33] What Ahmed describes converges with yet another trend: the corporate colonization of a political system that increasingly operates as little more than an organized machine in the service of narrow elite interests. The operation relies heavily on ideological manipulation and combines the work of diverse sectors: party elites, corporations, media, the government, lobbies, and an assortment of think tanks and foundations.[34] In this corporatist milieu what has historically been called propaganda extends across the entire social and political landscape. In polls conducted during and after the Bush run-up to the Iraq war, for example, a strong majority of Americans was shown to believe the repeated outlandish lies and justifications behind the invasion. In fact the whole stratagem of "regime change" was stage-managed by the government and military, with total media complicity. In the field reporters were "embedded" and muzzled, fully beholden to Pentagon agendas, while those few outside the patriotic stable were often targeted and in many cases assaulted or killed. Framing of the Iraq war as a moment of "liberation" represents the pinnacle of a media culture bringing together war and entertainment in pursuit of corporate profits, the subject of such documentaries as Robert Greenwald's *Outfoxed* and Danny Schechter's *Weapons of Mass Deception.*

James Bamford has documented the trail of propaganda that paved the way toward a war that Bush and the neocons had decided to launch months and even years before the March 2003 invasion, indeed well before 9/11. The Pentagon, the Central Intelligence Agency, and the White House utilized the sprawling public-relations network of the John Rendon Group to carry out "perception management" of epic proportions, helping establish the ideological conditions for war against Iraq despite the lack of UN authorization and the absence of any clear threat posed by the Saddam Hussein regime. The campaign depended on large-scale saturation of the media with false reports, lies, distortions, and a variety of contrived pro-war stories with the collaboration of writers like Judith Miller of the *New York Times*. Bamford writes that "never before in history had such an extensive secret network been established to shape the entire world's perception of a war."[35] That is not all: with the U.S. occupation in full force, it was revealed that Pentagon contractors regularly paid Iraqi newspapers to publish glowing stories about the war and the role of U.S. troops as benevolent "liberators"—a propaganda enterprise that, though costly, was completely hidden from the American public. The Washington, D.C.–based Lincoln Group was given tens of millions of dollars to infiltrate the Iraq media over a period of nearly two years.[36] The war, from the outset unpopular around the world, was conducted within a framework of sustained domestic and international media manipulation. Its initial ideological success, at least on the home front, cannot be doubted, but the protracted occupation and insurgency—along with continuous revelations of flagrant Bush administration deceit—began to erode even domestic supports for a costly and losing intervention.

In the aforementioned 2005 documentary *Why We Fight*, Eugene Jarecki builds his indictment of the U.S. war system on President Eisenhower's 1961 warning about the dangers of an out-of-control military-industrial complex, which by now comes across as rather understated. Neither Eisenhower nor Jarecki, however, calls attention to a crucial pillar of the system: a militarized popular culture that has only deepened over the past few decades. If the Hollywood war machine does not fully constitute a modern propaganda apparatus, its role in the legitimation process no doubt *surpasses* that of any such apparatus, since its spectacular images and narratives, produced and marketed as "entertainment," probably are more effective than any heavy-handed attempts at media censorship and control. Meanwhile, the big studio productions, part of a thriving cinematic culture, have become integral to the very state-corporate order that underlies both the film industry and Eisenhower's nightmare of a military-industrial complex.

# CHAPTER 1

# Militarism in American Popular Culture

At the start of the twenty-first century the United States has emerged as the greatest military power in history, an empire possessing all the features of a mature warrior society: permanent war economy, expanded security state, vast armed presence around the world and in space, a militarized order unlike anything ever known. It is a system increasingly grounded in—more accurately, addicted to—the deadly but profitable mobilization for warfare, a system that celebrates the spectacle, technology, great successes, and above all *power* that militarism brings to a political order bent on global domination. While such an order cherishes and indeed fetishizes the ethos of armed power, its reproduction demands a far-reaching *culture* of militarism that enters into and transforms the daily life of a population willing (under definite conditions) to give its consent to imperial adventures. Militarism appears as a form of *ideology,* a rationality that deeply influences the structures and practices of the general society through storytelling, mythology, media images, political messages, academic discourses, and simple patriotic indoctrination. While the intimate connection between institutional and cultural modes of power, between the military and daily life, is scarcely new, it has taken on new dimensions with the dramatic growth of media culture (including film) over the past few decades. If the culture of militarism endows warfare agendas with a popular sense of meaning and purpose, it also represents the hegemonic facade behind which corporate and Pentagon domination can more or less freely assert itself, both domestically and worldwide. The decay of American economic, political, and social life cannot be understood apart from this destructive cycle, bound to worsen owing to the frightful consequences of 9/11 and what is expected to be an endless U.S. war against terrorism that, in effect, amounts to a desperate struggle to maintain all the advantages of empire.

The phenomenon of war and warmaking both reflects and gives further impetus to a developmental pattern associated with this deepening culture of militarism. Beneath the "civilized" or "enlightened" norms of democratic society and modernity it is possible to detect a legacy of domestic and global violence that brings out some of the darkest impulses and contradicts familiar expectations of human progress tied to industrial and technological development. This was the compelling message of Michael Moore's Oscar-winning 2002 documentary *Bowling for Columbine,* which established a close linkage between regularized outbreaks of violence in everyday American life and continuous U.S. armed interventions around the world since World War II. A long history of aggressive foreign policy—carried out in the name of grandiose ideals—has been made possible not only through the workings of the political system and economy but also through the legitimating mechanisms of culture understood in the broadest sense. Here "culture" incorporates a syndrome of beliefs, attitudes, and myths running through the mass media, popular culture, education, the workplace, family, and community life. Militarism is integral to an ultrapatriotic, Manichaeistic view of reality in which the forces of light and goodness are destined to confront evildoers seen as lurking everywhere, with the United States (by definition) representing the forces of light and goodness on a global scale.

The evolution of a permanent war system reveals just how deeply ingrained and multifaceted the military realm has become, involving the systems of production, consumption, work, communications, politics—and, inevitably, collective psychology. The Pentagon labyrinth has firm roots in historical and cultural patterns going back to the first Indian wars of conquest. If the United States does not yet qualify as a "warrior society" at the level of Sparta, ancient Rome, Nazi Germany, or even contemporary Israel, its military influence is surely just as pervasive, likely even more so owing to the unique international scope of American power. While few Americans strongly identify with outright U.S. pursuit of armed conquest, invasion of foreign countries, and empire, the vast majority do remain intensely patriotic, easily seduced by ideological justifications for continued U.S. military adventures abroad. Indeed for many decades the United States has been a kind of fortress order sustaining popular beliefs around expansionary goals: nationalism, ethnocentrism, rights of intervention and entitlement to resources, the use of massive armed violence in the service of political ends. Never in history has a culture and ideology of militarism been so far-reaching, so sophisticated, and yet so illusory, dependent upon powerful myths.

## Patriotism as Secular Religion

The second Gulf War demonstrated, like Desert Storm before it, the extent to which a rabid patriotic mobilization has been sustained by American mass psychology—in popular fears, needs, aspirations, and prejudices. The ordinary person encounters a seemingly monolithic wall of myths, lies, distortions, and celebrations that it would be tempting to attribute to the propaganda apparatus alone, but which goes far beyond the discrete functions of the media and the political system in manufacturing consent, vital as that is. Spectacular celebrations of war, violence, conquest, and triumph have a profoundly cathartic, empowering dimension grounded in discourses of patriotism, American exceptionalism, and racism, in the midst of a society that prides itself on its special enlightenment, its wondrous educational and technological achievements, its sophisticated civic culture. While systematically ignored throughout the intellectual and academic culture, military discourses in reality become fully integrated into the vast framework of ideological hegemony, crucial to the reproduction of corporate and imperial domination.

The web of military institutions and belief systems in American society demands a simple yet highly romanticized image of the national interest and mission, an ideology strong enough to call forth heroism, conquest, and armed missions in faraway places. Seen in this light, probably no country in the world is more intensely patriotic than the United States, where the mass media, educational system, culture, and politics converge to generate pervasive hegemonic ideals. As Mary Wertsch writes: "In the theatrical world of the warrior society, where costumed actors rehearse their movements and their lines, patriotism is in the atmosphere of every set."[1] The doctrines of Manifest Destiny and the American Century were organically tied to such notions, justifying the early colonial push westward and then (beginning around 1900) outward toward Asia and Latin America. Patriotic sentiments reached their zenith during the "good war" against Nazi Germany and Japan but later sank to its low point during and after the Vietnam War, followed by a resurgence during the two Gulf Wars, when national military pride become an all-encompassing media spectacle.

In upholding war and warmaking as a noble, heroic calling, patriotism serves to rationalize the horrors and irrationality of military action: death, destruction, uprooting of local populations, environmental chaos, the very threat of planetary extinction. The ideology of warfare justifies, even celebrates, moral atrocities such as the saturation bombing of civilian areas or use of terrible weapons that would ordinarily be met with scornful outrage. Pursuit of "national interest" is invoked to legitimate the atomic leveling of Hiroshima and Nagasaki, harsh economic sanctions and blockades directed at civilian populations, the torture of prisoners, scorched-earth policies, and occupation of distant nations. Patriotism furnishes a convenient framework defining common objectives, shared fears and dangers, agreed-upon enemies. Barbara Ehrenreich refers to the "sacralization of war" in which patriotic feelings take on the character of a "civil religion" endowing large populations with a sense of loyalty, solidarity, commitment, and empowerment.[2] As both the ends and means of war become sacred, enemies are readily demonized while mass killing is all too often turned into a heroic obligation.

Americans' national identity has been shaped by a long history of military engagements sustained by a complex variety of experiences, attitudes, beliefs, and myths. From the outset patriotism converged with militarism, both having deep foundations in the early revolutionary and settler periods and continuing through the twentieth century. As Ward Churchill observes, "Racially oriented invasion, conquest, genocide and subsequent denial are all integral, constantly recurring and thus defining features of the Euroamerican makeup from the instant the first boatload of self-ordained colonists set foot in the 'New World.'"[3] The legacy of colonization tied to military conquest has been reproduced endlessly in literature, art, music, film, TV, and ultimately within the daily lives of ordinary citizens; this is no strictly elite phenomenon but resides within the larger collective national psyche. Chris Hedges writes that this pattern of warmaking amounts to a powerful drug peddled not only by business leaders and politicians but by writers, journalists, filmmakers, and others within the popular culture: "It dominates culture, distorts memory, corrupts language, and infects everything around it."[4] Tied to the twin legacies of patriotism and militarism, the idea of war has provided Americans with a large ensemble of impulses: sense of purpose, adventure, heroism, nobility, superiority. Warmaking permits, indeed encourages, depiction of other nations and cultures as alien, primitive, uncivilized, barbaric—eligible to be attacked, conquered, occupied—always framed by a self-conception that is noble and benevolent.

Patriotism is usually understood as a higher value, a source of unquestioned political truths, yet as a mass belief system it typically embraces the worst of human behavior, legitimating ethnocentrism, racism, and violence while sanctioning any variety of atrocities and war crimes. It offers a simplistic, anti-intellectual, parochial view of a world reduced largely to "us" and "them," "friend" and "enemy," "allies" and "demons," liberators and terrorists. It lifts popular spirits, especially during war mobilizations, furnishing a sense of collective empowerment that, however, is neither genuinely empowering nor very durable. It inspires and glorifies warfare as a virtuous human activity, rationalizing conduct that, as Hedges writes, "breaks down long-established prohibitions against violence, destruction, and murder."[5] In the United States this syndrome has become more pronounced over time, as patriotism mobilizes popular support for the Pentagon system, military priorities, and pursuit of global power. Here the Gulf Wars represent a turning point, helping rekindle American patriotism linked to armed adventures, glorification of weapons technology, and celebration of war as media spectacle.

The impact of the military on American political culture thus turns out to be just the opposite of its benign representation in high-school textbooks. Military action that stimulates mass xenophobia not only legitimates the war economy but also protects elite governance by deflecting attention away from urgent domestic issues. This works most effectively where military campaigns are waged against a well-defined diabolical enemy with a demonized leader (Noriega, Milosevic, Hussein), are dramatically and quickly successful, and result in minimum (U.S.) casualties—as in the first Gulf War and the Balkans. We know that warfare by its nature requires mass subordination to norms of loyalty and obedience, but for the United States, with its entrenched war system, the ideological consequences are more profound, more long-term than elsewhere, having transformed crucial elements of popular consciousness and culture. Hence the widespread jingoism (stirred up by the media), the ease with which a majority of Americans can be mobilized behind military ventures, the willingness of so many (up to 45 percent during Desert Storm) to consider use of nuclear weapons against the designated enemy, the often-callous indifference toward foreign casualties, the public celebrations of armed violence. While such attitudes can be attributed to the power of media and governmental manipulation, in reality they have a strong resonance within the popular culture and national psyche. Both Gulf Wars, for example, revealed a virulent nativism embedded in a mass psychology that stereotypes and demonizes Arabs and Muslims. The conclusion of the first Gulf War brought Bush I a resounding 91 percent approval rating, not quite reached by Bush II in 2003, when military victory (short-lived) produced a 73 percent rating. It seems that the mass public was prepared to believe any lie or myth spun by politicians and the media, allowing warmakers greater flexibility.

American politics has always been informed by a messianic belief in national destiny merged with notions of historical progress—a sense that people could have mastery over the course of events, a certitude about national supremacy and its entitlements, a unique civilizing mission. Here we have an ideology, simultaneously elite and mass, embracing American exceptionalism, religious fervor, and national supremacy, mixed, inevitably, with the idea of attaining virtue through military action. No U.S. president epitomized these values more than Theodore Roosevelt, with his fervent belief in Manifest Destiny and its colonizing agenda. Bush II fits perfectly within this trajectory, holding to the idea of a uniquely American crusade to establish global hegemony, ostensibly to rid the world of evil. For Bush and a small group of neoconservative ideologues, military power and imperial expansion become the centerpiece of renewed fundamentalist, messianic goals, a recycling of the "white man's burden" in which theocratic and humanitarian ideals help crystallize and justify the struggle for domination. In January 2003 Bush said, "We'll do everything we can to remind people that we've never been a nation of conquerors; we're a nation of liberators." It follows that such "liberation," as experienced by the Indian tribes, the Vietnamese, Koreans, and Iraqis, would have to be a matter of considerable death and destruction.

From all we can glean from Bush's personal background and outlook, what emerges is a fierce patriotism associated with Christian evangelical notions of good triumphing over evil, U.S. global ambitions being endowed with the blessings of a higher power. Empire, though scarcely acknowledged as such, is the manifestation of God's will, justified as religious imperative. Where monstrous evils must be extirpated by any means, where biblically inspired apocalyptic visions of the future are embraced with great fervor, then reliance on military force cannot be far from sight. For Bush and his circle, therefore, the United States possesses not only the right but also the *obligation* to remake the world in its own image—a sentiment reflected in the president's bizarre contention (in early 2003) that it would be immoral for the United States *not* to attack Iraq. While it has been argued that a small nucleus of neoconservative "defense intellectuals" were able to "hijack" American politics after Bush II's ascension to power, in fact the values they represent and the policies they advocate have strong resonance throughout U.S. history, shown in the strong bipartisan support for the illegal invasion of Iraq. The agenda is roughly the same, the main difference being how aggressively it is pursued. Here Bush has not really deviated from well-established imperial priorities, as can be seen from a reading of Bob Woodward's *Bush at War*.[6]

The two Gulf Wars galvanized patriotic feelings on a scale rarely seen in U.S. history, owing in part to the jingoistic influence of the mass media, in part to efforts to purge the Vietnam syndrome, in part to the spectacular appeals of technowar. Seemingly new departures in foreign policy made war fashionable again, indulging the popular attraction to spectacles, games, heroic victories, and technological gimmickry. Outpourings of patriotism come with quick military conquests of weak yet easily demonized opponents. For a populace conditioned by media culture, war is easily reduced to seductive *images* of combat violence that saturate people's living rooms, where they remain at a safe, passive, sanitized distance from the immediate horrors of combat. Political and ethical concerns are readily jettisoned, leaving the "audience" in a state of catharsis linked to the miracle of military victory with its destruction of a hated enemy. As Hedges writes: "We dismantle our moral universe to serve the cause of war."[7] It is a world where media *representations* of armed intervention help aestheticize acts of human violence to an extent previously unknown in human history. The aftermath of war brings not horror, shame, and forgiveness but rather the celebration of war itself, now increasingly commodified and glamorized. Thus following the second Gulf War, vast merchandizing operations came to the fore to take advantage of the (destined to be temporary) triumphal euphoria: on eBay alone it was possible to buy three thousand war-related items, including Iraqi coins and bills, Hussein condoms and puppets, wristwatches, terrorist body bags, wacky T-shirts, talking military dolls, Iraqi most-wanted playing cards, and special flavors of Iraqi ice cream.[8]

For the United States as unchallenged world superpower, patriotism and militarism underwrite the increasingly overt struggle for world domination. The narrative of military adventure and conquest—often denied or obscured in the official discourse—winds up fixated on a particular target (mostly Arabs and Muslims today) that can be defined as irrationally hostile to the West, modernity, and democracy. It follows that American patriotism is tightly interwoven with the presumed civilizing process itself, a bulwark against brigands, criminals, outlaws, gangsters, and terrorists, indeed against the historical legacy of irrationality and barbarism. And the logic of this connection seems absolutely overpowering: the stronger the armed power of the state, the stronger must be the patriotism, which legitimates virtually any U.S. military intervention regardless of its distance from American shores. Such political ideology at the start of the twenty-first century is the belief system of a chosen nation, to some degree internalized by the vast majority of the population, justifying its peculiar historical destiny that can only be realized by means of awesome global power.

## Gun Culture and Civic Violence

Owing in great measure to its long history of imperialism and militarism, to its endless fascination with guns and combat, the United States had by the 1980s easily become the major hub of global violence: repeated armed interventions abroad found their domestic parallel in the world's largest prison system, an epidemic of civic violence, an out-of-control gun culture, home-bred terrorism, gang warfare, militias spread around the country, domestic violence, spontaneous outbursts of youth violence like that at Columbine High School in Colorado, mass media saturated with images of violence and chaos. There is hardly anything new in all this—just its expanding scope and its increasingly transparent connection with the military-industrial complex. The tight linkage between military and civilian forms of violence is the outgrowth of the role the Pentagon has come to play in so many areas of politics, the economy, culture, media, and everyday life. If the governmental and military elites appear as regular purveyors of death and destruction worldwide, then a comparable ethos can be expected to develop locally, within civil society, as ordinary people follow the lessons taught by the power structure. As a government-supported mode of violence, armed intervention brings with it a definite form of legitimation that, as one of its consequences, gives added impetus to individual and small-group violence. Such violence results not only from an aggressive foreign policy but also from a social order riven by social inequality, anomie, fragmentation, and powerlessness where "politics" has lost its capacity to inspire or mobilize people, to get them involved as civic participants.

At the turn of the new century the United States was already the most violent of nations even as its political leaders customarily stressed high-sounding themes: peace, human rights, civic culture, law and order. This shameful condition grew out of a strong convergence of trends—global and domestic, military and civilian, national and local. And a culture nurtured on violence, on the resort to weapons and guns in solving conflicts, seems to require increasingly heavier doses of the medicine, as the 2003 war on Iraq once again confirmed. It could be that this culture has in some fashion become "addicted to war," as the title of one book on U.S. foreign policy suggests.[9]

As Richard Rhodes argues, civic violence is typically rooted in human experiences that desensitize people to suffering, pain, and death—harsh economic realities, media images, personal encounters, prolonged exposure to war and/or civil insurrection. Foremost among personal encounters is military training and service, designed to induce transformative individual changes that make killing more psychologically and ethically permissible, while even romanticizing and glorifying it. Combat experience in particular tends to strip away social and moral constraints historically related to violence and killing.[10] Acts that produce death and destruction need not have any relationship to immediate combat, of course, especially in the age of technowar in which the military is more likely to produce its deadly effects from a safe distance, its process more detached, impersonal, clinical. The point is that military training instills in recruits a preparedness to kill with few questions asked. This dynamic of psychological conversion, according to Rhodes, has shaped the lives of tens of millions of Americans whose return to the civilian world carries with it the fruits of that conversion. Those who served in Vietnam, Korea, and the two Gulf Wars were no doubt uniquely and permanently transformed by such brutalizing experience. One result is that the distance between combat violence and everyday criminality in the United States has been narrowed considerably, as the military ethos spills over into civic life in myriad ways.[11]

Rhodes speaks of "unmitigated violent phantom communities" that, to varying degrees, can support all manner of horrible actions or at least desensitize people to such actions. Indifference toward suffering and pain is a product of military socialization and is reinforced by harshly violent messages contained in the mass media and popular culture. Combat experiences, moreover, usually engender feelings of anger, revenge, frustration, and cruelty that reproduce codes of violent conflict elsewhere, including militias, cults, gangs, murders, domestic assaults, and terrorism. Many veterans of military life returned to the civilian world intoxicated by images of armed combat, as shown dramatically by the case of Oklahoma City bomber Timothy McVeigh. As a general statement it seems that the more violence the individual or group experiences, the more that individual or group is prepared to engage in further violent acts—a phenomenon that applies equally to those whose surface lives may appear quite normal, replete with comfortable jobs and homes, families, and strong religious ties.[12] Beneath the surface of a liberal, pluralistic society can be found a wide range of dark impulses capable of producing the most terrible deeds, which, though surely visible in any culture, have uniquely pervaded the American landscape.

A major phenomenon associated with civic violence is what might be called "reactionary populism," first noticeable on a large scale in the mid-1980s in the form of a bizarre variety of cults, sects, militias, and enclave groups. Attractive to the familiar "angry white male," its diffuse ideology embraces diverse impulses: the gun culture, xenophobia, conspiracy thinking, nativism, Christian fundamentalism, racism. It is fueled by many of the same conditions that gave rise to historical fascism, such as joblessness, intense fear of change, hostility to progressive social movements, and alienation from politics. With the decline of the two-party system and the increasing corporate stranglehold over government, many local groups came to view politicians and officials as corrupt, untrustworthy, incompetent, remote from immediate social problems, and indifferent to the ordinary person's needs. Violent confrontations erupted between local groups and the state—the FBI assault at Ruby Ridge, the Waco standoff and massacre at the Branch Davidian compound, the Oklahoma City bombing, the lengthy holdout of the Montana Freemen, the Amtrak train derailment in Arizona, and hundreds of lesser episodes involving angry public encounters, shootouts, and bombings. Federal agents were frequently victims of threats, acts of intimidation, and verbal attacks. Reactionary populism of this sort went into decline by the late 1990s, hastened along by the impact of 9/11, but given its deep roots in U.S. history and the persistence of conditions that foster such local mobilization, the eclipse could well be temporary.

The paramilitary groups carry forward a long-standing American tradition of disenfranchised people fighting for identity, recognition, and local control against distant, impersonal, elite interests. Most see themselves as bearers of renewed citizenship to be won with great difficulty in a harsh, threatening world. Their obsession with conspiracies, with mysterious schemes and plots, and their glorification of gun culture often draw them into a zone of domestic terrorism. The militias' hostility to state power, officialdom, and international agencies is visceral, going beyond the targeting of specific officeholders and politicians, beyond any simple hostility to bureaucracy. Their grassroots impulses are compromised, however, by a sometimes virulent racism, staunch social conservatism, intensely parochial defense of turf not too different from that of gang culture, and superpatriotism. They rarely energize people toward any positive, transformative ideals, dwelling instead on popular fear of disruption, material insecurity, and scapegoating of minorities, immigrants, gays, and others defined as "outsiders," often leading to a kind of Rambo syndrome—macho revolt against elites that draws on the frontier ethic of the outlaw hero and rugged individualism.

The importance for the militias of a weapons subculture, of preparation for armed combat, based on the idea of everyday people locked in struggle against mortal enemies, can hardly be stressed enough: these groups are simply taking to extremes the worship of guns and violence already embedded in postwar American social life. In the year 2000 there were an estimated 240 million guns in civilian hands across the country, including several million combat-grade weapons owned by people roaming freely across the rural and urban terrain. The hard-fought and well-financed lobbying campaigns and propaganda efforts of the National Rifle Association have done much to legitimate and solidify this gun culture. Add the influence of a mass media and popular culture saturated with images of violence, along with a turbulent civil society that feeds into a multiplicity of angry, paranoid responses, and the resonance of messages predicting apocalyptic warfare involving ordinary citizens (as in Larry Pratt's *Armed People Victorious*) becomes fathomable.

As William Gibson observes in *Warrior Dreams,* guns and violence have become a distinctly male obsession in the United States at least since the Vietnam war.[13] The weapons fetish has spread rapidly across regional, class, and ethnic lines; more than 5 million assault rifles alone were purchased between 1980 and 2000. Destructive male behavior has been on the upswing since the 1960s, from street crime to domestic violence to serial murders and terrorism. Hollywood films devoting macabre attention to mass killings—and just regular everyday mayhem—like *Silence of the Lambs, Reservoir Dogs, Pulp Fiction, Natural Born Killers, Very Bad Things, XXX,* and the *Terminator* episodes have become objects of cult fascination. The immense popularity of TV coverage of the two Gulf Wars is well known. Reflecting on the origins of this trend, Gibson points to the emergence of a "new warrior hero" in American society that mirrors a shifting masculine ethos, focused not only on soldiers and cops but also on an everyday warrior life in which the disenfranchised take up arms, join quasi-military groups, and "prepare for heroic battle against the enemies of society."[14] So the modern male warrior, whether in the guise of the Montana Freemen, patriot organizations, gangs, skinheads, or even a hermetic figure like the Unabomber, becomes the archetype of the renegade hero who in earlier times tamed the frontier, robbed trains and banks, or simply took the law into his own hands to fight various alien intruders.

This search for a male warrior identity can be traced back to the Minutemen, frontier settlers, and foreign adventurers like Teddy Roosevelt's Rough Riders, who recruited men looking to conquer the world, or at least hoping to defend their own turf, through the medium of armed combat. It runs through the myths and rituals of the Mafia and organized crime as well as urban street gangs. During the 1980s and 1990s it appealed more to young white men than to any other social category—to men feeling threatened by a heartless and encroaching urban world and often driven by feelings of racial superiority, sexism, male bonding, and ultrapatriotism. As Gibson notes: "American men—lacking confidence in the government and the economy, troubled by changing relations between the sexes, uncertain of their identity or their future—began to dream, to fantasize about the powers and features of another kind of man who could retake and reorder the world."[15] Here we witness a convergence of trends at both the elite and mass levels of American society.

Paramilitary culture was shaped in part by a national mood of defeat and pessimism stemming from the failed Vietnam War—a mood seemingly ameliorated by the euphoria of the first Gulf War. The Indochina debacle was a great blow to the collective American psyche, the end to a long tradition of U.S. military victories; it eclipsed, at least momentarily, the national sense of manifest destiny, of "progress" achieved by means of armed intervention abroad. U.S. military power was fiercely challenged and defeated, in one geographical locale and for one historical moment, creating broad psychological disruptions leading to a "crisis of self-image" in the general culture that was most disorienting to those in and around the military subculture. During a period of rapid, far-reaching change, including the impact of feminism and erosion of traditional gender roles, a large percentage of men felt driven to recapture the patriarchal ethos of an earlier time. Many sought out images of violent power, which they found validated in diverse arenas of popular culture: film, MTV, video games, comics, and so forth. But for such drives to make sense, to have real credibility, they would have to confront purported enemies: Communists, foreign terrorists, drug dealers, illegal aliens, nebulous conspirators, even the federal government itself. In this paranoid milieu the national predicament intersected with a variety of identity crises and material hardships that seemed to cry out for direct action.

As with cult organizations like the Branch Davidians, a conspiratorial siege mentality came to typify right-wing extremists who formed the backbone of rural groups such as the militias, survivalists, Aryan Nations, Christian Identity, The Order, and The Order II, often based in Far West areas like Idaho, Utah, Montana, and eastern Washington. Richard Butler, long a fixture in the white supremacist Aryan Nations, set up an enclave of twenty acres behind barbed-wire fences in northern Idaho where members could meet, practice target shooting, and generally vent their rage at disparate aliens, enemies, and conspirators. Butler's goal: a "ten-percent solution" that would save one-tenth of the United States for a "white homeland" while letting the rest of the country rot in its corruption and decay. Funded partly by Silicon Valley high-tech money, Butler and his followers rejected the Klan and John Birch Society for being "too liberal"; by 2000 they had established close contacts with various neo-Nazi groups worldwide. Referring to the Bible as a "book of separation," displaying photos of Hitler, and fascinated with both punk rock and German marching music, the Aryans envisioned a protracted "war of freedom" involving armed combat and insurgency. The Aryans and kindred groups derive much of their inspiration from survivalism, looking for refuge in the wilderness made possible by tightly knit, isolated communities intent on preserving conventional lifestyles. The term "survivalist" was coined by Kurt Saxon in the early 1960s to refer to people bonded together in remote areas, prepared to outlive cataclysmic events such as nuclear war. By the 1990s survivalist ranks grew to tens of thousands, drawing mostly from marginalized, poorly educated white males, and the groups took on increased organizational and ideological coherence. Their élan was boosted by the influence of neo-Nazi texts like William Pierce's novel *The Turner Diaries*.[16]

Already in the 1980s survivalists had merged with some militias and other right-wing populist forces, building upon a base that included tax resisters, Posse groups, religious fundamentalists, gun enthusiasts, and the ever-present cults. Within this increasingly violent subculture many adopted the veneer of military structures complete with uniforms, chains of command, ribbons and medals, large arms caches, shooting ranges, and the lingo of an armed outfit. Judging from their abundant literature and videotapes, some militia groups believed that "urban warfare" and "race war" were imminent, that American citizens were obligated to prepare for the coming Armageddon—an outlook shared by more than a few gangs and cults. At the same time, militia partisans liked to present an image of simple folks just out for fun and games in the woods or desert. While many groups had disbanded by the late 1990s, hundreds of others remained, often adopting a lower profile at a time when the war on terrorism began to limit their room to maneuver.

The culture of violence naturally extends to acts of domestic terrorism, which in the 1990s found fertile soil in reactionary populism. Protofascist episodes of violence directed at public targets were frequent, the work of seemingly ordinary people taking some very ordinary American ideas (freedom, rugged individualism, patriotism, the right to bear arms) to fanatical excesses. Such actions have been, at least indirectly, encouraged by the gun lobby, mass media, urban gang subcultures, generally high rates of violent crimes, the revitalized war economy, and plentiful examples of U.S. military intervention abroad. Local incidents of terrorism proliferated throughout the 1990s: according to the Bureau of Alcohol, Tobacco and Firearms, in the peak year 1993 there were almost 2,400 bombings across the nation, leading to 70 deaths and 1,375 injuries. Reportedly hundreds of other actions were intercepted by the FBI and police agencies. The heightened interest in bombs and guns, including sophisticated assault weapons, was fueled by mail-order companies that cater to paramilitary enthusiasts, not to mention what is available through the Internet, shortwave radio, fax systems, and talk radio programs hosted by militia sympathizers. Aided by the Internet and alarmed by perceived domestic and global threats, "hate" groups multiplied after the late 1990s. In 1998 observers from Klanwatch and the Militia Task Force documented an all-time high of 474 hate groups in the United States, an increase of 20 percent from 1996. The targeting of Arabs, Muslims, and immigrants by many groups was sharpened in the aftermath of 9/11, and the number of crimes directed against those minorities also multiplied. This orbit includes biblical doomsayers, often inspired by violent rock and hip-hop lyrics; collectors of high-powered weapons; builders of chemical devices and bombs; and architects of Web sites that coordinate literally hundreds of reactionary groups.

Right-wing terrorism was responsible for the bombing of Murrah Federal Building in Oklahoma City in April 1994, but this bold attack was simply the tip of the iceberg; politically motivated violence became a durable element of the culture, though it virtually disappeared on the left after the 1970s. Recurrent assaults on women's health clinics took place, along with increasing attacks directed against minorities, gays, Arabs, and Muslims. The violent mood has been nourished by a mounting sense of powerlessness in American society resulting from several factors: economic globalization, growth of bureaucratic and corporate power, influence of the media culture, and popular cynicism over the boring, meaningless character of normal politics. It is exacerbated by the spread of paranoid, conspiratorial beliefs that often comes with fear of nebulous intruders or some kind of imminent apocalypse.[17] Paranoid obsession with black helicopters, alien creatures, drug cartels, and secret military missions—all seen as possible elements of a tyrannical "New Order"—can be understood in this milieu. Such beliefs can produce a violent demonology that, when combined with genuine fears of terrorist attacks, furnish a convenient substitute for familiar cold war images of the Communist devil.

Domestic terrorism is hardly synonymous with reactionary populism, but the ideological milieu established by the latter helped nourish the former. As noted above, thousands of politically motivated acts of violence were carried out in the United States during the 1990s, with no doubt thousands more intercepted before they could be launched—figures dwarfing anything carried out by Al Qaeda—but this homegrown terrorism has received little media attention. At the time of the Oklahoma City bombing by Timothy McVeigh and his accomplices, militia groups were at their peak, with membership estimates as high as 4 million (including over 400,000 paramilitary activists). Just before the bombing former CIA director William Colby said, "I watched as the anti-war movement rendered it impossible for this country to conduct or win the Vietnam war. . . . This militia and patriot movement is far more significant and far more dangerous for Americans than the anti-war movement ever was. . . . It is not because these people are armed that America need be concerned. They are dangerous because there are so many of them."[18]

According to standard reports, McVeigh was just a regular kid from a blue-collar family in upstate New York. He developed an intense love of guns at an early age, obtaining a .22 caliber rifle at thirteen and a shotgun when he turned sixteen, at which time he began stockpiling food and large barrels of water in his basement. In 1986, upon graduating from high school, McVeigh and a friend bought several acres of property where they could camp out, wear army fatigues, build bombs, and carry out regular target practice. As Joel Dyer writes, during this period "McVeigh continued his survivalist behavior. He would camp out on the property at night and practice his shooting from sunup to sundown."[19] He joined the army in 1988, was quickly promoted to corporal and then sergeant, compiled an overall excellent record, and served in the first

Gulf War, in which he received battlefield commendations. He became an avid reader of survivalist and gun-related magazines and was fanatical about the right to bear arms, at one point complaining that the NRA had not taken a strong enough stand against gun control. He read the Christian Identity newsletter, *Patriot Report,* filled with antigovernment conspiracy theories, and then got hold of Pierce's *Turner Diaries,* which, by several accounts, transformed his life. For McVeigh, however, the Waco events in 1993 were the most traumatic: he saw the federal assault as a government-sponsored massacre, directed against the Second Amendment. He visited the Waco site on numerous occasions. Here McVeigh apparently turned to Pierce's novel, in which Earl Turner decides to fight back after the government passes antigun legislation. Turner blew up a federal building that housed the FBI with a fertilizer-and-fuel-oil bomb concealed in a truck—almost identical to the Oklahoma City scenario.[20]

In his correspondence with Gore Vidal spanning three years, McVeigh justifies his actions as a necessary moral and political response to an authoritarian, oppressive, and militarized government that was waging war at home and abroad. He writes: "For all intents and purposes, federal agents had become 'soldiers' (using military training, tactics, techniques, equipment, language, dress, organization, and mind-set) and they were escalating their behavior. Therefore, this bombing was also meant as a preemptive (or pro-active) strike against those forces and their command and control centers within the federal building. When an aggressor force continually launches attacks from a particular base of operations, it is sound military strategy to take the fight to the enemy." He adds: "Bombing the Murrah Federal Building was morally and strategically equivalent to the United States hitting a government building in Serbia, Iraq, or other nations. Based on observations of the policies of my own government, I viewed this action as an acceptable option. From this perspective what occurred in Oklahoma City was no different than what Americans rain on the heads of others all the time."[21] Elsewhere in his correspondence McVeigh writes: "Our government is the potent, the omnipresent teacher. For good or ill it teaches the whole people by its example."[22] From this standpoint McVeigh's brand of terrorism can be seen as *doubly* the product of a militarized culture—the gun craze and a government/military that encourages violence through its own actions.

Violence within the paramilitary milieu has parallels in sectors of youth culture including gangs, skinheads, and various roving groups across urban, suburban, and rural landscapes. Often reactionary in ideology, the skinheads—in contrast to militias and cults—have been more closely linked to the urban (and suburban) gang subcultures. Their origins go back to the Teddy Boys, a youth subculture that spawned the rival Mods and Rockers in England during the early 1960s. The Teddy Boys came together around dispersed gangs of young males alienated from social convention, feeling hopeless about the future, and looking for scapegoats to attack as the presumed source of their economic misery and social powerlessness. Their targets were mainly immigrants and racial minorities, symbols for them of a corrupt, oppressive, and threatening world. Skinheads first established a presence in the United States during the late 1970s, when they were associated with punk rock, "screwdriver music," episodic acts of violence, and gestures toward white supremacy. While not overtly ideological, they adopted the rhetoric of a racist, sexist, xenophobic subculture bent on reproducing the division between initiates and outsiders, between (usually homogeneous) youth groups and stereotyped "others."[23] They frequently took on the symbolic paraphernalia of historical fascism, adorning themselves with swastikas, German Eagle medals, and tattoos; listening to German marching music; celebrating Hitler's birthday; and so forth. Like many cults and militias, skinheads attracted youth from poor, marginalized, semieducated sectors, above all young males without strong roots in family or work, although their influence eventually spilled over into the suburban middle class. In a context where few good jobs and careers seemed available to young people, where family life had deteriorated as a source of cohesion and identity, and where politics was viewed as boring and meaningless, skinheads epitomized the anomie and nihilism of youth in general. Much like cults and militias, violent youth groups furnish solidarity where it might otherwise be absent. By the end of the 1990s the skinheads (loosely defined) numbered probably no more than three thousand across some thirty-one states, mainly in the West, but their social impact was no doubt greater than these numbers suggest.

On April 20, 1999, possibly in commemoration of Hitler's birthday, two students at Columbine High School in Littleton, Colorado, went on a shooting rampage, killing twelve students and a teacher before committing suicide. Michael Moore's documentary *Bowling for Columbine* depicts the suburban, middle-class environment where the students—Eric Harris and Dylan Klebold—lived and presumably were socialized into their violent youth subculture, such as it was. Both became attached to neo-Nazi ideas and symbols, listening to heavy-metal music, playing video games that celebrate violence and guns, and watching movies like Oliver Stone's *Natural Born Killers*. Both were former Boy Scouts but then in high school formed the "Trenchcoat Mafia," which focused hatred on blacks, Latinos, Jews, and other minorities and on the in-group of school elites. At a bowling class just before the killing spree, Klebold wore a T-shirt that read "Serial Killer," flaunting a symbol that would soon achieve its bloody realization. In the film Moore visits the nearby Lockheed-Martin plant, which manufactures and sells a huge arsenal of high-powered missiles and other weapons of mass destruction, setting up a strong parallel between the two cultures of violence. The parents of many students at Columbine High worked for Lockheed-Martin, carrying out their routine business in the midst of a seemingly peaceful suburban community.

If, as Rhodes argues, violence directed against human beings is in great measure rooted in people's exposure to certain brutalizing experiences and images, then we should hardly be surprised to find that the United States—with the world's largest military machine and prison system, the most violence-saturated media, a fanatical gun cult, and a civil society permeated with criminal activity of all sorts—is the global leader in mass murders and serial killings, among other violent crimes. The episodes are continuous, many perpetrated by individuals with military training and/or combat experience, or who have done extensive jail time. Clearly war and preparation for war thrive on an ethos that extends to the civilian population; the quick readiness of elites to use military action, or threaten such action, inevitably leaves its psychological imprint on the general population. It is no coincidence that a dramatic upswing in violent crimes occurred in the 1970s, coming on the heels of protracted U.S. warfare in Indochina that destroyed three countries and killed at least 3 million people, including fifty-eight thousand American troops. Hundreds of thousands of veterans returned after exposure to the horrors of a brutal war, with predictable consequences for everyday life in families, workplaces, and communities. We have already noted how both the Oklahoma City bombing and the Columbine shooting spree bear some relationship, direct or indirect, to the deepening culture of militarism. As for serial killings, they increased at a tenfold rate in the 1970s alone and have shown no signs of abating since.

As Darrell Hamamoto has shown, the huge increase in mass murders and serial killings in the United States has much of its origins in a military apparatus that pervades virtually every sphere of American life.[24] We know that Night Stalker Richard Ramirez, who brutally killed at least thirteen people in the Los Angeles area during 1985, was "coached" into violence by an older cousin who served in Vietnam and boasted of freely slaughtering large numbers of "Vietcong." A dedicated war hero, the cousin took credit for twenty-nine confirmed kills in Vietnam, and inspired in Ramirez a hatred of Asians while teaching him secrets of guerrilla warfare that he used for his nighttime attacks.[25] One of the most notorious serial murderers, Dr. Michael Swango, who relished poisoning dozens of patients under his care at several hospitals, had been a diehard marine with a fancy for combat and guns. His father, Col. John Virgil Swango, had been stationed in Vietnam and passed on his glorification of military life to his son. The younger Swango enjoyed being at the scene of gruesome disasters as a paramedic, was obsessed with firearms, kept a small arsenal at home, and dwelled on news reports of mass murder such as the July 1984 shooting spree at a McDonald's restaurant in San Ysidro, California. In his book on the Swango case, James B. Stewart writes: "Serial killers typically betray a fascination with the military and law enforcement, careers in which people are armed, and they often fantasize about violence and disasters in which they emerge as heroes."[26] Swango fit this profile almost perfectly. Stewart adds: "Swango spoke often of his absent father, glorifying Virgil's career in Vietnam [while] . . . his fascination with disasters, with killing, and with weapons echoed similar interests he perceived in his father, as when he learned that Virgil also kept scrapbooks of disasters."[27]

Yet another serial killer, Arthur Shawcross, rationalized his murder of eleven women between 1972 and 1989 by claiming it was a result of "posttraumatic stress disorder" following his duty in Vietnam. While in Vietnam he claimed to have murdered two girls, raping one and roasting and eating the severed leg of the other, setting him off on a pathological killing mission.[28] The man who came to be known as the "Genessee River Killer" admitted to having killed at least twenty-six Vietnamese in cold blood. The famous Zodiac Killer, who went on a murder rampage in the San Francisco Bay Area during the 1980s, was believed to have been on active military duty. More recently, John Allen Williams (Muhammed), the 2002 sniper killer in the Washington, D.C., area, was a Gulf War combat veteran. Just as U.S. military intervention around the globe has no historical precedents, just as government and military elites have often been able to commit war crimes with impunity, so too can it be said that the hundreds of documented serial murder cases in the United States since the 1970s have no parallel elsewhere.

The militarization of culture permeates other areas of daily life in American society. In 1991 Operation Desert Storm set in motion a new craze for large, powerful, aggressive vehicles—sport utility vehicles, manufactured by every automobile company, and the even more awesome Hummers, originally designed for military use. AM General began making Hummers in 1992, the first vehicle going to the king of male action films, Arnold Schwarzenegger. A major idea behind SUVs and Hummers was to give drivers a stronger command of the road, but the result was an increase in violent behavior behind the wheel including manifestations of road rage. As Sheldon Rampton and John Stauber observe, SUVs and Hummers "exploit fear while actually doing nothing to make people safer. They make their owners feel safe not by protecting them, but by feeding their aggressive impulses."[29] Not only do the huge luxury vehicles (costing up to $125,000) get far worse gas mileage than cars, they also have a 6 percent higher death rate, so the feelings of command and intimidation turn out to be illusory. Throughout the 1990s SUV sales skyrocketed in the United States, tied in part to fear-based marketing and a subliminal appeal to violent impulses that have no parallel in any other society. After 9/11 SUV and Hummer sales further exploded, but by 2004 Hummer sales began to drop significantly as gas prices increased.

If the widening ethos and practice of violence against other humans (and indeed against nature) is part of a transformed world, it takes place *within* modernity, not *against* it. There is much to suggest that barbarism is in many ways facilitated by the tools and modalities of advanced industrial society, in contrast to what is generally assumed. The main instruments of violence—high-tech military, weapons of mass destruction (WMD), bureaucratic structures, communications systems—have become more refined and concentrated, more capable of bringing massive death and destruction across the globe. Horrendous acts of violence become more routine, connected with modern forms of planning, calculation, and technique that easily widen the distance between perpetrators and objects or victims of violence. The idea of a civilizing, pacifying Enlightenment ethos has turned out to be a cruel myth. As Zygmunt Bauman writes: "Contemporary mass murder is distinguished by a virtual absence of all spontaneity on the one hand and the prominence of rational, carefully calculated design on the other. It is marked by an almost complete elimination of contingency and chance, and independence from group emotions and personal motives."[30] Hence the militarized culture, reflected in its great reliance on aerial terrorism, the setting up of terrorist regimes and death squads, the domestic gun craze and serial killings, and celebrated media images of vast destruction in real combat situations (the Gulf Wars) or in simulated warfare *(Star Wars, Black Hawk Down, Behind Enemy Lines),* is bolstered and legitimated by the very workings of modernity.

The refined practice of technowar, pushed to its routinized maximum in the United States, could just as easily be carried out by computerized robots and pilotless drones like those in sci-fi and action films, video games, and TV spectacles of the two Gulf Wars—all glorifying violence in a setting that separates actors from their victims, rendering the object of military action impersonal, detached, clinical, even invisible. Impediments to terrible acts of violence are stripped away as barbarism is integrated into the everyday structures and norms of modernity itself. In Bauman's words: "Reduced like all other objects of bureaucratic management to pure, quality-free measurements, human objects lose their distinctiveness. They are already dehumanized."[31] Here the institutionalization of violence within modern society readily places the human targets and victims outside any ethical or social consideration. The triumph of U.S. military power over weak, defenseless "enemies" is approached with the same kind of moral detachment as a Super Bowl contest. Rather than providing greater restraints and safeguards against the horrors of militarism, the technocratic ethos embedded in modernity erodes such restraints and safeguards, whether ethical, political, scientific, legal, or religious.

For the U.S. war machine, the notion that it would have to adhere to universal legal, political, and ethical precepts enshrined in the UN Charter and international law is considered preposterous, beyond the realm of discussion. Violence becomes a purely technical or strategic question, immune from normal countervailing pressures, just the way it is presented in the corporate media. Where the instruments of modernity are turned toward barbarism, the culture of militarism elicits less commentary and criticism, less outrage within the political system and mass media. Mechanisms and relations of power are all that seem to matter to elites who manage the war economy. In this context protofascist tendencies within American society—militarism, authoritarianism, xenophobia, racism, the weapons cult—can be assimilated into a rationalized state capitalism that already possesses a vast concentration of economic, political, and military power. This kind of power structure hardly requires the familiar accoutrements of historical fascism like swastikas, medals, concentration camps, organized military processions, and dictatorial führers. Geared to corporate domination and imperial expansion—and legitimated in part by the culture of militarism—this system embodies many features of previous fascist states behind a liberal-democratic facade. The long association of modernity with progress and civilization is a superficial veneer concealing the U.S. drive toward global supremacy through expanded military and economic power.

## Warrior Culture and Patriarchy

With few exceptions the military has been a domain of patriarchal, masculinist traditions—social hierarchy, violence, conquest, sexism, homophobia, gun worship—and the United States has never been one of the exceptions. The warrior culture (from training to combat) has always been a repository of patriarchal values, from the early Minutemen to the frontier settlers, cavalry, and cowboys to the later uniformed participants in global wars and more recent gangs, cults, militias, terrorists, and weapons fetishists. It is within and around these historical activities and legacies that the predominantly male mythology of warfare has evolved, built upon the motif of fighting off demons and evildoers with maximum force, on imposing order by violent means in a chaotic world. This is a milieu dominated by masculine action-heroes looking to make history, to achieve redemption by means of conquest and domination. Warfare has routinely provided an opportunity for men, as warrior protagonists, to rebuild psyches beset with some combination of anxiety, crisis, defeat, and impotence.

The Rambo phenomenon, dramatized in a series of 1980s Hollywood films starring Sylvester Stallone, was simply one example of male warrior heroes being endowed with iconic status in American popular culture, Arnold Schwarzenegger in his *Terminator* series being another. A superpatriot and gun cultist, Rambo embodies a heroic individualism won through protracted military action. Aligning strong masculinity with the power of the gun, the films construct a larger-than-life mythic personality who relishes violence as an instrument to rid the world of evil—a narrative falling within the tradition of Superman, the various *Star Wars* heroes, Indiana Jones, *Top Gun,* and literally hundreds of combat and Western films or TV shows. Wars giving visceral expression to patriotic valor, technological virtues, and masculine conquest fit this pattern. Within such a narrative the Vietnam war wound up frustratingly messy and confusing, while the first Gulf War easily fit into the desired historical pattern, reinvigorating the national psyche (deflated by the Vietnam syndrome) in a triumphal war over a demonized opponent (Iraq). Desert Storm furnished some of the most dramatic, compelling images of technowar replete with sophisticated gadgetry, flashy spectacles, graphic explosions, victory celebrations, and male expertise used to decode (and justify) the events witnessed by mass audiences. If Vietnam disintegrated into a terrible "quagmire," then the Gulf Wars could be understood as clean, neat, resolute, and technically efficient, with obvious winners and losers, all packaged within the masculine philosophy of victorious military power standing for moral rectitude.

In her path-breaking exploration of military life, Mary Edwards Wertsch analyzes a socialization process that is distinctly patriarchal, rooted in norms of discipline, order, and obedience in the service of a (masculinized) national ideal. She refers to a "fortress morality" known for its uncompromising rigidity, where easy acceptance of violence is combined with a "purity of vision" regarding duties and obligations.[32] An indelibly male vision saturates the military world, with women deemed valuable in nothing more than supporting, adorning roles. Thus: "Women are tolerated inside the fortress on one all-encompassing condition: in appearance, dress, speech, and behavior a woman must at all times reflect her complete acceptance of the ultimate patriarchy and its implications for women. By that rule any woman inside the fortress is automatically an accomplice in her own devaluation."[33] Within such a patriarchal culture—caricatured in the film *The Great Santini* —women are expected to live out male expectations and fantasies. Wertsch's generalizations are based on dozens of interviews with members of military families conducted in the early 1990s. While more recent socialization patterns have been altered by increased entry of women into the armed forces, the change seems not to have fundamentally transformed gender relations in the U.S. military.

Wertsch observes that within military culture it is male authority figures who prevail in both professional work and everyday life, where virtues of duty, conformism, and hierarchy operate to keep women and children in line. The sense of powerlessness experienced by women, and above all wives, can be rather extreme in the military setting.[34] Moreover, all this is exacerbated by other dysfunctions permeating military family life: rigid controls, alcoholism, frequent travel and separation, fear of intimacy resulting from constant loss of friendships, and so forth. It goes without saying that the trauma of war itself, with its emotional horrors, uncertainties, and exposure to violence, creates added tensions and conflicts that inevitably further marginalize women and children; family relations are commonly harmed by feelings of guilt, rage, and violence. The armed-services milieu gives rise to extremely high rates of domestic violence and child abuse insofar as the familiar dysfunctions of "normal" family life and gender relations are greatly aggravated. As Wertsch states: "One of the things characterizing life inside the fortress is the exaggerated difference between masculine behavior and feminine behavior, masculine values and feminine values. Macho maleness is at one end of the spectrum; passive receptive femininity at the other."[35] Conflict often turns out to be especially harsh and violent. The problems that arise within military families—domestic violence, child abuse, alcoholism and drug abuse, relationship breakdowns—are rarely if ever adequately handled by the military brass, which remains trapped within the same "fortress." The capacity of women to confront marital distress is undermined by their already devalued role within military culture. In the end, the ongoing travails and miseries of military family life are concealed (not always effectively) by an elaborate social facade of order, harmony, duty, patriotism, and outward status. Everything takes on greater significance as the military comes to occupy an increasingly central place in American foreign policy and social life.

In the conjuncture of an expanding war economy, empire, and recurrent U.S. armed interventions, one can detect a merger of corporate, bureaucratic, military, and patriarchal forms of domination. The stubborn fact is that military institutions continue to be ruled by men and pervaded by masculine norms; at the start of the twenty-first century men make up more than 90 percent of U.S. armed-services personnel, and fully 100 percent of those entering direct combat. The historical impact of the feminist revolution on Pentagon culture has been limited. As Claire Snyder observes, militarism in American society reinforces a wide range of conventional social and sexual values, a tendency strengthened by antifeminist backlash linked to official fears that a large-scale influx of women into the military will inevitably compromise training standards, weaken morale, create sexual tensions, and disrupt combat situations.[36] The dominant Pentagon thinking is that a kinder, gentler armed forces cannot win wars: it is best to rely upon the skills of men, with their supposedly innate drive toward aggression, violence, and martial exploits. Given tough leadership, military organizations can harness those masculine traits into forms of bonding, heroism, and brute physical strength required for combat—although the shift from conventional ground warfare to new modes of technowar would seem to render such assumptions obsolete. In any event, deeply entrenched patriarchal values defining military life can easily shade into misogyny, as reflected in the canons of basic training in which drill instructors often use woman-hating ridicule to shame recruits seen as lacking "manhood" and sexual potency. As depicted in films like *Full Metal Jacket,* femininity is repeatedly deprecated while the weapons of combat are identified with male genitalia; sexism becomes a medium to secure male bonding and preparation for killing. As elsewhere, the U.S. armed services thrive on authoritarianism, conformism, a cult of violence, and misogyny that, in civilian life, are generally regarded as signposts of fascist ideology.

As the military extends its presence throughout governing institutions and civil society, it further contributes to gender inequality and a social hierarchy consonant with increased violence against women; militarism and patriarchy together generate an even more explosive culture of violence. The forms of sexist outlawry in wartime are well known: women routinely become victims of combat, atrocities are visited upon civilian populations, homes and neighborhoods are destroyed, people are dislocated, and prostitution spreads along with sex-trafficking, rape, torture, and domestic violence.[37] Established social and moral restraints against extreme patriarchal violence usually disappear in warfare, giving women fewer protections and fewer safe havens as they often wind up the targets of ideologically and sexually charged acts of violence. It might be argued that women actually suffer more grievously with the advent of modern technowar characterized by aerial bombardments, long-distance attacks, and destruction of civilian infrastructures.

Domestic violence seems to have become an enduring feature of military family life even in the absence of wartime experience. The hypermasculinity and misogynism that flourish in and around battlefield situations often enter directly and tragically into the household. Wertsch's interviews reveal dozens of such violent episodes. A more recent case in point is five highly publicized domestic killings at Fort Bragg, North Carolina, in the summer of 2002, three of which involved elite Special Operations troops. The murders grew out of extreme marital conflict resulting, in part, from harshly aggressive behavior that military men so regularly bring home from work, from their entire hypercharged milieu. In many instances common taboos against violence simply disappear as the warrior mentality gives men permission to behave as if they are above the law. Problems like marital infidelity can be met with such extraordinary anger that they can, as at Fort Bragg, lead to brutal attacks and even murder. Those killings were no doubt the tip of the iceberg, made visible because they fell into a cluster of actions spanning a relatively short time.[38] Marital conflict in the armed services is aggravated by regular (and sometimes lengthy) periods of separation and by the fact that men—themselves victims of suffocating hierarchy and discipline—have very little control over their lives, a power they can easily reassert with a vengeance in the household. In the tragic Fort Bragg episodes, marital conflict quickly got out of control, helped along by the army's own code of silence as well as a traditional devaluing of therapeutic solutions. Military culture serves to inhibit families from getting badly needed help. The Pentagon brass, moreover, usually turn a deaf ear to reports of distress that might harm the image of the U.S. armed forces.

The predicament of women in the military academies reflects this pattern. At the Air Force Academy in Colorado Springs, for example, several years of reports by women claiming rape, stalking, and general harassment were ignored or downplayed by administrators and students steeped in patriarchal military values and the code of silence surrounding them. This history of charges came to light when a female student in the 2002 class, Andrea Presse, filed charges against a male classmate who was accused of stalking and harassing her for more than a year. In the end, her desperate complaints were turned against her by the academy: she was charged with dishonesty and summarily expelled. Subsequent investigations discovered an educational milieu largely devoid of

respect for women—a milieu actively fostered and defended by the male officers in authority. Officials found no less than fifty-six reports of rape and sexual assault that were not acted upon; perhaps hundreds more were never reported to what had become an unresponsive bureaucracy. As Presse's mother stated: "These boys just don't get it. They are being raised to have no respect for
women, and the attitude is fostered by the male officers in charge. My daughter asked for help, and they ignored her all the way up the chain of command."[39] As in the case of Presse, who had spent four (wasted) years studying
to become a pilot, charges brought forward by other women were frequently
turned against them, as victims. After dozens of reports, in fact, not a single air
force cadet was court-martialed. The situation was reportedly no better at West
Point or Annapolis, where an entrenched code of silence was maintained by
patriarchal gatekeepers to avoid "scandals" detrimental to the upper echelon of
the armed services.

Many features of patriarchal militarism thus remain firmly embedded in
American society, despite the historic gains of feminism and increased entry of
women into the different services. It is staunchly defended by such intellectual
figures as Christina Hoff-Sommers, Robert Bork, Lionel Tiger, and Stephanie
Gutmann, not to mention the vast majority of male politicians across the ideological spectrum. It continues to draw cultural strength from the male warrior
mythology that serves the Pentagon's elitism so well. If women are valuable to
the U.S. military, it is mainly in peripheral, subordinate, devalued roles consonant with the traditional sexual division of labor, exactly the pattern of gender
relations that has been challenged (and to some extent overturned) within the
larger society.

## Corporate Media: Reservoir of Militarism

If the familiar ideal of an open, diverse, accessible popular media is the sine qua
non of a thriving democracy, prevailing trends at work in American society
have for many years been moving in just the opposite direction: corporate
megamedia structures now colonize the political and cultural terrain, including
TV, radio, film, cable TV, print journalism, and the Internet. Through giant
multinational business empires like General Electric, Viacom, Disney/ABC,
and News Corporation, elites have achieved greater capacity to influence the
flow of ideas, information, and entertainment than at any time in the past,
increasing the power to shape governmental decision making and mass consciousness. The mainstream media have become an extension of corporate
interests, not to mention government and military agendas, hardly a recipe for
viable democratic politics based in active citizen participation.

The erosion of media culture in the United States can be attributed to multiple factors: corporate mergers and growing concentration of media power;

commodification of the entire public sphere; continuous expansion of the war economy; globalization and the collapse of popular, democratic leverage over vital areas of decision making. Add to this a protracted right-wing crusade to transform the popular media into agencies of conservative ideology (a point we return to later). Today we have a communications system mostly designed to serve the needs of Wall Street and Madison Avenue, with any notion of the public interest jettisoned owing to increased privatization and deregulation of the entire media structure. The result is a narrowed, commercialized, increasingly undemocratic political culture that is thoroughly stifled by profit-driven corporate media. American journalism at the start of the twenty-first century suffers mightily under the weight of these trends, unable to provide a genuine diversity of sources and outlets, much less critical investigations into major news stories of the day. What is generally true, moreover, is even more telling when it comes to the critical issues of foreign and military policy. As Robert McChesney writes in *Rich Media, Poor Democracy,* the "corruption of journalistic integrity is always bad, but it becomes obscene under conditions of extreme media concentration, as now exist." Such "obscenity" is now endemic to what has become a largely one-dimensional media culture, prompting McChesney to ask: "What types of important stories get almost no coverage in the commercial news media? The historical standard is that there is no coverage when the political and economic elites are in agreement."[40] The reference to "no coverage" might be amended to include the probability there will be uniform coverage in support of elite priorities where the news in question concerns international politics (and most emphatically where U.S. military action has been initiated).

As David Brock shows in *The Republican Noise Machine,* the mainstream media have been the focal point of an ideological shift engineered by right-wing partisans over the past three decades. This epochal shift is the product of a well-organized, lavishly funded, sustained, politically driven crusade to completely transform the contours of American public life. Brock speaks of "a deliberated, well-financed, expressly acknowledged communications and deregulatory plan that was pursued by the right wing for more than thirty years—in close coordination with Republican Party leaders—to subvert and subsume journalism and reshape the national consciousness through the media, with the intention of skewing American politics sharply to the right. The plan has succeeded spectacularly."[41] One outcome of this crusade is Republican control of all three branches of government for the first time since 1929. Meanwhile, "free market" myths associated with Reaganomics have become the prevailing wisdom, deregulation motifs have overtaken the political culture, the idea of U.S. global domination linked to exorbitant military spending has gained currency among the elite—and "liberalism" (including the social contract inaugurated by the New Deal) has fallen into disrepute. By the 1990s Democrats, taking their cue from the transformed ideological terrain, moved to assimilate these conservative views, campaigning and governing essentially as moderate Republicans—witness the presidency of Bill Clinton.

Right-wing efforts to colonize the popular media, as Brock argues, were inspired by a fierce sense of ideological *battle,* a form of cultural "guerrilla warfare," rooted in a patient, long-term strategy that, in effect, derided long-standing notions of media objectivity and genteel debating etiquette. The battle respected few ethical or political limits. The elaborate strategy was tied to a marketing of ideas, relying on the most sophisticated advertising and public relations techniques, aimed at discrediting liberalism and capturing the political landscape for the right, now able to frame the terms of public discourse. It was a no-holds-barred propaganda campaign pure and simple.[42] Supported by such wealthy scions as Adolph Coors and Richard Mellon Scaife, the mechanisms of this cultural revolution were many: right-wing think tanks (American Enterprise, Hoover, Cato, Hudson, Heritage Foundation, etc.), book publishing, public relations firms, political-action committees and lobbies, talk radio, magazines like *Commentary, National Review,* and the *Weekly Standard,* the Internet, and a growing presence within the print and electronic media generally owing to the largesse of think tanks and the rise of TV giants like Fox.

Carried along by a "savage partisanship," right-wing objectives were sweeping and comprehensive: deregulation of corporate power, tax breaks for the rich, an assault on the welfare state, attacks on gains made by sixties' and seventies' social movements (including affirmative action), loosening of gun controls, revitalized law enforcement and intelligence, an aggressive foreign policy dependent upon vast increases in the Pentagon budget. While the new generation of conservatives, bolder and more ideologically driven, loved to speak of reducing "big government," in fact they eagerly embraced vast increases in government bureaucracy when it came to the military, intelligence, and criminal justice systems. They championed an expensive Star Wars program, agitated for a stronger worldwide U.S. military deployment, and pushed for new weapons programs as part of an overall technological restructuring of the armed forces. They were, and continue to be, champions of a greatly expanded security state. This milieu provided the ideal breeding ground for the rise of a new stratum of neoconservative "defense intellectuals," themselves skilled at manipulating public opinion on foreign-policy issues, who came to shape Bush II's global agenda, which gained new momentum in the wake of 9/11.[43] The lies, myths, and distortions used to advance the war on Iraq—indeed to justify the entire Bush Doctrine of preemptive attack—probably never would have triumphed had not this deepening militarization of the political culture laid the groundwork.

The vast majority of Americans receive the bulk of their "news" and its interpretations from TV and talk radio, hypercommercialized venues that depend almost entirely upon advertising for their revenue. These outlets are not only emphatically conservative but also generally (except for times of crisis or war) devote little actual coverage to foreign affairs. In global politics the focus turns toward images of chaos, corruption, and violence that are usually considered ordinary facts of life for other nations and cultures—especially those (like Russia, China, and the Middle East) seen as potentially hostile or threatening to U.S. geopolitical interests. The larger consequences of media culture, both domestic and global, are depoliticizing where they are not conservatizing, the exception being those moments when warfare consumes public attention. As McChesney notes: "The commercial basis of U.S. media has negative implications for the exercise of political democracy: it encourages a weak political culture that makes depoliticization, apathy, and selfishness rational choices for the citizenry, and it permits the business and commercial interests that actually rule U.S. society to have inordinate influence over the media content."[44] At first blush this closing of the public sphere might seem to be contradicted by the national frenzy generated by round-the-clock coverage of war and its preparation; the outcome would seem to be greater collective political intensity. Such "intensity," however, is linked to media-inspired spectacles, an essentially manipulated process inducing an altogether different kind of involvement. Its overcoming of fragmentation and privatism, made possible by the glorification of military prowess and national triumph, is not only ephemeral but false, instilling a parochial zealotry hardly compatible with a progressive, engaged citizenry. In effect the media war spectacle of the sort witnessed during the two Gulf Wars gives rise to a caricature of politics.

The American media offer the public an entirely mythological view of the world, one populated by foreign demons and evil monsters plotting to bring terrible harm to a benevolent, innocent, peace-loving country. While the existing order is celebrated as a beacon of democracy, prosperity, and enlightenment, the global terrain as seen through the lenses of Fox and Disney appears riven with anarchic chaos where corruption and violence rule, where dark "others" regularly violate human rights and norms of democratic governance. This is a world, predictably enough, requiring U.S. economic and political involvement and (where that turns out to be inadequate) military intervention. These views are rather uniform across the mainstream media, a taken-for-granted representation allowing for only minimally divergent opinions. TV, radio, and print media are colonized by officials and "experts" drawn mostly from the corporate, government, and military sectors—a severely limited range of voices usually falling within the patriotic consensus. On *Nightline* and similar news shows, discussion of foreign policy is framed by distinctly U.S. interests, outlooks, and values, the rest amounting to a nebulous totality that vanishes into a Hobbesian nightmare where competing or dissenting viewpoints are routinely devalued.[45] If there is more than one side to any military discourse, the difference is usually reduced to matters of tactics and phrasing, especially once the United States is engaged in warfare. Media coverage has all the character of a propaganda spectacle.

In the case of military operations the spectacle often becomes something akin to a sports extravaganza, with its epic contests, winners and losers, heroes, and huge crowds, all reflecting the extent to which media culture becomes subservient to the imperatives of power, relying on double standards, myths, and self-serving platitudes. Thus the label "terrorism" as commonly employed has relatively little informational or analytical value owing to the manner in which the term is simply meant to describe the actions of designated "enemies"; more useful references to agencies that use violent methods toward political ends are strenuously avoided insofar as they would inevitably extend to *state* as well as substate terrorism, implicating military powers like the United States and Israel. Moreover, gruesome combat episodes are sanitized or aestheticized, transformed into remote, mediated experiences. In the electronic media age all the production values of TV advertising and digital imaging, notably useful in depicting warfare, are used to the fullest. This is imperative, for, as Norman Solomon and Reese Erlich write: "No product requires more adroit marketing than one that squanders vast quantities of resources while slaughtering large numbers of people."[46] Combat operations carried out by a high-tech military turn out to be effective marketing, with staged events and exciting viewing for audiences already saturated with sports images, reality TV, and true-crime programs; in warfare, life and media seem to converge. Leading TV commentators like Bill O'Reilly and Brit Hume on Fox speak freely about bombing Afghanistan and Iraq to rubble, as if the carnage will mean little to viewers, especially *young* viewers weaned on militaristic video games and action movies. If Iraq can be personified by a Hitler-like monster in Saddam Hussein, then when combat to destroy the monster is initiated, all is rendered possible (bombing civilian targets, raiding people's homes and places of worship, committing massacres, torturing prisoners) in a war made larger than life by the media embellishment of an epic moral crusade pitting good Americans against evil (foreign, terrorist) scoundrels. Referring to the prolonged media-charged buildup to the second Gulf War, former UN weapons inspector Scott Ritter, disgusted with repeated lies by the Bush administration and the media, commented: "We made it impossible for anybody to talk about Iraq in responsible, substantive, factually-backed terms."[47]

Although the U.S. media have faithfully served patriotic ends and imperial agendas since at least the Spanish-American War, which marked the advent of Hearst's famous "yellow journalism," it reached a pinnacle during the first Gulf War—in great measure a TV war glorifying American high-tech military exploits through repetitive, graphic, live depictions of modern warfare.[48] Crowning each victory as a great extravaganza, the media emerged as a powerful agency of the war hysteria that swept the country, creating a milieu in which the dreaded "Vietnam syndrome" of defeat, humiliation, and impotence could finally be put to an end. One result of this was a deepening militarization of American culture, already set in motion during the cold war but having been practically reversed during the 1970s and 1980s owing to the Indochina deba-cle.[49] Never in U.S. history had media power turned so flagrantly propagandis-tic, so technologically seductive, so capable of molding public opinion. At the time of Desert Storm and throughout the 1990s the media succeeded in colo-nizing social life largely along lines theorized much earlier by Marshall McLuhan and Guy Debord—a reality never achieved at the time they were writing. Following the Iraqi invasion of Kuwait in 1990, the political conse-quences would be ominous, as Douglas Kellner points out: "And so, George Bush, the U.S. military, and the military-industrial complex were the immedi-ate beneficiaries of the Gulf War. Bush was transformed from wimp to warrior and the U.S. military was able to overcome its humiliation in Vietnam and its past failures. The United States appeared to be the world's sole remaining superpower, a high-tech military colossus dominating Bush's New World Order."[50] It would be a remarkably short-lived, rather pyrrhic victory for both the senior Bush and U.S. global policy, as foreign and domestic problems (momentarily obscured by Desert Storm) would quickly reemerge, though the structure and ideology of militarism was not about to disappear from the U.S. landscape.

Since the first Gulf War, and particularly since 9/11, the American press has taken up its patriotic role and pushed it to new heights. Where foreign pol-icy is concerned, the increasingly conservative media have dropped all pretense of journalistic objectivity and fairness, embracing instead a one-dimensionality in which a (civilizing, democratic, peace-loving) United States is reluctantly compelled to face off against a wide array of demonic forces. Since its incep-tion Fox TV has been especially shrill in its jingoism, although a similar pat-tern is readily visible at such outlets as CNN, NBC, ABC, and CBS, along with the bulk of newspapers, magazines, and talk radio. This fiercely intense parti-sanship means that the general historical *context* of events will never be addressed by enterprising media. Events surrounding 9/11 offer a case in point: from the terrorist attacks onward, the media did little to situate and interpret the news, investigate its circumstances, scrutinize Bush's mistakes, report egre-gious intelligence lapses, or question the efficacy of a single-minded military solution to terrorism—though matters would begin to change once the occu-pation of Iraq turned into a political quagmire for Bush. The effects of blow-back—that is, the negative, counterproductive consequences of U.S. foreign policy—were never confronted, as if to do so was somehow "anti-American." Instead, the media chose the simpler path of national celebration, focusing on wondrous American freedoms that people around the world so angrily resent-ed.[51] The terrorist episodes were framed as the work of demonic Muslims lack-ing a moral compass or political motive, a narrative willfully overlooking the clear ideological significance of the targets selected. Events were depicted so as to justify immediate military response, a pattern duplicated later as the media culture helped legitimate the mobilization toward war in Afghanistan and Iraq.

The patriotic media came fully into action as Bush's drive toward the invasion of Iraq picked up momentum by later summer 2002. It was an ideological campaign based upon a series of half-truths and lies that elites and pundits across the political spectrum repeated ad nauseam: false statements about an imminent Iraqi military threat and possession of WMD, ridiculous claims about Hussein's collaboration with Al Qaeda, phony evidence brought forth to support the myth that Iraq was rapidly accumulating nuclear materials, shameful coercive methods (often futile) used to win UN members' support, disinformation about projected costs and consequences of war and occupation, and so forth. Few media outlets paid attention to these issues, dispensing with any watchdog or investigative role—long a journalistic staple—in favor of unabashed warmaking propaganda. The ostensibly liberal media derived their initiatives mainly from government and Pentagon sources, avoiding even mild dissent, which the guardians of public opinion considered particularly noisome as U.S. military operations got under way. As in the case of Desert Storm, TV now shifted to nearly round-the-clock coverage of U.S. military operations, dwelling on the Pentagon's initial "shock and awe" tactics, which targeted Baghdad alone with more than four hundred cruise missiles just during the first days of war. The campaign, labeled "Plan Iraqi Freedom," was now uncritically packaged as the liberation of Iraq from despotism and its transformation into a political democracy. The media lens focused largely on the logistical and technical aspects of military action, with political and ethical questions pushed aside. Guests on TV news programs, interview shows, and talkfests were drawn from the familiar stable of right-wing pundits: Fred Barnes, George Will, Charles Krauthammer, Ben Wattenberg, William Kristol, Ann Coulter, Max Boot, Robert Kagan. Many pro-war intellectuals were anointed media stars at Fox and other networks. And the "defense experts," as on the occasions of Desert Storm and Yugoslavia, were omnipresent. The antiwar side of the debate was basically ignored until popular demonstrations in the United States and around the world became much too large to ignore, at which time they were grotesquely caricatured. As the Pentagon was getting ready to invade, spurred on by resource and geopolitical aims, the inevitably costly material, human, and global consequences of the U.S. imperial gambit were overlooked or downplayed.

In the period 2002–2003 the *Washington Post* ran a series of op-ed pieces, editorials, and news reports that, taken together, helped fuel the push toward the second Gulf War. The paper served as essentially a mouthpiece for government and Pentagon agendas, voiced by such writers as Jim Hoagland, Henry Kissinger, James Baker, Richard Holbrooke, and Robert Novak. The ensemble of pro-war articles and op-eds seemed moved by a sense of imperial arrogance, indifference toward the costs of war, and rigid intolerance of anyone dissenting from the decision to invade. A few critical voices making their way into the *Post* were concerned with mostly tactical issues of timing, logistics, and the need to mobilize broader support. Most contributors were present or former Washington insiders, typically referred to as "experts" in world politics, terrorism, or the Middle East. Foreign viewpoints were extremely hard to locate.[52] The *Post* series established the prevailing trajectory for U.S. print journalism in the lead-up to war. The *Wall Street Journal* enthusiastically joined in the ideological mobilization for war, as did the *New York Times, Newsweek,* and *Time,* which devoted a number of special issues to the imminent threat of Iraq and the evils of Hussein's rule, while glorifying the blessings of U.S. military technology.

Diversity of opinion, long understood as fundamental to American democratic politics, now largely vanished from a public sphere increasingly saturated with outpourings of patriotism, militarism, and imperial arrogance. Opposition to Bush was smothered by the patriotic onslaught, dismissed as outright propaganda or siding with the "enemy." Some media outlets felt a responsibility to cover official Iraqi statements, but of course anything coming from Baghdad was immediately discredited as the diabolic machinations of Hussein or Al Qaeda. In January 2003 CNN was preparing to cover a live press announcement from Baghdad where Iraqi officials wanted to refute Bush's warmongering statements and policies—the very statements and policies that were carried nonstop throughout the U.S. media. Soon after an Iraqi spokesperson began laying out the case against war, the network cut away to "breaking news" from the White House: Bush would be giving a preview of his State of the Union address. But there would never be any return to the Iraqi official, whose argument had been interrupted in midstream. Although Bush said little beyond what was generally known, the abrupt break gave CNN a plausible excuse for ignoring a strong, vocal counterpoint. There was also Dan Rather's famous interview with Hussein in late February 2003—itself roundly condemned as an unpardonable indulgence of the enemy. Giving his first extended foreign interview in several years, the Iraqi leader made a passionate appeal for peaceful solutions, for stepped-up diplomacy, even for friendly relations with the United States. A nearly full-page report of the interview in the *Los Angeles Times* (February 27, 2003) began with the bizarre observation that Hussein's statements could not be regarded as newsworthy (they were just propaganda), then proceeded to totally ignore what was said; the report strangely contained no quotes of Hussein's responses to specific questions. In their place was a lengthy series of attacks on Hussein, five in all, by hawkish supporters of Bush's policy, including White House spokesperson Ari Fleischer. Hussein's views, for better or worse, gained attention only by virtue of their negation—an unconscionable journalistic practice, but one that would become all too familiar during the rush to war.

Even the slightest inclination toward media objectivity is abandoned once we enter the sacred "bipartisan" realm of U.S. foreign and military policy; official propaganda comes to the fore, transforming "news" into the modality of a sports contest and political discourse into expressions of patriotic conformism. Rival governments are vilified for exactly the same international behavior the

United States carries out with much greater regularity, on a larger scale, and with impunity. Media coverage dwells on a long list of abuses in Russia, China, and Iraq, while more grotesque violations by the United States and its client states go unreported or, where reported, are downplayed and "contextualized." Thus possession of WMD by other nations is treated as an unmitigated horror, a threat to human civilization, while the taken-for-granted and infinitely larger WMD arsenal of the United States fades into the natural terrain, scarcely worthy of notice. When embarrassing realities cannot simply be ignored—for example, the Gulf War syndrome or the Abu Ghraib prison scandal—government spinning of events warrants more attention than basic fact-finding investigations. The very *idea* that U.S. leaders might be guilty of war crimes is simply never contemplated by the media. What occurred during the prewar situation in Iraq constitutes just one of many recent examples: U.S. military action, routine bombings, and harsh economic sanctions for more than a decade, leading to hundreds of thousands of casualties, scarcely registered on the media radar scope.

Partly owing to an increasingly one-dimensional media, American political culture seems to have less space for genuinely open debates and diverse sources of information: "terrorism," for example, has become merely a shibboleth referring to an evil scourge, the work of foreign monsters addicted to hatred and violence, while supposedly good intentions underlying U.S. military actions remain a simple matter of faith. As Sardar and Davies observe, American public opinion is today shockingly provincial, reflecting a widespread lack of curiosity about how people around the world live, think, and act.[53] Despite unprecedented affluence, mobility, and access to information, despite huge enrollments at institutions of higher learning, Americans at the start of the twenty-first century are shockingly insular and ethnocentric, inclined toward superpatriotism. Surveys reveal a frightening ignorance of global affairs. It is easy to see how, with the end of the cold war, the label "terrorist" could so routinely be fastened onto individuals, groups, and states deemed hostile to U.S. interests or policies, just as the "Communist" stigma was successfully invoked before it. The frequently asked question in the media "Why do they hate us?" says volumes about the political culture. While "they" now typically refers to Arabs, Muslims, and terrorists, the "us" part of the equation assumes a wounded innocence, a victim status appropriate to a nation surrounded by threatening enemies. If the focus shifted to the real policies and actions of an aggressive superpower, entirely different sets of questions would have to be posed, directed at issues of why and how the United States so routinely intervenes in matters outside its own borders, why it has been so quick to use ruthless military force on behalf of its geopolitical interests, and why it so often violates international laws and agreements.

In any truly balanced forum, such questions would inevitably enter into public discourse in a manner that would enhance the general political culture.

One reasonable point of view within such an open debate would be that "hatred" directed at U.S. leaders might be the understandable reaction of people who are the victims of destructive superpower interventions over which they have no control. That some people might want to channel their hostility in violent directions will not be surprising to any informed observer. Yet this very idea is dismissed as crazy, even treasonous, by the mainstream media. For those tens of millions of people in some way harmed by U.S. imperial power, the same "terrorism" is automatically taken as a justifiable (if not always efficacious) response to *state* terrorism. History is of course replete with instances of violent popular struggles against governmental oppression: American and Irish independence movements against the British, the Algerians against the French, the antiapartheid movement in South Africa, partisan battles against the Nazis in World War II, to name only a few. Within the U.S. corporate media it seems comforting to frame violence committed by others as nothing but random, unmitigated evil, devoid of human rationality or motive. Sardar and Davies point out that the well-worn media fixation on *foreign* evil ultimately serves as a useful cover for willful ignorance, xenophobia, and, in the end, military action against the designated malignancy.

In the weeks preceding the second Gulf War, the airwaves of the major TV networks were colonized by virulent pro-war voices, according to a well-known study of the American media by the watchdog group Fairness and Accuracy in Reporting (FAIR). Of 397 total guest appearances during that period, fully 75 percent of U.S. sources were present or former government officials, often national-security and military people, all strongly behind Bush's decision to wage "preemptive" war on Iraq. Just *four* voices from what had become a massive, global antiwar movement were given even a limited forum. A few antiwar critics (just twenty in all) were chosen from largely *foreign* sources, many of them Iraqi government officials—the implied message being that such views were not to be taken seriously. The bulk of TV broadcasts covered the quest for distinctly *military* solutions—"solutions" to a "crisis" that was, in the final analysis, clearly American-made. Official news releases and press conferences, many from the Pentagon, State Department, and White House, were routinely and uncritically passed along by the patriotic media, taken wholly at face value, as were Bush's endlessly repeated pretexts for war.[54] Such intense media partisanship was visible at a time when opinion polls in the major industrial nations showed an average of 80 percent of the population opposed U.S. military intervention, with more than half of the *American* respondents also taking an antiwar stance. Given the historical trajectory of U.S. media culture, most of the public now receives news and information almost exclusively from mainstream outlets—their sources directly tied to government, the military, and right-wing think tanks along with a small circle of academics with hawkish military views. One problem here is that news organizations that want ready access to the centers of power, especially vital during wartime, are forced to go along with the hegemonic limits set by those same centers of power. Pentagon influence on the corporate media has grown measurably, especially since 9/11, a trend reflected in the increased glorification of military power common at Fox, CNN, ABC, *Time* magazine, the *Wall Street Journal,* and most talk-radio stations (the majority owned by right-wing Disney/ABC and Clear Channel)—not to mention the more frequent release of Hollywood combat movies dramatizing good-war themes since the late 1990s, a theme we shall take up in the following chapters. The dominant media culture, organically tied to corporate power and the war economy, has become more integral than ever to the legitimation of U.S. imperial and military agendas.

# CHAPTER 2

# War and Cinema: The Historical Legacy

The term "the Hollywood war machine" refers to the production of studio films depicting and glorifying U.S. wartime heroic exploits while embellishing the military experience itself in all its dimensions, from the Revolutionary period to the present. While our focus is primarily on the contemporary movie industry, familiarity with the century-long evolution of what has been called the combat genre—a centerpiece of American popular culture—provides the needed historical and conceptual backdrop to the analysis developed in later chapters. We argue that the motion picture tradition has from its inception at the turn of the last century been fascinated with military action as a vital part of the American patriotic tradition. For most of cinematic history war films have rivaled the Western genre (itself arguably a variant of the combat form) in terms of box-office appeal. A survey of the Hollywood film legacy reveals that an astonishingly large proportion of studio films have dramatized U.S. wartime experiences, heroics, and triumphs, often indirectly within the framework of other genres such as the male action-adventure picture that gained popularity in the 1980s. In exploring the rise and impact, both culturally and politically, of the Hollywood war machine, several questions inevitably emerge: Why do U.S. filmmakers remain so intensely interested in the phenomenon of armed conflict? Why do producers and directors emphasize some wars over others? Above all, why at the start of the twenty-first century are war films, as well as closely related genres, enjoying such a powerful renaissance? The answers to such questions will help illuminate the intimate historical connection between the U.S. military and the film industry—not to mention the broad contours of a militarized culture that we laid out in chapter 1.

In helping sustain a deep culture of violence, the legacy of the Hollywood war machine has been something of a reciprocal one in which warfare has provided filmmakers with some of their most exciting, lucrative storytelling material while the studios have furnished the military with continuous, free, highly effective advertising and marketing that has often done wonders for recruiting. With few exceptions, the movie industry has presented an image of the U.S. armed forces as heroic, noble, all-conquering, and above all *exciting,* with World War II furnishing the ideal example of a "good war" fought by good, civilized people for exalted causes against hated, barbaric enemies. This was indeed an image that simultaneously benefited Hollywood and the military: the films, trading on fascinating action narratives, male heroics, and patriotism, generally made profits while at the same time audiences became conditioned to accept real-life U.S. armed interventions wherever they occurred. Despite the occasional appearance of movies that put forth rather negative images of the military—for example, the bulk of those portraying the Vietnam experience—it is probably fair to say that the American filmgoing public today embraces an overwhelmingly *positive* view of the U.S. armed forces along with a patriotic willingness to support their foreign ventures. This is the product of a reconstituted and oligopolistic studio system in which corporate interests have engineered an unprecedented merger of entertainment and politics, money-making and global agendas. Within what has become a vast, globalized megamedia structure it is easy enough to see that warfare has emerged as a kind of sacred activity befitting the broader culture of militarism. Building on the time-honored tradition of the male-warrior ethos, it extends in Hollywood movies well beyond the familiar combat genre to Westerns, action-adventures, sci-fi films, horror pictures, comedies, and ordinary historical dramas. Since the late 1970s many blockbusters have been war-themed films. In all of these, to one degree or another, military action serves as the setting for uplifting, patriotic, violence-saturated narratives and myths, all the while rendering large-scale acts of violence more legitimate, more socially acceptable—the larger the acts, one is tempted to add, the greater the legitimacy.

From the Revolutionary War period and the ruthless campaigns against native tribes to the recent Gulf Wars, Americans have shown a consistent love of warfare and its call to patriotic duty and military heroism articulated by the likes of Andrew Jackson, Theodore Roosevelt, General George S. Patton, President George W. Bush, and a long list of film military protagonists portrayed by such actors as Gary Cooper, John Wayne, Errol Flynn, Henry Fonda, Clint Eastwood, and Tom Hanks. Even those movies in which the mantra is "war is hell" in fact usually carry forward a martial spirit that glorifies the action, camaraderie, adventure, and technological wizardry of the war experience. To simply label the combat genre as escapist diversion is therefore completely inaccurate; the addiction to military violence and armed conquest runs across the historical panorama, shaping the political culture and mobilizing people for the real thing. Indeed, military films have from time to time contributed enormously to particularly virulent expressions of nationalism and militarism, perhaps never more so than at the turn of the twenty-first century as the United States moves aggressively to consolidate its global hegemony.

Warfare and its glorification in Hollywood cinema speaks to a recurrent common impulse, especially salient in U.S. history, to transcend the *ordinary*—those frustrating, boring, anxiety-ridden features of daily life that violent struggles against threatening evil forces might seem to overcome. Thus, to legitimate war and its horrific consequences, powerful enemies are needed, and these of course have been furnished in great abundance by a long list of producers, writers, and directors in Hollywood: Indians, Mexicans, Asians, Arabs, Communists, Muslims, terrorists, drug traffickers, serial killers. Without such real or imagined enemies there can be no war mythologies, indeed no war *movies* as we have come to know them. Enemies are by definition demons, forces of darkness and evil that inhabit a world of anarchy and savagery—forces that appear all the more threatening because of their mysterious character. For combat narratives to work effectively, a Manichaeistic framework is required, pitting good against evil, light against dark, order against chaos, democracy against tyranny. In this scheme of things, villains generally are cold, remote, ghostly, and elusive while heroes are immediately *knowable,* concrete personae who embody the whole range of everyday feelings and emotions, who inhabit the real world of families, neighborhoods, and workplaces. A villain who kills is filled with unmitigated evil, devoid of purpose and rationale, which fits the media stereotypes of Nazis, Communists, and terrorists, whereas the hero is identified with fully intelligible and laudable goals or ideals—true of Gary Cooper in *High Noon,* John Wayne in *Sands of Iwo Jima,* George C. Scott in *Patton,* and Sylvester Stallone in *Rambo.* Owing to such an immense social and moral gulf between the two, killing becomes not only justifiable but praiseworthy, perhaps an existential moment on the path toward individual and collective self-actualization. Few Hollywood movies that address warfare narratives, whatever the genre, significantly depart from this structural pattern.

## Hollywood Mobilizes for Combat

The symbiotic relationship between Hollywood and the U.S. military was first solidified at the time of World War I, labeled the "Great War" in the press, but soon enough the focus turned to disillusionment and second thoughts—both in the film world and in American society as a whole. Even before the United States entered the war in 1917, motion pictures had become great recruiting vehicles for the armed forces, especially for the navy in the wake of its decisive victory over Spain. Not only had the navy grown rapidly after 1900, it also provided a colorful, exotic, adventurous backdrop for movies that rarely departed from formulaic romance tales, buddy stories, and comedic meanderings onboard ships. Routinely approved by the military, such films presented the navy in a highly glamorous, patriotic light, filled with images of handsome, dynamic, competent officers and men even as overtly pro-war messages were typically resisted. In lending the studios military facilities, men, and equipment, as well as logistical support, Washington was able to exercise rather strict control over filmmaking, always vigilant regarding any deviations from established military codes and norms. It was a relationship that worked splendidly for both sides.[1]

While military-themed movies of this period tended to romanticize life in the armed services, never failing to indulge feel-good patriotic sentiments, they rarely glorified warfare as such, preferring a more nuanced approach. When the popular mood of the country seemed to favor pacifism and nonintervention—as during the years immediately preceding both world wars—films rarely stressed the war motif. Before the United States entered World War I, several films actually conveyed something of an ethic of nonviolence, an outlook far more plausible at a time when the famous military-industrial complex was barely in its infancy. One such film was Thomas Ince's *Civilization, or He Who Remembered* (1914), in which the spirit of Christ returns to earth in the body of a great soldier who restores world peace as he sets out to redeem all humanity. This movie reputedly helped elect Woodrow Wilson to the presidency on an antiwar platform. During the election campaign, he was often compared to the film's Christ-like pacifist hero.[2] D. W. Griffith's epic depiction of the Civil War, *The Birth of a Nation* (1915), contains powerful scenes that illuminate the senseless brutality of warfare. While Griffith devoted massive footage to battle-field carnage, his major preoccupation was with the horrors of combat, its debilitating effects on soldiers from both sides, and the devastation of civilian life—even as he winds up romanticizing the Ku Klux Klan. Griffith followed this enormous box-office success with *Intolerance* (1917), which constructed elaborate images of war that were bound to instill jaundiced views of military violence in audiences. Unfortunately for Griffith, *Intolerance* reached theaters just as the United States was mobilizing for war, when a previously isolationist public was being transformed into a flag-waving, jingoistic mass. The antiwar message was drowned out by an outpouring of superpatriotic sentiment. The production of films like *Intolerance* would be unthinkable during and immediately after the Great War.

The decades between World Wars I and II marked something of a retreat from the jingoistic mood of the late teens—a shift at least partially reflected in the cinematic output of the period. Just a small number of movies fit the combat genre strictly defined, and these, while presenting largely positive views of military life, were not especially known for their outright xenophobia or militarism. Some dwelled on the peacetime mission of what was still a relatively small global deployment of U.S. armed forces. Those few productions that re-created the Great War gravitated toward the "war is hell" motif, featuring spectacles of death and destruction that, terrible as they were, could nonetheless be justified by resorting to such a noble cause as Woodrow Wilson's claim to be "making the world safe for democracy." Along these lines, Griffith's *Hearts of the World* (1918) depicts the general horrors of an especially brutal (and futile) World War I while at the same time showing German troops as especially demonic as they invade and terrorize a peaceful French village. Some local inhabitants resist and are quickly tortured and murdered by the Hun barbarians. The heroine (Lillian Gish), the daughter of an expatriate artist, meets the son of another expatriate (Robert Harron), who enlists in the French army to defend his adopted homeland. The two fall in love and on their wedding night are bombarded by a German assault: Gish survives but her husband is killed. Driven mad by his death, she spends the entire night with his corpse. Behind Griffith's graphically depicted abhorrence of war lies another, perhaps more compelling, theme: whatever the costs of military conflict, the German beasts simply had to be defeated. Rex Ingram's film *The Four Horsemen of the Apocalypse* (1921) follows roughly the same narrative structure, dramatizing the carnage of warfare while showing American objectives to be noble and heroic.

The Great War did inspire a series of more emotionally patriotic and militaristic films in the immediate aftermath of the armistice. The Edison Company's *Star Spangled Banner* appeared in late 1917 but was viewed for several years afterward as a powerful recruiting device for the U.S. armed services. Its focus was less on the combat experience than on the more seductive, adventurous elements of military life (here the marines) such as training, marching, drilling, and ceremonial activities. A huge commercial hit in 1918, *The Unbeliever* presented an array of perilous but inspiring trench-warfare scenes in which the Germans were shown in all their Prussian ruthlessness. A major U.S. distributor of the film, George Kleine, is quoted as saying that *The Unbeliever* was "inspired with patriotism of the kind that leaves you restless and eager to do something, whether enlisting or assisting the government in other activities that are necessary to win the war."[3] Anticipating later World War II combat pictures, *The Unbeliever* graphically portrayed, in scenes of bloody encounters at Belleau Wood and Chateau-Thierry, an enemy so unspeakably barbaric that the worst suffering of combat was easily justified. For this reason *The Unbeliever*, when viewed alongside *Star Spangled Banner*, established something of a paradigm for future "good war" epics, enlisting the passions of military life and warfare—although here in much cruder form than the more smoothly propagandistic movies of World War II. And these films, like the later productions, received the full blessing and support of the U.S. military.

After 1921, Hollywood produced few movies that embellished or glorified warfare in this fashion. Returning to the "war is hell" theme, King Vidor directed *The Big Parade* (1926), which depicted the lives of soldiers struggling to survive the horrors of World War I. Known for its powerful realism and emotional intensity, this film straddled both sides of the fence: war has few redeeming virtues but nonetheless comes across as something natural, part of the human condition. In refusing to glamorize combat, Vidor's work was widely understood to be an "antiwar" statement, although the filmmaker himself disavowed this label, presenting the film as simply a more rational, intelligent expression of patriotism. If war brought few rewards to its participants, victors and victims alike, it would be utopian to think it could ever be eradicated; peace and disarmament were the pipe dreams of a few misguided pacifists. In *What Price Glory?* (1926), Raoul Walsh presented a highly comedic but still romantic image of marine life in an entertaining movie that served the goals of military recruitment. While mocking some aspects of service life, Walsh adhered strictly to the War Department code, which required that no play or film bring discredit to the U.S. military—the sine qua non of winning needed military assistance. The strong critical and box-office success of *The Big Parade* was followed by William Wellman's spectacular air force epic, *Wings* (1927), a realistic rendering of World War I aerial warfare that won the first Academy Award for best picture. A patriotic film dedicated to "young warriors in the sky," *Wings* too served for many years as an effective recruiting device for the nascent U.S. Army Air Force. A precursor to such later combat extravaganzas as *Twelve O'Clock High* (1949), *Midway* (1976), and *Top Gun* (1986), Wellman's classic, according to Suid, "became the yardstick against which all future combat spectaculars have had to be measured in terms of authenticity of combat and scope of production."[4]

During the 1920s only a few military-themed films were produced, and fewer yet attracted large audiences at a time when Westerns and comedies were on the rise; the public seemed anxious to forget about the horrors of the Great War. This pattern continued throughout the 1930s as a mood of international disengagement swept the country as people grew fearful that the United States might get immersed in yet another meaningless conflict. By the late 1930s the combat genre had reached its low point, surpassed now by musicals, screwball comedies, gangster films, Westerns, and historical dramas that appealed to a mass of viewers looking to escape the harsh material realities of the Depression. Military pictures made in Hollywood during this period in fact incorporated some of these trends, turning to romance stories, comedies, and a variety of personal dramas against the backdrop of peacetime military life. The studios embraced movies about the navy, attracted mostly to the idyllic setting of the U.S. Naval Academy at Annapolis, relying on depictions of marching midshipmen, a beautiful campus, dances, gorgeous women, and football weekends to present a romanticized image of the military world outside combat. Examples included *Shipmates Forever* (1935) and *Navy Blue and Gold* (1937), both filled with formulaic stories about rites of passage in which young men encounter minor obstacles on their way to full adulthood marked by professional status and exciting relationships. Consistent with the Hollywood code, such movies ignored or downplayed the more problematic aspects of military life, its boredom, long hours, regimentation, and so forth. Made at low cost and approved by the Navy Motion Picture Board, these films still resonated with patriotism even in the absence of wartime scenarios, offered glorified versions of the armed services, and were ideal recruiting vehicles. John Ford's *Men without Women* (1930), another film revolving around peacetime navy life, fit this motif, as did a series of submarine-disaster pictures like *Submarine D-1* (1937), starring a young Ronald Reagan, and Frank Capra's *Dirigible* (1931), the first movie to depict the glories of naval aviation.

Many of these films were shot in Hawaii, which, like the military academies, furnished the perfect milieu for tried-and-true formulas: exotic physical settings, handsome men in uniform, weekend romances, rites of passage, happy endings. As wartime narratives and themes vanished, navy and army personnel were shown leading the good life in locales devoid of armed conflict, excessive hardships, unsavory characters, and, of course, harrowing story lines. *Dress Parade* (1927) became the model for such fare. An accurate subheading for these pictures—again, fully monitored and sanctioned by the War Department—might have been "The Army and Navy in Paradise." Everything corresponded nicely to the spreading ethos of isolationism, deeply reflected in such later films as Victor Fleming's *Gone with the Wind* (1939), which painted a bitter portrait of the Civil War and its aftermath in the South. Indeed, Scarlett O'Hara's (Vivien Leigh) first lines in the movie, directed at two of her suitors, perfectly illustrate this detachment from war: "Fiddle-dee-dee. War, war, war. This war talk is spoiling all the fun at every party this spring."

The outbreak of World War II in Europe in 1939 did little to change American public opinion, but it did give rise to a resurgent patriotic consensus at the studios, permitting something of a return to the familiar combat genre. Films dramatizing male battlefield heroics appeared in 1940 *(Flight Command)* and 1941 *(Dive Bomber)*, regarded as jingoistic propaganda by the isolationist crowd preoccupied with avoiding another U.S. entry into global conflagration. Critics viewed the studios, notably Warner Bros., as seeking to push the United States into war against Germany and Japan, to the point where the Senate began in late 1941 to investigate Hollywood war-themed pictures as "subversive." It was Howard Hawks's popular narrative of World War I, *Sergeant York*, released in 1941, that was most harshly accused of fomenting extreme nationalism and militarism, thereby aiding Franklin Roosevelt's scheme to mobilize the United States for war. Of course it took the Japanese bombing of Pearl Harbor to finally bring the United States into the war, after which essentially propaganda films like *Sergeant York* gained favor. There was the return to a Manichaeistic worldview in which the noble, heroic forces of American democracy were pitted against an array of brutal, menacing enemies in a struggle to protect civilization from the hordes of barbarians. The old "peacetime" military pictures vanished entirely from the scene.

# The Western as Combat Genre

From the earliest days of Hollywood the Western emerged as the quintessential American film genre—part historical drama, part colonial saga, part military epic, part folk mythology. It might be argued that Westerns, in their dominant form, were always most representative of the combat picture, complete with all the battlefield mythology that attracted millions of viewers to the standard military productions. Across many decades this output has glorified something else: in more than two thousand movies American Indians have been the victims of a brutal, cinematic process of colonization, their history distorted and mangled by a film industry moved according to its own ideological agendas. The Hollywood myth of the Western was built on the epic frontier expansion of white Euro-American settlers who stopped short of nothing—including genocidal rampages—to ensure their conquest of North America. This reality was inverted by hundreds of filmmakers anxious to show the "civilizing" effects of an idealistic westward migration that would eventually overcome the resistance of Native American savages. The Hollywood myth, in other words, depended on obliteration of the historical record, giving the myth full rein. In Ward Churchill's words: "Having attained such utter decontextualization, filmmakers were free to indulge themselves—and their audiences—almost exclusively in fantasies of Indians as warriors. Not just any warriors, mind you, but those of a most hideously bestial variety."[5] Thus, if it is true that Westerns represent "without question the richest and most enduring genre of Hollywood's repertoire," as Thomas Schatz writes, this legacy has been an overwhelmingly false one tied to discourses of colonialism, racism, and militarism.[6]

The combat and Western genres share a venerable cultural myth: courageous warriors fighting noble battles against demonic foreign savages, enemies lacking any shred of humanity. The myth is galvanized by bold, creative protagonists, usually white men, prepared to sacrifice their lives for common patriotic objectives. One thinks of the Concord irregulars leading a guerrilla insurgency against the British Redcoats, George Washington crossing the Delaware River to take on the Hessians, Civil War generals like Ulysses S. Grant fighting valiantly to save the Union, and later combat heroes like Sergeant York, Eddie Rickenbacker, Colonel James Doolittle, and Audie Murphy. Movie icon John Wayne's long series of warrior roles in both combat and Western pictures— from *Stagecoach* to *Sands of Iwo Jima* to *The Green Berets*—fits this pattern to perfection. The virtues of such warrior champions are well known: tenacity, tough-mindedness, honor, selflessness, nobility, and of course patriotism. Combat heroes have become an inseparable part of the American cultural landscape, occupying a special niche within cinematic history.

A large percentage of Westerns correspond to the combat pattern in their own right, especially those romanticizing the campaigns of settlers and the U.S. Cavalry during the nineteenth-century Indian Wars. A few depict Civil War episodes in the West, including *Shenandoah, Santa Fe Trail,* and *They Died with Their Boots On,* while others draw their narratives from events in the aftermath of the Civil War (Ford's *Searchers,* Eastwood's *Outlaw Josey Wales*). Still others focused on U.S. warfare against rival military forces, including army combat against Pancho Villa and scattered local wars against cattlemen, homesteaders, and law-enforcement agents (*Shane, The Wild Bunch, Silverado*). All of these films employ dramatic structures virtually identical to the established combat genre, in which patriotic military groups confront an array of brutal, despotic enemies on the road to human progress. They share spectacular movie settings, attractive heroes, predictable story lines, and despicable villains—the very stuff of Hollywood box-office success. Unlike conventional Westerns such as *High Noon* and *The Virginian,* which chronicle the exploits of individual "outlaw heroes," combat-defined Westerns depict relatively small groupings of warriors involved with collective military enterprises as in the famous Cavalry/settler campaigns to wrest control of the frontier from the Indian tribes. Here the protagonists are endowed with extraordinary personal virtues (love, dedication, honor, strength), while the enemy, as in all standard combat pictures, is objectified and demonized.

All the stock combat figures from classic war-related films naturally appear in the combat Westerns; the uniforms of course vary, but the familiar motifs come fully and dramatically into play. We encounter the predictable conflict between idealistic but naïve junior officers and rigid, tough senior officers, the usual struggle over issues of strategy and tactics, vast obstacles to be surmounted, treacherous romantic entanglements, and ordinary soldiers ready to sacrifice their lives for the larger good. This formula has appealed to filmgoing audiences since the advent of motion pictures. No doubt the most popular of these have been renditions of the great westward push involving fierce armed conflict between white conquerors and the eventually subdued Indian warriors. Classic Hollywood fare along these lines included *Stagecoach, The Iroquois Trail, Fort Apache, Red River, She Wore a Yellow Ribbon,* and *Apache,* many of these directed by outstanding filmmakers like Ford and Hawks and all of them told from the standpoint of the victors. In episode after episode the settler groups and the U.S. Army emerge not only gallantly triumphant—thanks to their organizational shrewdness and technological supremacy—but resolutely virtuous.

Cecil B. DeMille's *Union Pacific* served as one particular model for later Westerns—a narrative in which colonization is seen as part of the natural, inevitable march of progress. This picture chronicles the laying of the transcontinental railroad during the post–Civil War period as the audience is informed that "Indians redden the rails with the blood of tracklayers." The workers struggle mightily to complete the line before a congressionally mandated deadline. Jeff Butler (Joel McCrea) takes charge of the precarious railroad security and quickly encounters the grave menace of several hundred Sioux warriors determined to obstruct the line running across Indian territories. In familiar combat-Western style, the Indians use clever tactics to derail a Union Pacific train. When they go through the cargo in the overturned train, they become inebriated and start behaving like stereotypical drunken Indians. Butler and a few friends manage to conceal themselves in a railroad car long enough to send a primitive telegraph message to alert the cavalry, which rides in at the last minute to save the day. The sound of bugles blowing to accompany the charge and images of mounted troops riding full speed at the last possible moment to rescue besieged whites became the hallmarks of subsequent combat Westerns.

In similar fashion, Ford's *Drums along the Mohawk* (1939) harkens back to the Revolutionary period, with upstate New York its picturesque locale. The pioneer families farming the Mohawk Valley must overcome poverty, hostile Indians, and a sinister Tory named Caldwell (John Carradine). As the film opens, a young couple, Gil Martin (Henry Fonda) and Lana Borst (Claudette Colbert), set off on their honeymoon in the Mohawk Valley but soon meet Caldwell at an inn, where they are informed of an imminent Indian uprising. The uprising eventually takes place, at the instigation of Caldwell, whereupon Martin joins the community-defense militia and Borst joins other civilians heading for the nearest army fort. When the attack comes, a Christianized Indian named Blueback (Chief Big Trees) sounds the alarm by yelling "Indians on the warpath!" He shouts this warning, as Robin Wood observes, "as if he himself wasn't one."[7] In Ford's picture Blueback appears as the quintessential "good Indian," having renounced his roots and identity, while all other Indians are presented as undifferentiated one-dimensional villains out to destroy the white settler life. After vast spilling of blood the colonists (men and women together) are able to militarily prevail. As Wood points out, even as the audience sees a young couple bravely setting out to forge a family life together, to build a vibrant civilization, an otherwise idyllic enterprise ultimately conceals a sinister political reality that "is no less than American imperialism, the seizing of land as private property, the extermination of nature."[8] Ford's movie, like other combat Westerns of the 1930s and 1940s, serves to ideologically justify the Euro-American conquest of Indian lands and peoples.

Ford's *Stagecoach* (1939) is rightly considered the first masterpiece of the classic Westerns, representing (as Bazin notes) an "ideal balance between social myth, historical reconstruction, psychological truth, and the traditional theme of the Western mise en scene."[9] Here Ford combines an intricate, character-driven plot involving stagecoach passengers traveling through Apache territory with stunning cinematography of sweeping panoramas in Monument Valley—shots that effectively dwarf the carriage as it moves across zones of imminent danger. The passengers are a microcosm of Western society: an alcoholic physician, an embezzling banker, a young pregnant woman, a prostitute, a gambler, and the young outlaw Ringo Kid (played by John Wayne in his first major role). This ensemble embarks on a long, torturous journey between frontier outposts, eventually running into an Apache detachment that attacks the coach. The men, with Ringo Kid in the lead, suffer casualties as they hold off the intruders until they run out of ammunition—and are saved at the last minute by the Seventh Cavalry, which drives off the Indians. In the final scene Wayne, having fallen in love with one of the passengers, proposes marriage to her and expresses his desire to start a family. This narrative twist, where romance and family follow a period of great crisis and trauma, became a defining motif of the combat Western; once the menace has vanished, apparently, it is time for routine, ordinary social life to resume.

With the fading of the old Westerns starring the likes of Gene Autry and Tom Mix, Ford moved to resurrect and extend the Western myth in *Stagecoach.* Here the civilizing mission of white settlers taming native savages and a hostile environment reaches its apex. It served as a model for later pictures by Ford and others that glamorize the process of imperial conquest. The narrative structure revolves around pacification of a lawless, violent, chaotic frontier, the ruthless extension of "eastern" virtues into the Hobbesian West. *Stagecoach* is filled with unsavory, flawed protagonists whose very idiosyncrasies and weaknesses are covered up by the greater civilizing agenda. The film depicts the dangerous Apaches lurking everywhere, natural avengers devoid of any moral or social constraints. Of course the travelers were actually facing one sector of a long Apache guerrilla insurgency led by such warriors as Geronimo (who appears briefly in the picture) in a losing battle to save their homelands. This tragic history is fully obscured by Ford's larger-than-life re-creation of the Western myth as seen through the eyes of the colonists. As Andrew Sinclair observes, *Stagecoach* "set the pattern of the classic Western for all time, making archetypes of its characters, primal conflicts of its situations, dream landscapes of its backgrounds."[10]

Ford's great output of epic Westerns continued for another three decades, making a definite imprint on American popular culture. Another Wayne vehicle, *Fort Apache* (1948)—the first of Ford's trilogy about the U.S. Cavalry—is the tragic saga of a tough, arrogant, fiercely militaristic colonel named Owen Thursday (Henry Fonda) who, despite his Custer-like suicidal mistakes, ends up as one of the powerful legends of the Indian Wars. Thursday expresses nothing but contempt for the Native American tribes, and after setting a trap for the Apaches decides to move his regiment closer to a larger standing force, against the strong counsel of experienced Indian fighter Captain Kirby York (Wayne). Calling York a coward, the colonel leads his men into a suicidal attack where, in a trap laid by Sitting Bull and Crazy Horse, every soldier is picked off by Indian sharpshooters. Thursday emerges as a hero despite having foolishly ensured the terrible defeat of his own regiment at the hands of "savages" he despised so much he became blind to their military prowess. Earlier films—most notably Raoul Walsh's *They Died with Their Boots On* (1941), with Errol Flynn playing Custer—had whitewashed Custer's role in the great defeat at

Little Big Horn in 1876, transforming the general who once had presidential aspirations into a Western hero.

The second part of Ford's trilogy, *She Wore a Yellow Ribbon* (1949), further exemplifies the white colonial spirit in the period just after the Custer debacle, when the West is slipping into chaos and anarchy. Every settlement appears vulnerable to Indian uprisings. The film's narrator asserts (improbably) that "Pony Express riders know that one more such defeat as Custer's and it would be a hundred years before another wagon train cared to cross the plains," noting with alarm that "one thousand Indians are united in common war against the U.S. Cavalry." At this stage the conflict assumes epic proportions as the Herculean task of keeping the West safe for white settlements falls on a small outpost of the famous Seventh Cavalry run by Capt. Nathan Brittles (Wayne again). The narrative leads us to believe that nothing less than the fate of the entire West for the coming century rides on the big shoulders of Brittles, who symbolizes the struggle of white civilization against hostile primitive forces. The third picture of Ford's trilogy, *Rio Grande* (1950), was the last of his classic combat Westerns, this one set at a remote cavalry outpost in Arizona at roughly the time of the Civil War. Here Colonel Kirby York (Wayne yet again) pursues Apaches into their Mexican sanctuary; the story ends with a long shootout in a Mexican Catholic church, where the cavalry naturally prevails. The few "good Indians" in *Rio Grande* stand against the much larger horde of bad ones, depicted as bloodthirsty, sadistic killers who, in the period leading up to combat, get drunk on tequila and carry out acts of rape, torture, and kidnapping of children.

Having begun to question his own classic Western motif in such pictures as *The Searchers* (1956) and *The Man Who Shot Liberty Valance* (1962)—both critical of the values and practices embedded in the westward push—Ford returned one last time to the genre with *Cheyenne Autumn* (1964). In this rambling epic we encounter a courageous band of Cheyenne Indians led by chiefs Dull Knife (Gilbert Rowland) and Little Wolf (Ricardo Montalban), who flee their desolate Oklahoma reservation for Montana some 1,500 miles away. Reputedly based on historical events, this tale is a stark departure from the more famous Trail of Tears journey. As they travel, the Indians are helped by a few principled whites including the film's main protagonist, Captain Archer (Richard Widmark). Archer, an idealistic army officer, learns to respect the Cheyenne after having pursued them with his company of soldiers. He breaks with his fellow officers and goes to Washington to lobby the secretary of interior (Edward G. Robinson) in support of the uprooted Cheyenne. As a result, the Indians receive an official apology and are permitted to reclaim their ancient homeland.

If one relied on just this film to draw conclusions about the trajectory of white imperial conquest of the West, one might believe that Indians, helped along by well-intentioned whites (including both the army and high government officials) could, with the proper dedication, return to their homelands and live at peace with Euro-Americans. History, of course, informs us that nothing could be further from the truth. Neither high-minded white settlers nor steadfast "noble savages" were able to stem the tide of violent colonization that exterminated the vast majority of Indians and forced the remainder onto small reservations in remote wastelands. Ford based *Cheyenne Autumn* on Mari Sandoz's 1953 novel of the same title, but the film deviates critically from the novel, twisting events to favor white heroes. Above all, there was no Captain Archer to serve as advocate for the Cheyenne. Indeed, none of the idealist white characters who pervade *Cheyenne Autumn* appear in Sandoz's book; they were entirely fictitious. Ford's movie tells us much less about the heroic struggles of a proud band of Cheyenne to regain their historic lands than about the saga of courageous, selfless whites who risk everything to bring justice to long-suffering tribes. This narrative is wonderful salve for liberal whites who had begun to feel uneasy about their historic role in the destruction of native peoples, but it is total myth.

In *Cheyenne Autumn,* moreover, the tribal figures are depicted in the usual Hollywood racist stereotypes, flat, one-dimensional characters devoid of recognizable human qualities. Ford employed no real Indians—Chief Dull Knife and Chief Little Wolf were both played by non-Indians, the Spanish woman by Delores Del Rio, and Red Shirt by Sal Mineo. The three leading male characters sported improbable coiffures: shoulder-length hair and large forehead curls never seen on tribal men, whose hair was always straight. Red Shirt's wardrobe consisted of a blazing red costume resembling more closely something from a Paris fashion show than usual Cheyenne apparel. Here as elsewhere, the Hollywood Indians speak English with little or no accent. Richard Maltby points out that "whoever these characters are supposed to be, it is evident that they make no attempt adequately to represent the tribal nations whose names they appropriate." He adds that "the Hollywood Western has obliterated the ethnic and cultural distinctions between indigenous peoples of North America and imposed upon them by stereotype."[11] In fact Ford saw no reason to pay much attention to historical veracity, believing that he himself was the ideal interpreter of Native American culture, asking, "Who better than an Irishman could understand the Indians?"[12]

Much the same pattern holds for DeMille's film *The Plainsman* (1957), featuring Wild Bill Hickok (Gary Cooper), Buffalo Bill Cody (James Ellison), Calamity Jane (Jean Arthur), and the ever-present General Custer (John Miljam). Here Hickok and Cody team up against villainous gun dealers who smuggle rifles to menacing Indians in exchange for furs. The protagonists come across as larger-than-life heroes protecting white civilization. Cody is depicted as a wonderful fellow, in contrast to his actual despicable role in leading the slaughter of buffalo herds in his capacity as expert Indian fighter. And Custer, for his part, is shown as obediently following Washington's orders to launch his suicidal attack at Little Big Horn. All figures in *The Plainsman* look like they just stepped out of a comic book. Of course the Indians under Cheyenne chief Yellow Hand are uniformly portrayed as vicious and bloodthirsty, intent on destroying white society; they fit the image of the brutal savage. DeMille's picture constructs a narrative of embattled, innocent white settlers fighting to defend American civilization from hordes of demonic intruders. Hickok tells Cody that should a large band of Cheyenne warriors manage to unite with Chief Sitting Bull's Sioux fighters, "they'll be no more white men," since whites would be pushed all the way back to the East Coast. The final scenes of this racist, militaristic picture eulogize the heroic sacrifices of Hickok, Cody, Custer, and other agents of genocidal colonialism.

In a later rendition of these motifs, Robert Aldrich's *Uzana's Raid* (1972) focuses on a rogue Apache warrior and his guerrilla band who threaten white outposts. Here the warrior Chief Uzana (Joaquin Martinez) is pitted against a grizzled U.S. Army scout named McIntosh (Burt Lancaster), who teams up with a young, naïve officer, Lt. Garnett DeBuin (Bruce Davidson). As the two men set out into Arizona backcountry in search of Uzana, they soon encounter the horrors of Apache brutality: homesteads ransacked, a settler's wife raped until nearly dead, and a man tortured for hours before being left to die. Moved by this brutality, the troops resort to the same kind of violence, stabbing and mutilating the corpse of Uzana's son for revenge—an act understood to be fully justifiable in the larger scheme of things. Aldrich's film conforms to the time-honored formula of an older, wiser leader educating and toughening a younger initiate protagonist, the outlaw-hero mentoring the initiate-hero. In this case DeBuin's socialization involves learning to make intelligent decisions and give authoritative orders, but McIntosh is mortally wounded before the process is complete: the older hero dies to make way for the younger. Within the narrative, it follows that the older world inhabited by mountain men dressed in buckskins and looking like Fenimore Cooper heroes is destined to pass from the scene, to be supplanted by a new order dominated by the U.S. military, with the native peoples the inevitable victims.

Later in the twentieth century it was possible to view films presenting more sympathetic images of Native Americans; the best examples are Arthur Penn's *Little Big Man* (1970), Charles B. Pierce's *Winterhawk* (1976), and Kevin Costner's *Dances with Wolves* (1992). By the 1970s, in the wake of sixties radicalism and a counterculture strongly influenced by indigenous traditions, it was no longer fashionable to depict Indians—or indeed any other historically oppressed group—in demeaning, stereotypical fashion. (The one exception was Arabs, as we shall see in chapter 5.) The classic Hollywood Western had run its course. Not only Penn, Pierce, and Costner but also Ford himself had come to question the simplistic, racist view of history embodied in the Western myth. Yet, while the images and narratives changed and the extermination of Indian tribes was no longer glorified, the problem was never understood as a function of Euro-American colonialism and militarism but rather as the consequence of mistakes, excesses, and a few bad leaders (including Custer). In some of these later pictures Indians were portrayed as noble savages, the precise inversion of the long-standing cinematic stereotype.

These few movies, however, scarcely make a ripple in the overall Hollywood output spanning many decades in which Indians consistently appear as one-dimensional, angry, subhuman primitives who stand in the way of historical progress. The West constructed by the film studios was a mythical land threatened to its very core by Indian savagery—a world made inhabitable only through the hard work and courage of U.S. Army officers personified by John Wayne and others. Charged with keeping the barbarians from destroying civilization, such Western heroes recall earlier prototypes like Moses, Joshua, and Charlemagne. Whereas many earlier Western protagonists lived far less exciting and heroic lives, drifting around the barren landscape, playing poker, hanging out at saloons, and womanizing, the leading combat figures moved around with great physical vigor while riding out on patrol, disciplining troops, and of course fighting hostile native bands. And the combat scenarios inevitably call forth not only an anarchic milieu of chaos and violence but a strict dichotomous narrative of good (white settler, U.S. military) versus bad (Indian) forces struggling for the future of civilized life.

Combat Westerns like those directed by Ford revolved largely around the exploits of the U.S. Cavalry, often marked by courageous actions in the face of seemingly insurmountable obstacles. While the settings of such films alternated between the vastness of the Southwestern desert landscape and the more confined quarters of remote cavalry outposts, there was never any question about sovereignty, about who actually had the *right* to the frontier. Every inch of land is understood to be U.S. territory, owned by the settlers and policed by the military, while Indians were shown as having strayed from their proper place on the reservations. Despite the familiar rhetoric about democracy and rights, nothing remotely resembling these values could be found during the westward push—in history or in cinema. As for popular audiences, the Western combat subgenre was appealing because it simultaneously celebrated traditional "American" virtues of rugged individualism and the outlaw hero along with the familiar martial ethos of the combat film in which racial "others" could be easily objectified and demonized, all in the interest of Manifest Destiny.

## The Myth of the Good War

"Good wars" are U.S. military struggles for unquestionably noble causes, all-out wars pitting good against evil, democracy against tyranny, peace against barbarism. No military campaign fits this description more perfectly than

World War II, when the United States and its allies fought a bloody, heroic war to defeat the Axis powers (Germany, Italy, Japan), which embodied the darkest forces of history: militarism, racism, imperialism, a mortal threat to human civilization. The ultimate good war gave rise to the most sustained patriotic mobilization in American history, signaling a dramatic end to the isolationist 1920s and 1930s, when the scars of World War I were still vivid. Wartime industrial development and military deployment required deep support within the popular culture for all the hard work, sacrifices, and dedication to victory. And nothing was more important to this epochal cultural shift than the Hollywood studios, which produced hundreds of feature pictures and documentaries over a span of only five years.

The good-war discourse has been central to the culture of militarism since just after Pearl Harbor, keeping alive public memories of those dramatic history-altering victories over the Nazis and fascists while going even further, glorifying the entire legacy of patriotism and warfare, which remains firmly embedded within the American national psyche. What has been called the "martial spirit of Hollywood" derives much of its energy from this watershed historical moment.[13] Indeed the studios have come to cherish war movies for their endless action sequences, their focus on male heroism, their riveting patriotic emotion, and their consistent profitability. This helps explain why films like *Saving Private Ryan, Pearl Harbor,* and *The Thin Red Line* could be made and watched by so many millions of Americans nearly a half century after World War II ended. Today as then, there remains a strong political and cultural impulse to celebrate good-war narratives and themes. And today as then, the relationship between Hollywood and the U.S. military is tight enough to be regarded as a partnership, if at times a tense one.

In fact World War II was not initially presented as a good war in the United States when fighting broke out in Europe in 1939. At this juncture both elites and the public expressed overwhelmingly neutralist, noninterventionist sentiments, with President Roosevelt's unwavering assistance to Britain actually at odds with the American popular consensus, which cared little about the rising fascist threat in Germany, Italy, Japan, and Spain. The "war is hell" motif contained in Lewis Milestone's classic *All Quiet on the Western Front* (1930), which recalls the horrors of the Great War, seemed to dominate the popular consciousness. In September 1941 the debate over military intervention flared up in the U.S. Senate, provoked by trends in Hollywood toward antifascism and armed engagement. Democratic senators D. Worth Clark (Idaho) and Gerald P. Nye (North Dakota), favoring "isolationism," convened hearings to investigate the political influence of "Motion Picture Screen and Radio Propaganda." The studios hired as their counsel and spokesperson none other than Wendell Wilkie, the 1940 Republican presidential nominee. During the hearings Nye charged that Hollywood films were becoming overtly pro-war, "what I consider to be the most vicious propaganda that has ever been unleashed upon a civilized people." Nye identified some twenty motion pictures released in the late 1930s that he considered particularly offensive.[14]

In defense of Hollywood, Wilkie argued that most of the hundreds of films produced by the studios during the period in question had no ideological content but conceded that "some fifty do portray Nazism for what it is—a cruel, lustful, ruthless, and cynical force."[15] It turned out that the Roosevelt administration did foster "interventionist" films just after the outbreak of war, at a time when FDR's son James, head of Global Productions, sponsored John Boulting's *Pastor Hall* (1940), depicting Nazi storm troopers terrorizing German civilians, with a prologue written by Robert Sherwood and read by First Lady Eleanor Roosevelt. In August 1940 FDR himself asked studio chieftain Nicholas Schenck to produce a movie dramatizing the need for a more aggressive U.S. foreign policy; the result was *Eyes of the Navy,* a two-reel documentary with a pro-military theme shown widely across the country. By 1941 the president was congratulating members of the film industry for their "splendid cooperation with all who are directing the expansion of our defense forces." It was only after Germany invaded Poland, Norway, Holland, and France, however, that Hollywood started conveying images of Nazi fanaticism and violence. Anatole Litvak's *Confessions of a Nazi Spy* (1939) was an early motion picture of this sort—precisely the kind of statement that some guardians of the elite consensus would label "premature antifascism."

Immediately following the Japanese attack on Pearl Harbor on December 7, 1941, combat film production in the United States surged, given new encouragement by FDR and his newly created Bureau of Motion Pictures (BMP)— soon to be followed by the Office of War Information (OWI). By establishing these agencies the president was responding in part to requests by the motion picture industry itself to step up its involvement in the war crusade. At this point the BMP insisted upon the power to review every studio script related to the war, intent upon fostering "accurate" and "positive" messages from the standpoint of the U.S. military—power that was effectively granted and a mission that was, over time, wildly successful. The director Delmer Daves, head of the OWI, hoped to plant what he termed "propaganda seeds" within the film industry in order to fan public emotions around war mobilization and patriotism, with the idea of finally achieving a break with "isolationism." The main goal was to forge a deep cultural orientation toward warfare as a method for protecting U.S. national interests—in other words, to instill in the vast majority of Americans an ethos of the good war. Among Daves and his colleagues there was little sentiment that such "propaganda" ought to be subtle or even respectful of historical accuracy.

Within weeks after the Japanese attack, the mass media and film industry moved into high gear, establishing what can only be understood as a vast propaganda apparatus enlisting radio, newspapers, magazines, and book publishing as well as movies. Pro-war films geared to simple patriotic messages were produced quickly by all the major studios and were seen by millions of troops and civilians alike—and were routinely forced to pass muster at the War Department. The shock and disgust of Pearl Harbor generated popular feelings of hatred and revenge toward the Japanese (and secondarily the Germans), inspiring the return of a fierce martial ethos, and this naturally found its way into the cinema of the period. In contrast to most war films of earlier decades, in which powerful images of battlefield carnage were common, the good-war approach romanticized combat by diminishing its harsh, bloody side while stressing the larger conflict of values and the threat to democracy and freedom that had to be fought. The combat picture took on a more melodramatic character along with formulaic plot structure, as World War II films became a kind of genre unto themselves. These included John Farrow's *Wake Island* (1942), Howard Hawks's *Air Force* (1943), Delmer Daves's *Destination Tokyo* (1943) and *Pride of the Marines* (1945), Lewis Seiler's *Guadalcanal Diary* (1943), Mervy LeRoy's *Thirty Seconds over Tokyo* (1944), Lewis Milestone's *Purple Heart* (1944), Harold Schuster's *Marine Raiders* (1944), Edward Ludwig's *Fighting Seabees* (1944), William Wellman's *Story of G.I. Joe* (1945), and John Ford's *They Were Expendable* (1945). Directed for the most part by experienced, skillful filmmakers, these movies were overwhelmingly propaganda efforts tied to U.S. war aims—and they suffered accordingly from rushed production, simple and predictable story lines, corny dialogue, and limited camera shots. Later films that replicated the good-war pattern—for example Henry King's *Twelve O'Clock High* (1949), Alan Dwan's *The Sands of Iwo Jima* (1949), and Raoul Walsh's *Battle Cry* (1955)—went only slightly beyond the wartime Hollywood fare.

What might be defined as the good-war formula contains several indispensable motifs. First, the entire campaign is depicted as unquestionably noble, with the horrors of combat framed in morally imperative, urgent, heroic terms. In the case of World War II, filmmakers approached the dramas of military conflict with a uniform sense of ethical certitude. Second, warfare is shown to be a struggle between good and evil, between the forces of civilization and barbarism, where the (idealized) American cause must prevail over the ruthless goals of unspeakably demonic enemies—a corollary being that enemies are utterly devoid of human qualities or ultimate purposes. Third, the films revolve around typically (white) male heroism—always easy to construct in battlefield situations—often involving groups of heroes embarked upon life-and-death missions. Where female characters do appear in these films, they are presented in distinctly subordinate roles—as lovers, girlfriends, or wives, as women who love and support their combat men and thus at least indirectly contribute to the war effort. Fourth, military units (ground combat, ships, planes) are inevitably diverse in their social composition, reflecting a mythological religious/ethnic melting pot in which common patriotic goals are seen as rooted in, and accepted by, a broad social spectrum. Related to this formula is the notion that war is fought by regular guys, average GI Joes who speak in the everyday vernacular and have typical working-class lifestyles—a supposed reflection of American democratic and egalitarian values. Fifth, there is a pronounced soldierly professionalism and stoicism of military heroes in the face of terrible, life-threatening conditions, which only the most courageous are able to survive. Sixth, insofar as the (romanticized) armed unit occupies a highly cohesive, even hermetic world, outsiders entering the group are first met with suspicion and then are forced to prove their mettle by fully accepting the group ethos and its rules, which, again, are taken as the measure of absolute virtue.

This cinematic paradigm ensures that the bloody experience of combat will be turned into cosmetic images of the real thing, no matter how violent the on-screen representations. With a purpose so messianic and enthralling, and a dedication to save civilization from raving madmen, how could heroic military victories be presented as anything but glorious, as moments of national catharsis? War itself came to be seen as a positive human experience, made larger than life (and much less brutal than its actuality) by the expertise of the Hollywood studios. Of course World War II *was* the most popular war the United States ever fought, despite its initial unpopularity and its enormous costs. There was full-scale mobilization of the economy and armed forces behind preparedness for "total war." Nearly 20 million Americans served in the military. And the Axis powers did represent all the evils of fascism and militarism. The films, both features and documentaries, came to embrace a predictable jingoism with few limits, where enemy forces were routinely called "vermin," "monkeys," "rats," and (in the case of the Japanese) "Nips," "Japs," and "little yellow bastards." Courage under fire likewise recognized few limits. Thus, in *Thirty Seconds over Tokyo,* Colonel James Doolittle (Spencer Tracy) inspires his airmen on their secret mission to bomb Tokyo by promising, "You're going to do things with a B-25 you thought were impossible." The only blemish in the romanticized good-war scenarios was depiction of the ever-present atrocities, which, of course, were only carried out by the enemy, though such atrocities (like those of the Bataan Death March) just provided more fuel for the noble patriotic cause.

Missing from the Hollywood good war, then as now, was any semblance of balance, any effort to depict events with some degree of accuracy or historical veracity. The propaganda machine, overseen by the War Department, would never have allowed such complexity to enter into a filmmaking process designed to manipulate public opinion around U.S. military objectives. There was scant reference to brutal policies and actions initiated by the Allies: massive relocation of Japanese Americans into remote camps; firebombings of Hamburg, Dresden, Tokyo, and dozens of other Japanese cities; mistreatment and killing of prisoners of war; the nuclear annihilation of Hiroshima and Nagasaki. Where images of such atrocities did find their way into motion pictures—usually in features produced long after the war—they were generally sanitized, framed in a manner that transformed them into something necessary, legitimate. Above all, both filmmakers and the military feared the possibility of creating works that might lead the public to believe the war was something politically or morally troublesome.

In a few cases directors sought to impress viewers with precisely those more complex, troublesome aspects of warfare even as they remained firmly within a partisan framework. In this vein Alfred Hitchcock's *Lifeboat* (1944), which dramatized the ordeal of survivors from a torpedoed American passenger ship, met nothing but a torrent of critical and public hostility. One of Hitchcock's unpardonable sins was that his German submarine captain, far from being a demonic Nazi madman, possessed sufficient leadership (and presumably human) qualities to be able to take command of the lifeboat. The director explained that "at that time, 1940–41, the French had been defeated and the Allies were not doing too well. Moreover, the German . . . was actually a submarine commander and therefore . . . was better qualified than the others to take over command of the lifeboat. But the critics apparently felt that a nasty Nazi could never be a good sailor." One reviewer wrote that "unless we had seen it with our own eyes, we would have never believed that a film could have been made which sold out democratic ideals and elevated the Nazi superman."[16] Another critic was so incensed that she gave the film "ten days to get out of town."[17] Similarly, in 1945 John Huston sought to release a short documentary titled *Let There Be Light,* which crossed the cinematic line when it showed the battlefield experience in all its gory details. Alarmed at this transgression, the War Department prevented the film from appearing, shelving it behind a curtain of secrecy even while the critics in this instance praised it and advocated its distribution.[18] The military was far too enraged at Huston's work to permit its showing to armed-services personnel or the general public. The film was finally released decades later, emerging as something of a cult classic for its unfashionable antiwar sentiments.

As Hitchcock, Huston, and others learned, films that offered audiences even moderately complex or critical views of a popular war faced massive ideological and financial problems. Few directors, then or later, even *tried* to follow this route. World War II pictures were essentially forced into a narrow paradigm. In fact the combat formulas rooted in that period worked abundantly well, both in depicting (and romanticizing) warfare and in setting forth compelling narratives that sustain dramatic tension. In its most basic form this pattern has continued to attract viewers throughout the postwar years, although it has naturally been modified to suit changing tastes and styles. The structure is readily apparent in such contemporary films as *Saving Private Ryan, Black Hawk Down,* and *Pearl Harbor*—films that will be explored in later chapters. It also defined earlier movies such as Henry Koster's *D-Day, the Sixth of June* (1956), which celebrated the Allied landings at Normandy, and Ken Anaken's own version of D-Day, *The Longest Day* (1962), starring such veteran combat-genre luminaries as John Wayne, Robert Mitchum, and Henry Fonda. The battle scenes in Anaken's picture were superb enough to win two Academy Awards. Perhaps the quintessential setting for victory in the good war, the beaches of Normandy have been revisited frequently by American filmmakers.

Franklin Shaffner's well-received *Patton* (1970), an epic tribute to the hardened European theater general, cast George C. Scott as the brilliant and colorful war hero who played a key role in the Allied victory. In the film we see Patton framing war on a practical level, exhorting his troops to kill for their country rather than die for it. "I want you to remember," he instructs his gathered troops, "that no bastard ever won a war by dying for his country. He won it by making the other poor dumb bastard die for his country." Shaffner's movie follows the well-established genre convention dramatizing the exploits of courageous military units, but departs from the standard formula in focusing on a *single leader* in the person of General Patton. By showing the implausible deeds of such a gritty and outspoken leader, *Patton* touched a popular nerve, winning immense acclaim from an American public apparently longing to bask in reflected military glory. The film was reportedly President Richard Nixon's personal favorite; he kept a White House copy to show friends and visiting dignitaries. Released during the far less popular Vietnam War, *Patton* harked back to simple dichotomous categories of an earlier period, when warfare could be seen as noble, straightforward, decisive, and triumphant.

The film that surely most epitomized the good-war modality was *The Sands of Iwo Jima,* in which John Wayne as marine sergeant Stryker has come to personify the ideal, heroic American soldier willing to die for patriotic ends. Wayne, who also starred in *They Were Expendable* and later in such combat pictures as *Battle Cry* (1955), *The Alamo* (1960), and *The Green Berets* (1968), emerged from this role as a legendary marine icon whose love of the U.S. military surpassed that even of his wife and family. For him *Sands* embodied not just a battlefield triumph but a philosophy of life, a vehicle of heroic exploits in the cause of human progress. Iwo Jima, of course, was a major battle of the Pacific theater, and the flag-raising at Mount Suribachi turned out to be a crowning symbolic moment in the war. Suid writes: "By the time he played Stryker Wayne had been going after the enemy in films for about twenty years. But only in *Sands* did he become the symbol of the American fighting man, the defender of the nation."[19] Made with the full assistance of the marine base at Camp Pendleton, *Sands* remained several decades later an efficient recruiting vehicle for the corps.

Soon after Pearl Harbor the director Frank Capra began work on an ambitious series of "military orientation" documentaries titled *Why We Fight,* initiated by Army Chief of Staff George C. Marshall. These films, designed for troop viewing but quickly made available to the general public, became classics of wartime cinematic propaganda—ideal cultural instruments of the good war. These films were uniformly well-produced; Capra's first, *Prelude to War,* won an

Patton *(Franklin Schaffner, 1970, Twentieth Century Fox). A classic World War II combat picture, this paean to General George C. Patton (played by George C. Scott) ranks among the foremost "good war" films glorifying U.S. military exploits against the Germans in Europe, while showing all the flaws of Patton himself.*

Academy Award in 1942. Each script in the series had to be approved by no fewer than fifty military and other government agencies. Seven pictures were released, building on the frenetic patriotic messages that resonated during World War I. Throughout, Capra repeated the theme of a "free world" combating a "slave world," with the Allies carrying the "torch of freedom" for the entire globe. Skillfully employing German and Japanese footage, the series depicted an enemy willing to use every barbaric method to achieve its goal of world conquest. The war was an epochal struggle of life versus death. President Roosevelt was drawn to the *Why We Fight* pictures and urged their viewing by every American citizen.

Both the conduct of World War II and its cinematic representation took a more fiercely jingoistic and racist turn in the Pacific theater, where the Japanese were depicted as subhuman, regularly described as beasts, vermin, and yellow hordes. Japan was a nation without individuals, filled with conformist robots brainwashed by ruthless militarists out to take over the world; total war leading to large-scale annihilation was the only plausible U.S. response. In 1944 Admiral William "Bull" Halsey, commander of the U.S. Pacific Fleet, said, "The only good Jap is a Jap who's been dead for six months"—a sentiment that found its way into countless Hollywood movies.[20] Working on the *Why We Fight* series, the Capra team enlisted animators from the Disney studios to construct subhuman images of the Japanese, rendering them as reptiles, monkeys, insects, as "apes in khaki." Not only the "sneak attack" at Pearl Harbor but also the Bataan Death March was seized upon to dramatize the supposedly innate bestial qualities of the Japanese. Leading up to the merciless warfare across the Pacific, the firebombing of Japanese cities in 1945, and the nuclear destruction of Hiroshima and Nagasaki, the American wartime ethos could best be described as what John Dower calls "exterminationist sentiment," a recycling of attitudes that prevailed during the Indian Wars.[21]

This pattern of anti-Asian racism, forged earlier against Filipinos during the Spanish-American War, would later extend to other national groups, with equally grim results: Korea, Vietnam, Cambodia, Laos. Moreover, in portraying the Japanese as undifferentiated brute savages, the popular culture followed the way in which the Native American tribes were historically depicted in both politics and cinema. In 1944 the Capra group produced the documentary *The Battle of China*, which embellished the theme of Japanese barbarism; it was followed in 1945 by *Know Your Enemy Japan*, a film that dwells on the samurai tradition as the font of a society immersed in death and destruction. Here the Oriental threat, the Yellow Peril, is shown as a dire menace to a peaceful, democratic European civilization. Hollywood depictions of the European theater usually distinguished between evil Nazis and the great mass of Germans, ignoring or downplaying World War II atrocities committed by the Hitler regime, whereas the Japanese were always treated as one unitary horde. Indeed, the *Why We Fight* series never mentions the Nazi violence in Eastern Europe or against Jews, Slavs, and Gypsies, much less the Holocaust. The horrifying toll of death and destruction visited upon Japanese cities by U.S. bombing missions at the end of the war—all of little if any *military* value—makes sense in the more intensely racialized milieu of the Pacific theater. In contrast to the military campaigns in Europe, here civilian populations were deliberately and systematically targeted, the results made all the more gruesome by fearsome weapons (incendiary devices, napalm, atomic bombs) developed explicitly for use against noncombatants.[22]

As probably the most epic, transformative, and widely photographed matrix of events in the twentieth century, World War II naturally lent itself to a vast cinematic legacy. In the process the film industry and military established a tight relationship that has only been deepened across the intervening decades. This legacy, however, has not given rise to a particularly artistic or technically sophisticated body of motion pictures: typically the plots are simplistic and predictable, the characters wooden and one-dimensional, the scripts banal and stilted, the cinematography bland and unimaginative. The films routinely exude clichés of praise for American patriotism, the family, and the venerated principles of democracy, justice, and equality. In making hundreds of such good-war movies, the studio chieftains were never able to depict the grim realities of warfare; their contract with the War Department ensured their output was mostly propaganda as opposed to genuine filmmaking, with pictures serving as a massive "weapon of war."[23] At the same time, this marriage produced new and lasting changes within American popular culture. Thomas Doherty writes: "The unique, unprecedented alliance between Washington and Hollywood generated not only new kinds of movies but a new attitude toward them. Hereafter, popular art and cultural meanings, mass communication and national politics, would be intimately aligned and commonly acknowledged in American culture."[24]

In the end it can be argued that the good war, in politics as in popular culture, hardly reflected the far more complex social realities of World War II, not to mention any of the previous or subsequent wars conducted by the United States. As with the one-sided xenophobic propaganda churned out by *any* power structure during wartime, the Hollywood combat fare was shrouded in mythology and deceit. The good-war motif takes for granted that the Allied forces (the United States, Britain, the Soviet Union) waged war in defense of a superior civilization against the evils of imperialism, militarism, and racism that were supposedly the unique province of the Axis powers. As Howard Zinn writes, such an assumption scarcely corresponds to the historical record. The combined instances of British and American military aggression, going back to the nineteenth century, surpass anything carried out by the Germans, Japanese, and Italians. The war machines built by the Allies were gigantic models for the Axis nations to emulate and possibly match. As for racism, the United States and Britain had to be regarded as world leaders in their embellishment of white supremacy and its various practices—a legacy that quickly found its way into the ideology and conduct of the good war. Equally problematic for the good-war thesis, U.S. leaders did little to resist German and Japanese imperial advances in the 1930s, and American corporations remained fully involved in the German economy not only before but also *during* the war. Moreover, both the United States and Britain were rather soft on fascism until war broke out—fascism was, after all, fiercely anti-Communist—reflecting the dominant isolationist mood of both countries. The Allies did little to alleviate the plight of Jews and others victimized by the European fascists.[25]

At an even deeper level, the notion that the United States and other Allies upheld uniquely democratic ideals against the Axis tyrannies is easily overstated. As was generally the case, U.S. leaders pursued their own economic and geopolitical agendas despite the enormous risks and costs of war. By the end of World War II the United States, relatively unscathed by wartime carnage, emerged as a global superpower with a monopoly on nuclear weapons. Zinn writes: "Quietly, behind the headlines in battles and bombings, American diplomats and businessmen worked hard to make sure that when the war ended, American economic power would be second to none in the world."[26] And they were mighty successful, for reasons having nothing to do with democracy or noble ambitions or the myths perpetuated by the film industry. The postwar era opened up a whole new phase of U.S. economic, military, and imperial power that today remains the dominant fact of world politics.

## Cold War and Popular Culture

The end of World War II, with dramatic Allied military victories over fascism in Europe and Asia, was marked by patriotic euphoria and a general sense of national optimism. But this quickly gave way to a rather profound shift in politics and culture with the rise of the cold war, a wave of domestic anti-Communist hysteria, the bloody and futile Korean War, and then a nuclear standoff with the Soviet Union that came to be known as the "balance of terror." On the surface the late 1940s and 1950s appeared to be an era of conservative consensus, stability, revitalized sense of national purpose, and spreading affluence—but this barely concealed a darker side of the American experience: McCarthyism, a culture of fear and paranoia, images of nuclear nightmare, increased societal violence.

The onset of the cold war, Korea, and then McCarthyism ensured that the widely expected postwar military demobilization would never take place; the structure now known as the Pentagon was not about to be downsized, much less dismantled. On the contrary, what was evolving into a permanent war system would be a durable feature of American economic, political, and cultural life throughout the coming decades, just as President Eisenhower feared when in

1959 he warned of the perils of an out-of-control "military-industrial complex." An expanding and costly military structure performed several key functions, serving as a bastion of cold war ideological mobilization, a source of immense armed-services and civilian patronage, a font of patriotic unity, and, perhaps above all, a mechanism to stimulate continued industrial growth in the form of military Keynesianism. The growing reliance of the whole system on military production, deployment, and research and development (an engine of techno-logical innovation) would naturally have long-term consequences, giving the military unprecedented influence in American society. Hollywood reflected this changing ideological milieu, notably in its contribution across several genres to the legitimating of this permanent war system. In many ways the cold war *cultural* mobilization took its cues from earlier good-war formulas, as the film industry brought to the public a world of Hobbesian chaos in which various demons and aliens lurked about both internationally and domestically.

This cultural shift took place even in those military-themed films that departed from the good-war model. Postwar movies like *Twelve O'Clock High* (1948) and *Sands of Iwo Jima* (1949) continued along the good-war trajectory, but William Wyler's *Best Years of Our Lives* (1946), for example, dealt with the psychological chaos of three returning vets in their efforts to adapt to civilian life in a milieu of dizzying changes. Wyler never questions the virtue of fighting World War II, but he does subject U.S. military culture to rather harsh scrutiny. Much the same could be said of Fred Zinnemann's *From Here to Eternity* (1953), which brilliantly dissects the inner workings of army life in Hawaii in the period leading up to Pearl Harbor, portraying cynicism among the troops, carousing, sexual affairs, and questionable leadership. Inhabited by rich and fascinating characters, *Eternity* put on display more realistic images of the U.S. military but received little help from the Pentagon and was actually banned by the navy. By the end of the film, however, the unifying effects of the Japanese attack on Pearl Harbor bring everything back to the standard combat format. In the case of Edward Dmytryk's *Caine Mutiny* (1954), we have a wacky, paranoid navy commander (played to manic perfection by Humphrey Bogart), eventually removed by ship officers in the midst of a typhoon—a real 1944 episode chronicled by Herman Wouk. The navy had fiercely opposed the idea of turning Wouk's book into a movie, but Dmytryk's final product—more or less faithful to the original incident—did little to embarrass the military, especially since the behavior of Captain Queeg was far less unusual than the Pentagon claimed it to be. For the postwar era, however, films like *Eternity* and *Caine Mutiny* (and for the Korean War, *The Bridges at Toko-Ri*, 1954) were indeed rare exceptions to the formulaic combat rule. Yet even these films upheld the larger picture of a benevolent, well-disciplined but still democratic U.S. military out to slay all demons.

World War II, having given birth to an unprecedented scope of violence including horrendous aerial bombardment of cities and the dropping of atom-

The Caine Mutiny *(Edward Dmytryk, 1954, Columbia Pictures)*. Humphrey Bogart stars as Captain Queeg, a cowardly navy captain who mentally unravels during a heavy storm and is summarily replaced by his executive officer *(Van Johnson)*. As the mutineers go to trial, Queeg breaks down under cross-examination to reveal a frightened, insecure man beneath the disciplinarian officer. Copyright 1959 Columbia Pictures Corp.

From Here to Eternity *(Fred Zinnemann, 1953, Columbia Pictures). A classic post–World War II drama, based on James Jones's novel,* From Here to Eternity *depicts a peacetime U.S. Army set in Hawaii, riddled with personal vendettas, cheating, sadism, alcoholism, and prostitution. The film was banned by the U.S. Navy at the time. It stars Montgomery Clift, Frank Sinatra, Deborah Kerr, Donna Reed, and Burt Lancaster.*

ic bombs, would inevitably permeate the postwar cultural landscape, gaining perhaps its deepest expression in film noir. Although the noir sensibility, which reached its peak in the 1950s, took varied political directions, its abiding focus was on the dark side of modern urban life, a world of chaos, violence, and decay that can be connected with the horrors of 1940s warfare that broke down the distinction between military and civilian targets on all sides of the conflict. The millions of human casualties would not be easily removed from historical memory. The pathological effects of such military barbarism came to be associated with a downward spiral of social life, in the United States as in other industrialized nations, where (in Nicholas Christopher's words) "the delirium of violence produces its own aesthetics."[27] Beneath the surface of an apparently stable, peaceful, democratic order could be found a more threatening "noir" environment that quickly found its way into the film industry. In this as in other respects the war had come home.

The great wounds of World War II would find their way into the urban noir setting: civic violence, crime, poverty, corruption, community breakdown, social atomization, an emergent drug culture. Hardly novel, these phenomena were spreading rapidly and merging to create nightmarish landscapes of fear, paranoia, and depression. A fallen world of this sort was the inevitable outgrowth of global war, anti-Communist frenzy, and the arms race. It was a world filled with alienated people, corrupt politicians, crooks, gangsters, saboteurs, and the usual variety of subversives and Commies. The demons were everywhere—perfect material for Hollywood film scripts as well as for novels. Terrors of the noir city would provide the backdrop of dozens of movies during this period, including *Detour, Force of Evil, The Third Man* (all 1949), *Kiss Me Deadly* (1955), and *Touch of Evil* (1958). They would help define not only the noir lexicon as such but also a variety of other film genres: sci-fi, spy thrillers, historical dramas, documentaries. With American cities now emerging as heated ideological battlegrounds, threats once so easily identified with evil fascists were now more amorphous, more diffuse, both global and domestic. This was a time and place, lest we forget, where atomic annihilation seemed possible at any moment.

Against such a fearsome backdrop, noir classics resonate with harsh, moody, dystopic images of postwar urban existence. Thus in Abe Polonsky's *Force of Evil,* starring John Garfield, we find a dark, enclosed world of crooked politicians, cops, lawyers, and gangsters, characters in a violent thriller that appears to allow no exit. They inhabit a destructive capitalist system where all individuals are simply out for themselves, without moral or social constraints. In Carol Reed's *The Third Man,* set in postwar Vienna and featuring Orson Welles and Joseph Cotten, we see a complex web of murder and criminality, a harsh milieu of social decay and broken relationships in which individuals pursue their agendas with notable savagery. The bleakness of this film, with its grainy black-and-white shots, corresponds perfectly to the continuing horrors of adaptation and survival in the wake of a war that had devastated most of Europe. With Robert Aldrich's *Kiss Me Deadly* we are presented with a Mike Hammer vehicle and the portrait of sleazy individuals in a thoroughly debased society. In David Meyer's words, Hammer is "an amoral pig, which he freely admits. His contempt for the world is genuine and crippling. His personality makes him unfit for any profession other than private eye. That is, he's lazy, sadistic, likes spying on people, and feels morally superior. And in this universe, Hammer's the hero."[28] In perhaps the darkest (and best) of all noir classics, Orson Welles's *Touch of Evil,* starring Welles himself, Janet Leigh, and Charlton Heston, we are shown a menacing urban landscape, a "world spinning apart" in which every character seems capable of strange and frightening deeds and police corruption is the routine order of the day.[29]

In the noir universe of random, diffuse, often shocking violence there are few if any conventional heroes of the sort found in good-war combat pictures; on the contrary, the characters are more likely to have been damaged or broken by their war experience. This is the sort of urban jungle where new forms of technology (including warfare) seem to be spinning out of control, beyond recognizable moral, psychological, and even political limits—a setting more likely to breed existential angst than military-style protagonists able to save the world. In many ways a product of both prewar and postwar social turmoil, noir culture can be seen as a refracted critique of capitalism, at least of its basest manifestations. Yet it was also a reflection of the changing international situation in which the United States was confronted by new demons, often found in the cinematic narrative structures. Here we are likely to encounter acts of violence at any time and in any place—a motif familiar to such auteurs as Fritz Lang and Alfred Hitchcock—giving rise to yet further violent responses. Chaos begets struggles to reimpose order and normalcy. If urban life mirrors warfare, then the battle zones (the cold war, anti-Communism, the arms race, threats from rival states) become a durable feature of the noir setting. Along these lines film noir, and neo-noir, would generate new cinematic personality types found later in such pictures as *Cape Fear* (1962), *Taxi Driver* (1976), *Blade Runner* (1982), and *Pulp Fiction* (1995). Hovering over this psychological labyrinth was a deepening culture of militarism, part of an increasingly rigid and coercive power structure.

This culture of militarism was in fact rooted in a (largely white-male) fascination with guns that runs through U.S. history—the militias of the Revolutionary period, the frontier ethos, the Indian Wars, armed interventions abroad, mass media saturated with violence, and an expanding war economy. In the noir world of random, sudden, chaotic, sometimes unspeakable violence we know that guns appeared as a vital cinematic icon, nearly always present if not always used; they were symbolic of an urban milieu in which danger lurked everywhere. More than that: the noir gun cult was meant to reflect *mainstream* culture, something integral to the routines and challenges of everyday life—and given new life with the onset of the cold war. Thus in Joseph Lewis's cult classic *Gun Crazy* (1949), the two protagonists (Peggy Cummins and John Dall)—both obsessed, violent, sexually charged, self-destructive—were able to mix guns with romance, adventure, and rebellion in a wild existential journey. They were outlaws, but in their attraction to guns they were unswervingly American, fully indulging the frontier, nomadic, military impulse. As Jim Kitses writes, *Gun Crazy* skillfully merges diverse genres: the Western, noir thriller, gangster picture, love story. This is eminently possible since "in noir all of America is gun crazy, the inevitable side-effect of a ferociously aggressive patriarchal capitalism fuelled by a violent national history and ideology."[30] It is easy enough to affirm a definite continuity from *Gun Crazy* at the outset of the cold war to such later films as *Bonnie and Clyde* (1967), *Blade Runner, Natural Born Killers* (1994), and *Pulp Fiction*.

The peaceful state of international relations immediately following the end of World War II quickly gave way to rising tensions between the United States and the USSR, igniting a long era of mutual superpower hostility. For American elites this shift gave rise to virulent anti-Communist ideology, conveniently justifying continued high levels of military spending presumably needed to contain the Soviet (and worldwide Communist) enemy whose treachery knew no bounds. In the United States during the late 1940s and 1950s fear of "subversion" reached hysterical levels, stimulating the growth of right-wing, often conspiratorial politics. There was the spread of Communism across the European continent, an intense Greek civil war, the Chinese revolution, and the Korean War, which broke out in June 1950. Meanwhile, the Soviets had developed the atomic bomb, leading to a further intensification of fear and paranoia. One result of all this was McCarthyism, the revival of the House Committee on Un-American Activities, a crackdown on labor and the left, and blacklisting of Hollywood figures deemed subversive. In world politics, U.S. military responses in Europe and Korea were associated with the Truman Doctrine stating that the United States had the right to intervene anywhere in the fight against godless totalitarian Communism. By 1950, in place of armed-services demobilization, the Pentagon budget had actually *quadrupled*—a move that was vital to confronting the demons lurking in the fearsome political jungle.

The cold war balance of terror kept alive the permanent war system on a mass-psychological foundation of fear, paranoia, and conspiratorial fantasies.[31] After all, the proliferation of superbombs could mean the end of organized society within a matter of a few hours. An all-out cold war mobilization strategy had several consequences: perpetual military buildup, vast propaganda campaigns, covert actions around the globe, adoption of a first-strike nuclear policy, and of course intensive efforts to uncover and defeat Reds wherever they might be found—and they could be found in the most unlikely places (the State Department, the U.S. Army) despite the tiny, isolated, and embattled status of the Communist Party USA. Within this ideological matrix Hollywood, contrary to its militantly liberal/progressive reputation, produced scores of motion pictures reflecting (and also deepening) the Hobbesian zeitgeist.

An early, crude example of this theme was R. G. Springsteen's film *The Red Menace* (1949), in which a returning war vet is duped by the Commies as the script churns out a long series of anti-Communist lines that could have come from the pages of *Reader's Digest*. In 1952 Harry Horner directed *Red Planet Mars,* essentially a right-wing sci-fi vehicle depicting the spread of a ruthless atheistic Communism to outer space. Yet another sci-fi picture, William Cameron Menzies' *Invaders* (1953; remade in 1986), follows what would become a well-worn narrative: a small boy witnesses the invasion by fearsome aliens who capture and brainwash residents of a small American town. Probably the best known of the fifties-style sci-fi paranoid dramas, Don Siegel's *Invasion of the Body Snatchers* (1956) tells the story of small-town denizens being supplanted by duplicates hatched from alien "pods," made scarier by effective cinematography and music. Along more noir-influenced lines, Sam Fuller's *Pickup on South Street* (1953) features brutal imagery, an anti-Communist script, and a shady character, played by Richard Widmark, who inadvertently acquires top-secret microfilm and winds up the target of espionage agents in a narrative that somewhat anticipates Tony Scott's *Enemy of the State* (1998). A different sort of example is John Frankenheimer's *Manchurian Candidate* (1962), the harrowing, paranoid tale of right-wing machinations in the aftermath of the Korean War. Whatever their genre, these movies revolved around a distinct cold war psychology of fear, paranoia, and sense of imminent doom. They were filled with a variety of menacing figures—traitors, schemers, aliens, subversives—who opposed everything that American traditions and values presumably represented. As for Communists, they were typically semihuman, barbaric, ready to brainwash all the innocents, and unswervingly devoted to world conquest. While departing from the good-war motif, these cold war tales nonetheless carried forward many elements of the World War II combat formula, including the difficult plight of solidarity groups or ordinary persons battling to protect cherished values and lifestyles against hordes of godless, violent, life-negating Others.

The biggest nightmare confronting the postwar generation was, of course, the threat of nuclear catastrophe. Christopher is surely not too far off the mark in suggesting that the politics and culture of this period were shaped by the legacy of Hiroshima and Nagasaki, by deep fears of the new superweapons at the disposal of possibly maniacal government leaders.[32] This aspect of World War II unleashed demons that remained part of the American—and to a lesser extent, global—landscape. Not just the *memory* of nukes, however, but the very real phenomenon of the cold war balance of terror hovered over the world as a threat to survival. Three factors entered into this equation: U.S. adoption of first-use nuclear strategy against the Soviet Union, failure of politicians to seek genuine arms-control agreements, and the possibility of advanced technology spiraling out of control (including the very real prospect that an accident would trigger nuclear Armageddon). The world was living under the threat of both U.S. and Soviet dedication to a policy of "massive retaliation," which meant an end to the limits of modern warfare. Indeed U.S. leaders had promised to turn the USSR into smoking, radioactive ruins within two hours. Atomic madness was reflected in the deployment of tens of thousands of missiles and bombs, an overkill that stretched all human imagination.

Nuclear weapons had become such an integral part of American postwar military strategy that the film industry, already closely aligned with the Pentagon, was destined to follow suit by making films that defended or even glorified this policy. In many ways nukes were symbolic of the cold war in both life and film. In the wake of the 1945 atomic strikes—erroneously thought to have brought a quicker end to the Pacific war—and with intensification of the rivalry with the USSR, American elites were reluctant to question any kind of nuclear option. A series of films made in the 1950s and early 1960s, all with extensive air force assistance, embraced with few moral or political qualms the military efficacy of nukes, the role of the Strategic Air Command (SAC), and the technological supremacy that the United States had enjoyed since the Manhattan Project. Thus the propagandistic *Above and Beyond* (1952), directed by Melvin Frank and Norman Panama, portrayed with great flourish the story of Colonel Paul Tibbetts and his *Enola Gay* mission over Hiroshima, adding elements of drama and heroism that simply did not exist. While the picture took on the guise of a docudrama, the filmmakers took remarkable license with history for the sake of cinematic impact. As Suid remarks, "The technical advisors fought an uphill battle with the filmmakers, who consciously ignored history or . . . really did not care about creating an accurate story."[33]

In 1955 Anthony Mann directed *Strategic Air Command,* which was followed in 1957 by Gordon Douglas's *Bombers B-52.* Both pictures trumpet the theme "nukes for peace" and celebrate the role of B-52s as the new technological marvels of the atomic age flown by the true heroes of the cold war. Along similar lines, Bert Gordon's *Beginning of the End* (1957) chronicles the development of the atomic bomb, conveying the message that the doomsday weapon enabled the United States to remain vigilant against the dangers of totalitarian Soviet power, helping thwart any assault on the capitalist way of life. General Curtis LeMay, key architect of the firebombing campaigns against Japan and father of the SAC, was deeply involved in these and related cinematic projects, hoping to use Hollywood (despite his skepticism about the film industry) to effectively market the air force and also nullify fears of a nuclear holocaust. LeMay's anxiety over Hollywood's role in cold war mobilization would mount as films seeming to question the sanity of the nuclear strategy began to appear in the late 1950s. Frustrated, LeMay turned one final time to his friends in entertainment with a request to make another SAC movie. The result was Delbert Mann's film *A Gathering of Eagles* (1963), a quasi-documentary work with technically superb flying sequences but a rehashing of the same old narrative: the air force is relying on the power of nukes to protect the nation from vicious enemies, its fliers exhibiting a selfless professionalism and patriotism. As Suid observes, however, *A Gathering of Eagles* had little impact on audiences, who had grown more critical of the SAC ethos in the aftermath of the Cuban missile crisis that brought the world close to nuclear annihilation.

As the threat of nuclear warfare hovered over the cold war terrain, public fears and vulnerabilities generated a new mood countering the paradigm of right-wing paranoia and elite deterrence policies. Opposition to the arms race took the form of the 1950s Ban the Bomb movement and later campaigns that fed into the 1960s anti–Vietnam War mobilizations. Only a few movies produced on the margins of Hollywood expressed theses sensibilities, but their impact was surprisingly widespread. These filmmakers refused to frame the ideological conflict between the United States and Soviet Union as a noble crusade in defense of Western civilization, preferring a more jaundiced view that saw both societies in the throes of a deadly and insane nuclear arms race—and both in the grip of a military-industrial complex. The first of these, Stanley Kramer's *On the Beach* (1959), was based on Nevil Shute's best-selling novel about a submarine crew that manages to avoid nuclear destruction because the sub was underwater at the moment of detonation. With all continents except Australia laid waste by atomic devastation, the sub commander (Gregory Peck) and his crew head for Australia to spend their last days before they perish from radiation poisoning. Sidney Lumet's *Fail Safe* (1964) explored another nightmarish cold war scenario: a nuclear war set off accidentally between the United States and the USSR, a motif that the Pentagon managed to suppress throughout the 1950s. This picture too was based on a best-selling book, by Eugene Burdick and William Lederer, academics who set out to dramatize the potential horrors of an out-of-control arms race. The most powerful of these antinuclear films was the British black comedy *Dr. Strangelove* (1964), directed by Stanley Kubrick in the wake of his great antiwar classic *Paths of Glory* (1957). *Dr. Strangelove* confronts the real possibility of imminent nuclear catastrophe resulting from errors and "miscommunication" between U.S. and Soviet leaders. Dr. Strangelove (Peter Sellers, in one of his three roles) calmly envisions a postatomic world in which only a few hardy souls (including himself) would survive in an underground War Room. The survivors would ultimately be forced to repopulate the planet. Strangelove addresses the U.S. president, saying, "I hasten to add that each man will be required to do prodigious service along these lines, and the women will have to be selected for their sexual characteristics, which will have to be of a highly stimulating nature." Strangelove's words, meant to recall such hard-line cold warriors as Edward Teller and Herman Kahn, gave the impression that he fully welcomed the coming holocaust. Anticipating such later films as *War Games* (1983), *Dr. Strangelove* was perhaps the most cynical of all comedic statements about the possibility of scientific reason going awry.

Despite these efforts, films countering the main Hollywood trends were few and their antiwar content was usually muted. In Brechtian fashion, their humor amounted to an effective mockery of political leaders East and West, showing them to be vain, capricious, stupid, indeed laughable, even as the fate of the world hung in the balance. Nuclear war was presented as both catastrophic and monstrously irrational, no ideological goal conceivably being worth the price. Yet, perhaps owing to their very comedic structure, the narratives remained at a very general level: the horrible state of the human condition, technology taking control of politics, a failure of leadership, a plague on both the United States and the USSR for their hidebound doctrines. Lacking here was any cinematic focus on the *historical context* of the cold war and the arms race, the deeper global and domestic tendencies that fed into it, and a closer look at the power structures involved. The result was that, despite their often-biting satire, these pictures never rose above the well-worn "war is hell" theme, in this case of course with a nuclear twist.

The cold war also witnessed proliferation of the spy/espionage genre in which erudite, attractive, skilled agents work endlessly to save the (Western) world from evildoers—usually Commies and other subversives but often enemies too diffuse to clearly identify. The popular James Bond episodes (produced in England but viewed more widely in the United States) lent exotic, sexualized drama to intriguing tales of a universe torn between two superpowers, beginning with *From Russia with Love* (1963). This film depicts the dapper and elusive Bond (Sean Connery) scheming to steal a top-secret Russian decoding machine from the Soviet embassy in Istanbul. Never a reluctant hero in the tradition of familiar combat heroes, Bond takes on his assignments, displaying cool professionalism, even diffidence, in the face of death and at a moment when the fate of Western civilization is in jeopardy. When threatened at gunpoint by supervillain Red Grant (Robert Shaw), who intones "the first one won't kill you nor the second, not even the third—not till you crawl over here and kiss my foot," Bond calmly replies, "How 'bout a cigarette?" This remarkably detached attitude toward death is common to the more conventional war movies, but in this case Bond's exploits are strictly his own rather than those of some battle unit as in *Sands of Iwo Jima*. On the contrary, the narrative reflects the shadowy, at times nearly anarchistic moves of cold war intelligence agencies like the British M-15 or the CIA in the United States The lengthy Bond series, like the spy thrillers it would spawn, served to romanticize an espionage universe that in reality was dull, gray, and conformist.

The great Hitchcock, among others, added his own cinematic twists to this genre, producing such imaginative thrillers as *Torn Curtain* (1966) and *Topaz* (1969). In *Torn Curtain,* Paul Newman stars as a fake defector to East Germany whose real mission is to obtain Communist defense secrets, while in *Topaz*—

based on the best-selling novel by Leon Uris—Frederick Stafford plays a French intelligence agent who uncovers a vast spy conspiracy in high places. In both pictures we encounter gripping cold war fear and suspicion that quickly shade into paranoid hysteria, much along the lines of earlier noir classics. Hitchcock's films reveal the nasty, brutal side of a superpower competition marked by intrigue, duplicity, surveillance, blackmail, torture, and assassination—all the stuff of first-rate thrillers. The heroes fight nameless, shadowy villains associated vaguely with some form of international subversion. Indeed, Hitchcock's masterful thrillers revolved around cold war rivalries that could well have taken place during virtually *any* war, always presuming vast, labyrinthine networks of spies and counterspies. Unlike such directors as Lumet and Kubrick, Hitchcock seemed to view the cold war as just another extension of the good war: a struggle of good versus evil, an epochal conflict of ideologies endemic to contemporary global politics. But his approach always contained a strong element of jaundiced humor.

American film culture and the system of military power have followed an oscillating but nonetheless intimately connected pattern of development from the outset, with the relationship growing tighter throughout the postwar years. By the early twenty-first century it was possible to speak of a deepening culture of militarism in which Hollywood cinema—across a wide variety of genres and motifs—has played a crucial part. From the above historical analysis it is apparent that we are no longer referring simply to the combat genre strictly speaking but to a variety of cinematic expressions within which a good many military-related themes are visible. Although various counterthemes—"war is hell," antiwar pacifism, comedic savaging of political leaders—have from time to time entered into the cinematic discourse, for more than a century of filmmaking these representations have been few, generally confined to the margins. with only a sporadic influence on the larger popular culture. The recurrently dominant motif, benefiting from investment of massive creative, technical, and financial resources, has been (direct or indirect) celebration of U.S. military power and its interventionist role in the world. Precisely this ideological message, a legitimating mechanism for the entire power structure, has been the one directed at both domestic and international motion-picture audiences since the days of D. W. Griffith.

CHAPTER 3

# The Vietnam Syndrome: Politics and Cinema

The Vietnam War era, spanning roughly fifteen years from the early 1960s to mid-1970s, represented one of the most horrid and shameful chapters in American history—one that continues to play out in domestic and world politics three decades after its long-delayed and merciful ending. Those who engineered this war, beginning with presidents John F. Kennedy and Lyndon Johnson and extending to figures like Secretary of Defense Robert McNamara and General William Westmoreland, would by any objective criteria have to be considered bona fide war criminals. The torturous legacy of U.S. military involvement in Indochina produced the following: at least 3 million killed, nine thousand of fifteen thousand hamlets destroyed, virtually all urban areas devastated, 25 million acres of forest destroyed, nearly a million orphans left, vast ecological ruin caused by the most lethal bombing campaign in history, and 20 million gallons of deadly herbicides sprayed. Aerial terrorism, barbaric search-and-destroy missions, totalitarian "pacification" programs, and ecological warfare added up to an unparalleled war of attrition waged relentlessly by the U.S. war machine under three presidents. After the war ended in 1975—its outcome determined by sustained Vietnamese anti-imperialist struggles combined with years of domestic antiwar mobilizations—U.S. leaders were unapologetic, offering no regrets, no reparations, no aid, no recognition of any sort of what their technowar campaign had done to a poor, underdeveloped nation. Indeed the elites of both major parties were (and, for the most part, still are) convinced of the noble intentions that fueled their catastrophic policies, even after diplomatic recognition was extended to Vietnam in 1995. This escape from the past, including efforts to rewrite the actual history of the era, are part of the famous Vietnam syndrome, which remains very much alive, culturally and politically, more than forty years after the JFK counterinsurgency apparatus first emerged.

Any careful reading of contemporary American public life will show that the Vietnam syndrome persists despite repeated efforts to eradicate it, as the failed Iraq adventures of the senior President Bush and his son readily attest. The Vietnam era continues today as a zone of contested meaning within the public sphere, a struggle over historical interpretation and ideological understanding that is far from concluded. Contrary to popular myth, this syndrome reaches far beyond the well-known U.S. reluctance to carry forward a Vietnam-style warfare entailing heavy commitment of ground forces and the inevitable high casualty rates. In fact the war itself shattered central political narratives about the U.S. role in world politics rooted in long-standing doctrines such as Manifest Destiny, the conventional image of American troops heroically fighting and winning "good wars," a general recognition of Yankee noble intentions in spreading the gospel of freedom and democracy around the world. Within the span of a decade Vietnam changed all that, overturning such benevolent images in favor of harsher discourses: defeat; humiliation at the hands of a militarily inferior enemy; the specter of mendacious, scheming leaders; an imperial agenda gone terribly, disastrously sour. For many across the globe the United States now came to represent a global force of monstrous evil, driven to repeat the Vietnam horrors well into the new century. As for Vietnam itself, that nation and its people remain nearly totally invisible to the U.S. ruling stratum, their unspeakable suffering banished from public discourse as if the entire governing structure and media culture were trapped in a state of collective denial. To this date no U.S. leader or spokesperson has stepped forward to acknowledge guilt and responsibility for what happened in Vietnam. Occasionally the syndrome has been manipulated to serve narrow elite interests, as when the contrived MIA/POW spectacle came to the forefront in the 1980s. To his enduring credit, McNamara—in both his memoirs and the Errol Morris documentary *The Fog of War*—has expressed profound sorrow over a cataclysmic intervention that he knew at the time to be a disaster.

As we turn to films representing the Vietnam era, what stands out is the creative work of several influential directors (Coppola, Kubrick, Stone, Cimino, Ashby, et al.) that departs radically from the good-war motif that framed the combat pictures of World War II and later. Indeed the Indochina war was accompanied by such widespread criticism and social turbulence—by the breakdown of so many established discourses—that cinematic depictions of a heroic war spurred on by noble objectives would have seemed ludicrous to most filmmakers, especially among the New Hollywood generation that came into prominence in the 1970s. More than any other historical juncture, the Vietnam experience gave rise to harshly negative reactions not only to U.S. foreign policy but the larger power structure identified with that policy. The result was that the best-received Vietnam films, released between the mid-1970s and the late 1980s, appeared to capture the intense antiwar feelings of a generation influenced by the lengthy military debacle, the radicalism of the new left, and the experimental sensibilities of the counterculture. In movie after movie the familiar good-war theme vanished almost entirely. Gone were the larger-than-life military heroes of *Destination Tokyo, Sands of Iwo Jima,* and even *Patton.* In their place emerged a more open-ended body of cinema, more technically sophisticated than the earlier propagandistic works, that dwelled on the horrors and futility of warfare, the defeat and mood of disillusionment, the terrible costs of war at home and abroad. The historical reality, of course, was that there were few glorious military victories to report from the front. Only *The Green Berets* (1968), starring none other than John Wayne, sought to encapsulate the good-war narrative for Vietnam, and it failed miserably at both the box office and among critics. Replete with U.S. battlefield heroics against a demonic Communist enemy, *The Green Berets* resembled nothing more than a thinly disguised, recycled Western with its embattled military outpost of courageous American troops populated with comic-strip figures.

Yet, as we argue in the following pages, the most compelling Vietnam-era films ultimately shared many basic premises with the earlier tradition of one-dimensional combat pictures, reproducing several old discourses in new (more politically fashionable or "balanced") guise. Although the Hollywood war machine seemed to be relegated to the periphery, with Pentagon officials regularly alarmed by the sting of antimilitary narratives in the new movies, its guiding ideology in fact reemerged more or less intact. The undeniably antiwar content of the vast majority of Vietnam-era films was either seriously compromised and negated by incorporation of traditional combat-genre themes, or was countered by the appearance of works (often quite popular) that ran against the antiwar motif. These characteristics fall under several headings:

1. The Vietnam War is depicted as a primarily *American* experience, the horrors, suffering, and angst largely visited upon U.S. troops in the nightmarish field of battle or veterans as they return home. The narratives are told almost exclusively from a provincial, ethnocentric viewpoint, with Vietnam often little more than a dramatic backdrop for action/adventure scenes.
2. Typically U.S. military forces in Vietnam—fighting some ten thousand miles from their own soil—are portrayed as noble grunts, innocent and often illiterate kids just struggling for survival in the hot, dense, menacing jungles of an alien country, a place, moreover, that does not want them. This is far from the image of marauding, destructive imperial forces equipped with advanced military technology and prepared to destroy anything in their path, which of course was much closer to the truth. Here as in the above motif it is the Americans who are seen as the sad, unfortunate victims.
3. Vietnamese people in these films are with few exceptions stereotyped as the familiar (scheming, mysterious, demonic) Oriental threat, part

of the long-standing Yellow Peril—or they are simply ignored altogether. They are rarely presented on screen as sympathetic victims of a war they are fighting for their own independence and even more rarely as active subjects of their own history.

4.  Many of these films show the horrors and atrocities of the war in graphic detail, but such horrors and atrocities are nearly always localized or isolated—the product of a few rampant, sadistic troops as at My Lai—or the violence is framed within the war-is-hell theme where everything is understood to be part of the tragic human condition and blame is universalized, with the U.S. military no better and no worse than the people it is attacking and killing. Above all, one never finds scenes of the systematic destruction that took place routinely over many years in Vietnam, the result of a planned, comprehensive, mostly aerial war of attrition.

5.  For every picture that constructs a negative image of the Vietnam War, there is another that embellishes and carries forward elements of the Vietnam syndrome, turning narratives of defeat and failure into those of a Rambo-like, vengeful crusade for "victory this time." Here American victim status is combined with the triumphal militarism and patriotism of the good war.

6.  None of these films, however critical of the war, attempts to establish the broader historical and political context of the Vietnam era, which means that the cinematic narratives are fully detached from the crucial governmental and military decision-making apparatus. In the absence of such contextualization, which must include the role of U.S. imperial designs focused on worldwide counterinsurgency programs, the very meaning of the combat (or postcombat) representations is easily, and very conveniently, lost.

## Innocence, Defeat, Tragedy

As graphically critical of U.S. military operations as the majority of Vietnam era films might have been, few if any transcended preoccupation with strictly American interests and experiences; more often than not the Indochinese landscape existed as little more than a panorama for cinematic storytelling, with gruesome combat scenes added. This generalization seems most valid for the more celebrated of these pictures: *Apocalypse Now, The Deer Hunter, Platoon, Full Metal Jacket*. As Desser writes, virtually all Vietnam-related films share one overriding motif: "a focus on us, on what the war did to us, on how we entered Vietnam with either good or bad intentions, but never on Vietnam as historical site, never on the Vietnamese as genuine subjects, as people with a culture, a heritage, a political agenda, even a cultural and political confusion all their own."[1] The war in all its terrifying reality is presented as a moment of lost personal or national innocence *(Born on the Fourth of July)*, a hero's journey into the dark labyrinth of a Hobbesian jungle *(Apocalypse Now)*, a phase when the battlefield helped transform boys into men *(The Boys in Company C, Hamburger Hill, Full Metal Jacket)*, a moment where ordinary working youths were thrown into a tragic struggle for survival *(The Deer Hunter)*, a torturous discovery that the true enemy is located "within ourselves" *(Platoon)*, or the replay of yet another American tragedy *(Coming Home, Born on the Fourth of July)*. Only a small part combat genre, these films actually recall and in some ways extend certain elements of traditional American mythology: the voyage across frontiers, the epic struggle to overcome a chaotic state of nature, a coming of age, ordinary folk rising toward moments of courage and heroism. Through all these agonizing but often exhilarating exercises Vietnam scarcely figured in terms of its *own* human and political journey.

Probably the most critically praised, and most overwrought, of these works is Michael Cimino's Oscar-winning film *The Deer Hunter* (1978), described by some writers as the "great American epic." The main point of Cimino's brilliantly constructed narrative is to trace the lives of three working-class men in their journey from a small Pennsylvania steel town to the jungles of Vietnam. The director romanticizes the culture and the personal sagas of these men, depicting in great detail their everyday rituals tied to ethnic solidarity, community life, women, bars, and hunting, so that we come to identify closely with their humanity as they are sent off to do combat with a faceless, sadistic enemy that could only be understood as some rendering of the Yellow Peril. The noble intentions and pained innocence of these ordinary Americans extends into the battlefield, where the horrors they face (including torture by Vietcong captors) appear all the more grotesque given what we know about their roots and psychological travails. *The Deer Hunter* is shot entirely from the viewpoint of these three soldiers, their every move overlaid with a deeply pessimistic sense of powerlessness despite their obviously willing embrace of the warrior mission. Upon returning from the hell of Vietnam at the end of the movie, the two surviving men join in a powerful, uplifting rendition of "God Bless America," thus affirming a restoration of what had been a shattered national community—shattered above all by sharp divisions over an extremely unpopular war. Further, by constructing a scenario in which basically good American citizens are forced to battle a diabolical Vietnamese enemy, *The Deer Hunter*—whatever its populist sensibilities—winds up inverting the real legacy of the war. In the words of Quart and Auster, "The film suffers from a case of political and moral amnesia, forgetting that it was the Americans who were the aggressors . . . who carpet-bombed and napalmed the Vietnamese and adulterated and destroyed the social fabric of South Vietnam."[2] Along these lines *The Deer Hunter* emerges as nothing so much as an overblown cinematic tribute to a destructive and unpopular U.S. military campaign.

Francis Ford Coppola's *Apocalypse Now* (1979) is even more terrifyingly graphic in its portrait of the state of nature in the cauldron of Vietnam. The film involves a bizarre, surreal journey of Americans into the darkness of jungle combat, where everyone winds up submerged in a cycle of unfathomable violence, fear, and paranoia and where qualities of human goodness that might have existed before the journey have simply vanished. For Coppola, Vietnam was nothing short of a descent into hell, a noirish spectacle, as U.S. troops are sucked into the insanity of brutal warfare that turns ever inward. Following the trajectory of Joseph Conrad's *Heart of Darkness,* the picture meanders clumsily like an arcane detective thriller along a rather familiar path: that war is hell and human nature is wicked, much of it personified by renegade Green Beret Colonel Kurtz (played by Marlon Brando). The other characters, too, are mired in violence and nihilism—a commentary less on Vietnam itself than on some imputed human condition. Coppola builds his narrative deep inside Cambodia, where army captain Benjamin Willard (Martin Sheen), on a special operations mission, is sent deep into forbidden territory to discover the whereabouts of Kurtz with the idea of "terminating him with extreme prejudice." Willard's journey takes him deeper and deeper into chaos, suffering, and death, leading him to the ultimate embodiment of evil, Kurtz, who has surrounded his residence with decapitated heads of enemies. A fierce gun battle leaves most everyone dead but Willard. Amid the carnage Kurtz utters the film's final words, his chilling refrain encapsulating Coppola's simple message about war: "The horror! The horror!" The film thus presents war as evil in itself, the quintessential outpost of hell on earth. Once the war placed its grip on Colonel Kurtz, there was no letting go until he and everything around him were destroyed.

Filled with spectacular images of the Indochinese (actually Philippine) landscape, *Apocalypse Now* is presented as a distinctly American saga, replete with strains of the counterculture. Coppola himself was clear about this: "The jungle will look psychedelic, fluorescent blues, yellows, and greens. I mean the war is essentially a Los Angeles export, like acid rock."[3] Indeed, Coppola vehemently disavowed any political agenda, partly as a (futile) tactic to win Pentagon assistance to shoot his film in the jungles of Asia. In the end *Apocalypse Now,* though often viewed as antiwar, would depart little from the deeply conservative ideological outlook of *The Deer Hunter.* Despite all the film's pretentious moralizing, we ultimately come to see (as Quart and Auster put it) "that the particular historical and social reality of the Vietnam War and America's war there is replaced by a vaporous notion of civilization's madness. The terror is universalized—it is seen as part of the human condition, not as a product of concrete political forces."[4]

To varying degrees later Vietnam War pictures followed the pattern established by Cimino and Coppola. In Oliver Stone's Oscar-winning *Platoon* (1987), reputed to be one of the most powerful of all antiwar statements, the

Platoon *(Oliver Stone, 1986, Orion Pictures). This Vietnam War epic reveals intense culture clashes among army grunts in the field. Sergeant Barnes (Tom Berenger) is a redneck gung-ho warrior with a take-no-prisoners attitude toward Vietnamese villagers. Barnes is opposed by the more sensitive Sergeant Elias (Willem Dafoe), who tries to protect the villagers and inject a sense of sanity into a totally irrational warfare situation. Copyright 2003 Orion Pictures Corporation.*

storytelling uses the Vietnam jungles as a setting to depict uniquely American conflicts and tragedies—young men becoming battlefield mature, the struggle around military tactics, survival in an alien, hostile milieu—all tied in some way to the fabric of domestic culture at a time of rapid change. More than other films of the period, *Platoon* sets forth realistic images of combat horrors, the kind of horrors that are psychologically assimilated by ordinary grunts whose overriding mission is merely to survive. As in the other parts of his Vietnam trilogy, *Born on the Fourth of July* (1989) and *Heaven and Earth* (1993), Stone weaves together powerful cinematic sequences and deeper messages about the chaos and meaninglessness of war that, in their generality, fall into the war-is-hell category. As with *Apocalypse Now,* death and destruction are viewed as part of a broader human tragedy where everyone is trapped by events beyond their control; war is democratized. Of course where the source of evil is generalized in this way, there can be no *specific* culpability, no individual or collective agency responsible for the carnage. From this standpoint, Stone's work here as elsewhere is largely devoid of political content, shrouded in moral abstractions even as the movie seems committed to pursuing "the truth" by means of battlefield realism.

The great contribution of *Platoon,* as with *Born on the Fourth of July,* is that it offers realistic images of combat, stripped of the usual sanitized representations of warfare in Hollywood combat pictures. Stone's cinematography presents a Vietnam battlefield that is bleak and terrifying, where GIs face a ubiquitous, skillful, fearsome enemy; all moral and social constraints seem to evaporate. For embattled grunts, therefore, the jungle horrors are inevitably internalized and give rise to conditions familiar in other wars, where the "enemy resides in us." Put differently, Vietnam becomes a nightmare to purge America of its own self-destructive impulses and demons. Stone's powerfully emotional rendering of war—one he had experienced at length himself—is built around the persona of Private Chris Taylor (Charlie Sheen), an upper-middle-class college dropout initiated into manhood through the ordeal of battle. Taylor's fellow soldiers, however, are from mainly working-class backgrounds, and they, as in *The Deer Hunter,* are portrayed sympathetically, shown to be simple, innocent kids thrown into the heat of battle where, it follows, their lack of restraint toward acts of violence is fully understandable.

*Platoon* constructs its drama around two diametrically opposed platoon leaders: the well-intentioned, kindly, almost Christlike Sergeant Elias (Willem Dafoe) and the cynical, at times even sadistic Sergeant Barnes (Tom Berenger), who tells army troops stationed near the Cambodian border, "I am reality. That's the way it ought to be, and that's the way it is." Sergeant Elias, on the other hand, dresses down another sergeant for expressing a macho, dictatorial attitude: "O'Neill, take a break. You don't have to be a prick every day of your life, you know." Over time, the two antagonistic soldiers cannot coexist in the same platoon, and Barnes decides to murder Elias. The narrator, Private Taylor, explains that both men tried to dominate the entire platoon with their philosophy, a conflict naturally intensified in the heat of combat. Says Taylor, "There are times when I've felt like a child born of these two fathers. But those of us who did make it have an obligation to build once again, to teach others what we know, to try with what's left of our lives to find goodness and meaning." Stone's film thus reconciles the two sides of war—noble and savage—in his powerfully devastating narrative. Finally, Taylor says to the audience, "Somebody once wrote 'Hell is the impossibility of reason.' That is exactly what this place feels like—Hell. I hate it already, and it's only been a week."

As for the Vietnamese, once again they remain invisible aside from a dramatic scene where villagers are brutalized and killed by GIs. Here the Vietnamese are shown only as hapless victims when in reality they were collective agents in a successful fight for national liberation. The soldiers face shadowy Vietcong fighters who are rarely seen and therefore come to represent more abstract forces of destruction lurking about the jungle than actual social groups. Moreover, there is nothing in *Platoon* that situates the U.S. intervention historically or politically. The seductive power of this film lies entirely in its emotional immediacy.

Stanley Kubrick's *Full Metal Jacket* (1987) frames the Vietnam experience by first looking at the ordeal of marine boot-camp life, showing (in a number of obscenity-laden sequences) how the U.S. military turns ordinary youths into enthusiastic killers ready for combat. Marine training and indoctrination were designed to prepare men for all the horrors of warfare, stripping individuals of their previous identities, eroding their moral qualms about death and dying, and paving the way toward their becoming men as they eagerly join forces with the killing machine. For Kubrick, indeed, warfare by definition generates barbarism, something *Full Metal Jacket* eventually captures in Vietnam and shows to be endemic to human nature. Here the director follows a dual perspective: the terrible absurdity of combat is a condition the troops, having been fully trained and socialized, come to exemplify as they make their way through a fearsome milieu of demons and enemies where heroism is possible. Their very survival might well depend on such adaptation. Many, of course, go beyond adaptation and begin to relish the savagery imposed by combat. In any event, *Full Metal Jacket* embraces a narrative typical of many Vietnam War pictures, in which the military cauldron is presented as part human tragedy, part manifestation of a Hobbesian state of nature, part struggle for survival in an environment where all rules and norms have been torn asunder.

Kubrick establishes the first part of the picture around marine gunnery sergeant Hartman (Lee Ermey), a tough drill instructor whose only goal in life is to convert ordinary young men into trained killers who worship their rifles. They are taught to sleep with their weapons, which the recruits must regard as their best friend "without which life is useless." The marines must see themselves with their trusted rifle at hand as the ultimate defenders, indeed saviors, of America as they stand before God, country, and family. Further, "It is your killer instinct that you must harness if you expect to survive in combat. And it is the hard heart that kills." At one point in the indoctrination Hartman asks the gathered recruits to identify both Charles Whitman, who killed twelve people with his rifle from the University of Texas Tower, and Lee Harvey Oswald, charged with shooting President John Kennedy from the Texas School Book Depository in Dallas. The answer, of course, is that both were U.S. Marines, both were trained marksmen, and both were eager to kill. Toward the end of basic training Hartman intones that "the Free World will conquer Communism with the aid of God and a few good Marines." One of the recruits is Private Joker (Matthew Modine), a jaded narrator who immediately challenges Hartman by mimicking John Wayne in response to Hartman's intimidating repartee, asking sotto voce, "Is that you, John Wayne? Is this me?" Later another marine, Private Pyle (Vincent D'Onofrio), buckles under the pressure of Hartman's relentless harassment, goes crazy, and then shoots the drill instructor just after Hartman asks in his typical insulting style, "Didn't Mommy and

Full Metal Jacket *(Stanley Kubrick, 1987, Warner Bros.). A trenchant, dramatic critique of the Vietnam war, the film begins with the hypermilitaristic rigors of marine basic training. Real-life drill instructor Lee Ermey (pictured here) dominates the screen, only to be shot and killed by one of his trainees.*

Daddy show you enough attention when you were a child?" Private Joker later utters the final lines of *Full Metal Jacket* as elements of his platoon are moving through the carnage of a Vietnamese hamlet: "I'm so happy that I'm alive, in one piece, and short. I'm in a world of shit, yes, but I'm still alive and I'm not afraid." This bleak portrait of an American grunt's life in Indochina came roughly a year after *Platoon,* its images just as horrifying and jolting.

Of course in *Full Metal Jacket* as in *Platoon* and elsewhere one finds an unmistakable backdrop of patriotism, even if muted. More critically, any moral or political responsibility for decisions leading to carnage in Vietnam simply vanishes from sight, never to be encountered, much less debated, among the grunts or higher officers. In fact the Vietnam section of Kubrick's film, realistic and brilliantly shot, ultimately seems almost subordinate to the main (boot camp) drama, peripheral to the central focus on how the military transforms individuals through a matrix integrating aggression, sexual impulses, and killing—here again encapsulating a distinctly American frame of reference.

The earlier, well-received *Boys in Company C* (1978), directed by Sidney Furie, combines a number of these same themes—boys turned into men, the nightmares of combat, male bonding under fire, sense of entrapment in a world spiraling out of control, breakdown of social norms and moral limits. This picture offers no glorification of warfare, nor does it glamorize the marines in a context where officers are seen as bungling and incompetent. From all indications, the producers undertook the project to make a strong commentary on the insanity of war in general and the Vietnam War in particular. Like *Full Metal Jacket,* Furie's movie devotes considerable footage to the boot-camp phase, where recruits are browbeaten and brainwashed into becoming eager killers for their combat units, the marines, and the nation. Like *Platoon,* it dwells on the chaos and confusion within the military itself, anticipating the "enemy is us" thematic. And like *M\*A\*S\*H\** before it, *Boys* illustrates with comic absurdity the colossal irrationality and contradictions of military life. But this picture could have been about *any* war, so little did it contain regarding the conditions and consequences of U.S. intervention in Indochina. More than anything, we are left feeling warmly sympathetic toward this unique band of "boys" as they strive to retain their humanity in the midst of terrifying combat experiences.

John Irvin's *Hamburger Hill* (1987) furnishes another example of a film that projects the Vietnam reality from the viewpoint of the average (U.S.) soldier in the field. Yet whereas pictures like *Platoon* and *Full Metal Jacket* portrayed American grunts as largely young, naive, and ignorant, in many cases barely literate, this movie sets out to restore a mood of combat heroism to the Vietnam genre, showing in bloody detail GIs repeatedly storming a remote hill—daring and courageous maneuvers that would have done justice to *The Sands of Iwo Jima.* The story revolves around a ten-day assault in May 1969, when the Third Brigade of the army's 101st Airborne Division mounted no less than eleven fierce attempts to take Hill 937, resulting in 70 percent casualties even as the terrain was eventually vacated. Irvin wants the audience to see that U.S. troops in Vietnam exhibited precisely the same traits as those who fought at Guadalcanal or Tarawa, even in defeat. Thus *Hamburger Hill* could be interpreted as a narrative meant to make American GIs proud of their service in Vietnam, whatever the outcome and however unpopular at home, a reaction not likely to follow a viewing of *Apocalypse Now, Platoon,* or *Born on the Fourth of July.* It was this imagery, along with a harsh depiction of the antiwar movement in the United States, that gave *Hamburger Hill* its well-deserved reputation as a hawkish, superpatriotic picture. Consistent with *The Deer Hunter*—not to mention the *Rambo* films—the movie indulges the stereotype of a cruel, faceless, evil Oriental peril. If the film conveys a definite antiwar statement, showing the absurdity of GIs sacrificing so much in vain over a worthless piece of terrain, we are still left with feelings of empathy for outmanned American youth valiantly carrying out their assigned, nearly suicidal mission. No doubt for this reason *Hamburger Hill* is the only major Hollywood production about Vietnam combat to receive full Pentagon blessings and assistance.

When Barry Levinson directed *Good Morning, Vietnam* in 1987, he protested that he did not want to make yet another Vietnam movie to compete with the others; his idea was to shoot a war comedy with Vietnam essentially as the physical backdrop. Yet, having decided to set the film in 1965, when full-scale U.S. military mobilization was just on the upswing, Levinson ended up with a film that can easily be read as a metaphor for an ill-fated intervention with its peculiarly American sets of concerns. At one level *Good Morning, Vietnam* is a vehicle for Robin Williams's extended comedy routines as an Armed Forces Network disk jockey, a fury of good-humored criticism directed at the army lifestyle if not at the war itself. At another level the movie can be seen as a commentary on the mounting GI ferment that would later culminate in widespread alienation, dissidence, and even resistance. At still another level it portrays daily U.S.-Vietnamese interactions with a kind of sympathetic balance rarely visible before or since. No real combat is depicted in *Good Morning, Vietnam,* but the historical setting is richly laid out by Levinson and becomes the object of Williams's rapid-fire radio repartee that nearly sends his superiors into cardiac arrest. But that history, for the most part, comes across as fuzzy, with the politics muted and the human drama centered around distinctly American interests, as in *The Deer Hunter* and *Platoon.* As Suid remarks, "If *Good Morning, Vietnam* has anything to say about the nature of the American experience in Vietnam, it does so very subtly and from some inner truth rather than the historical record."[5] The picture did, however, provide Williams, playing real-life disk jockey Adrian Cronauer, with his most fitting role.

Despite his many well-publicized frustrations making *Apocalypse Now,* Coppola set out to win Pentagon assistance for another Vietnam film, this one less ambitious in scope but one that he hoped would convey antiwar sentiments. The result was *Gardens of Stone* (1987), based on a novel by Nicholas Proffitt. The narrative revolves around the military ordeals of Sergeant Clell Hazard (James Caan), an educated and enlightened NCO who had spent two tours of duty in Vietnam. The emotional centerpiece of the film—quite distant from the rhythm of combat—is the graphic depiction of daily, ritualized burials of soldiers who fought and died in Southeast Asia. On this basis alone Coppola manages to convey a far more striking antiwar message than anything visible in *Apocalypse Now,* though *Gardens of Stone,* with its emphasis on smaller tales of survival, has nothing like the same grand sweep or cinematic appeal. (One reviewer said that *Gardens of Stone* felt more like a little brother to *Platoon* than a companion to *Apocalypse Now.*) The picture focuses on the search within the army for routines of bonding and solidarity that become all the more vital as the war grows in unpopularity. If it stands to some degree as a pacifist work, in another way it comes across as a strong tribute to the military under fire—surely one reason the Pentagon extended its support. Fixating on some of the true victims of war, *Gardens of Stone* could (in Suid's words) be defined as "the paradigm of antiwar movies" insofar as "its images of death and lost potential pervade the psyche far more powerfully than the surrealistic images Coppola himself produces in *Apocalypse Now* or that Oliver Stone sought to produce out of the blood, gore, and chaos he was to put on screen in *Platoon*."[6] At the same time, Coppola's later work is even more confined to an American frame of reference than either of these films.

This same pattern of distorted, partial representations of war extended to the way filmmakers chose to depict the carnage—a carnage so vast in scope it could not be ignored. Few Vietnam-era movies tried to avoid the horrors altogether. Most confronted the images of death and destruction, refusing to downplay the battlefield chaos of the human casualties; indeed, this was always cinematically appealing to both directors and audiences, though predictably the Hollywood fare dwelled mostly on the American side of this nightmare. Atrocities committed by U.S. forces were even depicted on screen, at times with great emotional power, as in *Apocalypse Now, Platoon,* and *Casualties of War.* Some films even included strong political statements denouncing the evils of war, often focusing on the terrors that U.S. intervention brought to the civilian population in the sort of warfare wherein distinctions between combatants and noncombatants could not be sustained. In *Born on the Fourth of July,* for example, Ron Kovic (Tom Cruise) rails in anguish upon his homecoming, "Thou shalt not kill, Mom, thou shalt not kill women and children. Thou shalt not kill, remember? Isn't that what you taught us? Tell her, Dad, tell her. It's a fucking lie. There's no God. There's no country."

The chaos and tragedy comes across in these films in a way that is unlike anything to be found in World War II combat pictures. There is little glorification of the U.S. armed forces or their mission in Southeast Asia; everything is constructed as a matter of survival, of maintaining sanity and capacity to function in a maddening world that no one seemed able to comprehend, much less control. Naturally there are breakdowns of moral restraint on both sides, equally cause and effect of the widespread turmoil, nihilism, and atrocities. There is a pervasive sense that the untold suffering could have, and should have, been avoided. Within this cinematic milieu U.S. soldiers are shown raping, torturing, and killing Vietnamese civilians in a number of movies—scenes unimaginable in the good-war productions. A gruesome scene in Stone's *Platoon* stands out, one that suggests a revisit of the My Lai massacre in which hundreds of men, women, and children were slaughtered. In *Casualties of War* (1989), Brian DePalma brought to the screen Daniel Lang's account of a 1966 episode where a five-man army reconnaissance patrol abducted, raped, and murdered a Vietnamese peasant girl. For this the soldiers were court-martialed and convicted, but their sentences were reduced, as in the case of Lieutenant John Calley after My Lai. Characterizing this event as something of a microcosm of the entire war, DePalma referred to it as a "classical tragedy," adding—with inspiration from *Platoon*—that American troops turned out to be their own worst enemies.[7] Following the narrative of *Full Metal Jacket,* moreover, this picture dramatizes how ordinary Americans can be transformed into violent monsters virtually overnight.

The wartime horrors in Vietnam were duly portrayed within Hollywood cinema, but some questions remain: How were such horrors to be contextualized and interpreted by audiences? What was the scope of such horrors? Who was ultimately responsible? It is here that even the most "antiwar" Vietnam-era films wound up egregiously short of presenting anything close to a systematic, coherent picture of the lengthy war of attrition waged by the United States in Indochina, including its origins, nature, extent, and full consequences. Entirely missing was a view of the sustained, murderous technowar conducted by the Pentagon after counterinsurgency was begun by the liberal JFK elites in their global crusade against Communism. There were no graphic depictions of what took place *beyond* the local atrocities—for example, the years of strategic carpet bombing, the enclosed "hamlets" set up as part of the "pacification" campaign, ecological assaults on the forests and croplands, massive social dislocations, the vast death and destruction across the whole Indochina landscape. Indeed having lost the political war in Southeast Asia, the United States commenced in 1965 to wage an unprecedented "total war" with the inevitable catastrophic outcomes detailed at the beginning of this chapter. It is impossible to escape the specter of a rich and powerful country possessing the world's most awesome war machine laying waste to a poor, underdeveloped society. Everything that took place in Vietnam was systematic, planned, and murderous, the product of seemingly irrational but nonetheless deliberately harmful geopolitical ambitions embraced by U.S. leaders. In none of these enlightened, critically minded combat movies do we grasp even a hint of this reality.

These films reveal an important slice of truth about the terrors of war, yet the blatant distortions and omissions tell us even more about the films' failure to convey the larger Vietnam experience. Hollywood cinema dramatized everything from a uniquely provincial standpoint, one that is ethnocentric, inner-focused, and draped in the imagery of U.S. tragedy, victimism, and lost innocence. In the end these pictures reflect the arrogance of both American politics and popular culture, a privileging of U.S. interests, values, and experiences, or at least those filtered through the interpretive lenses of the power elite. The idea that U.S. military intervention ten thousand miles from its own shores, spanning fifteen years and waged against a nation posing no threat, could be more than a sad mistake or tragedy is never taken up in any form. The unfathomable suffering of tens of millions of people caused by a ferocious technowar is largely ignored. Who, indeed, *were* the Vietnamese Laotians, and Cambodians, whose very social fabric was ruthlessly destroyed? What did the war mean to them, their society, their history? Why, above all, was the United States in Southeast Asia in the first place? A close viewing of all these films combined will produce few if any answers to such crucial political questions.

## Post-Vietnam Traumas

The multitude of postwar traumas brought home from Indochina furnished ideal material for Hollywood filmmaking after the mid-1970s. Many films sought to integrate the psychological impact of the two fronts, the Southeast Asia battlefield and the cauldron of American urban life in the wake of momentous political and military catastrophe. In contrast to other wars, of course, Vietnam not only embodied the nightmarish experiences of combat but the humiliation of resounding defeat. American society, too, had changed drastically in the aftermath of Vietnam, political assassinations, turbulence of the 1960s and 1970s, Watergate, and the ongoing disintegration of social life. As for the immediate "casualties of war," they were not merely global or military but political, cultural, and psychological as well, penetrating the deepest interstices of the entire society which, fully three decades later, has yet to recover. The cinematic enterprise duly captured this phenomenon, becoming yet another part of the continuing Vietnam syndrome.

Films that set out to encapsulate some aspect of the Vietnam experience, including those that did so only indirectly or peripherally, followed two general paths: depiction of the costs to American society in terms of waste, the growing culture of violence, alienation, and broken people, and the framing of the syndrome to essentially rewrite history, recasting the narratives of war so that the United States could finally emerge as the victor. The larger implications of these two competing motifs would differ markedly, the first acknowledging and dramatizing the terrible consequences of war, the second looking for an escape hatch from the historical cataclysm by revising the script, using the traumas as a basis of national redemption. In both cases, however, the overriding frame of reference was the implications of Vietnam for American society; here as elsewhere the Vietnamese remain largely invisible. Viewed by huge audiences, this cycle of pictures would come to exert tremendous influence on the popular consciousness.

Martin Scorsese's *Taxi Driver* (1976) was the first movie to explore the life and world of a returned Vietnam vet, in this case the bizarre, psychotic travails of taxi driver Travis Bickle (Robert De Niro), who moves around the hellish streets of nighttime New York City in a perpetual state of paranoia, anger—and expectation. Shot in film noir style, the picture shows an urban labyrinth of drug addicts, hookers, pimps, and assorted riffraff, a setting where "all the animals come out at night." As for Bickle, he is shown to have become utterly disabled, mentally if not physically, presumably the result of his Vietnam duty, though we can never be entirely sure. The taxi driver, a twenty-six-year-old former marine, is aimless, cut off, lonely, and alienated, his brain filled with bizarre fantasies and demons, self-destructive to the core. His estrangement and wandering, his sense of disorientation, are accompanied by increasingly violent impulses that include a gun fetish. Above all, Bickle is desperately lonely. As he puts it, "Loneliness has followed me my whole life. Everywhere. In bars, in cars, sidewalks, stores, everywhere. There's no escape. I'm god's lonely man." Such a disabling condition might well fit any definition of "combat fatigue," a state of mental collapse brought on by lengthy exposure to the violence of warfare.

Viewed through such lenses, *Taxi Driver* can be understood as the quintessential statement of post-Vietnam war trauma, where the returning vet feels detached and alienated from an environment he or she cannot grasp; both the vet and the world that is experienced have changed drastically, frighteningly. Such trauma was no doubt encountered by hundreds of thousands of vets in the 1970s and later. Here Scorsese presents images of the noir city that are even more Hobbesian, more filled with chaos, violence, and danger, than those noir classics that served as models for *Taxi Driver*. The film stands as a metaphor for the kind of alienation—both individual and collective—that Vietnam, a U.S.-instigated war, brought to American society. Indeed the movie concludes with Bickle going off on a violent rampage, finally giving vent to a tormented life, signifying a form of personal and national psychological cleansing made possible by the cathartic release of pent-up emotions. The problem lies not with Scorsese's excellent cinematic representations of the noir city, but rather with its specific contextualization of Bickle's state of mind. For one thing, the connection with Vietnam is never clearly established but remains distant and refracted throughout the picture. This becomes even more problematic given what we know about Bickle's earlier (pre-Vietnam) mental condition. More to the point, the very notion of a Hobbesian urban milieu in the United States can hardly be considered novel, much less specific to the Vietnam aftermath, as could readily be seen in the gritty images of dozens of noir classics released many years before the Vietnam War. In fact the urban labyrinth, saturated with poverty, alienation, and violence, has deep roots in American history and its peculiar patterns of economic development, the product of many factors: capitalism, the military-industrial complex, social fragmentation, breakdown of the family, and so forth. All these are surely independent of whatever damage the Vietnam War might have caused. It is true that returning vets often wind up as broken people, but in reality the milieu Scorsese depicts in *Taxi Driver* (as in *Mean Streets* earlier) was exported from the United States to Vietnam, not the other way around. The Vietnamese never waged a long war of attrition against American society, convulsing and battering it in the process. The turbulence of urban street life, rampant individualism, and the culture of violence—all these were present long before the disastrous effects of the Vietnam debacle.

Several Hollywood films released in the late 1970s turned their narratives toward the issue of Americans being victimized by what happened in Indochina: not only *The Deer Hunter* but also John Flynn's *Rolling Thunder* (1977), Paul Kagan's *Heroes* (1977), Karel Reitz's *Who'll Stop the Rain* (1978), and Hal Ashby's *Coming Home* (1978). Although the United States initiated the carnage, in these films it turns out that through a complex dialectical process that same country—including its ordinary citizens employed by the military—suffered the most. In *Rolling Thunder,* we have the tale of an Air Force officer who returns home after seven years as a POW, only to find everything has changed—his wife has taken both a job and a new lover and files for divorce. Having been tortured by the Vietnamese, Major Charles Rane (William Devane) had already descended to hell, his terrors now exacerbated by domestic traumas. Adding to this nightmare, Rane is robbed and beaten by a gang of Mexican Americans, who proceed to kill his wife and son—yet another brutalizing experience at the hands of third-world demons. He naturally sets out on a path of vengeance, hunting those very enemies he could not effectively fight in Vietnam, recalling elements of Ford's film *The Searchers.* He finally tracks down the perpetrators at a brothel where, in a series of extremely violent scenes, he kills his tormentors in a shootout, giving at least partial vent to his long pent-up rage. Flynn shot the film to display emotional sympathy for the returning officer, whose resort to a bloody outburst appears rather normal. After all, Rane had become hardened to the brutality of war so that behaving in line with the norms of war could be understood as a natural psychological response. Moreover, Rane has already declared that he is fatally scarred, emotionally dead, in the aftermath of his combat horrors. Through all this Flynn reveals the tormented military figure to be a good patriot and dedicated officer, still committed to the war effort. This picture established the pattern for later cinematic works that focused on the emotional and physical scars of the Vietnam years.

In *Heroes* (1977), the director employs the same returning-vets-as-victims narrative to weave what might be construed as an antiwar statement. Henry Winkler plays a mentally deranged Vietnam combat vet who roams the country seeking answers to the chaos and doubt he finds both in himself and the larger society; the war lives deeply within him as it presumably did within Travis Bickle as well as Charles Rane and later figures like Ron Kovic in *Born on the Fourth of July.* Here Jack Dunne proceeds to walk into a New York City army recruitment center and drag away potential enlistees who are being told that parachute-jumping is better than sex. Along his tortured path he keeps getting sent back to Veterans Administration hospitals for "treatment," all the while haunted by demons, as shown in a flashback depicting his close friend's death in Vietnam. Upon visiting his parents, they scream that their son has already died in Southeast Asia, but the picture ultimately rescues him with a happy ending as he reunites with his girlfriend (Sally Field). The postcombat traumas are debilitating, but not entirely beyond reversal. Reitz's *Who'll Stop the Rain,* framed in the Vietnam aftermath but a more straightforward action picture with strong moralistic overtones, shows how it is drugs rather than war or violence that is corrupting America—with the twist that the drugs are an import from Vietnam, a symbol of third-world contamination. In fact it is drugs that wind up as the central metaphor for any damage the war had inflicted on the home front.[8] Depicting a culture that is essentially decaying from all the rot, *Who'll Stop the Rain* bases its storytelling on two interwoven myths: the war on drugs and the evils brought to America by demonic forces abroad.

In *The Deer Hunter*, we have seen how Cimino brings together narratives of combat and the home front into a broader cinematic statement about the damage Vietnam inflicted on American society. He employs the metaphor of Russian roulette to show the manner in which warfare becomes a "casino of death" where virtually anything can happen to anyone at any time, where survival is essentially a game of chance. We know that the actual playing of Russian roulette in Vietnam is fiction, but it works in the context of a picture where young American men are tortured and killed, while others are broken physically and emotionally once they return home. The three main protagonists—Michael, Nick, and Steve—leave their working-class routines for the casino of warfare. Each of them is dedicated to the cause when he is shipped out, only to be numbed and disabled by the experience. Michael returns obsessively to Vietnam in search of his friend Nick, who, semicatatonic by this time, winds up killed by the game of chance, while Steve becomes crippled in body and mind, incapable of continuing as before. Shot in noir-like flourishes, *The Deer Hunter* dramatizes the postwar traumas as powerfully as could be done. It is a film that could be read as a plea for healing the wounds inflicted on an entire generation victimized by the Vietnam syndrome (viewed psychologically as well as politically) of defeat and humiliation. Any antiwar message is obliterated, however, by the fact that everything unfolds fully within the dominant ideological paradigm of U.S. national righteousness mixed with strong images of family values and macho culture.

Two widely viewed post-Vietnam films, *Coming Home* and *Born on the Fourth of July*, feature the paralyzed vet as a symbol of enduring scars produced by the war. Both are self-consciously antiwar in their narratives and spirit, the first inspired by activist Jane Fonda, the second made possible by the collaborative effort of Oliver Stone and Ron Kovic, whose autobiography was the basis of the movie. In *Coming Home*, marine sergeant Luke Martin (Jon Voigt) is forced to adapt to his disability after being wounded in combat and returning to an indifferent milieu. He meets Sally Hyde (Jane Fonda), the restless wife of a marine captain played by Bruce Dern, whereupon the two fall in love and together become politicized in their opposition to the war. Sally's husband Bob winds up as a double casualty of war: Vietnam transformed him from a gung-ho officer into a disillusioned vet, while upon his return he finds his marital situation destroyed. Debilitated, Bob angrily confronts his wife and her lover, turns on himself, and eventually swims out to sea in a final act of self-destruction. In contrast, Luke and Sally turn outward in their response to the horrors of war, gaining strength from their own relationship and their decision to speak out. Luke talks to high-school students about the immorality of war, about the insanity of going off to a distant country to kill when there is no reason to do it. Combat, he informs the students, is nothing like the images presented in the movies, which aestheticize and romanticize what the participants experience as nothing but death and destruction. Here again we have American victims of war each confronting their own horrifying realities in different ways. A passionate appeal to end all the carnage, *Coming Home* offers a powerful antiwar message that is, however, diluted by virtue of the picture's much greater embellishment of the love story involving Luke and Sally and, more significantly, the vagueness of the moralizing sentiments contained in the script. The actual historical narrative of the Vietnam War scarcely enters the picture.

Inspired by the success of his hugely acclaimed *Platoon,* Stone carries forward and in some ways extends the same narratives in *Born on the Fourth of July*—on the surface clearly one of the most compelling antiwar films ever made. Kovic's disability resulting from a 1969 firefight turns what had been a superpatriotic, hell-bent marine into a broken casualty of war and then into an activist who founded Vietnam Veterans Against the War. Everything that Kovic experiences—the war, terrible conditions at the VA hospital, family strife, sexual impotence, a lifetime of paralysis—comes across as graphic depictions of how the pain and suffering of warfare are brought home, made part of American domestic life. In a nation torn apart by an irrational and costly war, Kovic the vet is torn apart in his own body and mind. Having grown up in small-town America, Kovic winds up intensely disillusioned with everything: the military, patriotism, political leaders who lied, family, friends, country. At yet another level the film explores the phenomenon of innocence lost and with it the eclipse of the American dream—a theme Stone would develop later in such pictures as *The Doors, Talk Radio,* and of course *JFK.* While much has been made of Stone's occasional excesses and distortions, the picture still works as a powerful cinematic statement that, as Suid observes, "incorporates virtually the entire American experience in Vietnam better than any other film about the war."[9] Yet even in *Born on the Fourth of July,* with its strong indictment of U.S. political leaders, the preoccupation is ultimately with the home front, the Vietnamese relegated to a distant, essentially invisible otherness, much as in *Platoon.*

With a parallel second cycle of Vietnam-themed films, Hollywood aggressively took on the syndrome in a series of revisionist we-won-the-war-after-all narratives filled with emotionally charged images of revenge, male heroism, violent rage, and racism. The ideology that fuels these pictures is a right-wing populism directed against the forces of betrayal and defeat: government bureaucrats, soft liberals, antiwar zealots—anyone who stood in the way of military victory. The *Missing in Action* films of the mid-1980s, starring Chuck Norris, feature a Superman-like armed hero who liberates American MIAs secretly held captive by the Vietnamese years after the war has ended. In the process he coolly and mercilessly kills hundreds of the enemy, framed here as ruthless and primitive—essentially a replay of the Western genre, where civilization triumphs over barbarism and modernity over backwardness, though now with even greater technological embellishment. As we have seen, the Western and combat genres share more or less the same formula—male heroes with noble causes defeat evil monsters after the requisite bout of bloody action. In Ted Kotcheff's commercially successful *Uncommon Valor* (1983), Vietnam is duly transformed into a good war as the protagonist, marine colonel Jason Rhodes (Gene Hackman), leads a group of rebellious prisoners who, betrayed by the elites, achieve liberation through their rediscovery of God, patriotism, and all-out cleansing violence. The prisoners are being held, it turns out, not in Vietnam but in Laos, imprisoned by elements of the Laotian military. The film actually blames the U.S. government rather than the Laotians for the impasse in negotiations over the MIAs—an impasse that forces Hackman's group to undertake its extremely risky mission. Here again the captivity myth suggests that the nation, its military unappreciated and subverted, is being corrupted by alien demons. It also signifies that the Vietnam War, a real-life military and political defeat, had never actually been resolved.

The much-celebrated *Rambo* films similarly played on a superpatriotic right-wing populism that has deep roots in U.S. history. In three episodes (1982, 1985, and 1988) Sylvester Stallone stars as John Rambo, an embittered vet determined to convert the humiliation and defeat of Vietnam into a glorious military triumph, unleashing a flurry of armed violence on an enemy long deserving of a bloody payback. An ordinary man turned into lethal warrior, Rambo quickly comes to embody a Superman persona able to wage devastating warfare despite obstacles placed in his way by weak, indecisive, incompetent political and military leaders. Perhaps more than any other cinematic enterprise, the *Rambo* series connects with the militaristic, xenophobic, racist zeitgeist of the Reagan years, an outgrowth of the Vietnam syndrome that was already simmering by 1975. Above all Rambo embodies the warrior virtues in his self-disciplined macho character, endowed with awesome physical and mental powers. During the Reagan-Bush years he emerged as a symbol of patriotic, betrayed manhood. Indeed Reagan's own public relations handlers made political use of this rugged national symbol by associating it with an aggressive anti-Communist foreign policy ready to take on the Evil Empire. And it would feed into the later action/adventure movies of the 1990s and beyond. Indeed the Rambo character still represents virtually every historic American right-wing fantasy: superhuman male heroics, ultrapatriotism, weapons fetishism, a return to simple frontier ethics, reversal of defeat, conquest of evil others (in this case Russians as well as Vietnamese). Moreover, it carries forward the time-worn conservative motif of betrayal and cowardice—here by liberals and others soft on warrior virtues—that had shaped McCarthyism and served now to transform the American superpower into a victim of its own failed, but nonetheless bloody, imperial crusade. Rambo as mythic figure exerted a deep influence on the political culture despite the shoddy cinematic productions,

Rambo: First Blood *(Ted Wotcheff, 1982, Orion Pictures). Sylvester Stallone plays John Rambo, former Green Beret Vietnam veteran out for revenge not only against Communist enemies but also against U.S. government bureaucrats, liberals, and others seen as having blocked U.S. military victory in Indochina. As Rambo puts it, "We get to win this time!" The film is a drama based on paranoia and violent revenge.*

cartoonish images, and lack of historical veracity (starting with the nonexistent POW-MIA "problem"). It made for a sequence of exciting, reaffirming, and self-serving narratives—another seeming "resolution" of post-Vietnam traumas. And it would be a theme that would help shape the emergence of neoconservative defense intellectuals little more than a decade later.

A rare exception to the strictly American focus on postwar victimhood was Stone's *Heaven and Earth* (1993), the story of a Vietnamese woman (LeLy Hayslip) who endures ordeals at the hands of both the United States and the South Vietnamese before her voyage (itself troubled) to America. Stone uses Hayslip's journey to depict a sense of spiritual awakening of the Vietnamese people as they struggled to free themselves from political bondage. While the director wants to construct a narrative from a distinctly indigenous point of view, the Vietnam he brings to the screen is a romanticized, nearly idyllic setting, a mythical premodern world in which peasants live in peaceful harmony with each other and with nature. The local inhabitants are shown as simple, innocent people attached to their land and religion with, presumably, little interest in the mundane encroachments of war and revolution—in other words, as more or less politically detached. While rather persuasive in the larger scheme of things—a recycling of the noble primitive ethic—this story turns out to be just as false as the others: far from being passive, innocent, and politically naive, the Vietnamese were for many decades involved in movements for revolutionary independence, opposing the Japanese, British, and French before the final cataclysmic encounter with the Americans. The nation had been on a perpetual, full-scale war mobilization long before the personal sagas of Hayslip, who came from a privileged background. In the process it had built one of the most effective mass-based insurrectionary movements in modern times. Stone's depiction of an idealized preindustrial order, embellished with lush cinematography, a depoliticized script, and new age music, therefore, bears no resemblance to the historical actuality, however well-intentioned his project.

In their myriad ways these post–Vietnam era films reflect the decline of American politics and popular culture, perhaps even the crisis of empire itself. The continued public dwelling on U.S. victimhood, on efforts to reverse the historical narratives of defeat while obscuring the war experience as such, illuminates a certain process of national denial, an inability to transcend the Vietnam syndrome even as politicians and the media tried for so long to overcome it. The syndrome clearly persists in Hollywood as in Washington, insofar as none of the cinematic works discussed above presents any true account of the war and its massive consequences for both Vietnamese and Americans. Even the most combat-savvy, realistic films like *Platoon* and *Hamburger Hill* share this glaring defect. For Hollywood, the complex and far-reaching Vietnam experience has been filtered through the conventional range of film genres, from Westerns and combat pictures to film noir, historical dramas, sci-fi, and the increasingly popular action/adventure category. From an ideological standpoint, therefore, the Vietnam film legacy is beset with the same limitations and distortions we find in the general political culture, however strong the antiwar pretenses of that legacy. The recurrent narratives affirm loudly and clearly that war is hell—but that hell is inhabited almost entirely by Americans, by troops composed of just good, ordinary kids doing their jobs and trying to survive the jungle nightmare and then, if they are lucky enough to return alive, coping with an assortment of post-combat traumas. As for the leaders who made and upheld the crucial decision to intervene, well, they are well-intentioned if also somewhat given to mistakes and incorrect tactical calculations. In any event, the war left behind a wounded nation that seems to have lost its way, stumbling toward empire, perhaps because, as Stone intimates in *Heaven and Earth*, it has become afflicted with the sins of modernity. Thus, while these pictures do not propagandize for this or any other war, neither do they convey any coherent statement of opposition to it, or to U.S. imperial domination in general. In the spirit of Hollywood filmmaking, they remain fully disengaged from any political discourse.

At the beginning of the twenty-first century—roughly thirty years after the Vietnam War ended—Vietnam surely lives on in American public life. More accurately, it persists as a powerful ideological and cultural frame of reference that remains at the center of political wars concerning the U.S. role in global affairs. In 1991 President Bush the elder declared that the "Vietnam syndrome has been kicked" in the wake of the spectacular (but eventually pyrrhic) Gulf War victory, but of course this psychological release was soon dashed by public realization that this was an ersatz victory, Bush's own defeat at the polls, and the growing neoconservative insistence on returning to Baghdad and "finishing the job." This move, which became the prevailing mantra once Bush II invaded Iraq in 2003 and declared quick victory, would presumably relegate the great Indochina loss to the dustbin of history. The ensuing nightmare of occupation and resistance, however, guaranteed that the syndrome would not only stubbornly refuse to die but also would no doubt be extended and deepened. The 2004 presidential election revealed just how pervasive the Vietnam legacy remained within the political culture, as both Bush and Kerry built their campaigns around the idea of capturing the warrior mantle, connecting Vietnam with Iraq and the war on terrorism. The leading question was, which candidate would make the most effective military guardian of empire? The answer, not surprisingly, favored the Republican who vowed to keep the United States militarily strong in the fight against terrorism. We know that Bush and leading members of his circle never served in that war, while Kerry did serve, was highly decorated, and then protested against a military disaster that the majority of Americans had come to view as exorbitantly costly if not outright immoral. Conservatives predictably challenged Kerry's record and behavior, along with his inconsistent voting record as senator leading up to the Iraq invasion. Kerry, for his part, not only wrapped himself in the aura of military heroism but desperately sought to finesse, even conceal, his leading role in early 1970s antiwar protests. In this heightened debate over military heroics Kerry was bound to suffer despite Bush's own absence of military service. The main point here is that, fully three decades after it ended, the Vietnam War continues to haunt the American landscape like an endless nightmare. It is the war that truly refuses to go away, even if Hollywood has finally moved on to new military horizons.

## Robert McNamara and the Fog of History

Errol Morris's documentary *The Fog of War*, a revealing if often painful narrative of the life and ongoing existential struggles of Robert McNamara, secretary of defense under John F. Kennedy and key architect of the Vietnam War—was richly deserving of its Academy Award. The director of such classics as *The*

*Thin Blue Line* and *Mr. Death,* Morris has woven an intimate, reflective picture of a central figure in the postwar expansion of the U.S. military-industrial complex. McNamara, a "hawk turned dove," acknowledges with great sadness in this film, as in his 1995 memoirs *In Retrospect,* the monumental errors he and others within the JFK and Lyndon Johnson administrations made when they set in motion and perpetuated the Indochina debacle. Here McNamara comes across as a sympathetic, introspective, troubled, apologetic human being long tormented by his role in the Vietnam legacy. In a fall 2003 appearance with McNamara at the University of California, Berkeley, their joint alma mater, Morris remarked, "McNamara is unique as a public figure. We don't have a lot of people who have gone back over errors they have committed." Compared with such hidebound leaders as Henry Kissinger, Morris observed, we can see in McNamara "a real attempt to reckon with the past."[10]

That past, of course, is one of the most horrid chapters in American history—one that continues to play out in domestic and world politics three decades after its long-delayed and merciful ending. Although *The Fog of War* is never clear on the issue, those who engineered the Vietnam War (McNamara at the forefront) would by any objective criteria have to be considered bona fide war criminals. The legacy of some fifteen years of U.S. military involvement in Indochina produced the following: at least three million killed, nine thousand of fifteen thousand hamlets destroyed, virtually all urban areas devastated, 25 million acres of farmland and 12 million acres of forest destroyed, nearly a million orphans left, vast ecological ruin caused by the most lethal bombing campaign in history and 20 million gallons of deadly herbicides sprayed. Aerial terrorism, barbaric search-and-destroy missions, totalitarian "pacification" programs, and ecological warfare added up to an unparalleled war of attrition waged relentlessly by McNamara's Pentagon and then by his successors in the Richard Nixon administration. After the war ended in 1975—its outcome determined by sustained Vietnamese anti-imperialist struggles combined with years of domestic antiwar mobilizations—U.S. leaders were unapologetic, offering no regrets, no reparations, no aid, no recognition of any sort of what their powerful war machine had done to a poor, underdeveloped nation. Indeed, elites of both parties were, and for the most part still are, convinced of the noble intentions that fueled their catastrophic policies, even after diplomatic recognition was extended to Vietnam in 1995. There was every reason to hope that *The Fog of War* would shed some light on this dimension of the Vietnam syndrome, or at least on McNamara's own legacy roughly forty years after the JFK counterinsurgency apparatus first emerged.

Any careful reading of contemporary American political life will show that the Vietnam syndrome remains very much alive despite repeated efforts to eradicate it, as George W. Bush's Iraq fiasco presently confirms. The Vietnam era persists as a zone of contested meaning within the public sphere, a struggle over historical interpretation and ideological understanding that is far from concluded. Contrary to popular myth, this syndrome extends far beyond the well-known U.S. reluctance to carry forward a Vietnam-style warfare entailing heavy commitment of ground troops and the inevitable high casualties. The war itself shattered central political narratives about the U.S. role in world politics rooted in the doctrine of Manifest Destiny, the conventional image of American forces heroically fighting and winning "good wars," a general recognition of Yankee good intentions in spreading the gospel of freedom and democracy around the world. Vietnam overturned such benevolent images in favor of harsher discourses: defeat, humiliation at the hands of a militarily inferior enemy, the specter of mendacious, scheming leaders, an imperial agenda gone terribly, destructively sour. For many around the world the United States came to represent a global force of monstrous evil, driven to repeat the Vietnam horrors well into the new century. As for Vietnam itself, that nation and its people remain nearly totally invisible to the U.S. ruling stratum, their unspeakable horrors and suffering jettisoned from public discourse as if the entire governing structure were trapped in a state of collective denial. To this date no U.S. leader or spokesperson has stepped forward to acknowledge guilt and responsibility for what happened in Vietnam. Occasionally the syndrome has been manipulated to serve narrow elite interests, as when the contrived MIA/POW spectacle came to the forefront in the 1980s. To his enduring credit, McNamara—in both his book and the film—expresses profound sorrow over a cataclysmic episode he knew at the time to be a disaster and that in late 1967 forced him to vacate his position as secretary of defense.

An unavoidable question raised by *The Fog of War*, however, concerns McNamara's willingness to accept guilt and responsibility—in fact criminal accountability—for military actions he helped plan and implement during the period 1961–1967. To confront this question fairly and thoroughly, it is useful to take up most of the eleven lessons McNamara says he learned from the Vietnam failure—lessons that furnish the organizing principle of Morris's film.

### Empathize with Your Enemy

Here in his first lesson McNamara articulates one of the great maxims of warfare—know everything possible about your battlefield opponent; try to see the world through the other's prism. The United States intervened in Vietnam with typically brutal imperial arrogance, running roughshod over an entire people and their culture, destroying virtually everything of value and still wondering why the Vietnamese became so unified in their nationalist resistance. McNamara argues, from hindsight, that U.S. failure was inevitable given the shocking inability to understand Vietnamese history, politics, and culture among those who would rescue the country from Communist tyranny—although, given what was generally known at the time, no hindsight should have been necessary. U.S. knowledge of its battlefield nemesis was sparse indeed, the predictable outcome of imperial hubris and, after 1965, an out-of-control military juggernaut. Whether, in historical perspective, it makes sense to refer to Vietnamese fighting for national independence as an "enemy" threat to America seems rather problematic. A more pressing concern would be how "empathy" might be translated into remorse over the unspeakable tolls of death and destruction the U.S. military machine brought to Indochina.

On this vital question McNamara has relatively little to say. Much is made of a statement made by the secretary of defense in May 1967, contained in the *Pentagon Papers,* lamenting the terrible costs of war suffered by the Vietnamese. He wrote, "The picture of the world's greatest superpower killing or seriously injuring 1000 noncombatants a week, while trying to pound a tiny backward country into submission on an issue whose merits are hotly disputed, is not a pretty one." In the next sentence, however, he adds, "It could conceivably produce a costly distortion in the *American* national consciousness and in the world image of the *United States.*"[11] Vietnamese casualties, in other words, turned out to be most troublesome for the nation responsible for producing them. Nowhere in the film, or elsewhere, does McNamara extend his empathy to the "enemy," still a remote construct, off the spectrum of concerns. In contemplating the lessons of Vietnam in his memoirs, McNamara states, "By the time the U.S. finally left South Vietnam in 1973 [*sic*], *we* had lost over 58,000 men and women; *our* economy had been damaged by years of heavy and improperly financed war spending; and the political unity of *our* society had been shattered, not to be restored for decades. Were such high costs justified?"[12] This is a superbly insightful sentiment, except that here again the Vietnamese people are confined to invisibility, obscured by the fog. McNamara's telling comment at the outset of his memoirs ironically rings as true for him as for others: "It is clear our nation has neither fully understood nor fully come to terms with Vietnam. The wounds remain unhealed and the lessons unlearned."[13]

## Rationality Will Not Save Us

When McNamara and his fellow members of the JFK liberal elite arrived in Washington in 1961, they claimed to be the harbingers of a new, "rational," more pragmatic outlook that would bring enlightened change to both the United States and the world. Rationality was always the catchword, though within an ideological framework that shaped and limited its contours. McNamara himself brought a technocratic, corporate rationalizing agenda to the Pentagon, transforming it into the most awesome military structure ever, a task he seems to retain pride in to this day. Recognizing the terrible menace of nuclear weapons even in the post–cold war milieu, in his second lesson McNamara expresses grave doubts about the efficacy of rationality in politics and above all in foreign policy, but such doubts seem never to have troubled his own reign as secretary of defense.

McNamara says that people ought to think more clearly about the deadly consequences of modern warfare—today. In the early 1960s he engineered arguably the world's first full-fledged technowar project, leading to a near-genocidal war of attrition against the Vietnamese. The ideological outlook was furnished by JFK's ambitious design for a "global liberalism," the centerpiece of which was a worldwide counterinsurgency strategy to be waged against Communism, radicalism, and wars of national liberation. Facing down Soviet power was central to this "pragmatic" agenda, justifying the most authoritarian, corrupt, and violent methods in defense of the global status quo. As McNamara stated in 1962, the crucial objective was "to prove in the Vietnamese test case that the free world can cope with Communist wars of liberation successfully, as we have coped with Communist aggression at other levels."[14] To this end McNamara moved to streamline the Pentagon, turning it into a high-powered engine of the permanent war economy and the most lethal agency of technowar ever. He further institutionalized the arms race and fed the disastrous illusion that massive armed strength can solve global problems—an illusion that still permeates Washington. The JFK mandarins portrayed themselves as technocratic managers acting as rational pragmatists, willing to unleash all the tools of militarism in the name of efficiency. But rationality was never the issue in a context where the ideological crusade dictated everything, from the Cuba missile crisis to the Bay of Pigs to Vietnam.

For the JFK cold warriors, ideology was paramount and rationality subordinate beneath the pragmatic facade. Viewed outside the paradigm of a global liberal crusade, the massive commitment in Vietnam was off-the-spectrum insane, ridiculed everywhere and clearly destined to fail. Yet McNamara argued in November 1961 that the United States could easily get "mired down in an inconclusive struggle" but that there was still no choice but to pursue military action since the "loss" of Vietnam would quickly turn all of Asia over to Communist control.[15] He saw imminent threats to the Philippines, Thailand, India, New Zealand, Australia, and Taiwan—a crazy scenario even by the most hoary cold war standards. In July 1965 McNamara was again pushing hard for further military deployment, including vigorous ground campaigns, stepped-up bombing of the south, and "pacification" programs to herd the Vietnamese into prison-like strategic hamlets. Agreeing with General William Westmoreland and the Joint Chiefs of Staff, he wrote: "If the military and political moves are properly integrated and executed with continuing vigor and visible determination, [our course of action] stands a good chance of achieving an acceptable outcome within a reasonable time in Vietnam."[16] To this day McNamara has never deviated from the belief that this course of action was guided by the most benevolent goals and intentions. In the memoirs he writes: "I truly believe that we made an error not of values and intentions but of judgment and capabilities."[17] Yet it was these very intentions, shaped by fanatical ideological commitments, that so deeply influenced issues of judgment and capabilities; the two were fully intertwined.

## Maximize Efficiency

This, McNamara's fourth "lesson," is a curious one to take away from the Vietnam debacle, where the most destructive war machine in history brought unfathomable carnage to a small, poor nation with frenetic efficiency, including relentless aerial bombing carried over from World War II and Korea, chemical warfare intended to destroy life-support systems, and minutely planned search-and-destroy missions across wide expanses of terrain. As William Gibson observes, McNamara's great legacy was construction of an efficiently organized Pentagon that could wage "cost-effective technowar" in the most coldly brutal fashion.[18] The military technicians under McNamara comprised a stratum of "experts" and "professionals" attached to discourses of productivity, calculated deployments, accounting, cost-benefit analysis, and efficiency-maximization—all instrumental categories detached from their political and human consequences. In Vietnam, of course, such "efficiency" turned not only barbaric but extremely counterproductive, as McNamara himself began to realize by early 1967, as intensified technowar generated widening insurgency and an increasingly insoluble political situation for the United States. Given the objective contradictions of a military superpower fighting a popular guerrilla revolution, the most efficient methods were precisely the ones most destined to fail.

## Proportionality Should Be a Guideline

This, the fifth in McNamara's list, is perhaps the most fruitful lesson of all to draw from Vietnam, and indeed from most wars, but McNamara's concrete understanding of it from his own experience seems obscure. In *The Fog of War* he refers to his World War II job as an engineering officer under General Curtis LeMay responsible for firebombing sixty-six Japanese cities at a cost of more than a million civilian lives in the waning months of the war. Reflecting on this unjustifiable carnage, McNamara concedes that U.S. strategic bombing, including the nuclear annihilation of Hiroshima and Nagasaki, would have made war criminals of its planners had the United States lost the war. The incendiary bombs dropped by B-29 Superfortresses in fact had little if any military significance; their targets were urban civilian populations, whose neighborhoods were deliberately set on fire. Not only did the aerial campaign go against any commonsensical rules of proportionality, it was in flagrant violation of the Geneva Protocols outlawing military attacks on civilian populations. McNamara comments in passing that "humans have never grappled with the rules of war," ignoring many decades of precisely such effort to codify limits of military behavior going back at least to the Hague Conventions of the late 1890s.

More problematic yet is McNamara's glaring lack of candor when it comes to the issue of war crimes the United States committed in Vietnam, where his own culpability as secretary of defense would have to be addressed. It was naturally easier to think of criminal responsibility for what took place in Japan, where LeMay was in charge and McNamara a relatively obscure subordinate. In Vietnam, where death and destruction was even more horrific but where McNamara's role was obviously a commanding one, all talk of war crimes is aborted and discourse of guilt and responsibility is supplanted by the narrative of entrapment in a historical tragedy. It is hard to imagine a case where reasonable laws of proportionality, including well-established rules of engagement, were more egregiously violated than in the U.S. war of attrition against Vietnam. McNamara refers in both his memoirs and the film to unfortunate nightmares of death and suffering that permeate all wars, as if this were some kind of natural, inescapable fate. When the Pentagon chief finally came to recognize the futility of the U.S. bombing raids during 1965–1967, he was troubled not by their excessive brutality or terrible casualties but by their failure to advance U.S. war aims, to secure the counterinsurgency effort. Despite understandable remorse, he has never expressed any sentiment contravening this narrow instrumentalism.

### Get the Data

It is difficult to believe that anyone, especially a figure at the top of the power apex, could derive a more preposterous lesson (McNamara's sixth) from the Vietnam disaster than the need to obtain more data. Here, as elsewhere, one must ask: what data? Or, data for what purposes? Of course, as the *Pentagon Papers* clearly showed, there was always plenty of data available on the Vietnam situation for anyone willing to pay attention—data on U.S. troop mobilizations, bombing missions carried out, casualties on both sides, percentage of countryside controlled by the National Liberation Front, amount of chemical defoliants used, the general state of morale among all parties, lack of support for regimes in the south, the failure of pacification efforts, and so forth. Much of this information was gathered by U.S. government sources. Above all, the staggering costs of the war could hardly have been a secret to someone in McNamara's leadership position. In fact all the data required to make wise political decisions was increasingly well known to American and world publics, the stuff of books, magazine articles, teach-ins, and media reports. The real problem resided not in absence of urgently needed data but in the willful neglect or distortion of such data by the likes of McNamara, Walt Rostow, Dean Rusk, and McGeorge Bundy, whose counterinsurgency mania transcended any concern for empirical reality. As supposed pragmatists, the true believers in reality had utter contempt for the actual data. After decades of apparently heartfelt reflection on the most ignominious military defeat in U.S. history, McNamara ought to know that data never speaks for itself but demands interpretation filtered through wisdom and contextualization. For this reason his protests over failure to conduct debates, to get more information, ring hollow.

A case in point is the massive Vietnamese casualty count, mostly civilian. Any strong, insightful critic of the war might have urged immediate cessation of the policies leading to such an outcome as both politically and morally intolerable. But in a memo of October 1966 McNamara writes: "The one thing going for us in Vietnam over the past year has been the large number of enemy killed-in-action resulting from the big military operations. . . . The enemy must be taking losses—deaths in and after battle—at the rate of more than 60,000 a year."[19] Here all the data is available and the official response is intelligible within a setting where U.S. military priorities enshrined large body counts as an indicator of battlefield successes. Compare this with three other administration responses at the time. As early as 1964 Under Secretary of State George Ball called for an end to a "losing war" that was racist, carried out by white U.S. forces against a poor Asian population, concluding that any victory would bring with it totally "unacceptable costs."[20] In 1966 Ramsey Clark, LBJ's Attorney General, said in reference to those in charge of the war effort: "I never sensed any concern for the other side. How many did the Vietnamese lose? How many people were killed in the villages? . . . It was *our* lives, *our* country; they didn't figure, those people."[21] And long before McNamara had concluded the war was probably unwinnable, Daniel Ellsberg, one of the compilers of the *Pentagon Papers,* stated publicly that the intervention was not simply a mistake but immoral, unconscionable. They were all looking at the same data, as were millions of people involved in the antiwar movement.

### Belief and Seeing Are Both Often Wrong

In the discussion of his seventh lesson, McNamara concedes that the United States made terrible, costly mistakes in Vietnam; "we" saw only half of the story, he says. Since he continues to believe in the goodness of American intentions, what then are the lessons to be learned here? A major preoccupation, it turns out, is the dismal failure of U.S. policymakers to win the hearts and minds of the Vietnamese people—in other words, to balance military operations with political efficiency so that American strategic efforts might succeed. Here McNamara remains blinded by a cold war, imperialist mind-set: since the Vietnamese naturally hated Communist tyranny, they surely ought to have been receptive to a foreign ideological campaign to win their consent. The United States could have, and should have, performed this all-important propaganda task far more efficaciously, so the reasoning goes. But the Vietnamese revolution was rooted in deep nationalist opposition to colonial invasion and domination that went back many decades, a logic that rendered impossible any U.S. design to win over hearts and minds. Every step in the military escalation served to intensify popular resistance, just as it had against the French, subverting any and all political efforts to stabilize foreign occupation. Anti-imperialist opposition to foreign intervention was already one of the great legacies of the twentieth century, but this legacy remained obscure to the arrogant, provincial U.S. elites who to this day continue to be mired in the Vietnam syndrome. Contrary to McNamara's enduring belief, there never could have been a political solution to the military quagmire adequate to satisfy U.S. cold war ambitions.

### Prepare to Reexamine Your Reasoning

This, the eighth lesson, is a wise enough maxim, especially when dealing with the horrors of a prolonged war involving endless policy misadventures mixed with terrible deeds. In the film McNamara says that American power was so immense as to overwhelm the degree of self-reflection needed to take up pressing moral and political issues of the time. What was morally appropriate at that particular historical moment? Such concerns appear quite disingenuous if not self-serving, as if the secretary of defense over a span of seven years could manage so little control over an unruly decision-making process that it took on a life of its own, operating beyond his desperate reach. The whiz-kid technocratic Pentagon manager, the former president of Ford, somehow found himself reduced to a state of passivity as events quickly raced past his gaze. In fact McNamara insists he never authored a policy but always served at the behest of a president, either JFK or LBJ. He was a solid organization man just doing his job. Were crimes committed in Vietnam? McNamara never brings himself to answer that question, but he does know he would never have authorized illegal actions. If such things took place—for example, the massive spraying of defoliants like Agent Orange—he clearly does not want to be judged morally or politically accountable for them. The crucial reexamining process thus falls short of fundamental soul-searching related to McNamara's individual actions as one of the few leading figures behind U.S. foreign and military policy throughout the Vietnam era. (His denial that widespread use of Agent Orange was criminal also lacks veracity—any planned destruction of civilian habitats and infrastructure and above all in the system of food production was and is a clear violation of international law.)

Frustrated by the lack of political and military successes, the Pentagon by late 1965 began to target huge expanses of countryside, including densely populated areas, with what can only be defined as weapons of mass destruction. When the B-52s targeted certain quadrants of land, they would first drop high-powered explosive bombs to "open the structures," then napalm the area to burn out as much as possible, followed by CBU-24 cluster bombs designed to kill large numbers of people running out to help those hit during the initial attacks. The cluster bombs were time-released to do maximum damage to human beings, emitting millions of tiny bomblets.[22] Such aerial terrorism was a flagrant violation of international laws obligating armed forces to distinguish between military and nonmilitary targets, between combatants and civilians, while avoiding use of weapons with such destructive power that they cannot be limited to specific military targets. Nowhere in the Geneva Protocols or elsewhere is the United States, or any other superpower, exempted from such canons of military behavior.

### Never Say Never

McNamara wants to be remembered as a leader with an open mind, willing to look critically at fresh evidence, possessing the fortitude to alter course in the midst of rapidly changing circumstances—thus his tenth lesson. By 1967 the situation for the United States seemed hopeless despite massive troop deployments and resource allocations, not to mention all the advantages of technowar. It was now time to cut losses, and the Pentagon leader turned dove. In a memo of May 19, 1967, McNamara lamented, to the disgust of most within LBJ's inner circle, that the bombing raids had produced few results, enemy morale remained high, and the political balance of forces was worsening while American casualties reached intolerable levels. Prospects for a military victory seemed dim. In this context McNamara argued for a scaling back of U.S. objectives and the move toward a "compromise settlement" permitting some kind of honorable retreat. This change of heart angered LBJ, who maintained an optimistic front, and McNamara was eased out of government later that year, just months before the Tet Offensive, after which insurgent victory was all but guaranteed.

McNamara's no-doubt-genuine shift from hawk to dove was, however, scarcely inspired by any sort of fundamental criticism of the ill-fated intervention; there were mistakes, to be sure, but the main problem was that the military campaign was deeply flawed and rapidly disintegrating. In *The Fog of War* he apologizes for errors in the conduct of policy but never questions the basic contours of that policy under either JFK or LBJ, to whom he pledged unending loyalty. As for his stint at the Pentagon, to this day he remains proud of his record. Moreover, in contrast to other critics, McNamara chose not to publicly air his opposition to the war—then or later—even when it might have hastened, albeit only slightly, an end to the bloodshed. He had every freedom, indeed every obligation, to speak out but chose not to do so. At his Berkeley appearance, McNamara was asked by the moderator, Mark Danner, if he could take lessons from Vietnam and apply them to the more recent catastrophe in Iraq, but he demurred, saying, "Look, you're smart. I don't need to apply them. You apply them."[23] Silence in the face of murderous imperial deeds is hardly a virtue. Morris himself was quick, and vocal, in drawing parallels between Vietnam and Iraq.

*You Can't Change Human Nature*

McNamara wants to believe that we live in such a Hobbesian jungle of ineradicable evil that military conflict and the terrors of war are endemic to the human condition, part of some abstraction called "human nature," which his eleventh lesson asserts is unchangeable. In the film he says that war is much too complex a phenomenon to think it could ever be eliminated from world affairs, conveniently intimating that Vietnam was just another of those episodes, one in a long series of tragic wars we are condemned to live and relive—made worse by mistakes, to be sure, but nonetheless an inescapable part of a tortured human history. Even if warfare can be seen as a logical extension of something called human nature—an extremely questionable claim—the generalization is as meaningless as it is self-serving. There was nothing inevitable about the Indochina debacle unless one believes that the JFK counterinsurgency elites were inexorably, fatally sucked into their dreadful decisions by forces totally beyond their control. The historical evidence supports no such thesis. Any reading of the *Pentagon Papers,* which McNamara himself commissioned, demonstrates this fallacy. The war was the outgrowth of a fervent ideological agenda with roots in postwar U.S. foreign policy. If wars in general are understood to be so complex as to be unintelligible, obscured by foggy vistas, the historical record shows that the Vietnam War was the product of a worldwide counterinsurgency doctrine blended with cold war anti-Communism championed by JFK and LBJ—and there is no evidence that McNamara ever questioned this outlook.

There is yet another way in which such a lesson, ostensibly drawn from rigidly fixed views of human nature, is entirely disingenuous. At his Berkeley appearance McNamara expressed revulsion over the horrific nature of modern warfare that, he now believes, should be countered by means of creative political intervention. Thus, "We human beings killed 160 million other human beings in the twentieth century—killed by conflict. Is that what we want in this [twenty-first] century?"[24] Here, contrary to simplistic platitudes regarding the inevitability of war, McNamara puts forth the notion that the fate of military conflict can indeed be altered, ideally through a global shift to the "rule of law," various multilateral arrangements, an expanded UN role, and so forth. Is this not what the eleven lessons derived from Vietnam, the centerpiece of *The Fog of War*, are precisely intended to achieve: a significant diminution, perhaps even abolition, of the horrors of modern warfare? It would be nice if these strictures had been applied, even retrospectively, to the war McNamara so energetically helped unfurl on the Vietnamese people.

McNamara's role as technocratic prime mover of the Vietnam War raises inevitable questions about his criminal responsibility—that is, whether and to what extent the Pentagon chief should be held accountable for war crimes or crimes against humanity, but Morris unfortunately never pursues this line of inquiry. At the end of *The Fog of War* Morris asks McNamara if he felt guilty for what happened in Vietnam, the very question posed by Christopher Hitchens of Henry Kissinger's actions pertaining to Vietnam, Chile, and elsewhere.[25] After a brief emotional pause, McNamara replies that he could go no further in the interview; anything he might say now would just stoke controversy and, moreover, the Vietnam War was just too labyrinthine, too complex to fully grasp. Better to be condemned for silence than to suffer the consequences of speaking out. The film concludes with a loud, reverberating silence.

What are we to make of such silence? Despite all the hand-wringing introspection we see in *The Fog of War,* despite the many "lessons" derived from the war, we end up with nothing regarding key issues of moral and political responsibility for what was undeniably one of the worst criminal ventures of the twentieth century. As in the case of a parallel documentary on Kissinger, one might have expected deeper probing on the part of both Morris and McNamara. In one revealing sequence, we see McNamara admitting the likely criminal nature of U.S. strategic bombing operations against Japan—this in a profoundly good war directed at a nation that had already attacked the United States and where casualties (though horrendous) would be dwarfed by those in Vietnam. The main difference, as mentioned earlier, is that McNamara bore no direct responsibility for crimes against the Japanese.

Far from being foggy, more than a decade of historical deeds and their consequences emerges with stark clarity to the careful, sensitive observer: the Vietnam War was planned and carried out by a relatively tiny stratum of JFK elites (later broadened under LBJ and Nixon) who should have shouldered direct accountability for what happened, despite any noble claims they might have put forward. McNamara's decisive role in this saga is beyond dispute—indeed it was fashionable in the 1960s to refer to it as McNamara's War. The United States attacked Vietnam, then Cambodia and Laos, with lethal military power to quell a nationalist insurgency ten thousand miles from American shores, where U.S. national security could never have been threatened. According to the Nuremberg precedent and the UN Charter, the unprovoked U.S. intervention was an unmistakable crime against peace, no different from what German and Japanese elites were accused and convicted of following World War II. The U.S. military subjected the Indochinese civilian population to years of wartime horrors—a clear violation of the Geneva Protocols and other international conventions protecting noncombatants from being militarily targeted. The long-term use of chemical weapons such as Agent Orange to destroy local infrastructures, food support systems, and the ecology contravene long-standing prohibitions against toxic warfare. There were large-scale, forced, illegal relocations of millions of Vietnamese into strategic hamlets. Finally, there were the recurrent local atrocities, of which My Lai was but one example. So far as we know, neither McNamara nor any of the other U.S. political or military leaders has apologized or taken responsibility for what they have done. Hence McNamara's glaring silence at the end of *The Fog of War* fits the familiar pattern of U.S. imperial arrogance, racism, and national exceptionalism that continues to the present day, shaping later aggression in Central America and the Middle East.

In accepting his Academy Award, Morris commented, "Forty years ago, this country went down a rabbit hole in Vietnam and millions died. I fear we're going down a rabbit hole once again [in Iraq]." It is too bad this connection is never made in *The Fog of War* and, more to the point, it is too bad McNamara has never been forced to depart from his awkward silence. At the Berkeley gathering, McNamara took refuge in a "personal code," deeming it somehow improper to speak out against decisions made by the U.S. government—an almost totalitarian notion of loyalty hard to imagine for someone engaged in decades of existential soul-searching. At earlier points he cited a deep obligation to the presidents he served as a rationale for not voicing his criticisms. Nothing of this sort, however, prevented such government figures as Ellsberg, Ball, and Clark from speaking their minds or questioning the morality of U.S. military actions.

The whole Vietnam episode cries out for answers regarding moral and political culpability: to what extent, and in what ways, were its major architects, including McNamara, guilty of war crimes? A brief look at the International Military Tribunal of Nuremberg is especially instructive here. When those trials were set in motion in 1946, the Nazis were charged with four interrelated types of crimes—conspiracy to carry out aggressive war; the actual launching of aggression; acts of killing, plundering, and destroying during the war; and various crimes against humanity, including atrocities against civilians. (Holocaust-related indictments were not brought forward.) While the Germans attacked several countries, just two decades later the United States carried out aggression against Vietnam, Cambodia, and Laos. And while the Germans accounted for more casualties—well over 20 million dead in the USSR alone—any impartial prosecutor would have to level exactly the same charges against the United States and would no doubt arrive at precisely the same conclusions of guilt as did the Bertrand Russell Tribunal even before the war concluded.

At Nuremberg, indictments were brought against twenty-three leading Nazis, including Foreign Minister Joachim von Ribbentrop, with the notable absences of Hitler, Goebbels, and Himmler, the main protagonists of German militarism. The tribunal adopted the principle that top leaders of the main governing organs should be held culpable, and that carrying out orders issued by a superior authority was no defense. Those involved in planning and implementing war, including high-level military officers, were all considered worthy of prosecution. When von Ribbentrop was charged (and later convicted) of war crimes, he responded that it was Hitler who dictated German foreign policy while it was simply his duty to carry out the Führer's wishes. The court's ruling was firm: the defense of following orders from higher officials was not acceptable. At Nuremberg the legal precept of individual accountability was strictly upheld. In the case of McNamara it should be noted that, although he too invoked the code of loyalty to the president, his role as architect of military intervention was far more pivotal than that of the German foreign minister. The indictment set forth at Nuremberg, and championed strongly by the Americans, could not have been more conclusive: "Not the slightest doubt could remain that Nazi Germany had planned and waged aggressive war, that it had fought that conflict with flagrant disregard for the rules of warfare, and that, independent of any military necessity, it had committed mass murder on an inconceivable scale."[26] The idea that these very charges ought to apply to U.S. behavior in Vietnam was persuasively argued long ago by the chief U.S. counsel at Nuremberg, Telford Taylor.[27]

One of the supposed great triumphs of Nuremberg was its decision to prosecute and convict leading government and military officials who, for the first time, could no longer hide behind protective bureaucratic structures; they were individually held accountable. While the defendants claimed they lacked real power, had no actual responsibility for criminal actions, the court ultimately found that all the men who went to prison or mounted the gallows were "willing, knowing, and energetic accomplices in a vast and malignant enterprise."[28] Indeed the entire Nazi leadership was found to be criminal in its planning and conduct of the war. Thus both von Ribbentrop and Field Marshall Wilhelm Keitel, chief of staff of the German armed forces, were found guilty on all four counts and executed. The same fate befell Field Marshall Alfred Jodl. Fritz Sauckel, organizer of the conscript labor program who actually did the bidding of superiors like Hermann Göring and Albert Speer, was found guilty and sent to the gallows. His boss, Speer, who charmed the judges with his educated demeanor, fluent English, and business acumen, was given twenty years in prison; Göring, in the upper echelon of Nazi elites, was convicted of all charges and sentenced to death, but then committed suicide in his cell.

The Nuremberg tribunal had several official purposes: to convict and punish those guilty of war crimes, to deter future military aggression, to codify rules of engagement in warfare, and to force the Germans to recognize the horrendous crimes of Hitler and Nazism. The UN General Assembly reaffirmed these precepts within its own charter as basic standards of international behavior. In the decades since the Nazis (and later the Japanese) were tried, the savage depredations of war have continued apace, none worse than the war of attrition waged by the United States in Vietnam. As secretary of defense and member of JFK's inner circle, Robert McNamara was by all accounts, including his own, central to the planning, implementing, and legitimation of this war until, after seven years (longer than the span of World War II) his doubts about its eventual success finally surfaced. How, then, could a military robot like Keitel or a second-rate bureaucrat like Sauckel, both working under the tyrannical power of Hitler, be convicted and executed for war crimes while a key architect of military aggression like McNamara, tearful recipient in 1967 of the Medal of Freedom, for so many years be respected as an honorable states-man, remain beneficiary of the Kennedy mystique, and be spared any account-ability? And what of such other coconspirators in the Vietnam War as Rusk, Westmoreland, Rostow, Bundy, and Kissinger, not to mention Presidents Kennedy, Johnson, and Nixon?

One depressing answer to such questions is that war-crimes tribunals were—and continue to be—courts established by military winners to try the losers. In this context the very definition of criminality inevitably embraces double standards, hypocrisy, and outright deceit. That such Allied nations as the United States, Britain, and the USSR committed prosecutable war crimes during World War II is beyond dispute—consider massive area bombardments, Hiroshima and Nagasaki, rampant attacks on civilian populations, the torture and shooting of prisoners, etc.—yet the very idea that victorious government and military elites might be tried as war criminals was never imagined. As men-tioned, even McNamara in *The Fog of War* concedes that U.S. firebombing of Japanese cities amounted to probable war crimes. A second reason for such double standards is U.S. exceptionalism—special entitlements for the most powerful, for those most capable of imposing their will and dictating canons of legality. This is why Slobodan Milosevic and other Serbs have been tried at The Hague tribunal while their counterparts in Croatia and Bosnia have largely been exempted from charges and NATO leaders who waged ruthless (but suc-cessful) aerial warfare against Yugoslav cities are lauded for their "humanitari-anism." It is also why the U.S.-led military invasion and subsequent occupa-tion of Iraq—flagrant violations of the UN Charter and international law, "crimes against peace," according to the Nuremberg trials—will never result in a special tribunal to try U.S. war criminals.

Regarding the Nuremberg legacy, the United States has shown no real interest in establishing international mechanisms—universal and impartial—to prosecute war crimes and crimes against humanity, or to contain human-rights abuses. The United States has rejected the International Criminal Court set up for just these purposes, refusing to participate because of its ethos of exception-alism along with a well-founded fear that its own political and military person-nel will be vulnerable to criminal indictments. This is the same outlook behind arrogant U.S. violation of a series of global treaties and conventions: on land mines, prohibition against militarization of space, arms control, the Kyoto accords, the bill of rights for women, and others.

As for McNamara, he seems to remain fully convinced that neither he nor any other American leaders were criminally responsible for what happened in Vietnam, that all their intentions were noble despite errors of judgment, that the death and destruction they caused was inescapable because of the innately demonic qualities of human nature. War is hell, but it is also complex and foggy. Such apparently is the vast power of collective psychological denial, the ideological pull of ultrapatriotism with its sense of national superiority, the capacity of elites to hide behind labyrinthine institutional facades. The necessary, morally compelling questions are never posed, much less confronted with anything resembling good faith. At the closing of the Nuremberg tribunal, the prosecution laid out its case regarding the issue of criminal responsibility, concluding that figures in a position of leadership were uniquely culpable, that "it is important above all else that responsibility be fixed where it truly belongs. Mitigation should be reserved for those upon whom superior orders are pressed down, and who lack the means to influence general standards of behavior. It is not, we submit, available to the commander who participates in bringing the criminal pressures to bear, and whose responsibility it is to insure the preservation of honorable military traditions."[29] In the United States, when it comes to military operations, who next to the president ought to be held more accountable than the secretary of defense?

The endless Vietnam nightmare goes back to JFK's crusade for a global democratic revolution, a crusade fervently taken up by LBJ, continued by Nixon, and then adopted by a later generation of neoconservative defense intellectuals who dictated years of brutal counterinsurgency warfare that, in the end, gave rise to tragic, criminal outcomes. The cold warrior liberal elites wanted to remake the world, or at least keep the dominoes from falling, so that capitalism could retain its global hegemony, whatever the human costs. While McNamara remains trapped in his own fog of war after many years of intense soul-searching, for untold millions of victims of U.S. militarism the very luxury, indeed possibility, of such a clouded vision never existed. Meanwhile, the Vietnam syndrome refuses to die.

# CHAPTER 4

# Recycling the Good War

**B**y the 1990s the United States had emerged as the lone superpower, with unprecedented economic, political, military, and even cultural power on the world scene. Although the vast majority of its people refused to acknowledge this reality, the United States had become a bona fide empire with aspirations for global domination, made possible by military spending at a level dwarfing that of any other nation, or combination of nations—indeed, larger than that of the next eight countries taken together. While the Vietnam syndrome and its mood of defeat and humiliation lingered, the United States was now able to move into a new phase of world hegemony reinforced by several developments: the end of the cold war and the eclipse of Soviet power, a quick and dramatic military victory in the Gulf War, the spread of technowar capabilities, a stranglehold over weapons of mass destruction, and continuation of a massive permanent war economy even in the absence of terrifying enemies. Moreover, the political culture was becoming increasingly conservative, marked by corporate media in which power was more concentrated and the ideology more constricted than ever, fueling a trend toward militarism and aggressive pursuit of American economic and geopolitical interests across the planet. The willingness of elites to intervene militarily grew more pronounced, favoring the rise of neoconservative intellectuals dedicated to U.S. global supremacy who would decisively influence foreign policy in the second Bush administration. Even before Afghanistan, Iraq, and the war on terrorism, the United States had begun to intervene quite liberally, in Panama, Iraq, Somalia, Haiti, and the Balkans. In fact the U.S.-NATO attack on Yugoslavia in 1999, sponsored by the Clinton administration, could be seen as a dress rehearsal for a second Iraq war given its bold geopolitical aims, its huge reliance on technowar, and its utter disregard for the United Nations and international law.

Yet what the politics of empire required, with its growing emphasis on military power, was a broad set of *cultural* values, beliefs, and myths that would confer legitimacy on the idea of perpetual intervention around the globe. Toward this end, American popular culture would have to be infused with the familiar motifs of the good war discussed in chapter 2: a world divided between good and evil, the presence of demonic enemies often framed as cultural Others, narratives of heroic victories with clear-cut outcomes, the United States as bearer of exceptionally noble purposes. The problem was that such a World War II–style motif was nowhere to be found in any of the more recent U.S. interventions. Full legitimation of growing Pentagon power and the expanded U.S. imperial presence had not been achieved. Sources of consensual support might well be located in the popular culture, above all the corporate media including the film industry, which could be expected to take on new meaning at the turn of the twenty-first century.

## World War II—Again, and Again

In cinema as in politics, World War II hovers over the landscape more than a half-century after the final surrender was signed aboard the USS *Missouri*. This is part nostalgia, part historical remembrance, part continued search for a "good war" to gratify the national psyche compromised by the Vietnam syndrome and dulled by a long-standing political malaise arising from a corporatized public sphere. The war, of course, was one of the epic moments of U.S. and world history, its consequences still deeply felt. But its meaning for American culture far transcends such historical specificity and is used today to justify contemporary wars and the institutionalized military. For Hollywood and the media in general, World War II persists as a source of action spectacles that gain new life with the advent of great technological refinements of military combat and communications.

The revival of good-war themes starting in the 1990s has been accompanied by a saturation of World War II images across the entire political culture. The sixtieth anniversary of the Normandy invasion of June 1944 was the occasion for a series of great anniversary celebrations, with new monuments and museums unveiled. President Bush compared the war on terrorism to the fight against fascism and Nazism. The 9/11 terrorist attacks were uniformly likened to "another Pearl Harbor." Bush's national security adviser Condoleezza Rice compared the U.S. occupation of Iraq, with its presumed mission of "liberation" for democratic ends, to the Allied postwar reconstruction of Germany, Japan, and Italy. British prime minister Tony Blair repeatedly invoked the legacy of Winston Churchill as the new "Allies" moved to secure geopolitical position in Iraq and the Middle East, hoping to "remap" the entire region. The neocons never tired of warning about the perils of "appeasement," arguing that the Iraq challenge should not lead to the same outcome as the ill-fated Chamberlain-Hitler Pact of 1938. Presenting the invasion of Iraq uncritically as a move to "liberate" the country, TV networks regularly portrayed Saddam Hussein as another Hitler, whose removal from power could be justified at any cost. (Both Noriega in Panama and Milosevic in Yugoslavia had similarly been referred to as modern-day Hitlers.) There were repeated comparisons to Normandy, D-Day triumphs, the travails and heroics of the "great generation" on the TV networks, in political speeches, in hundreds of op-ed pieces, in the writings of Stephen Ambrose, and of course in a multitude of cinematic narratives.

If only two of these films—Steven Spielberg's *Saving Private Ryan* (1998) and Michael Bay's *Pearl Harbor* (2001)—had appeared during this period, it would still be possible to speak of a World War II revival. Both pictures were expensive, widely viewed, and generally well-received and, most significantly, injected a sense of the good war into American culture at a time when the superpower was fervently looking to legitimate its Pentagon system and global aspirations. But of course there were plenty of others: Spielberg's *Schindler's List* (1993), Roland Joffe's *Fat Man and Little Boy* (1989), Michael C. Jones' *Memphis Belle* (1990), Terrence Malick's *Thin Red Line* (1998), Jonathan Mostrow's *U-571* (2001), and John Woo's *Windtalkers* (2002) among them. The cable TV series *Band of Brothers* was a spin-off from *Saving Private Ryan*. In most but not all of these movies some familiar themes reemerge, including a noble U.S. military mission carried out against despised enemies, heroic battlefield triumphs, an image (even if tattered at times) of unified patriotic spirit. The war is also sentimentalized and in most cases thoroughly *Americanized*, as when the Allied victory on D-Day is presented as a great turning point in vanquishing the Germans. Whatever the focus, Hollywood-made combat films tend to dwell almost obsessively on distinctly U.S. adventures, obstacles, and contributions.

In a special issue devoted to the D-Day anniversary, *Time* magazine (May 3, 2004) reported: "World War II remains the model Good War and D-Day its greatest day—one of those rare hinges of history that might have bent the other way." It surely might have bent the other way had not the Soviets won grueling victories at Stalingrad, Kursk, and other fronts well before Normandy, resoundingly defeating and demoralizing the Germans. Referring to the legacy of "the Great Crusade," *Time* goes on to draw parallels between World War II and Iraq, comparing Bush's visit to Iraq in summer 2003 to General Dwight Eisenhower's visit to the 101st Airborne Division on the eve of D-Day. Indeed, Bush had called for a rebirth of the Normandy spirit in his talk to U.S. occupying troops: "That spirit carried the American soldier across Europe to help liberate a continent. It's the same spirit that carried you across Iraq to set a nation free." Precisely the same message could be heard daily on Fox TV and other American media outlets. As with the worn example of the greatest generation, God was said to be wholeheartedly on the side of U.S. ambitions and interests. Here again the memory of the good war was invoked to keep alive spectacular images of an imputed benevolent U.S. role in world politics. To the extent such ideological maneuvers might work, the Vietnam syndrome could be extirpated once and for all. Bush the elder claimed this to be so after the first Gulf War, and the sentiment was echoed by his son little more than a decade later, but the Indochina legacy is far too stubborn, as evidenced by the central place occupied by Vietnam in the 2004 presidential campaign.

The recycling of World War II themes carries a special meaning for American leaders beyond simply reliving and romanticizing a time of crucial victories. First, it signaled the emergence of U.S. supremacy even if absolute domination was unthinkable at the time. Second, it seemed to validate the idea, running deep throughout American history, of a nation called to bring progress and enlightenment to the rest of the world, mostly deprived of the wonderful democratic virtues associated with Manifest Destiny. This idea was reinforced by U.S. technological and military superiority as convincingly demonstrated in the war, dramatically so by the atomic bomb. Further, the resounding victory appeared to renew a unique moral destiny of a nation anointed by God—a refurbishing of Manifest Destiny. Third, the motif of a triumphant good war could be used to affirm a U.S. exceptionalism already visible during the Nuremberg and Tokyo trials, where the Allied victors were considered ipso facto immune to charges of war crimes. Such exceptionalism continues today, in more virulent form, as the United States baldly places itself outside the UN Charter and international law, arrogating to itself the right to militarily intervene anywhere it chooses while refusing to sign, or violating, one global treaty after another. Of course virtually anything can be justified when the forces of good are called upon to repel and punish the forces of evil on the battlefield of destiny.

Genuinely competing images of World War II have been difficult to find in American popular culture. Within the combat genre, whether literature or film, the unwritten code is that Americans must be depicted as both victims and heroes, as the main protagonists in the greatest drama of the twentieth century; others appear as either villains (Germans and Japanese) or peripheral to the meaningful action (Russians, British). In fact only the Brits are permitted some portion of the glory, and even they—witness the distorted history of *U-571*—have often been denied their crucial role. A film like *The Thin Red Line* (Malick's version) offers a maddening view of the Guadalcanal conflict in which U.S. troops are presented as breaking down and even doubting the efficacy of their mission, but, as we shall see, Malick's larger theme remains confined to the good-war paradigm. Philip K. Dick's 1962 novel *The Man in the High Castle* stands alone in this regard: its dystopic narrative finds the United States having been *defeated* in World War II, capitulating to the Germans and Japanese, who take over thoroughly vanquished and humiliated America. No filmmaker has chosen to duplicate such a far-fetched negation of the conventional wisdom.

By the 1990s, as noted earlier, the mass media had become an increasingly vital mechanism of ideological hegemony and a conduit of the culture of militarism. Aside from the growing influence of the Pentagon system on American society as a whole, two factors stand out here: heightened conglomeration of megamedia corporate power and a dramatic rightward shift in the media culture owing to at least two decades of well-organized and lavishly funded campaigns waged by corporations, political action committees, lobbies, think tanks, and foundations to reshape public discourse around a broad range of issues (above all foreign policy). For the most part, these campaigns worked splendidly, to the point where "liberalism" had become an epithet in the political culture and a distinct liability on the campaign trail. Right-wing discourses had become more entrenched in such venues as TV networks (Fox leading the way), cable TV, talk radio, book publishing, magazines, and even the Internet. The film industry was hardly immune to such trends, especially in the arena of world politics, even as its liberal or progressive reputation remained more or less intact. The rightward turn has been most visible in U.S. foreign and military policy, as one might expect—a turn reflected in the spread of ultrapatriotism and celebration of military virtues even *before* the terrorist attacks of 9/11. Integral to all this was the long-standing national struggle to extirpate the Vietnam syndrome.

If the first Gulf War did not in fact vanquish the Vietnam syndrome—the limits and failures of Desert Storm were impossible to escape—it did represent a turning point of sorts insofar as it constituted the first true media combat spectacle. What Doug Kellner calls the "Persian Gulf TV War" was, if nothing else, an unprecedented technowar extravaganza, a momentous exercise in patriotic revival, national heroism, and military exploits that galvanized an entire nation riveted to TV sets for a period of several weeks. In contrast to Vietnam (filled with images of bloody defeat) and Panama (a brief military interlude), Desert Storm offered yet another form of popular entertainment that, incidentally, brought President Bush a (momentary) surge in popularity rating to 91 percent. Indeed the mass media made Americans feel good about war again, furnishing a collective sense of catharsis not available since World War II. And it provided a milieu in which the most brutal forms of violence and bloodshed could be legitimated and celebrated.

This convergence of media culture and technowar, mobilizing as it did popular sentiment against a hated enemy, further served to prepare Americans for subsequent military interventions, especially ones that were expected to be quick, dramatic, victorious, and relatively cost-free. After all, not only was patriotic military action a source of entertainment, it also provided great opportunities to test new weaponry and communications systems, to justify continued high levels of Pentagon spending, and to bring a sense of national catharsis to the American public. When such interventions did in fact take place—in the Balkans, Afghanistan, and then again in Iraq—they could more readily be marketed to a population already softened by years of fervently partisan, violence-saturated corporate media. To be marketed effectively, all such military actions would have to be sold as "good wars" reminiscent of the one fought by the greatest generation, by such revered generals as Marshall, Eisenhower, MacArthur, and Patton. Here the elites were helped along by the events of 9/11. To be a good war any military intervention would have to be framed as entirely "just," whether or not it adhered to the tenets of the UN Charter and international law. Historically, to qualify as a just war the resort to force would have to be sanctioned as *defensive,* undertaken against a mortal threat only after all venues of peaceful resolution were exhausted. Wars of conquest or aggression, usually fought in distant lands—for the United States the examples of the Philippines, Korea, Vietnam, Panama, and Iraq stand out—would never be considered "just," and therefore would be less likely to inspire public (or even elite) consensus, especially where the costs might be deemed high. From this standpoint, Vietnam counts as the quintessentially "unjust" war, although by late 2004 Iraq had begun to fit the same pattern. To be understood as just, wars in this category would have to be sold to a sacrificing public as something clearly worth fighting for; a rationale tied to obvious economic and geopolitical motivations alone probably would not suffice. In transforming a clearly unjust war into a just one, the propaganda apparatus would have to frame the military action in terms of the highest principles: democracy, freedom, human rights. In the wake of 9/11, the Bush administration has of course emphasized newer justifying discourses—the fight against terrorism and the spread of WMD. The return of cinematic good-war motifs, derived largely but not exclusively from World War II, makes sense in this historical context.

The worse matters become for the United States in its effort to occupy and pacify Iraq, the more desperately American leaders and the media are likely to cling to the good-war legacy to mobilize support where the public sees mainly sacrifice, costs, and failures. In any event, this ideologically rich legacy is being milked for all it is worth to help legitimate the U.S. pursuit of world domination—a pursuit destined to require nothing short of endless war. The dramatic growth of patriotism in the political arena, media, popular culture, and educational system helps bolster the aspirations and workings of empire, at least for domestic purposes and at least for the short term. They myth of the good war is indispensable to these hegemonic aims. As Hedges writes: "The myth of war sells and legitimizes the drug of war. Once we begin to take war's heady narcotic, it creates an addiction that slowly lowers us to the moral depravity of all addicts."[1] At the same time, the myth only works and addiction only sets in if people can be convinced of the very "goodness" of the war, if the image they have in mind is that of Normandy or Iwo Jima rather than Vietnam or Somalia. The mythic role of Hollywood filmmaking in this seminal ideological function should not be underestimated.

## Hollywood: War and Nostalgia

Within the film industry, the 1990s marked a rather significant departure from what had gone before. The Vietnam syndrome, as we have seen, gave rise to a period of filmmaking (roughly 1976 to 1990) somewhat removed from the familiar narratives of World War II: the prevailing image of the U.S. military was negative, often mocking, even as the larger goals of American foreign and military policy were embraced. Decades after World War II, in the wake of defeat and humiliation in Indochina, it is probably fair to say that *general* views of the armed services had turned somewhat sour and that Hollywood, with its new generation of progressive directors, was largely mirroring such attitudes. We have already surveyed a number of movies that portrayed this antagonistic mood, from *Apocalypse Now* to *Born on the Fourth of July,* that were the work of highly respected filmmakers. Other mostly noncombat films such as *Catch-22, The Great Santini,* and *War Games* extended this pattern, focusing on issues of inner conflict, weak or incompetent leaders, and breakdown in troop morale over such themes as solidarity, duty, heroism, and patriotism. Even such ultra-patriotic, right-wing pictures as the *Rambo* episodes conveyed harshly critical images of the Pentagon and particular branches of the armed services. During this period only *Top Gun* (1987) stands out as following in the line of familiar

The Great Santini *(Louis John Carlino, 1979, Orion Pictures). The film stars aging marine fighter pilot Lieutenant Colonel "Bull" Meacham (Robert Duvall), who exerts strict military discipline over his frightened family as a substitute for real armed combat. Copyright 1979 Orion Pictures Company.*

Hollywood combat pictures made popular during World War II, although less-er films glorifying the U.S. military such as *Delta Force* (1986) and *Iron Eagle* (1987) did appear. With the rise of postmodern sensibilities in cinema, even these pictures were infused with narratives of chaos, breakdown, and ambigui-ty not always consonant with the good-war tradition.

All this began to change in the 1990s, as Hollywood—again taking its cue from the altered historical situation—returned to the tried-and-true formula associated with World War II. Studios reissued a variety of standard documen-taries, including the Why We Fight series, *Victory at Sea*, and *The World at War*, frequently shown on cable TV along with films dealing with related topics: D-Day at Normandy, the race to build atomic weapons, biographies of Hitler and U.S. military heroes like Patton, reflections on the Holocaust. As the studios quickly learned, the good war, updated and refined to be sure, could be appeal-ing to modern audiences. It could also serve to galvanize popular enthusiasm for wars of empire. First and foremost it could provide an ideal dramatic back-drop for the male action-adventure films that had already enjoyed box-office success beginning in the 1980s, especially among teenage boys. Warrior virtues would be trumpeted, usually mixed with male heroics, formulaic tales of armed triumph, and all the blandishments of high-tech weaponry. If the Vietnam syn-drome could not be overcome politically, then perhaps it could be nullified on the big screen.

Already by the late 1980s World War II–inflected films began to make a comeback, their cinematic style decidedly less propagandistic than the earlier cycle, with the release of Delbert Mann's *The Last Days of Patton* (1986) fol-lowed by *Fat Man and Little Boy* (1989) and *Memphis Belle* (1990). Thomas Carter's *Swing Kids* (1993) revolved around the humorous flouting of a 1930s Nazi taboo (American jazz) by a small group of German teenagers, a picture that suffers greatly from clumsy overstatement and poor acting. Anthony Minghella's film *The English Patient* (1996), winner of nine Oscars, was based on the romance between a man and a woman thrown together by the horrors of combat, the setting shifting from North Africa to Italy in the early phase of the war. Other movies focused more squarely on battlefield scenes: aside from *Saving Private Ryan, The Thin Red Line, Pearl Harbor*, and *Windtalkers*, they included the cable TV production *Hiroshima* (1995) and Gregory Hoblit's *Hart's War* (2002), designed largely as a murder mystery set in a typical German concentration camp where American GIs perpetually try to outsmart their vil-lainous (but none-too-shrewd) Nazi captors. The decade of the 1990s was fur-ther saturated with box-office successes that glorified the U.S. military, among them John McTiernan's *Hunt for Red October* (1990), Roland Emmerich's *Independence Day* (1995), and Edward Zwick's *Courage Under Fire* (1996), although none of these is set in World War II.

On the surface, *Fat Man and Little Boy* chronicles the intensely emotional struggles of scientists and military personnel to develop the A-bomb under the aegis of the Manhattan Project led by General Leslie Groves (Paul Newman) and J. Robert Oppenheimer (Clyde Schultz). At a deeper level the film delves into the moral doubts and conflicts that infused the project from the outset, building toward the end of the nineteen-month enterprise when success in creating a doomsday-type weapon seemed likely. Brilliantly directed by Roland Joffe, the picture embraces good-war themes at the higher level of theories, concepts, and ideas: the Herculean mobilization of science and technology to outsmart and defeat the Germans (themselves thought to be on the verge of an atomic breakthrough) and the Japanese (considered scientifically backward but suicidal in their will to defend their homeland to the bitter end). At virtually every turn *Fat Man* depicts a fierce struggle between freewheeling, bohemian, leftist scientists and rigid, often paranoid army discipline exemplified by the crusty, rule-obsessed Groves. As new problems surfaced almost daily, it remained for the military structure in New Mexico to impose essential order and planning so that the bomb could be delivered in timely fashion, which strategists believed would guarantee overwhelming U.S. military supremacy at a time when the war itself was actually winding down.

True to historical events, the film shows a mounting crisis of conscience among most of the scientists, many of whom seemed willing to leave or even subvert the project. At one point, with the Germans already vanquished in April 1945, Oppenheimer is depicted as expressing severe qualms about ever *using* the device against Japan, opting instead for a "demonstration of the bomb." Military figures, on the other hand, are shown to be enthusiastically prepared to drop the bomb on Japan because, as one officer is heard to say, all Japanese are kamikaze fighters and will never give up. The "device," presumably, would break the military impasse—although, as the movie never entirely makes clear, the Japanese were already prepared for nearly unconditional surrender. For General Groves, there were absolutely no moral or political questions to be debated, only military priorities: we can end the war with "one shot" if you scientists just give me the bomb. He added: "I can give the President Japan—no invasion, no conditions." In the end, after painful temporizing, Oppenheimer goes along, concluding that scientists could be held responsible only for the technical job at hand while politicians would have to take up the life-and-death political and military decisions. At one point Oppenheimer fantasizes that a doomsday weapon might ultimately make war forever obsolete. Just before the final climactic test at Alamogordo, General Groves is heard to say, "I always believed the Lord was on our side. And I think now we're going to prove it." Within a few weeks Little Boy was dropped over Hiroshima and Fat Man over Nagasaki, destroying two cities, killing more than two hundred thousand people, and leaving tens of thousands more injured and homeless. The Manhattan Project, obsessed with the instrumental values of power and control and dedicated to unleashing the most awesome military technology, had worked admirably, and General Groves had the last word. Not only was the nuclear age born, but also a new era in which the United States would be emboldened in its pursuit of global hegemony by its possession of weapons of mass destruction. While many considered deployment of such weapons unthinkable, they could be and indeed were used precisely as the ultimate instrument in pursuit of the good war.

*Memphis Belle* depicted in harrowing detail a final, tense, heroic B-17 Flying Fortress raid over northern Germany in May 1943, just when the air war was beginning to swing in favor of the Allies. Coproduced by Catherine Wyler, whose father, William, made a 1944 documentary on B-17 combat, the film traces the saga of a plane crew, grown unbelievably weary from its previous twenty-four missions, brought together in the midst of fighting to overcome one obstacle after another: their slow, lumbering bomber running into quick German fighters and withering antiaircraft fire, treacherous weather, a rigid and unforgiving Air Force Command based in Britain. The picture dwells on the personal conflicts that erupt among a diverse crew facing terrifying conditions, but such conflicts—following the good-war pattern—are easily outweighed by the power of male bonding and the need for team solidarity under fire. Director Michael Jones skillfully trains his narrative on how the crew is assembled and then molded into a single cohesive unit out of a fractured medley of characters, all ordinary folk: son of a farmer, reform-school graduate, religious person, poet, a couple of U.S. Army Air Force officers. As in earlier cycles of World War II films, it was a motif constructed around average American service members, fearful but dedicated, going to war in defense of an embattled nation (here both the United States and Britain), ready to sacrifice their lives—though in this case on huge Flying Fortresses—knowing the casualty rate was terrible. The characters were humanized along the way and pitted against a distant, faceless, and ruthless Nazi enemy.

At the end of *Memphis Belle* we are informed that more than twenty thousand U.S. airmen lost their lives in the World War II European theater. For its last mission, the *Belle* is assigned the task of bombing factories in Bremen, a heavily fortified port city. Before the bomber slowly flies off across Europe, majestic in its own cumbersome way, we hear emotionally gripping strains of "Danny Boy" (the name of a crew member) and "Amazing Grace." There is an almost mystical quality to the final mission, which encounters a bevy of Messerschmidts and then the anticipated heavy flak. We see many B-17s going down. The *Belle* is hit repeatedly and suffers a casualty but manages to drop its bombs (seemingly with daylight precision) and then returns home guided by its resourceful pilot (Matthew Modine). A piece of its tail section shot out, the plane approaches base with two and finally three of its engines out, miraculously landing in front of a wildly cheering crowd of airmen—the dramatic centerpiece of the film. Marred only slightly by recurrent elements of maudlin sentimentality, *Memphis Belle,* powered by some excellent aerial photography, is unsurpassed in its narrative rendering of the good-war legacy. By turning the

*Memphis Belle (Michael Colin-Jones, 1990, Warner Bros.). Based on William Wyler's famous documentary about the final European mission of a B-17 Flying Fortress bombing crew based in England, starring Matthew Modine and Eric Stolz. Copyright 1990 Warner Bros. Inc.*

tide against the Nazis in the European air war, by defeating the Luftwaffe and severely damaging the German urban infrastructure at great cost, the Allies now appear to be in position to execute the final kill.

Mostrow's entertaining, fast-moving submarine warfare thriller *U-571* gets so fully absorbed in celebrating World War II as the ultimate good war—with American heroics at center stage—that it rewrites history in a manner that seems preposterous, virtually Orwellian. The filmmaker renders the epic achievement of British submariners in stealing the all-important German Enigma secret code, located aboard the *U-110* in May 1941, as the work of a U.S. submarine crew. A hyperdramatized, often wildly unrealistic framing of sub combat in the North Atlantic, the picture suffers from lack of historical veracity: in May 1941 the United States had not yet entered the war, there were *no* U.S. subs *or* German destroyers (both centerpieces of the movie) in the North Atlantic, and no American submariners ever commandeered a German sub as shown in *U-571*. Most significantly, by giving credit to the U.S. Navy for the heroic exploits of the British, Mostrow seems intent on falsifying actual events, with the result that the U.S. military, an emergent global force, takes precedence over the fading British military, which at the time was fighting a largely defensive battle against the Germans at sea and in the air.

Having constructed an overblown but still compelling dramatic narrative, Mostrow seemed rather indifferent to questions of historical authenticity, which provoked an uproar in England. He was mainly looking for an exciting storytelling device that would revitalize good-war scenarios. Indeed the film nicely satisfied all the requirements of the good-war paradigm: a vital strategic goal, superhuman efforts of a small combat group against impossible odds, male bonding, solidarity won in the midst of unbearable psychological pressures, the struggle to vanquish a bestial enemy. Few World War II combat films, classic or recent, can be said to fit this pattern so ideally. After the film was released, Mostrow himself stated: "If it's possible to call a war a 'good war' that label would have to apply to World War II. Never before in our history was there such a clear-cut case of good versus evil. There was no ambiguity about our involvement in that war, and we rose up as a nation to defeat Hitler." At another point, reflecting on audience reaction to *U-571,* he added that he wants "people to feel proud and patriotic about the men who fought in that conflict."[2] In contrast to such futile experiences as Korea and Vietnam, this war has a happy ending. The film is dedicated to "the brave Allied sailors and officers who risked their lives," an obvious concession to the British. Unfortunately, Mostrow's embellishment of the good war for the *American* military legacy is bought at the price of historical truth, a propagandistic move that appears more strained in the 1990s than it would have in the 1940s.

John Woo's *Windtalkers* revolves around the combat sagas of World War II Navajo (Dine) "code talkers," U.S. Marine radio operators who called in coordinates of Japanese targets during the battle of Saipan in June 1944 using the Navajo language to confound interceptors fluent in English. An overaged Nicolas Cage stars as Sergeant Joe Enders, a hard-bitten soldier assigned to protect Navajo code talker Ben Yahzee (played by Adam Beach). Woo sets out to captivate modern audiences by means of frenzied, wildly excessive, nonstop "hamburger" scenes dominated by hand-to-hand fighting at a level never actually encountered in the Pacific theater. The picture shows U.S. and Japanese troops shooting, bombing, stabbing, and frying each other with such fierce regularity that the viewer's senses are quickly overpowered and then dulled; the carnage, excessive even for battlefield footage, is mind-numbing. Obsessive attention is devoted to special effects, including flying bodies and severed limbs and heads. Woo's pained efforts at combat "realism" brand the movie a product of the action-adventure genre that became Hollywood's greatest source of box-office appeal in the 1990s. In this case the combat film merges with the male adventure epic to give audiences the kind of graphic carnage and repetitive violence they have come to expect from other genres: Westerns, sci-fi, gangster, and horror pictures. All of these reflect the increasing militarization of society most visible in media culture, and *Windtalkers,* aside from its glaring lack of authenticity, embraces virulently pro-military images that correspond to this trend.

*Windtalkers (John Woo, 2002, MGM). A World War II tale of Navajo "code talkers" who translate radio messages into the Navajo language to confuse the Japanese, in this case at Saipan. A sergeant (Nicolas Cage) is assigned to protect the Navajos. Source unknown.*

The drama in Woo's film centers around two characters, Enders and Yahzee, with Enders assuming the main role. Although Native Americans are supposedly the focal point and furnish the necessary storytelling content, here they wind up at the periphery, subordinate to the white male star. It might be argued that Enders becomes just the most recent incarnation of the Lone Ranger, with Yahzee playing his sidekick, Tonto, recalling a long history of subordinate nonwhite screen figures. Woo does twist the conventional ending in which the Indian sacrifices himself for the white hero by having Enders save Yahzee's life—but not until Yahzee begs Enders to shoot him rather than let him be taken prisoner and jeopardize the code. Woo evokes this time-tested though implicitly racist dichotomy in a transparent appeal to modern viewers still uncomfortable with Native Americans in crucial roles: their place in Hollywood cinema, as in society, remains fully subordinate. What we have in *Windtalkers* is a replay of military glorification in the tradition of John Wayne, in the very setting (Pacific islands) that served as the backdrop of Wayne's greatest film exploits. In a movie ostensibly about Native American heroism on Saipan, Woo, himself an Asian, although he depicts elements of racism within the marines, ends up reaffirming the racist discourses that characterized

Hollywood throughout its history, beginning with D. W. Griffith's *Birth of a Nation.*

With its bloody, overblown images of battlefield conflict meant to capture yet another gallant marine victory in World War II, *Windtalkers* is far more a tribute to the U.S. military in general than to the Navajo code talkers, whose stated role in any case is exaggerated. Cage, even though he is an emotional wreck and a candidate for battle fatigue, emerges as a laconic and righteous but mostly unwilling hero; both he and Yahzee are shown to be courageous and skillful soldiers. The Japanese, for their part, are portrayed as flat, cartoonish, one-dimensional characters whose combat abilities are nothing short of woeful. Their frenzied banzai charges are presented as not only suicidal but also pathetic, useless, the sign of a totally inept and fractured army (quite in contrast to the disciplined, efficient, courageous Japanese troops who fought and died on Saipan). Woo gives the audience scene after scene in which Japanese soldiers are mowed down by the hundreds, hardly putting up a fight, most of them blown to pieces by just a few good marines—ironically reminiscent of how the U.S. Cavalry slaughtered Indians by the hundreds in the classic Westerns. Enders and Yahzee alone kill scores of Japanese by gun and by hand, not to mention the hundreds more who died because the pair was able to radio enemy coordinates to call in heavy attacks by ships and planes. Sadly, Woo makes little attempt to probe the complexity of Japanese motives and tactics, and the film contains not a single Japanese character with a thought to express or line to speak, consistent with images of a racially objectified, demonized enemy. Still less does he draw parallels of combat action on both sides, something visible in more balanced pictures like Lewis Milestone's *All Quiet on the Western Front* (1930). Rather, we end up with yet another version—grossly overstated and flawed—of the quintessential good war.

Hollywood again revisited World War II—surely not for the last time—with Gregory Hoblit's *Hart's War* (2002), which recycled the familiar POW camp motifs seen in *The Great Escape* (dark, cold setting; sadistic Nazi commandant; conflict among prisoners; escape attempt). Although the picture is set in the final months of the war in Europe, at a facility in Augsburg, Germany, in reality this is no combat film; rather, it is constructed as a noir-style thriller about a murder (involving Americans) at the remote stalag. Indeed, the main drama focuses on personal struggles among GIs: between the men; between the ordinary POWs and the ranking U.S. officer, Colonel McNamara (Bruce Willis); between Lieutenant Hart (Colin Ferrell) and McNamara as the two wrestle for control over the court-martial proceedings. These conflicts are intense and relentless, heightened by the hardships of camp life and frayed personalities of the detainees. A subtext of the narrative involves the arrival of two black U.S. Army Air Force officers, shot down over Germany, who become victims of a virulent racism at the hands of Nazis and Americans alike; one of the black officers is summarily executed after a setup in which a "weapon" is discovered beneath his bunk. In a larger sense, however, *Hart's War* turns on some familiar combat themes, above all the struggle of good-hearted, patriotic American troops to cope with a tyrannical structure imposed by the Nazi commandant, urbane and witty yet ruthless and sadistic, leading (for some) to predictable escape through a tunnel. The draconian POW camp represents the cruel totalitarianism, with its outright contempt for *Untermenschen,* that the Allied forces have been sent to destroy—even as their own racism comes to the surface throughout the movie. The war's imminent conclusion, of course, emancipates all detained troops from the Nazi horrors. Before this can happen, however, Colonel McNamara is killed at the camp for planning the escape as he courageously trades his own life for those actually involved in the plot.

Terrence Malick's surrealistic combat epic situated in the final stages of the Guadalcanal battle in 1942, *The Thin Red Line* (1999), departs radically from the good-war pattern. More than a remake of Andrew Morton's 1964 version, based on James Jones' novel, it goes far beyond the standard battlefield guns-and-guts spectacle, probing with some philosophical depth the very meaning of war as it surveys the natural landscape with a penetrating cinematic eye. Although combat is shown throughout in surreal and impressionistic terms, the film is no less powerful as a depiction of one of the bloodiest battles of the Pacific theater.

At one level *The Thin Red Line* fits the war-is-hell motif, a terrible journey into the heart of darkness that recalls elements of *Apocalypse Now,* though Malick's rendition focuses on a heroic U.S. Army victory in World War II rather than the "bad war" that was Vietnam. Malick's camera brilliantly depicts the chaos of jungle warfare, the utter descent into a Hobbesian labyrinth; the hellish conditions engulf everyone, officers and ordinary troops alike, thrust into it by some quirk of fate. At one point the voice-over narrator reflects: "This great evil, where did it come from? How did it come into the world? What seed, what root did it come from? Who's doing this? Who's killing us?" Malick never really answers such questions, nor does he try. Elsewhere the same narrator intones: "War doesn't ennoble men, it turns them into dogs. Poisons the soul." Such ruminations, predictably, are followed by no intelligible responses—no doubt exactly the way the director wanted it. Laudable as such pacifist sentiments might be, they remain abstract, cut off from any historical understanding of the Pacific conflict.

Malick's own abundant denials that *The Thin Red Line* in any way fits the good-war legacy, however, should not be understated. Above all, the surreal embellishment of combat, with its rapidly shifting narratives and perspectives, tends to blur familiar distinctions between good and evil, between democracy and tyranny, between the American invaders and the entrenched Japanese garrisons on the island. The very *logic* of warfare, of winners and losers, degenerates into chaos and meaninglessness, resulting in an existential quagmire for *both* sides. There is of course the omnipresent reality of nature itself—the lush

The Thin Red Line *(Terrence Malick, 1998, Twentieth Century Fox). A brilliant, in-depth, idiosyncratic look at the Battle of Guadalcanal, starring Woody Harrelson, John Cusack, Sean Penn, and James Caviezel. One of the best war films ever, it is driven by the "war is hell" motif and by a passion for capturing the everyday lives of both troops and local civilians. Copyright 1998 Twentieth Century Fox.*

but ever-dangerous tropical landscape—that engulfs and transforms everything that enters it, humbling the human actors in the drama. At one level, indeed, the film can be seen as embracing a complex dialectic between war and nature, between interlopers and the locale (which includes local inhabitants, them-selves an extended object of Malick's cinematography). If at times the movie renders the landscape entirely *too* pristine, this makes sense within the dialectic Malick is striving to establish: if nature is beautiful, it is also true, as one voice-over states, that "the jungle swallows everything." Sucked into this vortex, U.S. troops are inevitably beset by their own fears, phobias, and breakdowns, follow-ing a central theme of the "thin red line" where sanity and madness occupy the same continuum. This recurrent element of the picture is conveyed in its many dimensions by a strong cast including Sean Penn, Nick Nolte, John Cusack, Jim Caviezel, and Woody Harrelson. As in many Vietnam-related films like *Platoon* and *The Deer Hunter,* the Americans reach such a psychological impasse that heroism and courage are rare commodities, and leadership often fails or collapses in the midst of pandemonium—hardly consistent with the good-war narrative. Fear and death permeate the environment, shown from the point of view of the Japanese as well as American troops. *The Thin Red Line* never gets around to the privileged, time-honored warrior virtues of honor, courage, and heroism as the troops are swamped by all the doubts and fears and confusion. The film truly depicts a world on the verge of total insanity, leaving open the possibility, as one voice-over intimates, that in the craziness of battle people sometimes die for no good cause; that may be the common perception, at least, of the average grunt, who may regard patriotic entreaties with suspicion. For Malick, who also wrote the screenplay, the critique of war transcends the mundane concerns of politics, command decisions, and military tactics. In this respect, as in most others, *The Thin Red Line* is a clear exception to the prevailing mode of filmmaking within the Hollywood system, revealing what is possible within the combat genre while also illuminating ever more clearly the dominant patterns of the Hollywood war machine.

The U.S. film industry naturally has had ample reason to frame World War II as a distinctly good war. The Allies were engaged in a fight to destroy fascist expansionist regimes in Germany, Italy, and Japan, so the prevailing media representations contained in the good-war tradition might be considered accurate—but only so far. In actuality the U.S.-Japanese conflict in the Pacific had a long history that seemed destined to erupt into military confrontation over rival economic and geopolitical interests in a region where the influence of both nations was growing. This rivalry had nothing to do with democracy and was even less a matter of "civilization" fighting "barbarism." There is currently abundant research to indicate that the United States, specifically a Roosevelt administration doing battle with the isolationists, had worked to provoke military conflict, welcoming it as a perfect rationale for entering the war in both the Pacific and the European theaters. Historical evidence suggests that the United States, which had succeeded in breaking the Japanese diplomatic and military codes, had ample warning of the Pearl Harbor attack, which seemed imminent by late November 1941.[3] In any event, the attack compelled FDR to declare war on Japan, after which the Germans followed suit and declared war against the United States. The ensuing long battle in the Pacific was fierce and ruthless on both sides, a "war without mercy" as the title of John Dower's book indicates, with widespread torture and shooting of prisoners, atrocities visited on civilians, troop massacres, suicide attacks, and so forth.[4] The United States firebombed no fewer than sixty-six Japanese cities, targeting defenseless civilian populations, much of the carnage coming in the final days of the war—obvious acts of vengeful retribution that, as Dower suggests, had racist motivations. The horrific atomic destruction of Hiroshima and Nagasaki was likewise carried out after the conditions of surrender had already been decided. The historical record shows that the United States was guided by its own geostrategic designs in the Pacific, which were no less imperial than those of Japan—hardly the simple barometer of a good war.

In the case of Germany, U.S. leaders had established a rather tolerant attitude toward the Nazi regime in the 1930s, overlooking its military threats and interventions, closing off borders to Jewish émigrés, and maintaining a strong corporate and financial presence (including Ford and IBM) in Germany before and even during the war. American conservatives were pleased with the efforts of Hitler, as with Mussolini before him, in fighting Communism and cracking down on labor. Surely no "enemy" status was officially conferred until Hitler declared war on the United States in December 1941. As the war drew to a close, the Allies conducted merciless "area" or strategic bombing raids on several German cities (Berlin, Hamburg, and Dresden among them) killing hundreds of thousands of civilians in a deliberate attempt to undermine Nazi morale and destroy the social infrastructure—violations of long-established international law. The prewar U.S. stance toward Mussolini's Italy had been even friendlier than toward Hitler's Germany. After all, both regimes emerged as bulwarks against Soviet power, which the United States believed was ready to sweep westward in Europe. After World War II, moreover, the United States had no ideological qualms about recruiting leading German scientists and technicians (mostly Nazis) to help bolster its own formidable war machine. (The Soviets, whose role in defeating the Nazis was far more decisive than that of the United States or Britain, refused such a move on political grounds.) The war in the European theater, owing in great measure to the horrors committed by the Nazi regime, no doubt better qualifies as a struggle between good and evil, but even here the boundaries are murkier than what the audience sees in a typical Hollywood rendering of the war.

What seems to be at issue here is that Hollywood's return to good-war motifs—elaborated further in the next sections of this chapter—is meant to help recast contemporary U.S. military actions in a distinctly Manichaeistic framework, with the Noriegas, Quadaffis, Milosevics, Husseins, and bin Ladens today standing in for Hitler, Mussolini, and Tojo. Such is the refrain of U.S. leaders and, at least indirectly, of the contemporary American film industry. Yet the historical reality at the turn of the twenty-first century is infinitely more complex as the United States moves to secure unchallenged global domination. Surely the vast majority of people around the world do not view the United States as a benevolent power motivated by selfless, democratic, pacifistic values; such claims are universally viewed as mere propaganda. Today U.S.-initiated wars have generally been fueled by aggressive economic and geopolitical interests, from Latin America to Asia to the Middle East. There are plenty of demons in the world, to be sure, but they cannot be held responsible for anything close to the scope of death and destruction that the U.S. behemoth has produced. Moreover, as the empire broadens its worldwide reach—especially its military operations—blowback in the form of different types of resistance is inevitable: insurgencies, local movements, nation-state antagonisms, terrorism. Under these circumstances, military conflict is anything but a simple opposition between freedom and tyranny, civilization and barbarism, peace-loving democracies and murderous dictators bent on world domination.

The entire framework of global politics has been fundamentally transformed since the heroic days of the greatest generation, though even then the seeds of change had been planted. But nowhere have signs of this transformation entered American media culture, including the film industry.

Beyond any questions of ideology, cinematic images of war—continuously put before film audiences—perform a deeper function, turning episodes of violence and death into exciting spectacles akin to sports contests. It might be argued that killing has become an enduring feature of the modern society of the spectacle, of which the Hollywood war machine is an integral part. The result is that Americans are uniquely desensitized to the terrible consequences of war, especially when the victims are understood to be remote Others: Native Americans, Asians, Arabs, those labeled "terrorists." A convergence of war and entertainment in the media culture, discussed in chapter 1, gives rise to an ethos in which life can appear very cheap, easily dispensable under the right conditions, thoroughly devalued within the prevailing moral discourse. The advent of technowar (itself now part of the media spectacle) reinforces this thinking as the very phenomenon of great technological or military advantage seems to confer a sense of moral-political supremacy on those who possess it. Such power, moreover, is often sexualized insofar as its hegemony is enshrouded in patriarchal as well as imperial, militaristic, and racist myths. The rekindling of good-war images and discourses within the film industry today, at a time of expanding U.S. global domination, feeds into these powerful trends.

## Steven Spielberg and the Spectacle of War

If World War II continues to hover over the media landscape, it takes on special meaning in the work of Steven Spielberg, arguably the most popular film director in the world since his mid-1970s blockbuster *Jaws*. No fewer than five of Spielberg's pictures have focused on the war, while several others engaged it peripherally. Allowing for significant variations in narrative and thematic content, Spielberg's body of war movies has created something of a wide-screen legacy in which some dominant themes in American popular culture converge: media technology, the entertainment spectacle, a sense of historical optimism, the power of warrior mythology. One need look no further than the Oscar-winning *Saving Private Ryan* (1998), already a combat film classic, which brought to mass audiences powerfully emotional good-war images of a triumphant U.S. military built on the momentous D-Day events at Normandy. If there was ever a historical moment when the United States could feel justifiably noble about its military deeds, this was surely it, and Spielberg chose to film those deeds, mediated through personal narratives in all their graphic immediacy. In the milieu of the 1990s and later U.S. leaders have looked to re-create a positive, heroic sense of political mission against a growing postmodern mood of ambiguity, relativism, and pessimism, with the Vietnam syndrome still alive despite the ephemeral (and illusory) achievements of Desert Storm. Epic morality tales grounded in dramatic battlefield victories over monstrously evil forces seemed to be just the remedy needed, and Hollywood filmmaking turned out to be the perfect vehicle.

Spielberg's impressive body of World War II–oriented cinema, each picture inflected with different narratives and technical styles, displays rather consistent aesthetic and ideological motifs that have strongly influenced both mainstream filmmaking and popular consciousness. It is further marked by Spielberg's distinct approach to filmmaking, which follows several basic lines of development.

First, Spielberg's cinema contains a deep nostalgia for the past reflected in the director's unmistakable homage to earlier auteurs such as Hitchcock, Ford, Capra, and Eisenstein, with frequent play on classical movies in an endless variety of scenes, from *1941* to *Empire of the Sun, Always,* and *Saving Private Ryan,* just to identify four of his most well-known war-related pictures. In Spielberg's case, Hollywood nostalgia is tied mostly to the 1940s, the war, the battle against fascism, the greatest generation. A sentimentalized history has furnished the inspiration behind his most ambitious projects, just as it has for directors like Robert Altman, Martin Scorsese, Francis Ford Coppola, and Woody Allen. This dimension of Spielberg's work extends beyond the combat genre to include blockbuster spectacles like the Indiana Jones episodes and *Close Encounters of the Third Kind.* Referring to the 1940s, Spielberg confessed, "I love this period. My father filled my head with war stories—he was a radioman on a B-25 fighting the Japanese in Burma. I have identified with that period of innocence and tremendous jeopardy all my life. It was the end of an era, the end of innocence, and I have been clinging to it for most of my adult life."[5]

To lay the groundwork for his spectacular war sequences, Spielberg diligently studied old World War II documentaries produced by John Ford and Frank Capra, and these sequences—involving battlefield chaos, the drama of combat, and carnage—found their way into *Saving Private Ryan* and a few other war films. Though fascinated by powerful technical flourishes that could render on-screen combat larger than life, Spielberg always looked for methods to enhance "realism" and authenticity, a tendency he shared with many earlier practitioners of the combat genre. Thus for *Private Ryan* he drew on William Wellman's superb combat epic *Battleground* (1949), along with Wellman's *Story of G.I. Joe* (1945), which in quasi-documentary style told the story of an ordinary infantryman from the viewpoint of legendary war correspondent Ernie Pyle. Lewis Milestone's film *A Walk in the Sun* (1945), regarded by some critics as the finest World War II picture, clearly left its impression on Spielberg. His frequent journeys into the world of fantasy, as in *1941,* with its comic mayhem, panic, and bumbling military figures, resemble the dark comedic features of Kubrick's *Dr. Strangelove,* with scenes from *Catch-22* and *M\*A\*S\*H\** thrown in. In the case of *Always,* Spielberg turned to a 1943 cult classic, *A Guy Named Joe,* depicting a fighter pilot who comes back from the dead to counsel his best friend, who in the meantime has fallen in love with the pilot's girlfriend. *Empire of the Sun* contains many dramatic sequences borrowed from Ford's *Searchers* and Hitchcock's war classic *Lifeboat* (1945), as well as *North by Northwest* (1958), all seemingly deliberate homages to great auteurs. In *Private Ryan,* the main protagonist, Captain John Miller (Tom Hanks), recalls the acting style of earlier quiet heroes in the lineage of Gary Cooper, James Stewart, and Henry Fonda, all of whom also starred in good-war classics. Examples of Spielberg's fascination with nostalgia can be multiplied several times over.

Second, throughout Spielberg's films can be found enduring portraits of especially despicable villains, often akin to the brutal, sadistic Nazis in *Schindler's List,* who in their pure but overstated embodiment of evil become choice targets to be fought and vanquished. World War II provided the ideal setting for such demonic constructions, but the panorama has a much larger sweep. Thus in *Indiana Jones and the Last Crusade* (1989), Spielberg introduces Hitler as the quintessential modern symbol of evil—obviously no difficult feat. The Nazi Führer is easily shown as a political monster intent on taking over much of the world, a beast from central casting whom anyone can easily detest (including those within his own circle). The Nazis in general appear as familiar upper-crust villains: classy, elitist, pompous, and almost charming in their barbaric plots and actions. In *Empire of the Sun* we encounter the persona of a ruthless and violent Sergeant Nagata, a camp commandant whose power is gradually whittled away by the guiles of an eleven-year old English captive (Christian Bale). Here as throughout Spielberg's work World War II is reconstituted as one large historical spectacle in which the horrors of fascism—the very darkest manifestations of the human condition—are finally crushed by benevolent military force.

It is in *Schindler's List,* as one might expect, that portraits of unspeakable evil reach their zenith, as Spielberg takes on the murderous years of Nazi genocide against the Jews. Set in Krakow, Poland, during the war and winner of several Academy Awards, the project was conceived by the director as a "film for this and future generations so that they would know and never forget that six million Jews were murdered in the Holocaust and that history cannot be denied." A cinematic masterpiece, the picture is filled with scenes of terror and murder: Jews are forcibly uprooted from homes and communities, arrested, tortured, enslaved, and shot indiscriminately, with most getting shipped off to Auschwitz and other death camps. Jews are shown as utterly debased and terrorized victims. Spielberg also sets out to capture a Nazi culture in which German elites spend considerable time acting as patrons to the high arts; partying with exquisite wine, food, and music; and dancing as genocidal policies are being carried out. The intricate dialectic connecting evil and good, tyranny and victimization, could not be more dramatically conveyed. The film's major villain, camp commandant Amon Goeth (Ralph Fiennes), is an overweight, sadistic, one-dimensional psychopath who enjoys shooting prisoners from his balcony on the slightest impulse. When a female inmate, an engineer, points out structural flaws in a new barracks, she explains, "I'm only trying to do my job." He then orders her shot, exclaiming, "Yeah, I'm just doing mine." Later, Goeth orders the prisoners to tear down their barracks and rebuild precisely according to the dead engineer's prescription. Viewers might find themselves wondering about such facile caricatures of barbarism, about whether even the Nazis might better be shown with a greater degree of humanity and two-dimensionality. Surely Hannah Arendt, describing the "banality of evil" in her classic *Eichmann in Jerusalem,* would have profoundly disagreed with Spielberg's simple one-dimensional imagery: the Nazis were on the whole rather ordinary figures who, as seemingly "normal" Germans, were nonetheless capable of the most terrible deeds in the service of an ultranationalist ideology.[6] Spielberg had a somewhat different political agenda, however, linking awareness of the Holocaust to its supposed modern-day reincarnations in such regions as Yugoslavia and Iraq—parallels seemingly drawn to fit the contours of recent U.S. foreign policy.

Third, Spielberg's films abound with an inspiring, often historically catalytic, heroism born on the terrain of warfare and given expression through the exploits of ordinary people, a part of American liberal mythology so often visible in the filmmaking of auteurs like Ford and Capra. There is a winsome youthful protagonist—privileged but young, innocent, and displaced—named Jim in *Empire of the Sun,* the familiar GI Joe figure of *Always,* the panicked but tenacious masses fighting Japanese incursions into Los Angeles in *1941,* the "accidental hero" Oskar Schindler in *Schindler's List,* the everyman Captain Miller who dies in the course of locating a designated soldier in *Private Ryan.* Some of Spielberg's protagonists can be seen as antiheroes or something akin to them, but they are still needed as dramatic agents of noble virtues in the struggle against tyranny, sadism, and mass murder. Virtue, moreover, connects to something much larger than particular leaders or heroes; it resides in combat groups, families, communities, a people or nation, thus lending added power to the good-war narrative.

In *Private Ryan* an army squad is trying to locate Private James Ryan (Matt Damon) in the aftermath of the Normandy landing, a long sequence brilliantly shot by Spielberg. The narrative is by now well known: Ryan's three brothers had been killed in action, and War Department policy dictated that a lone surviving son must be removed from combat. Squad members included Sergeant Horvath (Tom Sizemore) along with Privates Reiben (Edward Burns), Jackson (Barry Pepper), Mellish (Adam Goldberg), and Carpazo (Vin Diesel), and medic Wade (Giovanni Ribisi). In what turns out to be a treacherous mission, Ryan is found but refuses to leave the battlefield out of loyalty to fellow soldiers, instead urging his would-be rescuers to help repel the Germans in a fight to retain control of a bridge. The squad prevails because of its honed combat skills, subterfuge, grunt solidarity, and the courageous leadership of Captain Miller. The Germans, of course, emerge as faceless, demonic, and inferior troops desperately fighting for a doomed cause. Spielberg's point here is that heroic acts are performed at the end of *Private Ryan* by a small group of citizen-soldiers, a diverse but nonetheless cohesive unit of regular guys led by a captain who is just another member of the team and gives his life fighting the Nazis. At this juncture male bonding within the combat narrative takes on a distinct populist character following the pattern of 1940s war pictures like *G.I. Joe, Guadalcanal Diary,* and *Sands of Iwo Jima.*

Turning to *Schindler's List,* while the protagonist winds up a legendary figure for his courageous actions in saving 1,100 Jews during the last stages of the Holocaust, in fact Oskar Schindler was something of an ordinary German businessman determined to get the cheapest labor possible; as a result his heroic stature develops simply as a by-product of very routine activities. While charismatic and attractive, Schindler is no remarkable figure in his own right, just someone working to advance his own self-interest. The film begins with Schindler (played by Liam Neeson) asking Jewish businessman Itzhak Stern (Ben Kingsley) to find Jewish investors and recruit Jewish workers for a war-goods factory that Schindler would manage. The factory is set up, takes orders for ammunition from the German military, and hires workers who are saved from Nazi concentration camps. At the outset Schindler is brash, even callous, toward his employees but then develops sympathy for them, especially once he feels more emboldened to challenge Nazi authorities planning to carry out the "final solution." Schindler's nascent (and partial) anti-Nazism builds until he delays and even sabotages product orders while stalling for time to save his large Jewish labor force from certain death. "If this factory ever produces a shell that can actually be fired, I'll be very unhappy," he confesses to Stern toward the end of the movie. Schindler is eventually forced to close the factory, giving rise to a poignant moment when he gathers his long-suffering workers and exclaims, "We've survived. Many of you have come up and thanked me. Thank yourselves." By now the Germans have been overrun by the Allies, giving hundreds of thousands of Jews and others incarcerated by the Nazis new freedom. Critics have labeled Schindler a flawed hero bordering on antihero owing to his political ideology (a stubborn Nazism) and such personal failings as extreme womanizing, but a more accurate term would be *accidental* hero: serving his own needs, he happened to be at the right place at the right time.

Fourth, Spielberg's work can be appreciated as a kind of cinema of mayhem, made graphic through enduring images of chaos, upheaval, breakdown, and panic. His earliest pictures, beginning with the mid-1970s blockbuster *Jaws,* established this modality, embellished with dazzling special effects and a unique flair for violent action, like that in *Close Encounters* (1977), *Raiders of the Lost Ark* (1981), and especially *Indiana Jones and the Temple of Doom*

(1984). This last movie is saturated with technologically enhanced images of chaos and violence, with little concern for plot, characters, and setting. There is a definite logic to Spielberg's mayhem, however, insofar as it fits nicely his general narrative schema: disorder and breakdown converted into order and a return to normalcy through the intervention of groups and/or individuals—the ideal recipe for combat pictures.

Spielberg is usually at his best capturing a state of war-driven terror as it enters and recasts the human psyche: the military situation dislocates and disorients everyone (above all civilians) on both sides; cuts them off from family, neighborhood, and community; and throws them into angry, violent, amorphous groups struggling for survival. Although clearly enthralled by the unique spectacle of war, he returns time and again to its horrifying social and psychological consequences, to its peculiarly devastating impact on all that it touches. Spielberg's earlier work focuses mostly on the *exterior* dimension of chaos, but in the World War II–defined films he strives to get inside the social and psychological frenzy experienced by troops and civilians alike. In *1941,* for example, we see virtually uninterrupted street panic in Los Angeles, so fearful was the population of a follow-up Japanese attack in the wake of Pearl Harbor. Here Spielberg makes good comedic fun of war on the home front, with episodes so out of control that paranoid, frightened Americans actually wind up fighting each other. Panicked Angelenos wildly overreact to imagined threats and provocations, and the U.S. military itself falls into undisciplined confusion, as shown in one scene in which an American pilot flies over Hollywood Boulevard amid a hail of antiaircraft fire from trigger-happy troops convinced he is the enemy. The audience views an entire sweep of war-induced chaos, from food fights to bizarre sexual escapades to street riots, reflecting Spielberg's view of war as socially destabilizing and psychologically disorienting. The picture contains scenes of noisy confusion and mayhem from beginning to end. As Douglas Brode observes: "A fearful view of the crowd that can change moods in a moment is present; the people panicking on Hollywood Boulevard resembling the crazed swimmers in *Jaws.*"[7] Order eventually returns, of course, as it does in all of Spielberg's movies, but not before a Japanese sub surfaces off the California coast (an incident based on an actual event) and sets off even more frenzy among Angelenos.

These scenes of widespread panic would be repeated many times in later Spielberg pictures, where crisis and breakdown amount to a set of preconditions for the subsequent reestablishment of traditional values and social relations. If warfare gives rise to unfathomable nightmares, it likewise lays the groundwork for their transcendence. In *Empire of the Sun,* Spielberg depicts mass pandemonium in all its cinematic glory: street chaos and riots in Shanghai, disruption of families and communities with the resultant psychological traumas, the horrors of concentration-camp life, frenetic movements of large crowds both at the beginning and the end of the film. As the war in China

Empire of the Sun *(Steven Spielberg, 1987, Warner Bros.). An upper-class British boy (Christian Bale) is separated from his parents when Japan invades Shanghai. He is forced to survive on his own throughout most of the war. The film is based on J. G. Ballard's great autobiographical novel. Copyright 1987 Warner Bros. Inc.*

descends rapidly into barbarism, Spielberg stops at nothing to capture the accumulated human misery. "As the crowd riots in the Shanghai streets," writes Brode, "Spielberg envisioned a take-your-breath-away shot in which the camera would at first be trained on several thousand people, darting about in a panic at a key intersection. The camera would then slowly pull back until at last our view is from the top of the building, behind the shoulders of the Kuomintang rebels firing down into the crowd. In addition to the striking effect, the shot would also function thematically: we first see the chaos, then gradually learn its cause. But the shot was so complex that few believed it could be achieved. Undaunted, Spielberg had a newly built device, the Multicrane, installed on top of a ten-story office building . . . allowing for remarkable flexibility."[8] Not only did Spielberg's improbable technique work splendidly to transmit the chaos, it was perfected and put to use in subsequent films—dramatic shots of Jews being rounded up in Krakow in *Schindler's List* no doubt are the best example. Indeed this movie, with its noir-like documentary style, contains frame after frame of remarkable mayhem and panic: mass arrests, people being dragged from their homes, random shootings, trauma of every imaginable sort. In *Private Ryan,* the chaos is largely confined to the battlefield, but those scenes—including the twenty-seven-minute graphic depiction of the Omaha Beach landing—are filled with some of the most gripping representations of combat horrors ever shown on celluloid.

Where so much armed violence and social breakdown dominate the screen, the final (typically postwar) cinematic restoration of order and "normalcy" demands an uplifting solution to human conflict even though the victims of wartime brutality can never be brought back to life. Here Spielberg usually opts for something akin to a Hollywood happy ending, a device for which he has become justly famous. Dystopic motifs such as those in the work of Ridley Scott, Quentin Tarantino, the Coen brothers, and Oliver Stone, in such films as *Blade Runner* and *American Beauty,* are in the final accounting absent here. Spielberg's pictures have regularly conformed to the established studio pattern: happy endings inevitably follow the triumph of good over evil that is facilitated by some kind of old-fashioned heroic action. Chaos functions as a necessary stage on the path to ridding the world of evil and the monstrous figures responsible for it. We know that in both *Schindler's List* and *Private Ryan,* after long, harrowing scenes of wartime horrors, a return to order means that the Nazi beast has finally been defeated; war is surely hell, but it is the inevitable and necessary price to be paid. The same is true of *Empire of the Sun,* where defeat of the Japanese war criminals furnishes another happy ending as ordinary people are eventually united once the peril is exterminated—all to the accompaniment of John Williams's rousing musical score.

In *Schindler's List,* Spielberg manages to provide a happy ending to one of the great nightmares in history: the main protagonist, after all, is a Nazi good guy who single handedly rescues hundreds of Jews from sure death sentences. Not only do these Jews miraculously survive but so too does Schindler in spite of his risky shenanigans, as everyone walks off into a brighter future, presumably ending up in Israel since it will be rather difficult "going either East or West" once the war is over. A wonderful climax at the end of an orgy of mass murder? Apparently Spielberg wanted to show that even the darkest human episodes can give rise to positive resolutions, justifying a feel-good optimism, and indeed the final scenes of the picture take the audience years ahead to modern-day Israel as Jews and Israeli citizens are shown visiting Schindler's tomb. Tim Cole points out that in *Schindler's List* there is, finally, no banality of evil, only a narrative on power instead of on the powerless, about how one person or a small group of persons can make a difference in the bleakest of circumstances.[9] In *Private Ryan,* we are presented with enough carnage to be fully convinced that war is hardly worth all the misery and suffering, and Spielberg frames his ending at Normandy to replicate the way it looks today, dominated by countless rows of cemetery markers. What quickly follows, however, is a larger-than-life image of an American flag, symbolic of the quintessential good war carried out by the greatest generation to rid the world of Nazis. And in

*Schindler's List (Steven Spielberg, 1993, Universal). This Holocaust epic showcases the adventures of German businessman Oskar Schindler (Liam Neeson), who hired hundreds of Jews to work in his factory, thereby shielding them from being sent to concentration camps. One of several Spielberg pictures that deal with World War II. Copyright 1993 Universal City Studios Inc. and Amblin Entertainment Inc.*

such a world, riddled with human atrocities, there is ample room for eternal faith, hope, and optimism.

This raises perhaps the most enduring aspect of Spielberg's cinema: his deep attachment to traditional values—hardly surprising for a director commonly referred to as the "modern-day Disney." Like Disney, Spielberg has been adept at interweaving mainstream images and narratives with the power of cinematic spectacle, underpinned by a wide array of high-tech special effects. And like his predecessors Ford and Capra, he is an unabashed sentimentalist, his films often embracing the world from the assumed viewpoint of children, part of what Peter Biskind calls the "children's crusade" in his discussion of Spielberg and George Lucas.[10] Spielberg's World War II films come across as moral fables that turn on the goodness of human nature and, more generally, on the role of the common person struggling to overcome mayhem and evil. As with Ford and Capra, the result is a powerful sense of American innocence in what is a fearsome and chaotic Hobbesian world. There is a strong appeal to simple, unmediated feelings and emotions that readily crowd out thought and critical reflection—yet another hallmark of the Disney legacy and one that conforms to hegemonic American values and traditions. Spielberg's well-known nostalgia for the 1940s is organically connected to his love of conventional virtues (family, community, nation, religion) that incorporate but go well beyond the good-war narrative. In various ways these ideals enter into Spielberg's graphic images and narratives of warfare. As Brode writes in his commentary on *Always:* "While Spielberg has always mouthed the politically correct and ingenuously liberal platitudes required of today's hip, young Hollywood types, *Always* (like films which preceded it) reveals him to be essentially traditionalist, his movies serving as propaganda pieces for old-fashioned values."[11]

Against the backdrop of Spielberg's journey into the madness of war, it is easy to see how the translation of chaos into order, violent conflict into peaceful stability, makes sense exactly in accordance with the realization of traditional values in which community is healed, patriotism affirmed, families reunited, and established social and political life more or less restored. At historical moments of severe crisis and breakdown, endemic to warfare, prevailing rules and norms of social interaction tend to collapse, a collapse that Spielberg dramatizes in *1941, Empire of the Sun,* and *Schindler's List.* Psychological and moral restraints erode, to be reimposed at some later time, with the recovery of established institutions and social relations that were threatened by protracted military conflict.

Within Spielberg's larger body of work, the family recurrently appears as a bulwark of hope, solidarity, and purpose, as is effectively shown in *Empire of the Sun,* in which the Japanese defeat represents not only a reversal of fortune for the Chinese but also an emotional reunion of a young boy with his parents. Depiction of horrendous wartime events as seen through the boy's eyes also seems meant to convey a strong degree of Western innocence, a sentiment that is reinforced as the final battlefield victories are secured by squadrons of American P-51 Mustangs flying to the rescue. In *Schindler's List* too we find a deep mixture of community, religion, and hope grounded in a nationalist synthesis linked to the later founding of the Israeli state—at which cathartic point the film ends. As Norman Finkelstein and others have argued, this intimate connection between cinematic depictions of the Holocaust and political support of contemporary Israeli politics is consonant with what we know about Spielberg's own outlook. As for *Private Ryan,* we can appreciate one of the great patriotic experiences in U.S. history, a time when all the pain and sacrifice, all the patriotic and military mobilizations, produced an end to the Nazi scourge. The movie begins and ends with a billowing American flag, an emotional tribute to the thousands of fallen Allied soldiers whose pain, suffering, and death made possible this glorious outcome. In fact release of the film in 1998 coincided with a media-generated cultural rediscovery of World War II, Spielberg's own cinematic work intersecting with a series of best-selling books by writers like Stephen Ambrose. The director revisited Normandy no less than five times. In *Private Ryan* as in several other Spielberg pictures, epic moments of social, moral, and psychological renewal, often tied to the patriotic upsurge, are captured and dramatized with spectacular effect. *Private Ryan* would provide the inspiration for a good-war TV miniseries, *Band of Brothers,* which appeared in 2001. In *War of the Worlds* (2005), Spielberg expands his interest in war as spectacle to new levels, as high-tech cinematography heightens graphic images of entirely different modes of battlefield combat. Here again he revisits scenes of displaced people fleeing barbarian hordes—that is, invaders from outer space—one young girl asking, "Is it the terrorists?"

The Spielberg legacy of war films might be contrasted with that of Oliver Stone, whose brilliance in the making of combat pictures (while fewer in number) over the past few decades is roughly comparable. Also drawn to the great spectacle of war, Stone departs radically from Spielberg in his attention to more harshly critical motifs: terrible human costs and sacrifices, repeated political blunders, the arrogance of power, the futility of military solutions. In *Salvador* (1983), Stone explores the comic absurdity of U.S. political and military intervention in Central America; in *Platoon* (1986), to some extent a quasi-autobiography, he depicts the Vietnam War as a tragic, bloody, insane descent into hell in which the only protagonists are challenged antiheroes; this is far from the patriotic discourses of *Private Ryan.* In *Born on the Fourth of July* (1989), he links Ron Kovic's rejection of his patriotic upbringing with the general eclipse of the American dream that finds its way into other Stone films: *Wall Street, The Doors, Talk Radio, JFK.* Across his body of work Stone confronts a power structure that is increasingly antithetical to the interests of democracy, justice, and peace. As Susan Mackey-Kallis points out, in *Born on the Fourth of July,* Kovic emerges as "the classic Stone cinematic hero—maimed and disillusioned in a seemingly senseless sacrifice and railing against the injustices and meaningless life."[12] Stone's famous Vietnam trilogy (the third part is *Heaven and Earth* [1993]) sets out to cinematically deconstruct a national odyssey that, beginning with the Kennedy assassination and the Vietnam disaster, involves a trajectory toward defeat, humiliation, and impotence, all powerfully brought to screen in cinema verité style. With Stone we never find a justification for war; there is no embrace of the military or patriotism, only what he envisions as a painful search for historical truth, revealing the dark side of U.S. global (and to a lesser extent domestic) power. There is nothing resembling these kinds of critical sensibilities in any of Spielberg's pictures, no irreverence toward authority and tradition, no cynicism about military and government power, no distancing from good-war themes, which, in Spielberg's case, inevitably fall back on a deep nostalgia for World War II and the 1940s.

At risk of oversimplification, most of Spielberg's films—especially but not only those fitting the combat genre—might best be categorized as war spectacles. A product of diverse legacies, from Walt Disney to James Bond to Frank Capra, his work is thoroughly immersed in Hollywood canons of filmmaking, by now an integral part of the larger media culture. At one level it is an homage to mainstream American values filtered through sophisticated technology, the media spectacle, and stunning representations of violence—and of course the great drama of military conflict. A gifted director adept at merging artistic flair with box-office appeal, Spielberg has no peers today or probably in film history in his capacity to elicit awe and wonder. In weaving together morality tales and testaments of epic heroism with powerful special effects he has helped revolutionize Hollywood cinema. Drawing on his significant contributions to the sci-fi genre as well as the studio blockbusters, he has, whether intentionally or not, made pictures that, in their aesthetics and popular influence, converge with the growing American culture of militarism. With their lengthy, repetitive, and graphic scenes of bloody combat, they amount to a glorification of technowar, a central feature in the Pentagon's famous "revolution in military affairs" that has increasingly shaped U.S. war strategy since the Vietnam era. The blockbuster as profitable cinematic form, the modern society of the spectacle, and a popular culture generally saturated with ultraviolent images, all seemingly endemic to the corporate studio system, have a strongly conservative impact on mass audiences.

In directing historical pictures like *Schindler's List* and *Private Ryan,* Spielberg has maintained that his overriding interest was simply to "achieve reality" on screen. This cannot be doubted, but his was always a reality mixed with an overwhelming dose of fantasy and sentimentalism, enduring features of both the Disney tradition and classic Hollywood. His adaptation of technology does indeed furnish an aura of realism, but it does more to mesmerize mass audiences that nowadays are easily seduced by expensive cinematic extravaganzas. We end up with a dualism: the horrors of war are celebrated, made larger than life, while also shown in all their bloody realism. Military violence is first glorified and then, in the same process, fully legitimated. The critic David Ansen writes, commenting on *Private Ryan,* that "war, as a dramatic subject, is exciting, and the battles are the most exciting part [of any war film]. How do you depict violence without, in some way, promoting it?"[13] The sad but inevitable answer is that such promotion of warfare has been, and will continue to be, the likely outcome of sensationalized combat movies. Reflecting on Spielberg's general body of cinema, Thomas Doherty concludes: "Throughout all this, the guilty secret is that far from being horrifying and repulsive, the stunning spectacle of sight and sound is a joy to behold and harken to from a theater seat, pure cinema at its most hypnotic and intense."[14] In his "realistic," spectacular, larger-than-life images and narratives of the good war, Spielberg has probably done more than any other contemporary filmmaker—indeed more than any other media or political figure—to shape American views of the military while promoting the blessings of patriotic warfare.

## Pearl Harbor: Escape from History

As an epic moment in twentieth century history the Japanese attack on Pearl Harbor has few parallels either militarily or politically, for the United States or the world at large. It surely goes down in the lore of armed strategy as one of the most daring, risky, and audaciously successful armed maneuvers ever, all the more astonishing given the vastly unequal power relations between Japan and the United States. It brought destruction of the American battleship fleet in the Pacific—a fleet long viewed with awe and envy around the world. At a time of intensifying public and elite antiwar sentiment, the attack brought the United States into World War II against the Axis powers: in the words of Japanese admiral Isoroku Yamamoto, it "awoke a sleeping giant." Pearl Harbor gave the United States a fierce sense of dedication and wronged self-righteousness in its four-year pursuit of the war to its victorious conclusion. It no doubt fundamentally altered the way Americans came to view the global arena and the place of the United States within it. Finally, the attack set the United States on the path toward an institutionalized military-industrial system without rival, a war complex that would sink deep roots in the economy, political system, and culture, from which there would be no retreat. World War II set in motion forces that continue to influence American society into the twenty-first century. Although Pearl Harbor at the time symbolized defeat and humiliation for the United States, the event has been duly celebrated in an endless production of ceremonies, rituals, books, TV specials, monuments, and of course movies; it has become a defining memory of the good-war legacy.

We know that the Japanese naval armada, planned and assembled in the months leading up to December 7, 1941, pulled off one of the most remarkable tactical feats ever. On November 6 the naval assault forces—twenty submarines, six aircraft carriers, two battleships, three cruisers, eleven destroyers, eight tankers, and 423 planes—departed Hitokappu Bay in Japan, passing undetected on a northerly course to reach a point, two hundred miles north of Oahu, where they could deliver a devastating blow to the U.S. Pacific Fleet. The results (including the sinking of four battleships) are too well-known to demand recapitulation here. Aside from having been an embarrassing military fiasco, Pearl Harbor revealed a series of major U.S. political, military, and intelligence failures that led to several investigations, commissions, and reports that never satisfactorily resolved all the issues in doubt. Defined as a "date which will live in infamy" by an outraged President Roosevelt, December 7, 1941, came to symbolize the ultimate in military victimism: a dastardly "sneak attack" on an innocent, peace-loving nation just minding its own business. Since Pearl Harbor continues to signify the perpetual American search for good-war themes, the question is how this search might center on a terrible catastrophe where absolute defeat and failure marked the events of the day.

Michael Bay's blockbuster *Pearl Harbor* (2001) was just the latest in a series of films on the subject, though it was surely the longest, most expensive, most ambitious, and most technically sophisticated of the lot. Though Bay and producer Jerry Bruckheimer would surely deny it, this version may also have best fit the propagandistic contours of the standard World War II narrative, replete with themes of national heroism, individual courage, and military triumph, going well beyond the earlier attempts of Jonathan Mostrow and Steven Spielberg to romanticize and distort crucial events in the war. What preceded *Pearl Harbor* were several documentaries, including John Ford's Oscar-winning *December Seventh* (1944), and three features: Howard Hawks's *Air Force* (1943), Fred Zinnemann's *From Here to Eternity* (1953), and Richard Fleischer's *Tora! Tora! Tora!* (1970). The only remotely accurate, objective, and balanced account of the Japanese attack is contained in the last movie, although it too suffers from a failure to adequately frame events within their historical context. The release thirty years later of such a heavily one-dimensional, distorted spectacle as *Pearl Harbor* only underscores its ideological function in replicating the good-war discourse.

In *December Seventh* Ford (with collaborator Gregg Toland) wove together a series of still photos, documentary footage, and contrived scenes made on the back lot of Fox studios to produce an exemplary patriotic pro-war film, enhanced by the acting of John Huston. The bulk of the film is devoted to showing the unique "aloha culture" of Hawaii—a serene, happy, peace-loving, socially mixed culture that had become wonderfully Americanized as U.S. business interests, followed by the military, moved onto the islands. Hawaii was a land of sugarcane and pineapple fields, beautiful homes and hotels, a thriving tourist industry, diverse places of worship, warm and friendly people, a haven for passing ships. Schoolchildren are depicted singing "God Bless America." U.S. businesses flourish, made more profitable by the import of cheap labor from Asia and the Pacific Islands. Within this mecca of beauty and innocence, however, it was possible to identify a growing problem: the Japanese consulate in Honolulu, in its service to the empire, became a festering center of espionage and treachery: local inhabitants along with Japanese employees were observing and reporting on U.S. ship and troop movements in and around Pearl Harbor, preparing the way for subversion and a military assault that American officials were too naive and trusting to believe possible. Ford and Toland portray a Japanese enemy that is the very embodiment of two-faced scheming and diabolical intentions. The attack on the U.S. fleet, shown more realistically here than in most later films, comes as the people of Hawaii (including the military) sleep or attend religious services, striking at a happy tropical paradise with no logic beyond sheer evil. Virtually every subsequent documentary on Pearl Harbor has followed the script laid out by Ford and Toland.

Presenting a far more complex, variegated image of life (both civilian and military) in Hawaii in the months preceding the Japanese attack, *From Here to Eternity,* deservedly the winner of several Academy Awards, focuses mainly on peacetime military (army, not navy) narratives: the harsh discipline, rebellion in the ranks, personal hatreds and rivalries, wild bouts of drinking and womanizing, the inevitable sex triangle involving a sergeant and the wife of an officer. Based on James Jones's novel, the film offers one of the most penetrating critiques of U.S. military culture, in which infidelity, disloyalty, violence, and death appear as the predictable outcomes of a structure built on repression and discipline. At the moment of life-and-death crisis, however, the soldiers at Schofield Barracks are able to put aside all this for the sake of defending the unit. Like the book, the movie contains only a brief (if still dramatically powerful) sequence depicting the attack itself, and nothing on the battleship navy that was targeted in the bombing. In fact the Japanese operation is more an afterthought than the centerpiece of the film, which is concerned more with the plight of individuals caught up in their own tragic circumstances that had nothing to do with war. Overall, the U.S. military came across so negatively that the Board of Admirals banned the picture from being shown on any U.S. ships.[15]

Despite a number of serious flaws, *Tora! Tora! Tora!* remains today the best film ever made on the Pearl Harbor events. Produced at the height of the Vietnam failure, Schreiber's picture (codirected with two Japanese filmmakers) approaches historical accuracy, enhanced by its documentary style and genuine efforts to present the attack from both sides, with the Japanese language spoken where appropriate. Throughout, the Japanese military figures appear as something other than cartoonish villains—itself a significant departure for World War II movies. Although relatively weak in framing the larger context of events, *Tora!* does graphically present the American defeat in its breathtaking totality, including the strange lack of preparedness leading up to the bombings. Billed as the "most spectacular film ever made," it set out to put on screen the most authentic re-creation of military action, culminating in the awesome destruction of the USS *Arizona*. In contrast to *From Here to Eternity* and later *Pearl Harbor*, the particular human characters always remain subordinate to the action sequences, including the tactical planning, which were, after all, the underlying reasons for making the film in the first place. There are no contrived love stories or sex triangles, no maudlin scenes of personal tragedy, no emotional interspersing of scenes from the home front. The actual bombing of battleship row, however, is rendered no more credibly than in Ford's *December Seventh*. In the end, despite its powerful realism, *Tora!* never succeeded at the box office or even among critics, possibly owing to deep national preoccupation with the Vietnam War and the attendant mood of impending disaster.

Despite its enormous cost and sophisticated technology, Bay's *Pearl Harbor* is the most problematic of all Pearl Harbor films both cinematically and historically. In his statements about why he decided to produce yet another picture on the attack, the director said he was looking for a mixture of true stories and everyday heroes, military action and personal sagas—a perfectly solid foundation for any such project. In the *Pearl Harbor Movie Tribute*, Bay identifies the events as a narrative that needed to be told, built around a love story intermingled with a "serious piece about history."[16] Toward this end he and writer Randall Wallace set out to revisit Pearl Harbor with a sense of "utmost realism,"

Pearl Harbor *(Michael Bay, 2001). This blockbuster World War II epic showcases two American pilots, Josh Hartnett and Ben Affleck, who courageously (and somewhat implausibly) respond to the Japanese attack on Pearl Harbor by scurrying to their planes and shooting down large numbers of intruding planes. The narrative combines pilot exploits and a love triangle while downplaying the real action in Battleship Row. Source unknown.*

interviewing dozens of survivors, researching the events, and seeking out various elements of authenticity, for which they received abundant Pentagon assistance. Bay indicated that the film should be viewed as a "tribute" to the survivors and to the heroism of U.S. military personnel who fought against terrible odds. Perhaps looking at the *Titanic* spectacle, Bay and Wallace felt that mass audiences would more likely be drawn to a movie that combined elements of both a love story and real-life historical narratives. In *Pearl Harbor* as in *Titanic,* however, these narratives are overwhelmed (and thus grossly distorted) by the enormous weight of the personal melodramas.

Bay's significantly flawed epic manages to transform the great U.S. military defeat at Pearl Harbor into an improbable victory; the movie is filled with the usual variety of good-war themes. In discussing the film, writer Wallace says, "The fundamental question was, where does the story of Pearl Harbor begin?" His answer is that everything has its origins in the courageous actions

Pearl Harbor *(Michael Bay, 2001). Director Bay and producer Jerry Bruckheimer, architect of many war movies, are pictured here on the set of their World War II epic. Copyright Touchstone Pictures and Jerry Bruckheimer Inc.*

of U.S. Army fliers in the Battle of Britain—a suitable answer given that one of the protagonists in the drama, the fighter pilot Rafe McCawley (played by Ben Affleck) gains his combat experience dueling Nazis even before the United States has entered the war. The picture begins in rural Tennessee, where two young boys grow up fascinated by planes and dream of becoming combat pilots. Much later they do actually mature into expert air force pilots, with Rafe and his sidekick Danny Walker (Josh Hartnett) ready to attain hero status in the months leading up to Pearl Harbor. After training, Rafe volunteers to fly with the Eagle Squadron, a fighter group loaned to the British as they struggle to hold on against the German Luftwaffe. Before he leaves, Rafe falls in love with young nurse Lieutenant Evelyn Johnson (Kate Beckinsale), who promises to wait for his return. He quickly earns "ace" status by shooting down five German planes, then gets shot down himself over the North Atlantic and is presumed dead. News of Rafe's death ultimately brings Evelyn and Danny together after some reluctant, furtive initial moves; they fall in love and plan to marry. As the narrative begins to center on Hawaii, Rafe suddenly reappears: he was missing in action rather than dead and eventually fought his way back to British lines after being saved by a French fishing boat. Rafe explains that only his love for Evelyn gave him the strength to persevere but then abruptly abandons his claim on her when he learns she is pregnant with Danny's child.

As in *Titanic,* this heartrending romantic triangle occupies center stage in what is ostensibly a spectacular historical drama. Suddenly Bay interrupts the twists and turns of this relationship saga with the staged bombing of Pearl Harbor, brilliantly re-creating the horror, chaos, destruction—and astonishment—of the massive aerial bombardment carried out against navy and army targets, depicting the destruction of battleship row in all its fury. The film graphically shows pandemonium in and around the ships, with sailors swimming for their lives, being strafed on deck, and trapped in battleship hulls. Relying on the element of surprise and attacking early Sunday morning, the Japanese were able to sink many ships while also destroying the main elements of the U.S. Army Air Force on the ground; counterattack becomes virtually impossible, with planes taking to the air only at the tail end of the raids. At this point Danny and Rafe, close as brothers despite their love for the same woman, somehow manage to commandeer two fighters in the little time they have to change from their Hawaiian shirts into military uniforms. In their risky but skillful counterattack, the two pilots engage in a series of dogfights with Japanese zeroes, downing seven of them (quite a feat given that only twenty-nine enemy planes were shot down all told). Throughout Bay's forty-some minutes of combat sequences, the bulk of action is centered around planes rather than ships, army rather than navy targets—a scenario that fits his larger preoccupation with the two fliers. In contrast to those in *Tora!* the Japanese military personnel who appear in *Pearl Harbor* are remote and thoroughly objectified, visible only as the kind of evil schemers who would plan a sneak attack on a serene, innocent tropical island.

The final segment of the movie represents Bay's effort to rescue victory out of defeat, through depiction of the audacious raid on Japan led by James Doolittle in April 1942, with both Rafe and Danny gung-ho to take the battle to the enemy as retribution for Pearl Harbor. Here the United States would mobilize all the energy and skills of its elite pilots, attack the Japanese mainland from the carrier *Hornet,* reveal the enemy's vulnerability, and give the United States a badly needed psychological boost in the Pacific. Running low on fuel, most of the B-25s were able to unload their bombs over Japan, but the damage inflicted was minimal; at the time the Doolittle raid was considered a military failure. American pilots were forced to ditch, crashed, or were shot down. Rafe and Danny crash-landed in China, but only Rafe survived, bringing a tragic end to the romantic triangle. The Doolittle adventure, though entirely separate from the Pearl Harbor episode, ends up as a crucial uplifting (and redemptive) moment in Bay's picture.

If the goal of Bruckheimer, Bay, and Wallace was to achieve the "utmost realism," giving audiences a view of Pearl Harbor as never seen before, then the film was a complete disaster. It is riddled with distortions and inaccuracies, lacks historical mapping, dwells on peripheral stories and events at the expense of the main narrative, and presents visual images that are hardly compelling.

Indeed the special effects used to depict the attack convey nothing so much as a video-game quality. Anyone interested in the historical episode is best advised to forget *Pearl Harbor* and view *Tora! Tora! Tora!* which, despite its weaknesses, does seriously grapple with the complex series of causes and consequences surrounding one of the most fascinating military operations ever. Bay says he was mainly interested in weaving together elements of fiction and nonfiction. Fair enough, except that the filmmaker is obliged to adhere to at least minimum standards of authenticity if he wants the picture to be taken as anything more than one person's fantasy. Since Bay and Wallace repeatedly mentioned they set out to establish precisely such authenticity, their utter failure to even approach it is all the more noteworthy. And there was no excuse. As Suid writes: "Given the inaccuracies of fact and history in his script, Wallace probably should have visited his local bookstore and bought one of the many good histories about December 7 before he put a word onto paper. Except for the fact that the Japanese did bomb Pearl Harbor, his account of events bears little resemblance to what actually happened before, during, and after the date that will live in infamy."[17] In fact there is a certain logic to the plethora of errors, distortions, and omissions, the result of Bay's determination to cinematically transform Pearl Harbor into something it never was, another good-war episode.

Bay's film not only repositions Pearl Harbor as the ultimate good war, its preoccupation with a romantic melodrama—the love triangle involving two air force pilots and a nurse—is designed to broaden marketing appeal by targeting the widest possible audience. *Pearl Harbor* is simultaneously a combat and a noncombat picture, in the tradition of *From Here to Eternity*, but in this case the love story so dominates the screen that everything else becomes peripheral, with predictably bad ramifications for the historical narrative. By incorporating significant elements of other film genres, Bay was able to envelope his movie in the trappings of other motifs far removed from the realities of military action, or history in general. The result is a kind of cinematic hybrid that, combined with the familiar good-war motif, performs definite ideological functions, among them romanticization of the war experience itself.

Aside from the love story, the first thing that strikes the viewer is that *Pearl Harbor* is essentially about planes, American planes, and the men who flew them. The planes and their pilots are identified with the U.S. Army Air Force. This is rather astonishing insofar as the real history of Pearl Harbor involved altogether different military personae—the Japanese naval armada sailing toward Oahu, including its many squadrons that bombed and torpedoed mostly naval targets centered around battleship row. The U.S. Army, both ground and air forces, played a limited role in the events of December 7. In this context Bay's selection of two army pilots as protagonists seems bizarre and out of focus, much like dwelling on the role of the Soviet navy in a film depicting the battle of Stalingrad. Yet there is a certain twisted logic to this approach, which shapes the picture from beginning to end. First, it engages the image of daring, heroic, macho pilots who operate as skillful aerial gladiators, handsome and sexy officers willing to risk everything for country as seen in such films as *Top Gun*. Second, in what might pass for the "battle" of Pearl Harbor the filmmaker is able to show these same macho heroes taking to the air and fighting, against heavy odds, the swarms of Japanese bombers and fighters, even knocking down seven of them. At a moment of unprecedented U.S. military defeat, this subplot could readily be shown as a dramatic victory, always crucial to the good-war narrative. Finally, preoccupation with the U.S. air war is extended further within the cinematic production to a final, heroic climax: the Doolittle raid on Japan. This narrative shift gives Bay added opportunities to glorify the individual exploits of pilots, inspired by the Patton-like Doolittle (Alex Baldwin), all misleadingly constructed as a turning point in the Pacific theater. (The Battle of Midway some months later was the real turning-point, but this obviously did not fit Bay's priorities.) In a film ostensibly about Pearl Harbor, sequences capturing the Doolittle raid consumed more than a half hour.

The actual story of Pearl Harbor was, first and foremost, about the colliding fates of the Japanese and American navies—astonishing triumph for the Japanese, humiliating defeat for the Americans. This narrative is entirely lost in Bay's ideologically driven film. From the U.S. standpoint, the incredible saga of battleship row would be the natural starting point for any movie seeking even a modicum of authenticity. After all, the Japanese managed to destroy the Pacific battleship fleet, sinking four ships, disabling four others, and killing more than two thousand sailors and officers. What happened at Hickam Field and Schofield Barracks was of marginal importance. True enough, *Pearl Harbor* does contain lengthy sequences dramatizing the attack on battleship row, but these sequences come across as mere technical flourishes, detached from the general flow. The ships are visible mainly as distant objects, in contrast to the army bases where the attack takes on a sense of concrete, graphic immediacy; the horror and chaos and death on battleship row are revealed only in detached fragments. Nowhere does Bay's film try to capture what these battleships were—their gigantic and awesome presence, their unique culture, what they symbolized as naval dreadnoughts, what the attack did to annihilate all that. To visualize such epic drama, clearly more fascinating than anything contained in *Pearl Harbor,* the viewer must go back to *Tora! Tora! Tora!* which, although it was made thirty years earlier, endows the military action of December 7 with far greater historical authenticity and human drama.

Bay's radical deemphasis of the U.S. battleship fleet was no mere oversight but came from his obsession with the air force—though not, of course, the Japanese (naval) air force, which stands as the clear victor of the engagement. This is quite unfortunate from a cinematic as well as historical point of view, for there has been no military force as fascinating as the U.S. battleship fleet before or since. These ships were indeed unique: huge floating cities nearly three football fields in length, multitiered, and organized into a complex system of working compartments, graceful without parallel on the seas, with crews of more than 1,200. They were armed with fourteen- and fifteen-inch guns that could fire 1,500-pound shells more than twenty miles, requiring intricate guidance systems that first introduced the modern computer (aboard the USS *California* in 1939). They constituted something of a walled, medieval fortress manned by a special caste of maritime warriors imbued with very special norms and ideals.[18] The battleship sailors who lived, often for stretches of many years, on such naval behemoths as the *California* and the *Tennessee* were an arrogant, provincial lot, condescending toward all land creatures and those assigned to ships considered lower in the hierarchy: destroyers, cruisers, even aircraft carriers, which were viewed as ugly and clumsy. The ships' culture included such things as coffee rooms, musical groups, boxing matches and other sports events, massive drills, and cultural activities. Once the ships reached port for shore liberty—during the 1930s and later the Pacific Fleet moved back and forth regularly between the West Coast and Pearl Harbor—the battleship culture carried over into the bars, dance halls, and bordellos, and the fleet became notorious for myriad shenanigans. It was precisely these immense ships (and their culture) that were demolished with the events of December 7, after which the carriers would assume overwhelming tactical importance. It is hard to imagine a more fascinating, indeed more historically dramatic, setting for any movie that intends to capture the essence of the Pearl Harbor legacy than these ships, but Bay's agenda clearly pushed him in other directions.

What could possibly be a more riveting wartime drama than massive battleships under surprise attack, their crew members in a state of pandemonium and struggling to survive or, where possible, fight back? On December 7, of course, we have no fewer than eight ships under siege. If we cast a glance at *Tora! Tora! Tora!* we immediately encounter the full force of the bombardment and its hellacious aftermath, both within and outside the vessels, as the crews desperately respond to the series of devastating hits. In *Pearl Harbor,* on the other hand, the action is staged almost entirely outside the ships. Bay is more concerned with the characters he sees as the *real* heroes, the American fliers scurrying around to find their vehicle of combat adventure. The *Tora!* scenes are absolutely mesmerizing: battleships bombed while crews are attending reveille or having breakfast at Sunday morning mess hall or simply getting ready to face the day after drinking bouts on Hotel Street. The ships are quickly transformed into cauldrons of huge explosions, fire, smoke, and chaos as entire infrastructures—many years in the making—are reduced to shambles. Men are blown up, others forced overboard, others trapped in hulls, still others scramble to reach five-inch and antiaircraft guns. There are calls to abandon ship as the once proud and graceful vessels begin to list severely, capsize, or sink to the bottom of the bay. A break in the action is followed by renewed devastating attacks. Recalling his terrifying experiences aboard the USS *California* (which was eventually sunk), Seaman Theodore Mason writes: "The harbor was a scene from Dante's *Inferno,* evoking all the horrors of the ninth circle. Oil was spreading everywhere: spreading out from the sunken ships in pernicious rings, mottling the water, blackening the shore. Drifting the slow currents were life rafts, life jackets, pieces of boats, and other flotsam. The air smelled of bunker oil, fire, smoke, and death."[19] Five heroic men on the beleaguered *California* were honored for their bravery under attack by having ships named after them in World War II. If only Bay, with his supposed commitment to realism, had set out to capture the actual events along these lines, he would have produced a far more compelling piece of cinema. To do this, however, would have clashed with his overriding aim: reprise of the good-war motif.

Bay's failure to present the actual history of Pearl Harbor extends even further: the attack not only destroyed the Pacific battleship fleet but, more tellingly, revealed the obsolescence of the battlewagon itself as a major weapon of war while simultaneously highlighting the supremacy of the aircraft carrier. Such huge ships made easy targets for carrier-based planes, as the Japanese were the first to show. It was this carrier supremacy that, in the end, propelled the U.S. forces to victory at Midway and then later across the Pacific theater. Once a tremendous symbol of military power, the battleship now came to signify impotence despite its guns capable of demolishing an entire city. While some of the dreadnoughts sunk at Pearl Harbor would be raised and returned to service, their role would be increasingly limited; the assembly lines produced new carriers monthly along with thousands of planes but only a few modern battleships like the *Missouri.* Their passing from the scene was duly noted by Mason: "Never again would the mighty battlewagons of the Pacific Fleet steam off the California coast in line of battle ahead, their turrets trained out. . . . Never again would the 14 and 16-inch rifles speak in concert splitting the heavens with earthly thunder. . . . Never again would the once-revered battleships anchor in arrow-straight columns in the lee of the San Diego breakwater. And never again would the fleet landings at Long Beach and San Pedro come alive with thousands of battleship sailors bringing good news to bar and bistro and bordello."[20]

This eclipse of an already aging battleship fleet points to a central mythology of Pear Harbor that finds its way into Bay's film: while tactically audacious and stunning, and while it brought the United States into World War II, the attack did very little to immobilize American military capabilities in the Pacific, or even in Hawaii itself. Historians know this well, but filmmakers like Bay and writers like Wallace prefer to characterize the bombings as having decimated the Pacific Fleet, dealing a crushing blow to the U.S. military on the eve of war. Not true, as the Battle of Midway would soon reveal. It was surely a moment of great military drama, and the losses should not be downplayed, but the military impact has been drastically overblown. At the time of the raids the U.S. fleet had 106 ships out to sea and 103 in port, of which 21 were sunk. Of the 8 battleships hit only the *Arizona* remained permanently at rest; the others were quickly repaired, modernized, and returned to sea, where they saw only limit-ed duty. What would have been the main Japanese prize—three large aircraft carriers—was out of reach, the carriers having been sent out of port. Most sig-nificantly, ground facilities suffered little damage on December 7: the huge submarine base, oil depots, supply warehouses, dry docks, and repair shops emerged fully operational; these were crucial to restoring U.S. power in the Pacific. Outside Pearl Harbor the destruction was surprisingly light; Honolulu itself was hit only sporadically and sustained no more than sixty civilian casu-alties (resulting mostly from friendly fire). More than 160 planes were destroyed on the ground at Hickam Field and elsewhere, but these were large-ly obsolete fighters and bombers. Even the overall casualty level from the raids was not extraordinarily high when compared with later World War II aerial bombardments: there were 2,403 dead (nearly half of these aboard the *Arizona*) and 1,178 wounded, as opposed to tens of thousands of civilians routinely killed in U.S. bombing raids against Japanese cities toward the end of the war.

An even greater flaw of *Pearl Harbor* is its complete lack of historical con-textualization—nothing illuminating is presented across a span of nearly three hours. A brief passing reference to the U.S. oil embargo on Japan in 1941 is all that we hear about a crucial development in the buildup to war. Any such nar-rative would, of course, subvert a defining theme of the film: evil Japanese, motivated by imperial designs, carry out a sneak attack on peace-loving Americans at their tropical outpost. Viewers will be entirely clueless as to why the Japanese chose to mount an assault they knew would lead to protracted military encounters with a much stronger power.

Not much historical probing is required to show that several factors con-tributed to the Japanese decision to launch an attack, all part of the escalating rivalry between the United States and Japan over imperial domination in the Pacific—over access to raw materials, trade issues, geopolitical presence, and of course military influence. By 1941 this rivalry had generated intense competi-tion, rigidity, and arrogance on both sides, aggravated by expanded U.S. mili-tary deployment to the Philippines and to Guam, Wake Island, and Hawaii and then further heightened by the American embargo. U.S. demands that Japan withdraw from China and Indochina, part of its own imperial gambit, were summarily and understandably rejected. Meanwhile, Admiral Harold Stack, chief of naval operations, had in early 1941 decided to make permanent the stationing of a reinforced Pacific Fleet in Hawaii, a move both the Japanese and Americans regarded as deliberately provocative. In fact the scores of U.S. ships based at Pearl Harbor were used to monitor, harass, and test the Japanese navy while also disrupting trade routes, a stratagem that had to be considered as anything but passive or innocent.[21] By late 1941, Japanese elites felt they had no option but to respond militarily to the United States, an ominous shift in attitude well known to American leaders, who, according to reliable reports, had already anticipated this shift as an outcome of their policies.[22]

Conflict between the United States and Japan contained a powerful racial dimension from the outset. As John Dower writes, the Pacific theater quickly became a "spellbinding spectacle of brutality and death" marked by sheer hatred on both sides.[23] It appeared that no U.S. enemy was ever so detested as the Japanese, who became immediate objects of racial caricatures, reflecting attitudes that predated Pearl Harbor. Indeed the Japanese were viewed as irredeemably primitive and barbaric, so primitive in fact that U.S. political and military leaders doubted their capacity to carry out successful armed campaigns; they simply did not know how to manufacture good ships or planes, much less adequately train their crews. One military official was quoted as saying "we can lick the Japanese in 24 hours." Even once the United States came to possess information about a likely attack, there was contemptuous disbelief, which turned to outright shock on the morning of December 7. The conversion of such national hubris into a mood of terrifying shock ought to be a central historical motif of Pearl Harbor, more compelling than the racist notion of unspeakable treachery by architects of a "sneak attack"—as if military campaigns were supposed to be telegraphed to the enemy in advance. What Dower refers to as "exterminationist rhetoric" continued throughout the war, making possible the later firebombings of Japanese cities and the atomic devastation of Hiroshima and Nagasaki.[24] No accurate depiction of Pearl Harbor is possible without taking into account this larger historical backdrop.

There is far more to the story: abundant evidence shows that the Roosevelt administration was not only fully aware of the Japanese mobilization and buildup to war but also coordinated its foreign policy in a manner consciously designed to provoke an intemperate response. According to Robert Stinnett and others, FDR was prepared to enter World War II but needed Japan to take the first step in order to get an isolationist Congress (and nation) willing to join the battle. The United States was no innocent sleeping giant, nor was it caught totally off guard by Pearl Harbor—though it is true that officials in Washington failed to pass along vital messages to the armed forces command in Hawaii, leaving both General Walter Short and Admiral Husband Kimmel out of the loop. After reviewing some two hundred thousand documents Stinnett writes: "By provoking the attack, Roosevelt accepted the terrible truth that America's military forces—including the Pacific Fleet and the civilian population in the Pacific—would sit squarely in harm's way, exposed to enormous risks."[25] By means of well-planned covert and overt actions, the United States implemented an eight-point scheme to incite the Japanese to war, including the embargo, military support for the Chinese nationalist regime, expansion of the Pacific Fleet, and the dispatch of naval task groups into Japanese waters (a violation of international law), and then crudely dismissed all protests. Having run for the presidency on an antiwar platform in 1940, and having failed to sell Congress on the urgency of reversing course and entering the war, FDR decided to pursue a "backdoor policy" by forcing the Japanese hand, and history shows that it worked. Roosevelt had also steadfastly refused to go along with the Japanese proposal for a Greater East Asia Co-Prosperity Sphere, viewing it as a threat to U.S. economic and geopolitical supremacy. With the Japanese code broken and crucial messages intercepted, Washington officials knew by late November 1941 that an attack was imminent, the only question being exactly when and where the strike would occur.[26] In the days leading up to December 7, with thousands of messages intercepted, vast Japanese fleet movements were detected closing in on Hawaii, but this information was never passed along to Short and Kimmel, the commanders responsible for military preparedness who were later victimized as scapegoats for their weak leadership at Pearl Harbor. With the attack FDR had achieved his goal: U.S. entry into the war was now fully justified, indeed it was a matter of patriotic duty that all Americans could support. Pearl Harbor not only united the country behind war but also gave rise to a military-industrial complex that remains today.

None of these historical realities, of course, coincide with the demands of the good-war fairy-tale that Bruckheimer, Bay, and Wallace embraced in the making of *Pearl Harbor*. After all, films that revisit World War II tend to celebrate that tale in great measure because it so neatly fits the ideological parameters of present-day U.S. foreign and military policy. The war of attrition in the Pacific, with its fusion of imperialism, militarism, and racism and its massive shift of American armed forces into the Orient, followed a long historical trajectory of expansion and conquest originating in the ethos of Manifest Destiny. Motion pictures served as propaganda instruments of these objectives just as they would later in new geopolitical contexts.

World War II has been brought to the screen more as fiction than as fact, more as ideological construction than as historical reality—hardly surprising given the immense power of an increasingly conservative media culture in the United States. To be sure, filmmakers always laid claim to a certain graphic "realism" in making their war movies, but as we have seen with *Saving Private Ryan, Pearl Harbor,* and other combat pictures, it is a realism that serves definite aesthetic and political ends. Films about World War II have been popular and profitable while also exerting an ideological impact not immediately visible to audiences captivated by the high drama of combat. We know that epic moments of the war—Pearl Harbor, Normandy, the Battle of the Bulge, Okinawa, etc.—have been plumbed for all they can yield ideologically. As might be expected, the Hollywood war machine has missed few opportunities to celebrate, glorify, and (where necessary) reframe the spectacles of warfare so that the viewer is inundated with images of the good war. As in the case of Vietnam, with its altogether different outcome and consequences, it is easy to see that World War II continues to shape and reshape the American political and cultural landscape.

# CHAPTER 5

# Cinematic Warfare in the New World Order

The 1990s brought a new paradigm to both the U.S. global presence and Hollywood filmmaking, precipitated by the end of the cold war, the rise of America as an unchallenged superpower, renewed forms of worldwide intervention, the resurgence of Pentagon militarism, and the proclamation by the first President Bush of a promising New World Order shaped by U.S. interests. By the early twenty-first century all of this would take on new political expressions: the war on terrorism, ascendancy of right-wing neoconservative "defense intellectuals," consolidation of U.S. empire, the second President Bush's preemptive-war stratagem, and the war in Iraq. Beginning with Panama in December 1989, the United States carried out armed interventions no fewer than six times—twice in Iraq and in Somalia, the Balkans, and Afghanistan, with plans regarding Iran, Syria, and North Korea on the Washington drawing board. This period has been marked by a massive growth in Pentagon spending, a turn toward RMA ("revolution in military affairs"), reliance on technowar, and an increase in U.S. exceptionalism with its disregard for international customs, laws, and treaties, surely part of the ongoing struggle of political elites to extinguish the Vietnam syndrome once and for all.

Drastic shifts in the mood of the country are bound to be reflected in the kinds of films produced by the mainstream studios, and this period is no exception. We have already explored how media culture in general and Hollywood filmmaking in particular have revisited World War II with the aim of giving new life to the good-war legacy, which always serves Pentagon agendas. Here we devote attention to other related cinematic tendencies: a new cycle of films that burnish the image of the U.S. military while exalting such themes as high-tech violence, patriotism, ultramasculinism, anti-Arab racism, and Western supremacy. Such films might fit the classic warfare model identified with the combat genre, but just as often they are likely to fall within such categories as sci-fi thrillers, terrorist dramas, and male action-adventure movies that we refer to as "disguised militarism." Other pictures incorporate the motif of "distant wars," that is, military action removed in time and place but coded to represent forces at work in the contemporary world. Many of these films, including those made by established directors, are shrouded in the mythology of technological supremacy, racism, and imperial hegemony, and many of them are inspired by the well-known perpetual search for new enemies to replace the old Communists who inhabited the erstwhile Evil Empire. (To be sure, Communists of one stripe or another can still be found, but they no longer provoke the same national fears and paranoia.) The new enemy, not surprisingly, turns out to be an assortment of demonic Arabs and Muslims, fanatical, semicivilized, and violent, whose usual modus operandi is some form of irrational terrorism. This new cycle of filmmaking grew more popular once the earlier cycle of Vietnam-era movies, typically critical of the U.S. military, had run its course. In fact the origins of this phenomenon go back to the late 1980s as Hollywood began the search for more endearing portraits of the post-Vietnam armed services. Here the film culture has performed vital ideological functions in contributing to the expansion of U.S. global power.

Several mass-audience films produced in the late 1980s and early 1990s brought forward refurbished, celebratory images of U.S. military prowess, an obvious departure from the Vietnam cycle. Clint Eastwood's *Heartbreak Ridge* (1986) managed to present an uplifting, patriotic, triumphant account of the ridiculous U.S. military intervention in tiny Grenada, where a regime change was demanded by President Reagan to protect American "national security." This propagandistic work follows the career of grizzled Airborne soldier Tom Highway (played by Eastwood), who forges a unified combat group out of a motley assemblage of selfish prima donnas and takes them to victory, in the process exhibiting the most ruthless imperial behavior, including shooting unarmed Cubans and other prisoners. Much like Rambo before him, Highway is the kind of maverick hero the U.S. military finds both problematic and virtuous. In any event, Eastwood's patriotic intent was to make the army look good, to help restore its shattered reputation, and here he apparently succeeded despite conflicts with the Pentagon and major cinematic defects of his project.

Released the same year as *Heartbreak Ridge,* Tony Scott's *Top Gun* goes even further in glamorizing military life, in this case an elite stratum of navy fighter pilots stationed at Miramar Naval Air Station near San Diego. Starring Tom Cruise as the aptly named Maverick, the picture valorizes all the warrior virtues: individual daring and heroism, mastery of technology, patriotism, masculine power. Moreover, at a time when the United States could be said to have no military adversary, with the cold war waning, *Top Gun* succeeded in constructing combat scenarios in which the "top guns" (Maverick of course in the lead) blow away "enemy MiGs" in a series of dogfights over the Indian Ocean.

In this otherwise mediocre film Scott's dazzling aerial cinematography uses the sophisticated F-14 fighters as symbols not only of military power and efficiency but of the beauty of combat, in which glamour, sexuality, and technical proficiency are mixed with a gung-ho fervor. The most widely viewed picture of that year, *Top Gun* embraced the kind of cinematic militarism that would later find expression in the initiatives of presidents Bush I, Clinton, and Bush II.

As we have seen, the Pentagon has always sought to enhance the popular image of the U.S. armed forces, toward which end it has worked diligently to gain leverage within media culture by assisting filmmakers when its interests might be enhanced. In the case of *Top Gun*, glamorous depictions of elite fliers turned out to be a bonanza for navy recruitment even after the film received a host of negative reviews from critics. It seemed that the armed forces had been rehabilitated from their post-Vietnam doldrums, and the charismatic heroism of Tom Cruise was the perfect vehicle. Other movies of the period contributed modestly to this trend, laying the groundwork for a resurgence of cinematic militarism in the 1990s: *The Delta Force* (1986), *Navy Seals* (1990), *The Hunt for Red October* (1990), and in its own nuanced way, *Forrest Gump* (1994). Arriving at the end of the cold war, such pictures found heroic pursuits for the military and were able to locate serviceable enemies by either looking ahead to new confrontations *(Navy Seals)* or reviving old ones *(The Hunt for Red October)*. Many films, of course, would take up the lucrative motif of terrorism with its new staple of mostly Arab and Muslim demons, a development explored later in this chapter.

## Iraq: From Spectacle to Chaos

U.S. military involvement in Iraq began in 1991 with Operation Desert Storm as perhaps the most celebrated of media technowar spectacles, but by 2004 it had degenerated into one of the more sordid experiences in American history: two bloody wars, more than a decade of catastrophic economic sanctions, ongoing bombing and espionage campaigns, and a harsh military occupation that recalls the worst features of classical European imperialism. Corporate media, including the Hollywood studios, have both reflected and magnified this sad debacle, glorifying the new U.S. militarism at the very moment it dramatizes, without apparent intent, the limits and dysfunctions of that militarism. However one characterizes the U.S. presence in Iraq—"quagmire," "impasse," "debacle," or simply "imperialism"—the parallels with Vietnam seem increasingly difficult to avoid even for the most hawkish Pentagon strategists, evidence that the "syndrome" has yet to be fully conquered.

From the vantage point of early 2005, U.S. military aggression in Iraq can be traced back to the end of World War II, if not earlier, when Anglo-American efforts to gain hegemony over the resource-laden Middle East first began in earnest. The neocon strategy to "remap" the region to suit U.S. economic and geopolitical interests, outlined ambitiously after the first Gulf War, must be understood in this context. Such interests include not only pursuit of resource wars in the Persian Gulf and Central Asia but also the *control* of these resources—above all oil—for leverage against potential national competitors as well as protection of Israeli objectives. Actual U.S. military intervention was facilitated by several factors: the decline of Soviet power, Iraq's invasion of Kuwait in 1990, growing conservatism in the United States, and a renewed search for military enemies to justify continued high levels of Pentagon spending. It must be remembered that the Gulf region is home to no less than two-thirds of the world's known petroleum reserves, and nothing is more vital to the functioning of modern industrial and military regimes. At present the United States, with military spending equal to that of the next *eight* most powerful nations combined, consumes nearly 40 percent of global energy supplies. At the same time, the Middle East is gateway to the rapidly expanding economies of East and Southeast Asia, the northern entrance to the African continent from Europe, and the location of many strategic waterways. In the heart of the region lies Israel, crucial U.S. ally and power broker, which serves as a subimperialist power and requires constant political, diplomatic, and economic supports. It has become increasingly obvious to American leaders that strong hegemony, necessitating military control, over the Middle East is crucial to maintaining domination over the global market economy, an imperative shared by Democrats and Republicans alike.

For such imperial ambitions—sometimes referred to as the U.S. "grand strategy"—the powerful corporate media, moving ever rightward since the early 1980s, have emerged as a crucial ally and conduit, essentially a propaganda system. If the mass media of the Vietnam era brought to the American public graphic images of death and destruction, helping inspire harshly critical responses to the war, with Iraq the media have performed more celebratory functions, representing the wars as technological spectacles deserving of mass patriotic fervor. Already by the late 1980s, as we have seen, pictures like *Top Gun* and *Heartbreak Ridge*—not to mention the Rambo episodes—helped prepare the cultural ground for Desert Storm with the glorification of military heroism mixed with a fetishism of high-tech weaponry. Other films such as *Delta Force* and *Iron Eagle* and *Iron Eagle II* contributed by setting up Arabs and Muslims as the new cinematic enemy. The Middle East became the focal point of a new barbaric menace to Western civilization. Once the Gulf War was launched in January 1991, it became the ultimate media extravaganza, an unprecedented electronic worshipping of militarism and patriotism that seemed to reinvigorate the entire national psyche.[1]

At the end of this brief but frenetic "war"—in reality a massacre carried out against a totally overmatched foe—Bush was able to bask in the glory of military triumph, having proclaimed (and enforced) a momentary Pax Americana.

Within this order the United States gained firmer hegemony, validating the rise of a superpower without serious challengers, ready to punish any nation choosing to transgress against the rules of that order. Just as important, the Pentagon had now perfected a good many of the tools of technowar, which the TV networks dramatized and celebrated in an orgy of images: aircraft carriers mobilized, attack helicopters and fighters sweeping over enemy terrain, sophisticated command centers, Tomahawk missiles launched from ships and lighting up the skies over Baghdad. Technowar became the preferred mode of combat, intimidating foes and sending messages to would-be competitors while conveying moral and political supremacy. Technowar can inflict enormous bloodshed and destruction, both civilian and military, while simultaneously being presented as an entertaining spectacle, a kind of hyperinflated series of video games ideal for home-TV consumption. Everything that fit this format was duly recorded and indeed dramatized, including the infamous "highway of death" scenes where tens of thousands of retreating Iraqi troops were trapped and then pulverized from the air long after the withdrawal from Kuwait had begun. Those long-distance missiles, bombs, and artillery shells, of course, killed additional thousands, including nearly five hundred women and children who had taken refuge in a Baghdad bomb shelter. Not surprisingly, the carnage elicited very little emotional response, much less moral outrage, within an American public already hardened to the deepening culture of militarism.

Desert Storm contributed immensely to this further militarization of American society—a development solidified by U.S. ascendancy on the global scene. The 1990s witnessed a growing legitimation of the very idea of U.S. empire (long denied), accompanied by a revitalized language of American exceptionalism: the notion that the United States had the right to intervene militarily anywhere it chose in pursuit of its own interests, even if this meant trampling on the UN Charter, international law, or binding treaties. The celebration of military power, especially in its high-tech incarnation, took on new meaning in this historical context. As the ideological center of gravity shifted profoundly rightward even during the Clinton presidency, the media culture became an increasingly powerful conduit of corporate, military, and imperial agendas, best exemplified by the expanding influence of the Fox TV network. The culture of militarism also coincided with a growing concentration of economic and political power reflected in a strengthened war economy and security state and marked by a narrowing of public discourse (most notably in the sphere of foreign policy). Such trends, it should be emphasized, were well under way even before the events of 9/11 and the rise of George W. Bush to the presidency. And these same trends helped make possible later U.S. military adventures (in Yugoslavia, Afghanistan, and Iraq again) to enforce America's power within the New World Order.

Hollywood's approach to Iraq has been anything but straightforward or categorical, and on the surface it is far removed from the Gulf War TV flourishes. The few filmmakers who decided to take on Desert Storm resisted following the good-war motif. At the same time, they indulged elements of the militarized culture that motion pictures about the Middle East have carried forward in different guises since the 1980s. By 2004 the first Gulf War had inspired only two Hollywood features: Ed Zwick's *Courage Under Fire* (1996) and David Russell's *Three Kings* (1999). Interestingly, neither of these movies depicts actual U.S. military operations against Iraq to any degree, nor do they try to confront the actual historical or strategic backdrop of these operations, a pattern that in some ways replicates the Vietnam-era films. Both pictures can be read as offering an essentially critical view of the war insofar as they dramatize the limits and contradictions of an armed engagement that easily could have been avoided by a dedicated resort to diplomacy, but this reading should not be pressed too far. More recently, director Sam Mendes' picture *Jarhead* (2005), based on Anthony Swofford's best seller, chronicles U.S. Marine experiences in Desert Storm and is the third full-scale combat picture about the 1991 Gulf War.

The second Gulf War, quickly transformed into a regimen of U.S. military occupation and popular armed resistance, did not initially generate much interest among Hollywood studios, despite a renewed cycle of TV spectacles lauding the great blessings of "Operation Iraqi Freedom." One problem is that the "operation" did not turn out as predicted: a swift military victory followed by widespread Iraqi consent to American rule. Instead, the outcome was a bloody military regime that spawned intensified insurgency and cost the lives of more than a hundred thousand Iraqi civilians (estimated by a 2005 Johns Hopkins University report) and over 2,400 U.S. troops and civilian support personnel as of early May 2006. Another problem is the long-standing reluctance of the studios to make pictures about ongoing warfare, and here there is no end in sight, just as there is no end in sight to the war on terrorism. One exception to this media reticence is Steven Bochco's production of *Over There,* a rather gory TV program for cable network FX (owned by Fox) that follows six U.S. Marines in Iraq along with their families back home. As with many war-themed films and TV programs since the 1970s, *Over There* focuses mostly on the home front, on the trials and ordeals of American troops and their relatives exposed to the risks and hardships of armed service in Iraq, heightened by the harsh realities of occupation and resistance. The war itself becomes largely peripheral to the narrative structure Bochco and Gerolmo have established. A different modality has been pursued by HBO, which in 2005 aired a limited series based on Evan Wright's book *The Killer Elite,* revolving around a highly specialized marine unit as it drives toward Baghdad during the initial phases of war. Given their source materials, such programs can be expected to recycle good-war themes in an Iraq setting manifestly hostile to such themes.

Zwick's *Courage Under Fire* is the only film to date that devotes any serious attention to battlefield action in Desert Storm, and even here the action is peripheral to the main story line, focusing on the human anguish of battlefield ordeals. With Akira Kurosawa's 1950 *Roshomon* as inspiration, Zwick and writer Patrick Duncan created the story of Lieutenant Colonel Nathaniel Serling's efforts to investigate whether Captain Karen Walden should receive a posthumous Medal of Honor for heroic actions during the Gulf War—to be the first ever awarded to a woman in combat. Oddly, Serling (played by Denzel Washington) himself has become the object of military investigation after friendly fire destroys one of his own tanks. Walden (Meg Ryan) was killed after landing her medevac helicopter to assist the crew of another downed copter, but the events surrounding Walden's actions dissolve into chaos and ambiguity in a way that is quite unusual for a combat picture. Obsessed with his own sense of guilt, Serling renews his dedication to unveiling the truth about Walden's case while his own life begins to unravel.

Serling's efforts to discover the truth produce more confusion than enlightenment. Did Captain Walden act with great courage, as Specialist Ilario (Matt Damon) recalls, or was she a coward eager to surrender to advancing Iraqis, as Sergeant Monfriez (Lou Diamond Phillips) remembers the incident? As the investigation proceeds, the White House decides to manufacture political capital from the incident, hoping to bask in Walden's glory in breaking new ground for female combatants. Serling's commanding officer, General Hershberg (Michael Moriarty), echoes White House thinking on the matter: "Everybody wants it—senators, congressmen. One shining piece of something for people to believe in." Publicity-mad White House aide Bruno (Bronson Pinchot), planning a gala ceremony involving Walden's young daughter, jubilantly explains, "She's the first woman in history to be nominated for a Medal of Honor in combat. It means this is gold. It's gold! Unfortunately, it's posthumous, but I've got her little daughter." Despite the film's title, Zwick's work shows few examples of courage under fire, instead portraying not only ambiguity regarding Walden's own behavior but also a generally negative view of the soldiers' actions, which include a hint of mutiny against Walden's command and a general breakdown of military discipline that parallels scenes from *The Thin Red Line*. What we see in *Courage Under Fire* are abundant episodes of weakness, confusion, incompetence, and indecisiveness under fire, all filtered through Zwick's multiperspectival approach.

At the same time, the movie does not abandon crucial elements of the good-war motif. Zwick employs typical CNN stock footage of the Gulf War at the outset, thus carrying forward images of the war spectacle to frame the picture. Moreover, the narrative makes clear that President Bush had no recourse but to solve the crisis of Iraq's presence in Kuwait by military force (a complete myth). Colonel Serling goes into Desert Storm with a typical warrior mentality, calling out, "Let's kill 'em all, let's eat 'em up." In a scene where Serling is in charge of a tank column, U.S. gunners annihilate faceless Iraqis as if they were mechanical targets on a firing range. After Captain Walden's copter is downed,

Courage Under Fire *(Edward Zwick, 1996, Twentieth Century Fox). In one of the few films about Operation Desert Storm, Meg Ryan portrays a helicopter pilot whose nomination for a Medal of Honor is investigated by a senior army officer (Denzel Washington). The picture graphically shows the psychological horrors of warfare. Copyright 1996 Twentieth Century Fox.*

the crew somehow musters enough firepower to cut to ribbons dozens more hapless Iraqis who have the audacity to attack a medical unit. Iraqis are routinely dismissed as a bunch of stupid "ragheads." At the end of the combat scene, Apache attack copters are called in to shoot and napalm even more totally overmatched Iraqi soldiers. Despite its *Roshomon* quality, *Courage Under Fire* depicts just one Iraqi human actor throughout the entire picture.

What helps compensate for these flaws is Zwick's skillful inclusion of several crosscutting subplots that work against the good-war pattern. One subplot involves the role of women in the military, in this case the relationship between Captain Walden and her male subordinates, which degenerates into outright rebellion and possible mutiny once the copter detachment is on the ground. Clearly the men chafe under Walden's authority, at times fiercely resisting her orders; there is even the possibility that she was killed at the hands of one of her own soldiers—a phenomenon we know occurred with some frequency in Vietnam. The battlefield situation in Iraq, however, with its quick and decisive victory over an outmanned enemy, was entirely different, with few if any reports of fragging. In *Courage Under Fire,* Sergeant Monfriez did strongly challenge Walden's command and might well have been her killer, part of a mutiny that the army found objectionable when reviewing the script but one that seems credible in the context of intense male-female tensions throughout the U.S. armed forces. We know that a large percentage of men strongly resent the growing presence of women in the military, especially where the women are in positions of command as in Zwick's movie, and such resentment can easily veer out of control under the pressures of combat. In keeping with the *Roshomon* character of *Courage Under Fire,* however, Serling's investigation turned up enough "information" to show that Walden did indeed deserve the Medal of Honor, which she is duly awarded at the end of the film.

Yet another subplot, one with probably more enduring ramifications for the U.S. military role in the Middle East, involves the horrors that Desert Storm—brief and surgical as it was—visited upon American troops, more than 650,000 strong during the operation. Indeed *Courage Under Fire* can be interpreted as a manifestly dystopic view of the first Gulf War, not so much because it critically scrutinizes the larger U.S. geopolitical agenda there (that is never confronted) but because it dramatizes the myriad personal aftershocks emanating from the war. At this point Zwick's film seems to borrow heavily from those Vietnam-era pictures that explored massive postwar traumas extending across the battlefield to the home front. We know, of course, that Captain Walden faced her own series of nightmares: insubordination and possible mutiny among her troops, deadly threats from surrounding Iraqi forces, death in combat. At the same time, Colonel Serling himself—appointed to research the merits of Walden's medal nomination—winds up with his own terrifying postcombat dysfunctions, including the knowledge that he issued orders that led to the deaths of U.S. troops, a mistake that haunts him throughout the picture. Serling becomes a basket-case alcoholic increasingly estranged from his family and is so driven by guilt that he eventually decides to inform the parents of a soldier killed by his tank's friendly fire that he was the one culpable (a page taken from Ron Kovic's saga in *Born on the Fourth of July*). Meanwhile, Specialist Ilario develops his own combat-generated terrors leading to drug addiction while Sergeant Monfriez, driven to insanity by his extreme confrontations with Walden before she is killed, winds up committing suicide after being reduced to a nearly catatonic state. Finally, we are introduced to another Desert Storm veteran who is dying of cancer, presumably one of the thousands of victims of Gulf War syndrome who had been exposed to either depleted uranium (DU) or toxic substances released during U.S. military attacks on Iraqi targets. The syndrome has never been officially acknowledged by the Pentagon despite widely reported health consequences of DU and other poisonous agents that troops encountered during the Gulf War.

In the end, Zwick's film sidesteps the broader U.S. political and military role in the Persian Gulf while framing the horrors of warfare within a distinctly

*American* context—a partial view to be sure, but one hardly consonant with the good-war theme. In fact everything ultimately revolves around the question, what happens to U.S. troops under fire, and what are the psychological consequences? One result of constructing the narrative in this fashion is that American lives are emphatically valorized over Iraqi lives, a dynamic shown repeatedly as faceless Iraqi soldiers are blown away like so many insects. Viewed in its totality, *Courage Under Fire* contains elements of the combat spectacle: glorification of battlefield heroism, demonization of the Arab enemy, a powerful glimpse into the terrors of warfare, and depictions of postwar traumas endemic to any battlefield experience. Throughout all this, as in the case of the Vietnam-era movies, the geographical setting itself (Iraq) serves largely as a simple cinematic backdrop for the multiple U.S.-centered war dramas.

The second major film set in the Gulf War, *Three Kings*, deals only peripherally with battlefield action. Russell approaches it more as a caper movie in the desert, a kind of action-comedy with a military backdrop; little about the U.S. military mission is regarded as sacrosanct. A fast-moving, offbeat picture, it sets up many targets: CNN's Christianne Amanpour, the Hussein regime, the first Bush administration, Iraqi elite forces, the greed of American renegade soldiers, the army hierarchy itself. Like *Courage Under Fire*, Russell's picture departs significantly from the good-war formula while simultaneously highlighting central elements of it. By virtue of its quirkiness and its refusal to validate the claims of Desert Storm with straightforward battle sequences, *Three Kings* distances the viewer from the official moral and political rationale for U.S. military intervention, which included not only freeing Kuwait from Iraqi occupation (something Hussein was prepared to do *without* war) but also enforcing international law and removing Hussein from power.

In Russell's work three American soldiers (played by Mark Wahlberg, Ice Cube, and Spike Jonze) discover a map leading to millions of dollars in stolen Kuwaiti gold bullion. Upon learning that these men possess what is in effect a treasure map, opportunistic Special Forces Captain Archie Gates (George Clooney) assumes command of the renegade group, and the four embark on a clandestine foray across the Iraq desert to find and seize the stolen bullion for themselves. As its *Kelly's Heroes*–style action unfolds, the group encounters anti-Hussein Shiite rebels who help transport the gold in exchange for safe passage to Iran. Units of the Iraqi army offer resistance and are repulsed with ease by the Americans, and the group nearly manages to flee with the gold before facing a terrible moral dilemma: whether to assist the Iraqi rebels, presented here as pathetic, innocent, unarmed victims who desperately need military help to escape, at the risk of losing their fortune. The Americans of course decide to aid the rebels but are soon apprehended by U.S. forces at the border, where they trade their gold for both their own freedom (from harsh army discipline) and that of the rebels. While the renegade soldiers emerge with their honor intact, the U.S. Army is shown to be shamelessly *dishonorable* in its callous attitude toward the refugees as well as the breakaway group. At this point *Three Kings* attempts to expose the shallowness and duplicity of Desert Storm, notably its policy toward Iraqi insurgents whom the United States supposedly promised to help overthrow Hussein. At the same time, the picture exhibits recognizable features of the combat genre, showing U.S. troops victorious over every challenge by virtue of their cool, efficient, professional manner in readily dispatching a hapless, demonic enemy. When a soldier expresses fear to Captain Gates over an upcoming battle against the Republican Guards, Gates explains, "The way this thing works is you can do this thing you're scared shitless of and then you get the courage after you do it." In any event, the film depicts no overt manifestations of American battlefield weakness.

In other ways too *Three Kings* contains narratives usually identified with the good-war model. Although superficially it is something of an antiwar movie that erases certain damaging anti-Arab stereotypes found in standard pictures about the Middle East—we do indeed encounter some dignified, friendly Iraqis—the larger portrait is far less sympathetic. Thus in the first scene, in which Russell sets the tone for the entire picture, a U.S. soldier shoots and kills an Iraqi soldier who refuses to lay down his weapon (a bizarre suicidal act for anyone surrendering in combat). "Congratulations, my man, you just got yourself a raghead," exclaims one of his buddies. At another point Chief Elgin orders a soldier to stop using racist epithets to refer to Iraqis, but when the soldier expresses confusion, he is told to use "towel head" and "camel jockey" instead of "dune coon" and "sand nigger," the implication being, of course, that these terms of derision were fairly standard (and thus acceptable) among U.S. military personnel. More tellingly, throughout the film the Americans intimidate and blow away locals at every turn. The brutal killings are meant to contain an element of humor. In fact the Iraqis are treated with as much contempt as the myriad racist terms would suggest, undercutting Russell's professed antiwar intentions for *Three Kings*. At several points in the film Iraqis come across as inept primitives whose main role is to serve as cannon fodder for both Hussein and the U.S. military. As in most good-war pictures, the villains are shown as either completely unskilled or cowardly, or both, on the battlefield. For much of the picture the renegade Americans barge around the country as if they owned it—an aspiration which, as it turns out, would be fully realized at the time of the second Gulf War and occupation.

Media construction of events and manipulation of popular consciousness have become integral to American political culture, and this lies at the center of all recent U.S. military interventions. Increasingly, media involvement in government lies, myths, and distortions has contributed vitally to legitimation of war as a means to advance U.S. global interests. TV, radio, and print journalism have been central to this process, routinely carrying forward those false discourses, bolstering the dominant ideological framework, and failing to critically investigate the claims and pretensions of government and military officials. Media culture has evolved into a propaganda apparatus, especially in the realm of international concerns, where corporate and Pentagon interests are able to create their own version of "reality" for an American public already inclined to follow the prevailing discourses. In many ways, as Neal Gabler writes in *Life: The Movie,* the boundaries separating reality and fiction, actual events and media constructions, have broken down as the society of the spectacle comes to dominate the public sphere.[2] Recent films dramatizing this theme include *Bob Roberts* (1992), *Bulworth* (1996), *Wag the Dog* (1997), *The Truman Show* (1998), *Pleasantville* (1998), and *Enemy of the State* (1998). While reflecting the enormous growth of media culture in the United States, such cinematic fare demonstrates that widespread fear and paranoia are gripping the public, especially with respect to global issues.[3]

Barry Levinson's comedic *Wag the Dog* is probably the most germane of these films insofar as it dramatizes the way that media manipulation can serve two functions simultaneously: deflect attention away from a president in crisis and justify U.S. military operations against a manufactured foe patently falsely charged with transgressions. The movie features Robert De Niro as Conrad Brean, a political media mastermind who has the psychological will to impose his version of truth on the American people and is ruthless in his enforcement of power. Dustin Hoffman plays Stanley Motss, a Hollywood producer hired to enable the chief executive to survive the mounting storm engulfing him, reminiscent of the Clinton sex scandal throughout 1998. Brean and Motss team up by staging a "war" against tiny Albania, which, overnight, emerges as an imminent threat to U.S. national security. When that ploy stalls, the two create a phony war hero based on Larry Beinhart's 1994 novel *American Hero,* which intimates that the first Gulf War was largely a staged media event based on "atrocities" that never happened (for example, Iraqis yanking babies out of incubators in Kuwait) that could seduce an ignorant, provincial, intensely nationalistic public. As Ray Pratt writes: "*Wag the Dog* cynically illustrates how political illusion-makers could hoodwink a public only dimly aware of distant events and totally dependent on television news reports for knowledge of events."[4] The media skills of Brean and Motss were indeed so honed they were able to dupe an entire nation.

The military actions of the Clinton administration, at a time when the president was faced with a sex scandal much like the one depicted in *Wag the Dog,* could easily be interpreted along these lines. There were stepped-up bombings of Iraq in 1998 to face a new Gulf "crisis," followed by bombing raids in Sudan and Afghanistan. More to the point was the nonstop, seventy-nine-day U.S.-NATO aerial campaign against Yugoslavia in spring 1999, an operation justified by extensive reports (later shown to be false) of Serb atrocities in the form of "ethnic cleansing" and "genocide." At the time of these bombings *Wag the Dog* was routinely played on Belgrade TV, another reflection of the dialectical intersection of media culture and actual events. Indeed U.S.

intervention in the Balkans was preceded by a sustained, expensive public-relations effort in which Serbs were demonized as modern-day Nazis, a pattern that would be replayed in the lead-up to the second Gulf War. It should be emphasized that media manipulation of this sort, duly taken up by the film industry itself, cuts across the thin ideological line dividing liberals and conservatives, Democrats and Republicans. In this context the notion of a "liberal" Hollywood consensus extends only so far.

## New Rules of Engagement

The 1990s witnessed a resurgence of U.S. imperial ambitions opened up by the end of the cold war and given military articulation by the Desert Storm onslaught, which, among other things, established a durable American presence in the Middle East. In the absence of a Soviet counterweight, U.S. military actions—a continuous element of the permanent war system since World War II—took a more aggressive turn, reflected in the neocons' drive to remap the region while further extending U.S. global hegemony. At the same time, with the ebbing of the Soviet and Communist threats, new enemies would have to be framed as the political target: terrorists, rogue states, Arabs, drug traffickers, or some combination of these. To solidify these targets in the popular consciousness, to establish a firm grounding for Pax Americana, the media culture would emerge as a linchpin in the system of mass ideological legitimation. The rightward shift in the corporate media over this time span made them friendlier to such political demands. Widely viewed films that appeared from the early 1990s on typically fit this paradigm of U.S. imperial aims, whatever their setting, specific geopolitical focus, or designated enemy. For Hollywood, this meant—in conventional good-war fashion—that combat narratives would revolve around an eternal struggle between the forces of savagery (Arabs, Muslims, Serbs) and those of civilization (Anglo-American powers), with the demonized Others stereotyped as backward, fanatical, barbaric. As in the case of the Persian Gulf, the new settings from Yugoslavia to Somalia would provide the dramatic backdrop for the display of U.S. high-tech weaponry, ultrapatriotism, and masculine heroism. Excluding those movies specifically focused on terrorism during this period, we emphasize three major works: John Moore's *Behind Enemy Lines* (2001), William Friedkin's *Rules of Engagement* (2000), and Tony Scott's *Black Hawk Down* (2002).

President Bush's New World Order was conceived as an integrated global system dominated by one superpower, the United States. Independent centers of power were regarded with deep suspicion by Washington elites. If Desert Storm was the first major salvo in the new phase of imperial expansion, other interventions would quickly follow: Somalia, Yugoslavia, Afghanistan, and Iraq again, with threats against Syria, Iran, and North Korea to follow. Justification for military action varied, from "humanitarian" goals to curbing weapons of mass destruction to the war on terrorism, with the supposed commitment to democratic ideals always a handy rationale. In the case of the Balkans, the U.S.-NATO campaign was actually motivated by long-standing economic and geopolitical interests in southern Europe and, by extension, central Asia and the Middle East. A fierce aerial bombardment was intended to break the last holdout against full-scale corporate globalization in the region, epitomized by the Serb regime under Milosevic, which had been charged with genocide and other atrocities in the midst of a prolonged civil war. As Diana Johnstone writes: "The bombing of Yugoslavia marked the turning point in the expansion of U.S. military power."[5] Indeed all the features of U.S. militarism that would later surface at the time of the Bush II war on Iraq were already present in Clinton's war on Serbia in 1999: a preemptive strike, sidestepping of the UN Charter and international law prohibiting acts of military aggression, evasion of genuine diplomatic efforts, and phony claims about awesome "threats" posed by a designated rogue state.

The one-sided and devastating U.S.-NATO "war" against Serbia—like Desert Storm, more a simple *assault* than anything resembling military conflict—came directly (or so it seemed) from the story lines of *Wag the Dog*, except that the fictitious justifications for war were repeated so endlessly that they gained strong resonance with the American public. Questions regarding whether the United States (or any other power) had the legal, political, or moral *right* to intervene militarily were never taken up by the institutional elites or media pundits. Nor were issues of what groups might have been responsible for specific acts of violence in the long and complex Yugoslav civil war, itself in great measure provoked by Western powers operating in their own national self-interest. In fact the humanitarian pretext for intervention was severely undercut by the decades-long U.S. record of violating human rights throughout its own considerable sphere of influence. Moreover, the evidence reveals that Serb atrocities during the civil strife were no greater than those of the Croatians and Bosnian Muslims (both governed by essentially fascist regimes) and were surely minimal when compared with the U.S.-engineered bombardments that destroyed the entire Serb infrastructure. It turns out that the real "threat" to U.S. national interests is not imminent military attack but rather any *political* force that stands in the way of the country's capacity to assert hegemonic economic and geopolitical influence—and here the Milosevic regime (twice duly elected) was one of the few impediments remaining from Communist Eastern Europe.

The first mainstream Hollywood film set amid the Balkan conflict, *Behind Enemy Lines,* was released two months early to take advantage of the post-9/11 patriotic mood sweeping the United States. It was expected that a film dramatizing the remarkable courage and resourcefulness of an American navy pilot maneuvering toward escape in a savagely hostile environment would be gripping to mass audiences, and it was. With an all-star cast, the picture achieved tremendous box-office success. The work of first-time director Moore, it is a fast-paced, entertaining movie that owes just as much to the action-adventure as to the combat genre. It is loosely based on the actual experience of an air force pilot, Lieutenant Scott O'Grady, who was shot down in Bosnian territory and later rescued by U.S. forces; given cinematic definition by Moore, the episode is transformed into an action-packed, high-tech fantasy.

The seemingly indestructible hero of *Behind Enemy Lines* is Chris Burnett (Owen Wilson), who finds himself scrambling for survival after his F-18 fighter is shot down during what started as a routine Christmas Eve reconnaissance mission over snow-covered Bosnian territory. Burnett has taken off from the carrier USS *Vinson,* commanded by Admiral Leslie Reigert (Gene Hackman). With his copilot (Gabriel Macht), Burnett takes several aerial photos of Serb killing fields. Once downed, he must face a brutal Serb tracker (Vladimir Maskov) bent on terminating the U.S. mission after summarily executing the copilot. With Burnett desperately scurrying across dangerous enemy terrain, Admiral Reigert moves to order a carrier-based rescue operation but is quickly overruled by his NATO superior (Joaquim de Almeida), shown to be so coldly obsessed with likely political fallout from U.S. military provocations that he is willing to sacrifice the individual flier. At serious risk to his own command and career, Reigert defies the NATO orders by insisting that the rescue operations be set in motion. Meanwhile, Burnett is forced to scramble to a rendezvous point deep in Bosnian Serb territory where he continues to evade his pursuers, depicted here as quintessential Nazi-style villains. How he is able to survive and finally get rescued defies even the most audacious imagination: running furtively and relentlessly across the frozen terrain, lacking even minimum tools of survival, dodging withering automatic-weapons fire at virtually every turn. Never has an escape maneuver been presented as so harrowing—or so miraculous. Indeed the patriotic action motif of Moore's film achieves dramatic articulation through the Promethean efforts of no fewer than three layers of heroes: Burnett, emerging intact from his nightmarish escapades; Admiral Reigert, who sacrifices his career to save one individual U.S. flier; and of course the copter-based rescue troops who face ceaseless enemy fire as they save Burnett from the barbaric Serbs at the last possible moment.

One can identify several crisscrossing messages throughout *Behind Enemy Lines* that, to varying degrees, resonate with the imperatives of U.S. foreign policy. The narrative itself embraces virtually every cliché known to the combat genre. It winds up questioning the very efficacy of NATO peacekeeping operations in the Balkans, demonstrating that U.S. military authority is to be valorized above all else. As might be predicted, recurrent images of the Serbs as horrible demons serve to justify, at least post hoc, the U.S. decision to militarily intervene in 1999. The movie contains high-tech representations of American troops prevailing over the Nazi-like, but ultimately inept, Serb forces. All this is combined with the familiar happy ending in which U.S. troops save the day just when the rescue mission seems destined to fail—consonant with the well-established combat formula. *Behind Enemy Lines* concludes to choruses of uplifting rock music as the troops return to the USS *Vinson* amid resounding cheers from the crew, a replay of scenes from *Top Gun*.

Friedkin's *Rules of Engagement* is set broadly in the Middle East, this time in Yemen, but the combat narrative represents something more universal: the potential consequences of an expanded U.S. global military presence within the New World Order. Awesome military power accompanied by economic and political hegemony easily translates into a combination of local rebellion, blowback, and excessive use of armed force that subverts conventional rules of military conduct. In this case, the events are adapted from a story by Secretary of the Navy James Webb, but they could occur anywhere the United States maintains a strong armed presence, or where its embassies are protected by military detachments. The action centers on two marine officers, Colonel Terry Childers (Samuel L. Jackson) and Colonel Hayes Hodges (Tommy Lee Jones). An early flashback scene depicts the two young officers in a deadly firefight in Vietnam in 1968. Hodges finds himself pinned down by Vietcong machine-gun fire and is saved by Childers, who kills an enemy soldier and then gets the Vietcong commander to call off the attack. The story then abruptly shifts to Camp Lejeune, North Carolina, to Hodges's retirement party in 1996. Reflecting on the changed (post-Vietnam, post-cold war) situation, Childers says to Hodges, "You ain't missin nothin', Hodge. It's a whole new ball game: no friends, no enemies, no front, no rear, no victories, no defeats, no mama, no papa. We're orphans out here." In fact Childers's refrain is more revealing of the restless military mind, always searching for battles to be won over terrible enemies, than of global circumstances that would soon produce incendiary conflict.

From Camp Lejeune the action moves to Yemen, where the U.S. Embassy is surrounded by an angry mob of protesters: the conditions quickly turn ugly, whereupon the ambassador (Ben Kingsley) demands to be evacuated. The marines send Colonel Childers and his contingent in three copters to rescue the ambassador and his family, but once the copters arrive on the scene, the crowd turns even more hostile and snipers begin firing at the marines. Having evacuated the ambassador and his family amid a hail of bullets, Childers crawls along the embassy roof to assist a fallen man when the crowd suddenly breaks out automatic weapons and escalates its attack on the Americans. In retaliation, Childers orders his troops to open fire on the crowd, resulting in eighty-three deaths and more than a hundred wounded (all civilians). This touches off an explosive international crisis for the U.S. government in a context where its Middle East presence has already generated widespread outrage. Eager to get the United States off the hook, national security adviser William Sokal (Bruce Greenwood) sets up Childers for court-martial and assigns Major Mark Biggs (Guy Pearce) to prosecute a case in which rules of military engagement are said to have been seriously breached. Childers hires his old friend Hodges as defense attorney despite indications he may not be qualified for the job. Hodges travels to Yemen and observes the heart of the underground jihadist network. His investigation uncovers embassy video cameras that probably recorded the whole episode. Hoping to retrieve tapes that would have shown Childers acting in self-defense, Hodges learns that the national security official destroyed the tape once it surfaced in Washington. In the end, of course, Hodges as everyman lawyer rises to the occasion, his courtroom skills more than adequate to outduel the scheming but inept feds, and Childers is basically exonerated despite lingering questions about his excessive use of force.

What are we to make of the narrative established by Friedkin? The problems with *Rules of Engagement* are many, beginning with the stereotyping of Arabs as villains who, in this movie, possess absolutely no redeeming qualities. As Jack Shaheen writes, this is one of the most anti-Arab films ever shot, and that is saying a good deal: it validates nearly every cliché about Middle Eastern politics.[6] The crowd of protesters is shown to be full of venomous, evil-looking Others intent upon making life miserable for innocent, businesslike Americans simply trying to go about their jobs—marines no less than the embassy staff. Filled with veiled women, screaming and gesturing men, and out-of-control children, the mob appears onscreen as nothing more than a vehicle of hatred and destruction. Some Arabs in the mob have weapons and begin shooting; even the children are presented as potential enemies. Nowhere do we find any suggestion that these might be human beings with actual *reasons* to protest. Once the firing starts and a marine is hit, Childers decides to respond, yelling, "Waste the motherfuckers." In the massacre that follows, we are left with the conclusion that the mob, having initiated violence for no good reason, deserves its fate. We see that Childers ultimately behaved correctly—after all, American lives had to be saved and these were just a bunch of anti-American killers who merit absolutely no sympathy. Within the cinematic stereotyping we see large numbers of stock demons ready to be slaughtered, a motif with deep roots in the Hollywood combat Western.

At the same time, *Rules of Engagement* follows elements of the *Rambo* tradition in pitting the military against the government and setting up the latter as archvillain in its sleazy, dishonest, manipulative conduct after the embassy catastrophe. The U.S. Marines and their own code of behavior in the midst of crisis are valorized over civilian officials who simply want to scapegoat the military to defuse an international incident. It is the military that stands victimized after its Middle East ordeal: falsely accused, deceived, its mission subverted, blocked in its all-important freedom to act. In other words, much as in the revisionist Vietnam-era movies, the military is forced to endure yet another "stab in the back" scenario. Here too we are treated to one more happy cinematic ending when Colonel Childers and his attorney, Colonel Hodges, get the best of the scheming government authorities as Childers is finally set free. With

Childers's dramatic but hardly unexpected courtroom victory, not only do the armed forces wind up standing tall but still another familiar combat-picture theme is affirmed: strong male camaraderie between Childers and Hodges, depicted with emotional power in the final victory celebration before the two plan a fishing trip together. This bonding, after a period of intense stress and conflict between the two, signifies a convergence of enduring virtues—patriotism, efficacy of military action, marine solidarity, brotherhood shaped by combat (in the field and in the courtroom).

The film's representation of events at the U.S. Embassy raises a series of other problems. While the protest gathering and outbreak of violence at such a locale is quite conceivable given mounting anti-U.S. sentiment across the Middle East, the massive response by Childers and his marine detachment seems highly questionable, even allowing for a degree of cinematic license. The response was not only immediate and total but also was so lethal as to leave all but a few civilian protesters dead or wounded. Are we to believe that there were no alternatives to the massacre? Could not a few marines have shot rounds into the air to disperse the crowd, a routine procedure in such cases? Failing this, would it not have been possible to target a few of the protesters—if possible, those brandishing weapons—after which the mob surely would have broken up? More puzzling, is it conceivable that U.S. Marines have no guidelines whatsoever for armed response in such conditions? In the end, Friedkin's narrative leaves the viewer with the idea that this bloody massacre—a war crime by any definition—was a natural and legitimate mode of response, a notion reinforced by Childers's exoneration at court-martial. And this makes all the more sense if the demonized Arabs outside the embassy are shown to be lacking any coherent motivation.

Finally, *Rules of Engagement* conveys no message congruent with what it seems to promise: a cinematic reflection on ethical dilemmas related to certain lines of military conduct, in this case responses to an angry, threatening crowd made up almost entirely of civilians. What indeed *are* the rules of engagement for the circumstances presented in the film? Can the mass slaughter of civilians *ever* be justified according to canons of international law, or indeed simple military convention? By focusing on the deceitful villainy of government officials and the exoneration of Childers, the story completely sidesteps such crucial issues. The trial itself is nothing more than a dramatic flourish, its outcome predetermined. All this is unfortunate given how actual international events have raised anew questions regarding military rules of conduct, notably in the context of U.S. armed interventions in the Middle East and elsewhere. From early 2002 onward we have growing numbers of reports of U.S. military operations leading to huge civilian casualties, torture and killing of prisoners of war, and widespread atrocities at American-run prisons in Afghanistan, Iraq, and Guantanamo. In these cases the problem of moral and political responsibility is apparently just the opposite of what is shown in *Rules of Engagement*: the government has failed to hold the military personnel accountable for these violations and abuses while permitting growth of a culture of impunity within the armed forces. In other words, far from being overzealous, the U.S. government has done far too little to prevent massacres, atrocities, and other violations of international law. Indeed it has been possible to trace policies allowing for such outrages to the very summit of political power.

If *Rules of Engagement* is based upon fictitious episodes in an imagined but nonetheless believable setting, Scott's *Black Hawk Down*—a hugely popular film inspired by Mark Bowden's best seller—depicts actual events surrounding the disastrous U.S. intervention in Somalia in October 1993. A darkly atmospheric picture starring Ewan McGregor, Sam Shepard, Josh Hartnett, and Tom Sizemore, it offers the viewer rapid-paced images of urban combat spanning more than two hours, filled with scenes of incredible mayhem, entrapment, helicopters crisscrossing the skies, and horrific bloodshed. This is one of the most intense, if not realistic, combat movies ever shot, set in a capital city (Mogadishu) where battle lines are never firmly drawn. Scott's prologue refers to how the U.S. humanitarian mission quickly became an exercise in nation-building that would entail destroying a network of warlords that had prevented UN-sponsored aid from reaching hungry Somalis in the midst of civil war. At his base outside Mogadishu, U.S. Army general William Garrison (played with a bizarre sense of detachment by Shepard) interrogates a high-level militia member about Somali warlord Mohammed Farah Aidid, declares "This is genocide," and then orders his men to swoop down on the city and kidnap Aidid, ostensibly to achieve humanitarian goals. The American troops, numbering only 140 but confident of quick victory over what they see as ragtag gangs of primitives, quickly run into trouble. The mission spins out of control when elements of Aidid's powerful militia begin a fierce counterattack, shooting down two UH-60 Black Hawk helicopters and forcing U.S. soldiers into a hasty, desperate retreat, which is brilliantly framed by Scott. The sight of injured and bloodied comrades leads additional troops into the morass, and the tragedy is compounded. Many are trapped and out of ammunition; others are eventually pushed back into the confines of their own base. In perhaps the most intense fighting since Vietnam, 18 Americans were killed while the Somali death count probably rose to well over 1,000—a catastrophe barely recognized at the end of the film. A shocked President Clinton removed the U.S. troops from Mogadishu, General Garrison resigned, and the warlord Aidid was soon assassinated by one of his own men.

*Black Hawk Down* shows the U.S. military to be remarkably tenacious and courageous in battling against overwhelming odds—an essentially correct rendering, by all accounts. We further see an American operation in a poor East African nation centered around sophisticated high-tech warfare with electronic command centers, the latest in weaponry and communications, and of course the omnipotent Black Hawk flying machines equipped with fearsome gunnery. The

U.S. technowar apparatus stands in total contrast with the rather outmoded equipment of Third World Somalis, whose combat infrastructure is seen as relatively backward. As is often the case, however, it is the more lightly armed forces fighting on their own turf that prevail. In the film, the Somalis—labeled "skinnies" by American troops—are depicted as simply frenzied, brutal villains without any apparent sense of human community or political motives. We see their sadistic cruelty toward the only American soldier captured during combat. We never learn why they have such fierce hatred of the United States, as if the anti-American feelings came from a nationalist mania or ideological disease rather than understandable opposition to the U.S. intrusion into a local civil war. Here the parallels to later U.S. military intervention in Afghanistan are rather striking.

There are other problems with *Black Hawk Down*: U.S. troops did not behave quite so honorably or heroically as the film indicates, if we are to believe eyewitness accounts from Somalis present throughout the battle. One of them, a Mrs. Weheliya, described how she and her family were taken hostage by Americans trying to rescue men from a downed helicopter, their captors warning sternly that everyone would be killed unless the militia forces retreated. "We were clinging to each other," she recalled, "we were terrified."[7] Of course U.S. officials never acknowledged such episodes, nor did anything remotely like this enter into Scott's film. In fact, leaving aside General Garrison's command failures, everything in the picture merely reinforces a positive image of the Army Rangers, other U.S. troops, and the daring copter pilots. Yet if American forces were such paragons of skill and bravery, why the catastrophic battlefield failures despite great military superiority—and why the persistent reports of atrocities against civilians? What version of history do we believe, eyewitness reports or filmmaking imagery framed around a Hollywood patriotic consensus and searching for the widest possible audience? The creative figures behind *Black Hawk Down* naturally disavow any political or nationalistic intent. As screenwriter Eric Roth insisted: "For me, the film is less about patriotism and flag-waving. It's a study in heroism under fire, by a couple of soldiers who are outmanned and in over their heads. I found it stirring and, frankly, slightly apolitical."[8] The film might be everything Roth says it is, but apolitical? In reality every film—those dealing with U.S. military actions abroad perhaps most of all—cannot help but reflect the values and beliefs of producers, directors, and writers working within the contours of the movie industry; to imagine otherwise would be terribly naive, if not disingenuous.

## Hollywood and Terrorism

Many years before the events of 9/11 terrorism was already a central focus of Hollywood filmmaking, one reflection within popular culture of the increasing levels of political violence in American society, in U.S. foreign policy, and around the globe. Terrorist actions, both state and nonstate, have increased in both number and destructive power since the 1960s, spanning such diverse regions as North America, the Middle East, Asia, and Latin America. Terrorism has become a vital source of narratives, fantasies, and myths that contribute so much to highly entertaining cinema, with its international intrigue, exotic settings, graphic violence, and the putative conflict between good and evil. Scenes of terrorist and counterterrorist activity have a natural cinematic appeal, above all in the United States where the gun culture, civic violence, crime sprees, and the flourishing war economy shape the landscape. The attacks by Al Qaeda on the World Trade Center and the Pentagon inevitably heightened public fascination with terrorism, and this helped inspire a new cycle of films in which endless graphic images of on-screen terrorism capture elements of real-life terrorism, nowadays with the threat of weapons of mass destruction lurking in the background. The rise of jihadic terrorism largely associated with the Middle East, with its dispersed networks, sinister leaders and operatives, and extended international reach, challenges U.S. geopolitical domination while also helping to legitimate it. And President Bush's war on terror, driven as much by the U.S. strategy to remap the Middle East as by the events of 9/11, serves as the perfect backdrop for film industry productions of high-tech spectacles, which have evolved into the major staple of a violent media culture.

Within a New World Order shaped by U.S. economic and military power, both terrorism and the war on terrorism appear to have few limits in time and space, given how immersed these phenomena are in the global dialectic of militarism and terrorism. Antagonism to U.S. hegemony takes many forms, but political violence of some sort is endemic to a neoliberal global order enforced by the largest war machine ever. One outcome of specifically jihadic terrorism, however, is to strengthen this dialectic, as the post-9/11 situation amply shows, favoring a milieu in which an aggressive neocon foreign policy could gain wide political currency during the Bush ascendancy. Militant anti-U.S. sentiment in the Arab-Muslim world has spread as one manifestation of blowback against growing U.S. militarism. Against this reality, media culture upholds a simplistic "madman" thesis of global terrorism, its purveyors obsessed with small pockets of evildoers—larger-than-life villains like Osama bin Laden, Saddam Hussein, and Slobodan Milosevic—prepared to destroy Western values. The main political and media discourses stress an epic struggle between (Western, democratic, modern) "civilization" and (jihadic, Muslim, primitive) "barbarism"—a self-serving, hypocritical grand narrative that sees political violence as a monopoly of cultural/national Others whose modus operandi, mostly local attacks, contrasts with the institutional military actions of powerful governments launching long-distance missile strikes and bombing raids. The post-9/11 shift occurs at a time when the larger American political culture has grown more insular and provincial—a trend that owes much to the workings of the corporate media system.

The problem for cinema, as for politics, is that within the prevailing ideology the "Middle East" now exists as a quasi-mystical entity largely outside time and space, a convenient source of dark fears and threats. This kind of ideological bias shaped public understanding of the region (as well as terrorism) for many years in advance of 9/11, reflected in the new wave of Middle East–centered terrorist films beginning in the early 1980s. Patterns of terrorist activity were changing at this time, toward a new phase of dispersed global operations that differ markedly from earlier forms. As the *9/11 Commission Report* of 2004 states: "A new breed of Islamic terrorist has emerged from the downtrodden societies of the Middle East. Attached to no nation but infiltrating many, its strategy is to inflict mass casualties and their aim is to attack no less than the heart of Western civilization. The preeminent practitioner of modern terrorism is Osama bin Laden, and in the space of a decade he has managed to draw the United States into a declaration of global war: new tools of counterterrorism, more aggressive strategies and tactics—and an unprecedented focus on the threat of devastating violence in the American homeland."[9] While much of this statement is false or grossly distorted, it does stand as the overriding *perception* ruling elites have of the new terrorist challenge, while the "tools" and "focus" mentioned in the report obviously extend to the media culture.

Hollywood's fascination with terrorism—at least its foreign variant—actually goes back several decades, to the World War II era if not earlier. One classic of this genre is Alfred Hitchcock's *Saboteur* (1942), featuring a worker-hero who stumbles into a clandestine terrorist cell of American Nazi fifth columnists planning to sabotage aircraft factories, hydroelectric dams, and naval warships. Hitchcock based his dramatic structure—the bombing of a U.S. ship—on historical events surrounding the mysterious burning of the USS *Lafayette,* an ocean liner being refitted as a warship in 1942. The film contains a shot of the badly damaged *Lafayette* lying on its side at a Manhattan dock. Hitchcock turns to Charles Tobin (Otto Kruger), a wealthy businessman obsessed with gaining political power, to lead the saboteurs, who include a rich dowager (Alma Kruger) and several mid- and lower-level operatives. Their stated purpose is to create "a more profitable type of government" in the United States modeled on European fascism since, as Tobin proclaims, "the competence of totalitarian nations is much higher than our own. They get things done." And Tobin would love nothing better than to install himself as dictator: "Power, yes, I want it as much as you want your comfort or your job or that girl." In this wartime narrative filled with crude stereotypes, it is clear that Tobin would be ready to have thousands of people killed in order to satisfy his great power obsession. The fascist monsters, taking every advantage of constitutional freedoms, win a few victories but are summarily vanquished in the end. *Saboteur* reminds the audience of a familiar motif endemic to terrorism: evil can surface virtually anywhere, often in the most unexpected places. This narrative would reappear with a vengeance in Hitchcock's next film,

*Shadow of a Doubt* (1943), and would become a staple in dozens of future pictures dealing with terrorism.

If the 1950s saw the emergence of a cycle of cold war and sci-fi movies influenced by the classic noir thriller, the 1960s ushered in a new phase of terrorist-action films like the early James Bond movies, which fixated on shadowy terrorist groups out to subvert Western interests. Villains featured in such films as *Dr. No* (1962), *Goldfinger* (1964), *Thunderball* (1965), and *You Only Live Twice* (1967) were easily disposed of by the shrewd and wisecracking Bond, though he often had to rely on the resources of British intelligence. In contrast to fanatical ideologues later identified with Arab or Muslim terrorism, Bond's enemies were colder, more politically calculating figures working for the World Communist Conspiracy (like Dr. No). In Terrence Young's *Thunderball* we have a fiendish, swarthy terrorist (played by Adolpho Celi) who plans to detonate a stolen nuclear warhead unless he receives $280 million in ransom. Bond (Sean Connery) thwarts this plot thanks to clever tactics and his cool demeanor under great duress. His deadpan humor, the film's nonstop action sequences, and sophisticated underwater special effects make *Thunderball* an entertaining spectacle even if the plot is not remotely believable. Compared to later terrorist episodes, Young's handling of nuclear blackmail seems almost incidental to the ongoing repartee between Bond and special agents on both sides. The notion that a terrorist could get hold of a nuclear device and use it for blackmail, however, something barely thinkable in 1965, would be considered quite feasible by the 1990s—in real life as in cinema. Whereas the terrorist phenomenon was an exotic narrative device in the 1960s, within three decades far more cataclysmic scenarios would become prophetic, and by 9/11 the earlier fantasies morphed into imaginable nightmares.

By the late 1980s, with the cold war in its death throes, cinematic terrorism moved onto new ground, focusing on the Middle East, where Arab/Muslim militants were locked in battle with Israel and, to a lesser extent at the time, the United States. These groups replaced Communists and kindred time-honored demons as larger-than-life screen villains. Many such films, for example the *Delta Force* series (from 1986 to 1991), were made in Israel or with Israeli financing and/or backing. The terrorist enemy was seen as crude, semi-civilized, shady, violent, beyond redemption, capable of horrendous crimes—traits making them quite suitable for extermination. Lee Marvin, cast in the first movie of the series, *The Delta Force,* is quoted as saying: "I like what the picture says. . . . Audiences love to see the bad guy get it. We start blowing up everybody. That's good old American revenge."[10] In *Delta Force 3,* essentially a replay of the first episode, Palestinians are shown as nuclear terrorists ready to blow up Miami, assisted in their evil plot by a crazed sheikh. Shouting "Allah Akbar," a terrorist attempts to explode a nuclear bomb but is thwarted at the last moment. In Roman Polanski's *Frantic* (1988), starring Harrison Ford, several drunken Arab kidnappers set out to obtain stolen devices for triggering a nuclear explosion. Commenting on these and related films, Douglas Kellner observes that such harshly racist caricatures of Arabs were hauntingly similar to earlier fascist and Nazi depictions of Jews in European popular culture during the 1920s and 1930s.[11]

One departure from Hollywood's Middle East obsession at this time was John McTiernan's *Die Hard* (1988), the first in a trilogy of terrorist action films starring Bruce Willis as overworked New York policeman John McClane. In the premier, McClane travels to Los Angeles at Christmastime to visit his estranged wife and two daughters when he comes across a group of German terrorists led by Hans Gruber (Alan Rickman), who commandeer an office building and take hostage employees of the Nakatoni Corporation. The terrorists patiently wait while a computer expert unlocks a code that would make available some $600 million. McClane slips out of the party unnoticed and, armed with only a handgun, begins a counterattack that rapidly subdues the Germans. In these scenes the German villains evoke images of World War II Nazis, while McClane's one-man show of brute force sets new standards for the ultramasculine heroism typical of the modern action-adventure. McTiernan weaves together elements of terrorism and economic sabotage at a time when U.S. corporations were facing ever-stiffening competition from Europe and Japan. Renny Harlin's *Die Hard 2* (1990) sought to capitalize on its precursor's box-office success, this time with McClane transferring to the Los Angeles Police Department after meeting his wife (Bonnie Bedelia) at Dulles Airport, where terrorists—working for a Latin American dictator resembling Manuel Noriega—brazenly seize control of the facilities. McClane swings into action to crush the pathetic, one-dimensional villains.

Back to the Middle East, Lewis Teague's *Navy Seals* (1990) revolves around the theft by Arabs, or Palestinians, of U.S.-made Stinger missiles that occurs as an American helicopter crew is taken hostage. Seven Seals, led by Charlie Sheen, come to the rescue: the crew is freed and Israelis and Americans working in tandem slaughter dozens of Palestinians. The scruffy, sinister-looking Arabs are casually referred to as "scumbags" while Beirut is described as a "shit hole" filled with "ragheads." Other stereotypical portraits quickly follow. In *American Ninja 4: The Annihilation* (1991), a nuclear-mad Islamic sheikh, setting out to bomb New York City with the full blessings of Allah, finally receives his punishment at the hands of Delta Force commandos. *Patriot Games* (1992) depicts terrorists as a motley assemblage of Palestinians, Libyans, and Syrians, all rapidly decimated video-game style—wooden victims whose terrorist camp in Libya is bombed by the United States, anticipating the real Clinton-ordered aerial strikes in 1995. In a similar vein *Chain of Command* (1993), the work of Israeli producer Yoram Globus, shows Arab terrorists taking Americans hostage in the fictitious Republic of Quimir, where the evildoers blow up a station only to be bloodily vanquished, with just a single American operative at one point mechanically killing dozens of Arabs. The fact that Palestinians have never been involved in *global* terrorism—their operations always being local, directed against Israel—seems not to have troubled the producers, whose main concern is to bring to the big screen ultrapatriotic narratives and images tied to the "clash of civilizations" motif.

In James Cameron's critically acclaimed *True Lies* (1994), we have an Arnold Schwarzenegger action vehicle tapping into the cultural pillars of empire through a rare mixture of Hollywood genres: combat, gangster, Western, thriller, romantic comedy, and counterterrorist action film in the Bond tradition. Schwarzenegger plays undercover agent Harry Tasker, who works with sidekick Gib (Tom Arnold) to track a ruthless Arab terrorist (Art Malik) who has seized several nuclear warheads. Tasker surfaces from a frozen Swiss lake and crashes an elegant party thrown by an Arab tycoon for his fellow terrorist plotters. By hacking into computer data at the mansion Tasker is able to follow the criminal plans of the group Crimson Jihad. In familiar Bond style he disposes of all those standing in the way of his mission, including a small militia of well-armed security cops. The narrative informs us that Western global interests are threatened by Crimson Jihad, whose agents are happily prepared to use weapons of mass destruction. As the film unfolds, Cameron interrupts the global intrigue to introduce a complicated sexual subplot in which Tasker suspects his wife Helen (Jamie Lee Curtis) of having an affair during his extended absences. The husband's suspicions are borne out by a private investigator, although eventually husband and wife manage to patch things up—but not before Helen, who thought her husband was just a computer salesman, learns his true occupation, at which juncture the movie becomes more comedy than action-thriller. When Helen asks her husband if he was ever forced to kill anyone, he responds, "Yeah, but they were all bad." Tasker and his wife link up as a counterterrorist team, finally destroying Crimson Jihad after a series of wild military maneuvers (at one point Schwarzenegger pilots a Harrier jet) but not before the jihadists detonate a bomb on an island off Florida. Before their demise the terrorists are heard promising to explode a nuclear device in a major American city every week until U.S. military troops are pulled out of the Persian Gulf. In *True Lies* Schwarzenegger takes on the persona of a killer robot who cherishes family values and has a twisted sense of humor, while the Arabs are cold, rootless, and barbaric. In its clever mixture of film genres and staunch defense of patriarchal and military virtues, in its predictable demonizing of Arabs, *True Lies* can be seen as quintessential 1990s Hollywood counterterrorism fare.

The four years separating *True Lies* and the next major terrorist-oriented picture, *The Siege* (1998), witnessed a large number of mediocre but popular films within the standard counterterrorist-thriller genre. These included *Under Siege 2* (1995), *Die Hard with a Vengeance* (1995), *The Rock* (1995), *Executive Decision* (1996), *G.I. Jane* (1997), *Air Force One* (1997), and *The Peacemaker* (1997). Such movies gained favor among studio chieftains undoubtedly influ-

True Lies (*James Cameron, 1994, Twentieth Century Fox*). *Arnold Schwarzenegger is cast in a superman role as a master sleuth working for a top-secret government agency in the guise of a traveling salesman. The film is replete with superhuman feats carried out by Schwarzenegger, including piloting a Harrier jet to thwart Middle Eastern terrorists. Copyright 1994 Lightstorm Entertainment Inc.*

enced by the growing incidence of political violence in the United States, including the first World Trade Center bombing in 1993 and the Oklahoma City disaster in 1994, as well as fallout from the Gulf War and the Palestinian-Israeli conflict. During this period, a seemingly endless march of crazed Middle Eastern villains in Hollywood films seemed to resonate with the deepening anxieties of an American public already rendered fearful by routine violent images depicted by corporate media culture.

George Murphy's action-packed *Under Siege 2: Dark Territory* casts Steven Seagal as Casey Ryback, former Navy Seal and counterterrorism expert but now a chef traveling by train with his niece to visit the Mile High Restaurant in Denver. Ryback winds up pitted against Travis Dean (Eric Bogosian), an eccentric producer of advanced military weaponry and inventor of a powerful laser satellite who now manages to hack into its control system. Dean's goal: to target the Eastern Seaboard with a nuclear device buried under the Pentagon after being promised $1 billion by shadowy Middle Eastern operatives. He commandeers a speeding train with Ryback and his niece aboard, broadcasting over its speaker, "Good evening, ladies and gentlemen, this is your captor speaking. There's been a slight change in your travel plans tonight." Dean threatens to kill everyone aboard, then shows off his military prowess by destroying a fertilizer plant in China, an airliner, and incoming Stealth fighters armed with guided missiles. As Pentagon officials struggle to manage the chaos, one ranking officer wonders how such a "madman" could be given a contract to build a superweapon, commenting (nonsensically) that "sane people do not build weapons like this." Like many action protagonists, Ryback finds himself swept into the action by accident. He quickly maneuvers along the inner structures, passageways, and rooftops of the speeding train, waging a campaign of attrition against Dean and the terrorists with the help of a young porter, saving the world from total disaster.

In McTiernan's *Die Hard with a Vengeance,* the terrorist plot revolves around another madman (here without Middle Eastern ties), played by Jeremy Irons, who holds New York City hostage with subway bombings and relays further threats to ousted New York cop John McClane (Bruce Willis). As the fanatical militant befriends a Harlem storekeeper (Samuel L. Jackson), the terrorist action and counteraction degenerates into high-tech mayhem ending with the villain's brutal demise. A poorly made product with extremely contrived sequences, the entire *Die Hard* series still netted over $700 million in profits. In similar fashion Michael Bay's *The Rock* chronicles the takeover of Alcatraz Island by one General Hummel (Ed Harris), who steals military rockets loaded with deadly VX gas, takes eighty-one hostages, and threatens to annihilate the entire Bay Area unless the federal government gives him $100 million within forty hours. To stop an out-of-control Hummel without paying the money, the feds turn to John Patrick Mason (Sean Connery), who leads a team of Navy Seals working underwater to recapture Alcatraz and destroy Hummel's operation.

Under Siege 2: Dark Territory *(Geoff Murphy, 1995, Warner Bros.). The sequel to* Under Siege, *starring Stephen Seagal, this terrorist thriller features men commandeering a train to seize a secret doomsday weapon. The plot is thwarted by a Secret Ops agent (Seagal) in a series of very contrived, stylized actions. Copyright 1995 Warner Bros. Productions and Monarchy Enterprises.*

Returning to the more fashionable theme of Arab terrorism, Stuart Baird's *Executive Decision* (1996) pits eight ruthless Palestinians against an elite U.S. antiterrorism squad commanded by the frenzied Steven Seagal and the more low-key but more adept Kurt Russell. The terrorists hijack a Boeing 747 en route to Washington, D.C., with 406 passengers aboard and randomly beat and kill innocent people, all the while chanting "Allahu Akbar." The hijackers possess enough DZ-5 nerve gas to kill at least 40 million people. An American Stealth fighter maneuvers beneath the hijacked plane, allowing Russell's crew to board the craft and swiftly wipe out the terrorists. *Executive Decision* is a tense and creative thriller, which, however, taps into virtually every anti-Arab/Muslim stereotype while again falsely depicting Palestinians as international thugs. Throughout March 1996 this film was the highest-grossing big-screen product in the United States. Spokespeople at Warner Bros. defended the picture's stereotypes, claiming it was "portraying make-believe situations" but that it did roughly correspond to "the headlines of the moment."[12] In *G.I. Jane,* Ridley Scott takes a different approach, unveiling the inner workings of Navy Seals' counterterrorism units with a multicultural backdrop and a cast of

G.I. Jane *(Ridley Scott, 1997, Disney). Demi Moore is cast as a test case for determining women's fitness for violent military combat. GI Jane trains hard and pumps iron to assert herself against a variety of challenges, not least being male doubters among her own military ranks. Copyright Trap-Two-Zero Productions, Inc., and Hollywood Pictures Company.*

mostly women and minorities. Jordan O'Neill (Demi Moore) undergoes rigid combat training, determined to become a first-rate Seal able to vanquish terrorists who, in this picture, have taken control of a U.S. nuclear-powered satellite and its weapons-grade plutonium at the instigation of Libya. Eventually the Seals, O'Neill in command, manage to retrieve the satellite after a long sequence of fierce, gripping combat-action episodes that have become Scott's stock-in-trade.

Shifting the geographical locale to Central Asia, Wolfgang Peterson's *Air Force One* shows hijackers taking control of the president's airplane with the U.S. leader, his wife and daughter, national security adviser, and Secret Service agents on board. The terrorists belong to a separatist group from Kazakhstan and demand the release of General Razak, an ultranationalist Russian who hopes to resuscitate the Soviet Union. After Razak's agents, impersonating Russian journalists, seize control of Air Force One, President James Marshall (Harrison Ford) pretends to ride an escape pod to safety while secretly hiding in the cargo hold. From there the president, a former helicopter pilot and Medal of Honor winner in Vietnam, slowly begins to retake control of the plane, outwitting and killing one hijacker after another. But once the few remaining terrorists threaten his daughter, Marshall relents and asks for the release of General Razak. Soon, however, the president and his entourage retake the plane, whereupon the request for Razak's release is countermanded and Razak is killed while trying to escape from prison. It turns out that, following the superhero formula, Marshall himself has managed to subdue the terrorists, punching and shooting each of them before miraculously taking over the pilot's duties. Once at the helm of the liberated plane, he fends off attacking MiGs loyal to Razak although *Air Force One* is damaged so badly it cannot land, forcing him to abandon the craft—though not before everyone is rescued. The president too is finally rescued, seconds before the plane crashes into the ocean and just after he discovers and kills the mole inside his own Secret Service who masterminded the entire hijacking.

In Mimi Leder's film *The Peacemaker,* fast-paced action begins in Russia and follows a complex trajectory to Central Asia (Dagestan), Bosnia (Sarajevo), and finally New York City for a wild finale. A Chechen terrorist cell takes over a Russian train, neutralizes troops on board, and triggers a nuclear explosion with one of ten stolen devices. The motley unit, comprised of scruffy Muslims, sets out to attack nuclear plants in Russia while also sending much of its inventory to Iran, presumably so Islamic fundamentalists can use the materials in their global combat against Satan (the United States, Israel). The hijackers show nothing but hatred and contempt for everyone they confront. The U.S. response is quick if not immediately decisive, here combining the efforts of a naive but dedicated scientist (Nicole Kidman) and an arrogant, tough military counterterrorism expert (George Clooney), the two sustaining a tense and conflicted but good working relationship. Attack copters are brought onto the scene, orchestrated by action-hero Clooney, who clumsily oversteps his domain but still manages to dispose of the main terrorist operation and recover most of the nukes. One nuke somehow gets away, however, only to wind up in Sarajevo where new villains (Serbs, of course) enter the picture, intent on bringing weapons of mass destruction to New York City. Chaos erupts in the city, law enforcement is mobilized, and the Kidman-Clooney team shifts into high gear as it moves from Europe to the United States. The two finally trap and neutralize the threat at a New York church, deactivating a timed nuclear bomb just in time to avert massive destruction and the loss of up to 2 million lives. *The Peacemaker* deteriorates as it moves from one absurd scene to another, the viewer overwhelmed by multiple far-fetched climaxes. One questionable premise concerns both the intent and the capacity of Chechens and Serbs to carry out such global terrorist ventures. In the end, of course, the hate-filled, cowardly, barbaric terrorists are overcome by the efforts of resourceful Western action-heroes.

The most bizarre foreshadowing of 9/11 is Edward Zwick's popular 1998 terrorist action-thriller, *The Siege,* which dramatizes harrowing attacks on

Manhattan by Islamic fanatics organized into dispersed secret cells. The film starts with terrorists under radical Sheikh Ahmed Bin Talal (Ahmed Ben Larby)—a pale image of Osama bin Laden—assaulting a U.S. Army base in Saudi Arabia. When the CIA captures the sheikh, his enraged followers strike back by detonating high-explosive bombs across New York City. The resulting pandemonium sparks congressional calls for martial law, one senator demanding, "Find out who they are and bomb the shit out of them!" While speculation on the source of terror includes such "rogue states" as Syria, Iraq, Iran, and Libya, *The Siege* fixates on the Palestinian-Israeli conflict, suggesting (contrary to real-world evidence) that Palestinian groups like Hamas have taken their struggle across the Atlantic Ocean to the United States. In any event, the president declares martial law, whereupon the army officer in command, General Devereau (Bruce Willis), moves to seal off Brooklyn and other areas where Arabs are concentrated. Devereau stops at nothing to establish ironclad military control over New York, in the process relocating the Arab population into camps. His totalitarian methods are fiercely opposed by law enforcement officials, led by FBI counterterrorism agent Anthony Hubbard (Denzel Washington) and CIA agent Elise Kraft (Annette Bening)—both of whom prefer aggressive police tactics to Devereau's heavy-handed militarism.

Zwick's film is remarkably prophetic, although it might have seemed ridiculously improbable at the time it was released. The scenes of death, destruction, and chaos in Manhattan offer a frightening portent of future events. The terrorists first blow up a city bus and then destroy a Broadway theater, killing hundreds, before moving on to even richer targets, their fanaticism and thirst to kill apparently recognizing no limits. As the attacks continue, Devereau cheerfully violates the Geneva Convention when one of the cell leaders, Tariq Hussein, is arrested and then tortured to death, ostensibly to get information. The conflict between Devereau and law enforcement escalates, but it is Devereau's own harsh methods that lead to his ultimate downfall, as Hubbard is able to get a court order abrogating the general's authority and permitting the FBI to arrest him. The movie sets up a final standoff between Hubbard's agents and Devereau's soldiers, at which point the general agrees to surrender—just after the last cell leader is killed (by Hubbard himself) but not before agent Kraft suffers the same fate in a wild shootout.

*The Siege* departs from earlier terrorist-action plots owing to its more complex, nuanced range of narratives and motifs. For one thing, the quick turn toward martial law to short-circuit violence is shown to violate constitutional liberties, anticipating provisions of the Bush-Ashcroft Patriot Act passed in late 2001. The prisoner abuse attributed to General Devereau presages later U.S. prison scandals at Iraq's Abu Ghraib, Guantanamo, and Afghanistan. Zwick's film accurately places blame on the U.S. government (namely, the CIA) for training and funding those very jihadic movements that would later haunt the United States—almost exactly as laid out in the narrative. (In fact Sheikh Ben

Talal's group in the film had been directly supported by CIA agent Kraft.) Even more tellingly, *The Siege* offers a more varied picture of Muslim terrorists and their cultural milieu than can be found elsewhere in Hollywood cinema. In mainstream films of the sixties and later, villains had obvious self-serving strategies for waging terrorist acts, such as threatening the world with nuclear catastrophe or unleashing war between the United States and the Soviet Union. The perpetrators were cold, calculating international masterminds capable of heinous crimes, whereas in the later cycle of pictures villains were fanatical Arabs and/or Muslims shown praying as they plotted terrorist carnage. In both cases demonic enemies personify evil and lack redeeming qualities, yet in *The Siege* we encounter terrorists who, though still evil, are dedicated to what they believe are noble aims. Although Zwick's rendering of Islamic culture lacks depth, we do see militants acting out of political commitment, dedicated to repaying the United States for past grievances; their violent behavior contains a hint of an underlying rationale. And many "good Arabs" inhabit *The Siege*, often shown as victims of a draconian racist order imposed by General Devereau.

At the same time, Zwick paints a portrait of Islamic terrorism that turns out to be more fearsome than what is likely to be found in real life. Operatives are fiercely dedicated to their work, driven by some combination of religious and political fanaticism, moved by genuine claims against U.S. policies and actions spanning many years. They gladly commit acts that bring destruction and panic to an entire city, using methods of random, brutal violence that recognize few if any ethical restraints. Moreover, in *The Siege* we come to appreciate a certain mundane, almost random aspect of terrorism: violent death can occur anytime, at any place, from any quarter. Ordinary people are vulnerable as they ride buses, go to work in high-rise buildings, or simply walk along crowded streets—a reality hauntingly definitive of the new paradigm of warfare. At the same time, Zwick's terrorists bear a strong resemblance to the actual 9/11 hijackers, who, in contrast to Bond's old-fashioned villains, carry out scattered bombings but never threaten wider military confrontation. And consistent with the effects of blowback, it is possible to see in this film the long history of U.S. economic domination, military aggression, and covert action—barely hinted at by Zwick—finally coming back to haunt the imperial superpower. Viewed at the intersection of art and politics, the series of explosive real-world events since 1998 has greatly strengthened the power (and credibility) of *The Siege*.

While popular interest in distinctly nonstate terrorist-oriented cinema has grown since the 1960s, no doubt peaking during the 1990s, the more durable impact of 9/11 on Hollywood filmmaking remains (as of early 2006) rather ambiguous, although it might have begun to change with the appearance of Paul Greengrass's *United 93* in spring 2006. Films like *The Siege* dwell on terrorist scenarios that in the transformed political milieu would seem far too "realistic" to bankroll as anything other than made-for-TV docudramas. Despite more than a decade of periodic attacks on U.S. targets, filmmakers have yet to grasp either these episodes or the stepped-up American response to them now visible in Bush's war on terrorism—a "war" sure to guarantee protracted global military conflict. Indeed, scarcely any mainstream pictures have realistically engaged the profoundly changed historical situation. As we have seen, earlier films usually relied on absurd plot lines with cartoonish villains— fare that surely cannot be ruled out for the future. Such films were often inspired by a marriage of combat and thriller genres, with battlefield action driven by overheated narratives involving conflict between two powerful national or ideological forces. Today, however, and especially in the wake of 9/11, story lines have begun to shift as combat itself morphs into something considerably more diffuse, reflecting a situation where military battle can take place anywhere and everywhere in the absence of definitive front lines, clearly demarcated battle zones, and set boundaries between combatants and civilians. In movies as in reality, the point is reached where virtually any target becomes thinkable: New York subways, *Air Force One,* the Super Bowl, Alcatraz, theater gatherings, religious shrines, the streets of any major city. Yet while Hollywood does often capture such altered states of warfare, its continued reliance on the entirely familiar but stale combat genre—along with a strong residue of cold war myths—imposes strict limits on how far it can go in the direction of authenticity.

Philip Robinson's picture *The Sum of All Fears* (2002), resurrecting the nightmare of nuclear terrorism first captured in the Bond movie *Thunderball* three decades earlier, suffers from these very flaws despite some believable action sequences. The film had been in production even before 9/11, but its release was delayed by several months because of initial misgivings after the events of that day. It was produced for an audience that could view terrorist attacks within U.S. borders from a safe emotional distance, but of course the post-9/11 atmosphere made this impossible. However, *The Sum of All Fears* was neither as prescient nor as realistic as *The Siege,* in part because it emanated from an outdated geopolitical mind-set that has the United States and the Soviet Union still engaged in a struggle for global supremacy.

Based on Tom Clancy's acclaimed novel of the same name, *The Sum of All Fears* opens in the Middle East during the 1973 Arab-Israeli war but quickly segues into the present as Arab black marketeers, a lost nuclear warhead, and a South African gem dealer enter the picture, giving rise to a series of events that would have far-reaching consequences for the U.S. homeland. The central villain is Richard Dressler (Alan Bates), a German neo-Nazi out to conquer the world by instigating all-out war between the United States and the Soviet Union. Perennial Clancy hero Jack Ryan (Ben Affleck) is charged with heading off a catastrophe that could eventually trigger global annihilation. Under Robinson's direction, Ryan is transformed from a grizzled veteran into an inexperienced young man, a protégé of CIA director Bill Cabot (Morgan Freeman). Dressler's Nazi group hijacks nuclear devices and explodes one in Chechnya; the Soviets conclude that the United States is behind the attack and prepare to retaliate, but Ryan, in Moscow, begs the Russian leader to stay calm. The terrorists smuggle a warhead into Baltimore harbor and detonate it while the Super Bowl is under way, killing tens of thousands of people—an action meant to trick the United States into attacking Russia. As Dressler says regarding his scheme, "You don't try to fight Russia and America. You get Russia and America to fight each other." According to a timeworn and exaggerated terrorist "strategy of tension," the superpowers would annihilate each other, allowing neo-Nazis to seize power out of the ashes of destruction and chaos. Dressler theorizes that "Communism was a fool's errand, the followers of Marx gone from the Earth. But the followers of Hitler abound and thrive."

Often described as a stylish political thriller—in part because of the Tom Clancy pedigree, in part owing to the all-star cast—*The Sum of All Fears* is driven by an archaic motif further weakened by an implausible story line. The idea of stock Nazis conspiring to trigger nuclear Armageddon in a major U.S. city makes sense only in the context of Robinson's lame effort to resurrect World War II villains in the service of modern-day terrorist warfare. Why Hollywood remains so fascinated with aging Nazis (and Commies) and why anyone in the film industry believes even Nazis are so crazy as to envision a glorious new civilization arising out of global holocaust are questions best left for another time. (In this case, the film does establish a linkage between Muslim radicals and old-style Nazis, improbable as that might be.) Viewed in this light, *The Sum of All Fears* seems to be a cinematic throwback, the contemporary variant of tired cold war action-thrillers that were outlandish even in their own time.

Rob Cohen's hyperpaced *XXX* (2002), a slicker version of the director's earlier film *The Fast and the Furious* (2001), typifies the kind of high-tech blockbuster action picture nowadays so popular among teenage boys. Here international terrorism, though neither Arab nor Muslim, is decisive to the cinematic narrative, providing the backdrop to a frenetic, ultraviolent movie augmented by James Bond–style combat gadgets and a heavy-metal sound track. Vin Diesel stars as Xandar Cage, a shady underground sports figure who masters every moving vehicle from motorcycles and cars to skateboards and snowboards. Cage draws the attention of the National Security Agency (NSA) after he steals and destroys a politician's Corvette to protest his "anti–rock-and-roll politics." Faced with jail time, Cage allows himself to be recruited by the NSA, where his job is to infiltrate subversive groups by feigning a tough counterculture persona to gain legitimacy. He soon falls under the influence of NSA master spy Augustus Gibbons (Samuel L. Jackson), who puts him through a series of excruciating tests that he passes with little difficulty. Once Gibbons feels that Cage is the right man, the NSA sends him to Prague to infiltrate a terrorist gang known as Anarchy 99, run by a former Russian soldier named Yorgi

XXX *(Rob Cohen, 2002, Columbia Pictures). An action-thriller with elements of the combat genre starring Vin Diesel as a sports maniac recruited by a National Security Agency operative (Samuel L. Jackson) to work undercover in Prague to monitor sinister Russian plots. Source unknown.*

(Marton Csokas) and his girlfriend Yelena (Asia Argento). In the mode of *The Sum of All Fears,* it turns out that Anarchy 99 is planning to incite war between the leading military powers, in this instance by loosing massive doses of a deadly biological microbe.

At this juncture *XXX* morphs into another Bond-style action extravaganza, marked by several digitalized high-tech feats and athletic maneuvers pulled off with skill and charisma by Diesel, including some acrobatic motorcycling and snowboarding and, in a final duel with the terrorists, parachuting onto a speeding boat. Outnumbered and outgunned, he mixes athletic skill, personal wiles, and professional finesse to neutralize the terrorists and checkmate their efforts at world domination. While Robinson presents Cage as a brave fighter against evil, the hero is surely no patriot; on the contrary, he seems mostly self-interested, driven mainly by a desire to stay out of jail. In the final scene, however, Gibbons informs Cage that his life-and-death battle against terrorism is nothing but an *illusion:* the entire saga was staged simply to test his willpower. Here *XXX* deftly constructs illusion after illusion to the point where little "reality" is left to experience, or to contemplate. At one level the picture is nothing but pure fantasy, yet from the standpoint of present-day audiences, any such distinction vanishes insofar as mainstream media culture has become increasingly hyperreal, the boundaries separating the real and the illusory disappearing under the sway of the mass spectacle. If present discourses and images surrounding war and terrorism are indeed illusory, their capacity to reproduce intensely patriotic and militaristic feelings across the broad population are likely to be heightened rather than diminished.

High-profile Hollywood films dealing with terrorism may have reached their peak in the 1990s, but the genre, recast in a more sophisticated guise, is sure to extend its life and attract popular audiences in the United States while the militarism-terrorism dialectic moves along its deadly path. Since U.S. global military reach and jihadic terrorism are reverse sides of the same process, the war on terror can be expected to persist years into the future. Cinematic as well as political approaches to terrorism inevitably mirror recent shifts in world politics, just as they reproduce key elements of domestic ideological hegemony: patriotism, the cult of guns and violence, glorification of technology, the hypermasculine hero, obsession with "alien" threats. Such enduring motifs of American political and film culture are visible elsewhere across the entertainment industry—TV, video games, music, the Internet, comic books, and so forth—but the influence of cinema on popular consciousness has no equal.

Hollywood movies built around terrorist plots thus have significance far beyond their power of diversion, merging as they do with powerful images, cultural stereotypes, and ideological biases rendered all the more effective because of their seemingly nonpolitical content. The enemy Other is generally a foreigner of some type, home-grown terrorists associated with local militias and other right-wing groups—the same circles that produced the Oklahoma City bombers—rarely find their way into mainstream pictures since *domestic* terrorism is understood as having little to do with U.S. *global* priorities. The emphasis on alien demons, moreover, is congruent with long-standing Manichaeistic views of world politics in which problems are framed in such a way as to encourage military "solutions."

Although political terrorism is centuries old and spans virtually all ideological, national, religious, and ethnic groups, as we have seen, recent Hollywood cinema focuses on Arabs and Muslims. For the past two decades both TV and cinema have caricatured jihadic terrorism as irredeemably evil, the product of a deformed mentality lacking human or rational standards of behavior—its adherents perfect targets for vengeance. Such representations flow from an essentially metaphysical or religious worldview, devoid of historical analysis or political context.[13] In the real world political violence is universal, but in Hollywood it is reduced to the diabolical work of certain designated groups and identities. Visual images, plot lines, musical scores, and sound effects merge to convey an epochal "clash of civilizations" mood as unique personality types (irrational, fanatical, sadistic) hostile to the United States occupy center stage. The viewer will look in vain for any *political* backdrop consistent with complex, balanced views of how armed force is used by an array of state and nonstate forces throughout the world. Violent political encounters never occur in a vacuum, but such a vacuum is precisely what nowadays defines Hollywood cinema. Lost is the common sense that Arab and Muslim antagonism to U.S. imperial power, especially its recent efforts to reconfigure the Middle East, has been overwhelmingly secular and political, as revealed in dozens of public statements, not to mention the actual targets of choice. Religious fundamentalism surely plays a role, but there is no evidence to suggest it is decisive. Far from being mysterious or irrational, popular Arab/Muslim anger toward the United States turns on several mundane (and globally recognized) outrages: American geopolitical hegemony, a long history of bloody military interventions, unwavering support for Israel, enforcement of a neoliberal globalization regimen. These issues are routinely ignored or downplayed in Hollywood movies dealing with terrorism, as the more convenient "clash" scenario is preferred.

In a universe where terrorism is depicted as a monolithic scourge to be extirpated by maximum force, further expansion of U.S. global military power is the logical corollary. Insofar as world politics can be framed as the struggle of good versus evil, democracy versus tyranny, and civilization versus barbarism, the Bush administration has been able to legitimate its unilateralism and militarism while moving to upgrade the Pentagon's high-tech arsenals, rapid troop deployments, air and space capabilities, and intelligence systems—all vital to solidifying the permanent war system. While such representations are clearly visible within the film industry, for marketing purposes Hollywood still favors male action-hero narratives drawn from the legacy of John Wayne, James Bond, Rambo, and Schwarzenegger, whose warrior roles owe more to the hypermasculine, individualistic ethos of the frontier than to routine operations of the modern Pentagon war machine. For terrorist plots the difference between victory and defeat often comes down to the last-minute heroics of warrior-saviors. In *True Lies* it is Schwarzenegger who manages superhuman counterterrorist exploits in almost single-handedly rescuing the world from catastrophe, but in the end he must rely on updated combat technology (the Harrier jet) to prevail. Comparable scenarios unfold in *Patriot Games, The Peacemaker,* and *The Siege. Air Force One* contains a plot in which the U.S. president (Harrison Ford) thwarts a terrorist scheme by his own daring exploits. The new superheroes recall earlier figures who, like Wayne and Bond, could satisfy American viewers' desire to see male heroes triumph over menacing demons, whether from space aliens, ideological devils, or simply nameless enemies lurking about the landscape. As the capacity of nonstate terrorists to carry out real-life destruction increases—bolstered by their possible access to weapons of mass destruction—so too has the power of hypermasculine screen saviors. And as public fear of new terrorist episodes in the United States and elsewhere understandably lingers, that fear sooner or later finds resonance within a corporate media system that continues to transmit paranoid and frightful impulses.[14]

Images and narratives of "terrorism" within media culture reveal the extent to which American public opinion has become insular and provincial, the sign of a population shielded from knowledge about the global repercussions of its own nation's foreign and military (not to mention economic) policies. As Ziauddin Sardar and Meryl Wyn Davies write: "America has the power and resources to refuse self-reflection. More pointedly, it is a nation that has developed a tradition of being oblivious to self-reflection."[15] In this atmosphere Hollywood cinema has done its share to encourage a narrowly conservative political culture that nurtures the conditions (while sidestepping the consequences) of far-reaching imperial power. The film industry has engaged the durable legacy of U.S. colonial violence and conquest, visible in Westerns, combat movies, action spectacles, sci-fi pictures, and related fare. The recent cycle of terrorist- action films is simply another extension (and refinement) of this legacy. Within U.S. history different forms of violence, rhetorically denounced by established opinion as too "uncivilized" and "undemocratic," have been embraced fully as an instrument—often the preferred instrument—to achieve national interests. As might be expected of any campaign against evildoers, violence easily takes on cathartic and redemptive features, in warfare as in movies. At the same time, discourses on violence reflect the double standards permeating so much of the American public sphere: violence is sanctioned, even celebrated, in the service of U.S. power and wealth but is treated as a violation of civilized values when used by others. (In this vein, the acquisition of weapons of mass destruction by countries like Iraq and Iran is fiercely opposed, viewed as deserving of preemptive military action, while U.S. possession of its own vast arsenal of such weapons is regarded as normal, necessary, even praiseworthy, in defense of "democracy.") Larger-than-life images of threatening villains willing to destroy civilization are vital to the effectiveness of such propaganda, and nowhere are these images more powerful than in Hollywood movies with their dazzling technology, seductive cinematography, fast-paced action sequences, and gripping narratives.

Widespread, legitimate public fears of real-life terrorism enable the media to sensationalize one of the great icons of modern barbarism, with its visual constructions of savage Others bringing death and destruction to innocent populations for no reason beyond their own pathological disorders. The terrorist personality by definition is nihilistic, an outlook typical of deranged serial killers and mass murderers including the likes of Hitler, Stalin, Charles Manson, and of course Osama bin Laden. Within media culture sinister enemies of the United States seem to lurk everywhere, given new life on a daily basis while often living seemingly normal lives—a narrative shared by journalists as well as the vast majority of politicians and academics. Thus Walter Lacquer, a leading expert on terrorism, writes that "fanaticism inspired by all kinds of religious-sectarian-nationalist convictions is now taking on a millenarian and apocalyptic tone." In terrorism he sees recurring elements of criminality reflected in "the rise of small sectarian groups that lack clear agendas other than destroying civilization, and in some cases humankind," agents characterized by nothing so much as "blind aggression," "suicidal impulses," and "sheer madness."[16] In other words, the new terrorist personality is distinct from anything that went before it, so utterly sui generis and irrational as to defy historical or psychological analysis. Along these lines, Gabler writes of jihadic violence based on premodern, fundamentalist outlooks, a complete attack on logic and reason, utterly hostile to progress, democracy, and secular order.[17] How acts of political violence carried out by Al Qaeda and similar groups are supposed to differ qualitatively from varieties of state terrorism, or from the long history of nonstate terrorist operations, is never explained by mainstream writers like Lacquer and Gabler.

In American media culture (especially TV and film) terrorism has inspired the invention of an entirely new category of human being, a category that ostensibly captures the essence of contemporary jihadic violence. The personality type is one existing beyond history, beyond politics, beyond psychology, a type so irredeemably evil and crazy that no normal mode of interpretation is possible. Even historical Commies and fascists were typically shown to be politically motivated human beings with certain ideas, interests, and identities—craven beings, to be sure, but still part of an intelligible world. Even hardened criminals and drug addicts may be regarded as subject to social and psychological analysis, whereas "terrorists" are people whose sole purpose in living is to cause great pain and suffering. Following this discourse, the modern terrorist amounts to nothing more than a cancerous intrusion into an otherwise healthy body politic, and thus is immune from standard legal sanctions or efforts at rehabilitation and must be removed by maximum force. The physical habitats of such toxic agents—Fallujah in Iraq, for example—become open terrain for total warfare, an arena where all the horrors of technowar are permissible. This is why the torture of prisoners defined as terrorists is so easily justified, and practiced, and why the U.S. government can insist that terrorists have no rights under the Geneva Convention. This new terrorist personality—faceless, sinister, innately violent—has appeared hundreds of times in the recent cycle of Hollywood terrorist-action films that continue to reap enormous box-office revenues.

Situating the phenomenon of terrorism historically, Jean Baudrillard calls attention to the spectacular, mirrorlike features of political violence and its ideological representations within the expanding system of mass media. In 1993 he argued that "the violence of old was both more enthusiastic and sacrificial than ours," whereas contemporary violence is a product of hypermodernity, with political terror "a simulacrum of violence, emerging less from passion than from the screen, a violence in the nature of the image." Baudrillard observes that it is possible to specify a dialectical relationship between terrorist actions as such and the growing media fascination with them—a social process in which the two phenomena are intimately chained to each other.[18] In the present-day media system, what journalists and politicians routinely call "terrorism" is more accurately viewed as a mode of political activity that simultaneously reflects and helps create an increasingly violent society of the spectacle in which pervasive feelings of fear, anxiety, and paranoia are reproduced daily. Scanning the post-9/11 political terrain, one encounters the paradox that while radical Islam is uniformly associated in the popular media with a desperate return to preindustrial, fundamentalist, and anti-Western values, in some instances even fascism, it is a phenomenon that flourishes within a distinctly modern universe, that is, an urban, bureaucratic, high-tech, globalized system in which media culture continuously shapes and reshapes elements of popular consciousness. Baudrillard concludes that terrorism unfolds as one side of a globalized modernity made possible by advanced technology, geographical mobility, open flows of communication, and the breaking down of territorial divisions. It follows that the emphatically international terrorism of Al Qaeda and kindred groups ultimately corresponds to the very transnational corporate system it depends upon for expertise, funding, mobility, recognition, and, perhaps above all, the conditions generating blowback. Globalization as an economic, political, and cultural process thus ironically feeds into modern terrorism, both state and nonstate, as political violence extends its worldwide impact while sharpening its capacity to attack, disrupt, and surprise—the same features now so integral to the Hollywood film industry. Meanwhile, jihadic terrorism can be understood not only as a virulent form of blowback against U.S. imperial domination but also as possibly the darkest side of neoliberal globalization.

## The Cinema of Disguised Militarism

American movie history is replete with productions that share most or all of the elements of a military-themed cinema but that do not strictly fall within the established combat genre—what we define here as "disguised militarism" in film. The familiar combat model usually involves clear-cut battlefield scenarios, one set of armed contingents pitted against another, typically within a particular historical war (the Civil War, World War II, Korea, Vietnam, the Gulf War, etc.). In most of these classic pictures recurrent motifs are rather easily identifiable: triumph of good over evil, glorification of the male hero, the power of weaponry, simple narrative structures, patriotism, and of course positive endings. Such motifs, of course, are not always confined to battlefield situations; they commonly extend to various zones of civilian life, as in many films dealing with terrorism. Hollywood long ago found that the combat formula could be incorporated into other genres, ranging from Westerns to gangster, sci-fi, noir, and action-adventure movies. Although these other genres have often presented more refracted, indirect, mediated images of combat-style violence, their immense contribution to the expanding culture of militarism in the United States today cannot be discounted.

During and immediately after World War II, combat films accounted for nearly half of the total studio output, and this led to fatigue among both producers and viewers grown tired of the same predictable formats. However, it did not take long for filmmakers to carry forward roughly the same blood-and-guts approach into the genres mentioned above—a move designed to replicate the box-office success of war movies by other means. The idea was to satisfy popular demand for variety. Sometimes the allure of military themes could be sustained by simply changing uniforms from army or navy to police and relocating the action from remote battlefields in Europe or Asia to settings in urban America. Disguised combat pictures often feature armed protagonists facing off against evil but nonetheless awesome opponents. Adopting methods refined in war movies, studio heads seemed content to offer audiences an endless dose of mega-violence, serving up a large helping of blood, gore, and mayhem, but framed through new settings, costumes, icons, and plots. Some military-style protagonists, as in the *Rambo* episodes, morphed into "civilian" superheroes able to represent entire organized combat units. Such protagonists could be found within virtually any cinematic framework. Over time, the disguised military form turned out to be especially suitable to the blockbuster male action-adventure pictures that first gained currency in the 1980s, bringing the cinema of violence to levels scarcely imagined during the studio period.

The Western genre, as discussed earlier, typically paralleled the combat formula, substituting frontier landscapes for the conventional battlefield and having Indians stand in for standard military adversaries. Both Westerns and combat films, of course, have common features: violent action, charismatic male heroes, good defeating bad, happy endings. And while a certain subtype of the Western overtly fits the combat motif, the vast majority of pictures fall under the "disguised" category as defined here. This would include such postwar examples as *Rio Bravo* (1959), *The Good, the Bad, and the Ugly* (1966), *The Magnificent Seven* (1967), *Bandolero* (1968), *Butch Cassidy and the Sundance Kid* (1969), *The Wild Bunch* (1969), and *Silverado* (1985). Among these Sam Peckinpah's *Wild Bunch* represents perhaps the best classic example of the disguised (Western) combat film. It features a small band of outlaws led by the aging Pike Bishop (William Holden) who hijack a munitions train in order to sell arms to Pancho Villa's Mexican rebels. The outlaws meet their match when they are attacked by large units of the Mexican army, but in the end they display the kind of courage, coolness under fire, and male bonding that viewers are accustomed to seeing in the traditional combat genre. On the whole, Westerns lend themselves to military narratives and themes owing to experiences and challenges endemic to the frontier of Western mythology. There is always a precarious balance where the opposing forces of civilization and savagery, modernity and primitivism, order and anarchy are locked in a struggle for supremacy—themes familiar to the combat tradition.

The gangster movies likewise often follow the combat script but within a uniquely domestic setting, the modern urban labyrinth. First appearing in the 1930s, these productions, usually just as formulaic as the war films, gained an increasingly wide audience throughout the postwar years and enjoyed a strong revival in the 1980s and 1990s. Early postwar gangster pictures, including *The Gangster* (1947), *Key Largo* (1948), *White Heat* (1949), and *The Big Heat* (1953), were crafted by established directors: Gordon Willes, John Huston, Michael Curtiz, Raoul Walsh, Fritz Lang. Here organized gangs, always corrupt, duplicitous, and violent, carried out horrible actions that reminded audiences of German and Japanese atrocities during World War II; gangsters were the new cinematic barbarians, demons always easy to loathe. As screen antagonists, gangsters like Johnny Rocco, Joe Lugano, and Cody Jarrett served admirably as hardened, cold, sadistic criminals who deserved whatever terrible fate awaited them. In Walsh's *White Heat,* for example, gang leader Jarrett (James Cagney) eludes police by pulling into a drive-in theater showing the film *Task Force,* a standard war narrative. To reinforce the linkage between Jarrett's crime spree and the war against Germany, Walsh has Jarrett execute his dramatic escape from the surrounding army of cops while images of battlefield combat flash on screen. In Huston's *Key Largo* the main protagonist, Frank McLeod (Humphrey Bogart), is a decorated World War II veteran who runs up against a despicable gangster. He is heard to say, "We are not making all this sacrifice in human effort and human lives to return to the kind of world we had after the First World War. We're fighting to cleanse the world of ancient evils, ancient ills." The chief evil exposed in the film is Mafia-style gang leader Johnny Rocco (Edward G. Robinson), who shows little regard for life. Rocco and his mobsters are ultimately destroyed in a series of armed clashes.

Postwar gangster movies were built on a solid foundation of urban violence, armed conflict in a menacing world, and male solidarity. Encounters between mobsters and police often seemed to be patterned after episodes of battlefield combat—naturally with much smaller casts and less sophisticated weaponry. Francis Ford Coppola's *Godfather* trilogy contains scenes of this type, as do Brian de Palma's *Untouchables* (1987), the Coen brothers' *Millers' Crossing* (1990), and Martin Scorsese's *Goodfellas* (1990). Further, when in the *Godfather* episodes the Corleone family "goes to the mattresses" in its war against rival Mafia families, it conducts its actions essentially as a military unit. It matters little whether violent combat takes place on a battlefield deep behind enemy lines or in an urban neighborhood. Male bonding, collective violence, authoritarian edifices, and hostility toward outsiders (a form of local patriotism) are all writ large not only in the *Godfather* series but also in subsequent gangster films like *Prizzi's Honor* (1985), *Billy Bathgate* (1991), *Bugsy* (1991), and *Casino* (1995). Mafia bosses and their underlings generally come across as little different from army or marine commanders: all are obsessed with control, loyalty, and violent efficiency. At the same time, insofar as gangsters are associated with crime, outlawry, and social disruption, they—much like the familiar enemies of the combat genre—are set up for eventual annihilation, often by police forces employing military-style weapons and tactics.

The dramatic sequences that locate protagonists in alien territory, behind enemy lines, are akin to what is experienced in most science-fiction films: both situations depend on the elevated mood of alienation and danger that comes from being in strange, hostile territory. As we have seen, the sci-fi genre sets up an opposition between humans and aliens that must be resolved in some fashion at the end. (There are occasional friendly aliens, but that is another matter.) One of the first sci-fi movies to adopt the full-scale combat structure was Don Siegel's classic *Invasion of the Body Snatchers* (1956), the quintessential disguised military picture. Here aliens in the form of vegetable seed pods begin to duplicate human beings, kill them, and steal their identities. The idea is that beings identical to ordinary Americans were in fact involved in a secret, nefarious plot to overthrow the government and bring to power a group of "pod people," automatons devoid of human emotion. Of course the aliens resemble the prevailing fifties view of Communists: godless, cold, ruthless, seemingly omnipotent, a dire threat to American society. Future Hollywood filmmakers learned to make their villains correspond to this menacing stereotype drawn from cold war hysteria. In the case of *Body Snatchers,* of course, armed citizen mobilization would be needed to repel and defeat the alien subversives.

A later example of disguised militarism was George Romero's cult classic *Night of the Living Dead* (1968), which borrows heavily from the combat genre. Here we have a story that pits ordinary citizens against zombies that suddenly arise from their graves and begin to attack, kill, and devour humans. Made on a slim budget with unknown actors, *Living Dead* eventually became a hit on the midnight cult film circuit. Radiation causes vast mutations in the dead, transforming corpses into demonic, flesh-eating creatures. Survivors of the onslaught, who have taken refuge in a remote country house, learn from radio reports that "there is an epidemic of mass murder being committed by a virtual army of unidentified assailants." Dedicated to mayhem, the zombies, soulless killing machines, have only one fear: fire. Surviving humans manage to keep hordes of zombies at bay but only after suffering terrible casualties. In its narrative of a small, desperate band of humans fighting to hold off an invading army of subhumans, *Living Dead* clearly exhibits features of the war movie, once again confronting Americans with the menace of terrible alien monsters. Whereas Siegel in *Body Snatchers* appears to favor ideological subversives as villains, in this case Romero seems to prefer more traditional demons from hell. In both cases, however, the fearsome threat represents a form of barbarism to be resisted at all costs, leading to an epic clash between rival armed forces, between decent law-abiding citizens and ruthless monsters bent on total destruction. Such monsters, of course, could symbolize either Communists or Nazis, or (in later versions) terrorists or leaders of rogue states.

The several films in George Lucas's spectacular *Star Wars* episodes, combining elements of sci-fi and action-adventure in the modern blockbuster, can also be situated rather comfortably within the disguised combat pattern. Any serious effort to account for the growing culture of militarism in American society would have to explore the impact of Lucas's powerful work. Indeed the whole structure of the *Star Wars* series is modeled on motifs of warfare. We see that Luke Skywalker and his circle of aliens and robots as well as humans constitute something of an efficient combat group. In these films conflict erupts between the evil Empire (totalitarian, ruthless) and the courageous heroes who rise up against it, force against force. The setting of course is a highly imaginary one, located in the future and with the most outlandish scenarios and exotic costumes, but the combat is predictably fierce, relentless, and powered by the most technologically sophisticated weaponry.

Owing to their spectacular production values and enormous popularity, the *Star Wars* extravaganzas—which made Lucas one of the wealthiest people in the world—have epitomized the blockbuster phenomenon. From the standpoint of the disguised combat picture, the blockbuster furnishes virtually every ingredient: fast-paced action, male heroics, high-tech spectacles, violent confrontations, good versus evil, idealistic goals mixed with patriotism, happy endings. Within the framework of larger-than-life storytelling we encounter the usual run of glamorous heroes doing combat with any variety of demons, monsters, aliens, and tyrants. In Lucas's *Phantom Menace* (1999), we have perhaps the greatest of all cinematic extravaganzas, a powerful recycling of both earlier *Star Wars* themes and classical war formulas. Scattered throughout the Lucas sci-fi adventures is an array of epic, mythological figures patterned after Jason, Rama, King Arthur, Robin Hood, and Ivanhoe—all capable of Promethean deeds. The director regularly invokes Joseph Campbell as a source of heroic mythology, with a simple change in props taking the viewer to medieval Europe, ancient Greece, or the American West. Campbell lays out fairy-tale narratives that tap legendary myths in which heroes go against impossible odds to conquer evil, all combined with dazzling acts of valor, mind-bending special effects, and fearsome combat scenes. Simple plots are combined with visually overwhelming cinematography and digital imaging as combat hero Skywalker becomes a seasoned space fighter pilot able to harness the mysterious "Force."

At one level the *Star Wars* episodes represent a countercultural revolt against authoritarian power, directed against the vast, heartless Empire shown on screen to be an oppressive machine. The main authority figure, Darth Vader, glorifies order and discipline, enforced by a network of storm troopers, while Skywalker is the perpetual rebel who will never rest until a new order in the galaxy is established. Although Skywalker takes on the Empire as a kind of Nazi power structure, in the process becoming an outlaw-hero, as a noble character committed to his *own* galactic system he winds up more of a conventional hero—and surely one obsessed with all the techniques of violence and warfare. Viewed in this fashion, the "rebels" of *Star Wars* and comparable blockbusters like *Batman* and *Terminator* easily morph into agents of order and control embedded in new institutional systems that incorporate classic virtues of collective solidarity, combat heroism, technological acumen, and grandiose visions of the future. In many ways, too, military weapons appear as centerpieces of the films. In the first *Star Wars* (1977), we encounter armies, spies, warships, and air forces moving into uncharted territory, along with laser rifles, futuristic spacecraft, and a powerful Death Star that is essentially a galactic battleship. Despite all of Lucas's high-tech flourishes, however, it is the light sabers, reminiscent of combat swords, that become the most celebrated weapons, adding a swashbuckling flavor to the combat scenes. Obi-Wan (Alec Guinness) explains that the light saber provided "an elegant weapon for a more civilized age."

In the *Star Wars* narratives, moreover, there are always plenty of scurrilous villains to be identified and conquered, just as in conventional warfare drama. Many such villains, dubbed "Star Troopers," suggest the most futuristic variant of popular Nazi-style demons that inhabit most combat pictures. Lucas's Nazis provide muscle for the evil Empire, indicating that such a breed—decades after the end of World War II—is rather ubiquitous. When Skywalker (Mark Hamill) attempts to disguise himself by donning a storm trooper uniform, Princess Leia Organa (Carrie Fisher) asks sarcastically, "Aren't you a little short for a storm trooper?" This is probably true enough, especially when Skywalker is compared with the bigger, more athletic-looking leader, Darth Vader, whose persona has become so much a part of American lore that his very name has come to symbolize a supervillain. Indeed Vader's powers are so acute that he can strangle an enemy simply by his force of mind. After the rebels clash with Vader and his troopers, and after Skywalker destroys the Death Star with a missile, few viewers will need to be reminded that *Star Wars* possesses all the features of a combat film. As this blockbuster became a mini-genre unto itself, spawning popular sequels, the narratives and motifs continued along the same trajectory, pitting groups of rebels against the evil Empire.

Ridley Scott's *Alien* (1979), released in the aftermath of the great *Star Wars* success, refined the modern sci-fi genre as a reconstructed, and only slightly disguised, combat picture. The setting is an "off-world" colony on a remote planet; the film casts Sigourney Weaver as Ripley, an aide to a starship commander (Tom Skerritt) who lands on the colony in response to a distress call from its inhabitants, most of whom appear to have been murdered by someone or *something*. The culprit turns out to be a monstrous reptile that begins attacking the crew of the starship; Ripley survives, available to star in the sequel, *Aliens* (1986), this time directed by James Cameron. In the sequel Ripley returns to the planet hoping to discover whether the reptilian aliens still exist. Of course the alien species has not only survived but poses enough of a threat to wipe out all humans on Earth—assuming the aliens could negotiate the distance. One expedition member clandestinely captures an alien and smuggles it back to Earth, ostensibly for research purposes, resulting in new threats to the home planet. Both of these movies devote the bulk of their footage to fierce combat between aliens and humans as the earthlings fight to neutralize the subversive menace, with the second episode introducing a uniformed Special-Operations unit to do battle with the tenacious monsters.

Scott's later sci-fi thriller, *Blade Runner* (1982), is one of the outstanding examples of the disguised combat genre. Based on Philip K. Dick's popular science fiction novel *Do Androids Dream of Electric Sheep?* this film constructs a dark, menacing, dystopic Los Angeles threatened by a population of murderous superhuman androids or "replicants." One supervillain named Leon (Brian James) tells the protagonist Deckard (Harrison Ford), possibly a replicant himself, to "wake up, time to die!" Deckard not only survives but initiates a one-man crusade to destroy the androids, who had escaped from an off-world colony, presumably to wreak havoc on Los Angeles and other regions of the planet. Scott's narrative revolves around nearly continuous violent clashes between the hero Deckard and the ruthless villains, with action centered in a futuristic underworld. Los Angeles is populated by a mixture of recent Asian and Hispanic immigrants along with their android pets. Eventually, as the warfare unfolds, Scott depicts a series of armed confrontations between rival androids along with recurrent war between replicants and humans squarely in the tradition of *Invasion of the Body Snatchers*.

In Cameron's first *Terminator* movie (1984) we have yet another sequel to Scott's seminal work—appearing two years after *Blade Runner* just as *Aliens* followed *Alien* by two years. Although *Blade Runner* soon achieved iconic status, Cameron's film turned out to be an even bigger hit with American audiences. Following Scott, Cameron employs superhuman characters: the Terminator (Arnold Schwarzenegger) is a deadly android (or "cyborg") teleported from the future to carry out a terrifying mission, namely, to kill the future savior of humanity, played by Linda Hamilton. Opposing the Terminator is a character with equally superhuman features, Kyle Reese (played by Michael Biehn). The epic is driven by military-style combat between the two. The Terminator possesses a computer-like guidance system that helps plot his vicious attacks on humans, as well as a steel frame beneath his massive human physique. His vast system of armaments includes guided missiles, tanks, warplanes, and smaller but nonetheless deadly weapons. Here, as in many of his roles, Schwarzenegger evokes distinct aspects of Nazi *Übermensch* (superman) villains as well as hyper-masculine combat heroes of World War II movies, although Schwarzenegger's extremely bulked-up physique endows him with an added dimension. In a compelling flash-forward scene depicting a future war between machines and humans, *The Terminator* incorporates elements of the more conventional war genre: the figures have access to the latest assault weapons, while cars, trucks, and even a motorcycle substitute for the familiar tanks and jeeps. In the end Cameron's blockbuster anticipates a seemingly infinite cycle of future warriors—some machines, others human beings—doomed to battle each other repeatedly until, perhaps, the Terminator manages to obliterate humanity.

*The Terminator* became a box-office triumph, earned glowing critical reviews, and inspired a number of imitations that led to something of a new genre: the futuristic techno-action film replete with supertechno heroes and villains locked in epic combat. Cameron followed this initial effort with *Terminator 2: Judgment Day* (1991), in which Schwarzenegger plays a somewhat kinder, friendlier cyborg dedicated to helping humans. This served as a prelude to Jonathan Mostrow's even more ambitious *Terminator 3: Rise of the Machines* (2003), also featuring Schwarzenegger, on the eve of his audacious (and successful) run for California governor. All of these films can be described as male action-adventure blockbusters reliant on explosive and recurrent use of high-tech weaponry, only thinly disguised combat pictures.

Another kind of blockbuster, Tim Burton's *Batman* (1989), is set in a rather futuristic Gotham City like the one featured in the popular comic strip. *Batman* features Michael Keaton in the title role and Jack Nicholson as the Joker, a larger-than-life villain who (with his criminal gang) relishes his battles with the main protagonist. Like the Terminator, Batman possesses an imposing arsenal of high-tech weapons including the famous Batmobile, a powerful sports car with bullet-proof armaments, awesome guns, and the capacity to be turned into an attack aircraft. The Joker has access to less imposing technology, which includes a long rifle he unveils to shoot the Batplane out of the sky. Eventually, of course, Batman kills the Joker and frees Gotham City from the clutches of a brutal mob. In a final message to the people of the city Batman raises the specter of urban warfare, saying that the citizens have earned a period of rest from crime, "but if the forces of evil should rise again to cast a shadow on the heart of the city, call me." This is exactly what the Gotham denizens do in *Batman Returns* (1992), Burton's more polished sequel, which follows essentially the same narrative pattern: lethal combat between good and evil. The popularity of these two episodes inspired Eric Radonsky's *Batman: Mask of the Phantom* (1993) and Joel Schumacher's own follow-up, *Batman and Robin* (1997), starring none other than Schwarzenegger as the Freeze. These latter episodes contain unending warfare encounters and feature a host of flat, one-dimensional, cartoonish figures geared largely to young audiences.

Philip Noyce's *Patriot Games* (1992), a sequel to *The Hunt for Red October* and derived from another Clancy novel, follows the saga of retired CIA agent Jack Ryan (Harrison Ford). While on a lecture visit to London, Ryan finds himself in the middle of an Irish Republican Army (IRA) plot to assassinate a member of the British royal family: acting on his instincts as a marine vet, he shoots to death one of the gunmen, and the dead man's brother (Sean Bean) promises revenge on Ryan and his family. The movie follows extended combat, psychological and physical, between Ryan and the IRA, depicted here as a villainous, ultraviolent organization personified by an evil-looking Patrick Bergin. Ryan returns to the CIA hoping to legitimate and bolster his war against the terrorists. Eventually the assassins pursue Ryan, a sidekick, and his family to the waters of the Chesapeake Bay, at which point Ryan drives off and captures them, with some help from the navy and law enforcement, and then personally dispatches the leader at the end of some thrilling individual fights. The CIA hero is shown in *Patriot Games* to be above all a loving family man with strong feelings for his wife Kathy (Anne Archer) and daughter (Thora Birch), shown to be his greatest source of strength and motivation (as opposed to patriotism, anti-Communist ideology, or even loyalty to the CIA). Indeed Ryan's actions come across as mostly visceral; at one juncture he says, "There isn't any time to think, you just act." Throughout the movie, however, Noyce makes it clear that the protagonist embraces all that is good (including family values) while his enemies appear as brutal unfeeling terrorists who, in the real world, pose absolutely no threat to the United States. (More-realistic portraits of Irish rebellion can be found in *The Crying Game, In the Name of the Father,* and *Michael Collins.*)

One of the most hyped blockbusters of the 1990s, Roland Emmerich's *Independence Day* (1996), combines elements of the 1950s sci-fi alien-threat movies, later disaster films, and the generic combat picture. One might argue that *ID4* (as it was marketed) is the ultimate war narrative: a combat film with unprecedented martial scope and sweeping visual impact. Here awesome monsters from outer space maneuver huge vehicles over Earth, threatening three major cities and, we can only presume, the very survival of the planet. On the eve of the Fourth of July a massive counterresponse is engineered by three protagonists: a superfighter pilot (Will Smith), a nerdy satellite engineer (Jeff Goldblum), and a weak but determined U.S. President (Bill Pullman). It is the engineer, David Levinson, who figures out when the aliens plan to attack and who eventually comes up with a technological solution to the threat. In scenes of unmatched devastation, the aliens unleash their military capabilities, destroying New York City, Los Angeles, and Washington, D.C., as the president narrowly escapes in *Air Force One.* We see skyscrapers demolished in a matter of seconds, hundreds of cars flying through the air, and mass pandemonium. The aliens send off dozens of spaceships armed with powerful defense systems and weapons far beyond anything produced on Earth. After a series of failed U.S. military assaults on the alien fortress, the technician, the fighter pilot, and the president all wind up at Area 51, a secret military zone in Nevada, where they plot a counterattack. Cleverly, the engineer devises a computer virus that can infect the enemy communications system, nullifying the shields and permitting an effective counterstrike. Accompanied by the engineer, the pilot flies a captured alien spacecraft into a position so that the virus can be injected into the mother fortress. After repeated military failures, a renegade pilot (played as an out-of-control wacko by Dennis Quaid) finally manages to blow up the enemy craft. Earth barely survives this horrific onslaught, while the two heroes in the captured vessel naturally just manage to escape.

The ambitious combat narrative of *Independence Day* revolves around the capacity of *American* military and technological power to save the day, as the result of the largest armed mobilization ever. The clash between aliens and humans is of course nothing short of epochal, but in the end the human side is depicted only in the personas of Americans, even as Emmerich shows the entire planet coming under attack. Victory is delivered by all the ingenuity of the military-industrial-intelligence complex. For most of this superpatriotic film the president scarcely measures up to heroic status; he comes across more as an indecisive figurehead. Yet before the decisive clash Pullman's character delivers a rousing speech in which he intones that, to win this greatest of all battles, Earth's inhabitants would have to put aside their "petty differences" (read: class, racial, national, ideological). "We will finally all be united in our common interests," he says, adding that the human struggle for freedom has now become one for survival. In this, the President concludes, the Fourth of July will no longer be simply an American celebration; it will become an international holiday to be recognized by every person on Earth. Here we end up with not merely the ultimate patriotic trope symbolizing this most dramatic of all (U.S.) military triumphs, but its rather brazen extension to the entire world—a moment of grandiose imperial hubris where the United States, alas, emerges as the universal vehicle of freedom and survival.

Mostrow's *Terminator 3,* released nearly twenty years after the first episode and ten years after the first sequel, celebrates the images of technowar at a new level, in the context of a sci-fi adventure again showcasing the feats of Schwarzenegger. Insisting that "judgment day is inevitable," the film resonates with the motif "The machines will rise and war will never be the same." Indeed, whatever its other seductions, *Terminator 3* more than anything else hinges on the sounds, sights, motions, and outcomes of combat: fierce, violent, technological, repetitive. In the period after *Terminator 2,* Sarah Cooper had died of leukemia and her son John (Nick Stahl) is a recluse after having fought to avert a nuclear war that would have enabled the machines to take over the world. Suddenly an overpowering Terminatrix, the T-X (Kristanna Loken), enters the twenty-first century on a mission to kill John and his companion Kate Brewster (Claire Danes), paving the way for a final takeover by the machines. As an obsolete T-101 entity Schwarzenegger is sent to protect John and Kate from the beautiful but sadistic T-X, who, if successful, will be able to trigger a nuclear catastrophe. The enormous mass appeal of this movie, however, lies in neither its hackneyed plot nor its predictable characters but in its wild action sequences, including one where T-101 and T-X fiercely clash and one where a giant crane crashes through buildings, vehicles, and everything else standing in its way as it attempts to run down John and Kate. In the end, of course, Schwarzenegger is able to team with these two and avoid Armageddon, which is just about to be set off by a Skynet alert that would destroy all military command functions.

In the eschatological struggle between humans and machines constructed in *Terminator 3,* the technological beings, including those, like T-X, that also appear human, are shown to be the ultimate villains: emotionless, sadistic, ruthless, destructive. Such supervillains can have no redeeming virtues. The heroes are built with largely "human" features, are often ambivalent toward the violence surrounding them, and possess feelings like fear, anger, and despair. Yet there are situations where, as in the famous Jose Orozco murals in Mexico, humans and machines seem able to morph into each other, or at least to combine elements of each other. There is a definite continuity from one realm to the other, which is, after all, a feature of modernity itself. The film also reflects the great vulnerability of humans when it comes to the instruments of technology; that this is especially true of the military is shown in several powerful scenes. Further, Mostrow appears rather concerned about the degree to which technology has threatened to conquer human life, to take over the world, a threat best symbolized by nuclear weaponry. Ultimately, however, such motifs are trumped by what is far more central to the movie: the clash of robotic machines within awesome images of technowar, with prospects of total nuclear annihilation looming over all. The film is one long advertisement for the power of superweapons, vast killing machines of the sort the Pentagon has been quite willing to develop. Indeed warfare carried out by sophisticated combatants is what seems to have attracted such huge audiences, combined of course with the ultramasculine action persona of Schwarzenegger. Producers of *Terminator 3,* with the help of their "official" magazine, have celebrated their futuristic spectacle made up of a whole new generation of weaponry (far beyond anything imagined, for example, in *Blade Runner*). The most advanced humanoid robot ever produced was made by Honda specifically for this film. As the magazine suggests, modes of technowar highlighted here anticipate a reordering of battlefield combat facilitated by such innovations as nanotechnology and remote-warfare devices.

Quentin Tarantino's two episodes of *Kill Bill* (released in 2003 and 2004) build in several ways on the director's earlier work and, with some new twists here and there, further indulge his penchant for sustained graphic violence. The two "volumes" actually constitute one not very seamless four-hour film, incorporating Tarantino's inclination to borrow from established genres: thriller, gangster, action-adventure, spaghetti Western, kung fu. One thread runs through the entire narrative, disjointed as much of it is: images of bloody martial combat. We are told at the outset that "life is a series of mortal combats," and later we are informed that what lies at the heart of all combat is suppression of human emotion and compassion. The plot, extending across both segments, has enough twists and turns to imbue the endless bloody scenes with elements of mystery and surprise. Here as in other Tarantino films we are introduced to a series of exaggerated figures identified by impersonal nicknames such as the Bride, Black Mamba, Sidewinder, and Cottonmouth.

As the centerpiece of *Kill Bill*, the Bride (Uma Thurman) is a modern-day samurai warrior who had been active in the Deadly Viper Assassination Squad, a yakuza-style gang of warrior-assassins that prefers venerable Japanese swords to more conventional mob weapons like machine guns and automatic pistols. The killing process is said to be more dignified and honorable, even intimate, in its execution, in touch with premodern Oriental traditions. For Tarantino these swords and the flashy, swashbuckling swordplay that goes with them owe a debt not only to the yakuza films but also to the famous *Star Wars* light sabers. The story begins with the epigram chosen to introduce *Kill Bill: Vol. 1*: "Kill anyone who stands in the way, even if it be Lord God or Buddha." In a powerful flashback we see the Bride dressed in a wedding gown as she prepares to get married; she and the entire party are attacked gang-style and left for dead—the work of the Deadly Viper group—in an incident referred to as the "Massacre at the Two Pines Wedding Chapel" in El Paso, Texas. The squad includes Budd/Sidewinder (Michael Madsen), Elle Driver / California Mountain Snake (Daryl Hannah), and O-Ren Ishii / Cottonmouth (Lucy Liu) along with the Bride's former boss and lover, Bill (David Carradine). The Bride (also known as Beatrix Kiddo), who miraculously survives the onslaught and spends four years in a coma, upon recovering plans blood vengeance against the Vipers, first acquiring high-level samurai training as the ultimate weapon of justice. She compiles a list of people to be eliminated, with superman Bill the final stop. The Bride even travels to Okinawa, where she picks up a special sword, and Tokyo to exact her revenge against the villainous O-Ren Ishii, now head of a Japanese underground criminal gang. After a torturous journey she disposes of the deadly Vipers, reserving the last execution for the sadistic but nonetheless charming Bill—but not before he is able to deliver a speech on the virtues of Superman over Clark Kent.

The extended *Kill Bill* chapters exhibit both combat imagery and mythology, at times with impressive cinematic panache, as they move from one bloody scene to another marked by the athleticism of warriors dueling and slashing across the screen. In one lengthy scene in volume 1, the Bride implausibly manages to slay no less than eighty-eight skilled samurai on her way to dispatch her archenemy, the supremely arrogant Ishii. We see heads, arms, and legs cut off and blood gushing everywhere—graphic dismemberments that offer a brutal commentary on Tarantino's gory but otherwise simple tale of revenge. This narrative defines the Bride as the ultimate combat hero in the great samurai tradition, a role Thurman embraces with the requisite martial sense of confidence. Before her death O-Ren Ishii makes a dismissive reference to a "silly Caucasian girl who likes to play with samurai swords"—but of course the Bride has the last word. Bodies pile upon bodies in the first segment, while in the second (lengthier, talkier, and less bloody), that action revolves more around a series of martial encounters including one in which the Bride gouges out Elle's one remaining eye at the end of a fierce battle at close quarters. This scene comes just after the Bride uses her martial skills to escape being buried alive by Budd/Sidewinder. In volume 1 Tarantino incorporates anime sequences to dramatize the life of O-Ren Ishii, which further contributes to the cartoonish, rather comedic tone the director seemingly wants to capture. In both the animation and standard depictions, Asians are set up as the ultimate villains, shown consistently to be authoritarian, rigid, crude, and ruthless.

The kind of violence that permeates *Kill Bill* turns out to be just as much comedic as rational or militaristic, in the tradition of black comedy such as that in *Pulp Fiction*. It is the violence of wild and reckless fantasies, far removed from the highly structured (and far more subdued) violence of Hitchcock or Lang, for example. With Thurman as the main protagonist, moreover, Tarantino has selected a woman as combat heroine while building much of his storytelling around a series of "girl fights"—further indulging fantasies. In a twisted version of feminism, he apparently wants to show that women too can be brutal fighters, just as tough, confident, and violent as any man. As if to embellish the black-comedic dimension of his film, Tarantino has the Madsen character mumble a few words of wisdom before being struck and killed by a black mamba snake that Elle had placed in his box of reward money: just as warriors always need enemies, people *need* combat, for it gives them something to live for. And there should be absolutely no confusion on this point—*Kill Bill* is more than anything a combat movie, cloaked in other genres and framed against a darkly comedic backdrop.

# CHAPTER 6

# Pentagon Strategy, Technowar, and Media Culture

We have seen in earlier chapters how, with the growth of the imperial power and military reach of the United States, warfare today extends across the cultural as well as the institutional and battlefield terrains, the result of great technological changes now altering the very character of modern combat. Expanded military influence within the corporate media and popular culture is an inevitable outgrowth of the largest war machine the world has ever seen. The aftermath of 9/11, with its open-ended war on terror, reinforces this trend as the power structure turns increasingly to Orwellian methods of rule: media propaganda, technologies of surveillance and control, draconian law-enforcement methods, a warfare system that extends and deepens authoritarian politics. Renovated Pentagon strategy based on the high-tech "revolution in military affairs" (RMA), a defense-establishment article of faith since the early 1990s, underpins a more brazen, aggressive imperialism geared to heightened resource wars, geopolitical maneuvering, and efforts to crush political opposition. The likelihood of stepped-up armed intervention mounts, whatever party controls the White House, as U.S. global power increasingly depends on an ensemble of quasi-fascist ideologies—superpatriotism, worship of technology, militarism, national exceptionalism—for domestic legitimation. Yet, as we shall see, this glorification of technowar has its own limits and contradictions.

## Empire: The Movie

The U.S. pursuit of world domination gains crucial ideological support through the media, where images of superpower virtue can be seen daily across the sprawling entertainment industry and elsewhere. According to standard texts and discourses, the United States is and always has been a peaceful, dem-

221

ocratic nation forced to rely on military action only when threatened by demonic enemies. While there is little truth to such notions, they remain a staple of media and academic culture and are believed by enough Americans to ensure popular acceptance of a huge war-making machinery and security state. The U.S. media are today saturated with representations of violence and routinely celebrate the exploits of gangsters, terrorists, and warriors of all types, a pattern accelerated by the rightward shift in American politics that came with the end of the cold war and the events of 9/11. The neoconservatives, whose extreme hawkish views were only a decade ago confined to the political margins, had by 2002 gained control of U.S. foreign policy while moving to strengthen the media's role as a propaganda arm of corporations, the government, and the military. Their success is nowhere more visible than in foreign policy. The major TV networks, talk radio, and even most print outlets have degenerated into a cheerleading chorus behind whatever military venture Washington decides to launch.

Hollywood's recent film output mirrors this trajectory, even as producers and directors often fiercely defend their creative autonomy and liberal credentials. In 2003 and 2004 the studios spent lavishly on dozens of movies pervaded with combat motifs, including *The Last Samurai, Lord of the Rings, The Matrix Reloaded, Terminator 3, The Alamo,* and *Master and Commander,* all viewed by large audiences and praised by respected film critics. Also released were Quentin Tarantino's two martial *Kill Bill* sequences and the blockbuster epic *Troy,* with its many computer-generated scenes of war and bloodshed. In *The Matrix Reloaded* (2003), a marriage of kung fu movies, comic books, action-adventure films, and the combat genre, directors Andy and Larry Wachowski employ such high-tech devices as robotics, arriving at a new breed of cyber-thriller filled with ultraviolent imagery, lethal weaponry, and spectacular battlefield exploits interwoven with a fusion of humans and machines comparable to scenes from *Terminator 3.* Part of a planned trilogy, this *Matrix* episode won instantaneous cult status among young viewers, earning over $450 million the year after its release.

In Steven Spielberg's *War of the Worlds* (2005), based on the 1898 H. G. Wells novel that envisions aliens from Mars invading planet Earth, a new wave of killers from outer space threatens innocent, peace-loving earthlings—the perfect tale for an updated cold-war-style paranoia in the post-9/11 era. Apparently referring to modern-day jihadic violence, writer David Koepp comments: "We don't know where they're from. They're from somewhere far away and they don't seem to want to tell us where they're from. They don't seem to want to talk at all. They just want to kill."[1] Like Commies of an earlier time, these recycled demons symbolize an omnipresent threat that is supposed to bring to mind the grave menace of dispersed, elusive Al Qaeda operations. *War of the Worlds* continues Spielberg's long-standing obsession with war as spectacle, an obsession that goes back to *1941* (1979) and extends to *Saving Private*

*Ryan* (1998), where high-tech special effects heighten graphic images of warfare. As with *1941* and *Empire of the Sun* (1987), Spielberg relishes scenes of panic, of displaced people running from barbarian hordes, one young girl asking, "Is it the terrorists?" Here we have, for the first time, a cinematic spectacle bringing all the drama of 9/11, the "new Pearl Harbor," to the big screen. A sci-fi thriller that is also a combat picture, *War of the Worlds* conveys a shadowy, fearsome world of nearly invisible enemies, ideal for a cinematic war on terrorism. Unspeakable evil pulsates through every frame of the movie, in which villains have no identity, no motive, no rationality, absolutely no redeeming features; they are mechanical figures resembling the demons of old Western and combat pictures. Aliens materialize as war machines with two-hundred-foot tripods, so powerful they can instantly vaporize human beings. In the end, of course, the marauding invaders succumb, this time to voracious microbes, symbolizing potent agents in the epic struggle against terrorist evil.

The new cycle of martial films features high-tech innovations, special-effects wizardry, and nonstop violence combined with blasting sound. Combat furnishes the key dramatic vehicle, a stratagem that has worked splendidly at the box office. Filmmakers have traditionally sought Pentagon assistance for technical and stylistic enhancements, but as digital technology becomes cheaper and more sophisticated the need for such collaboration diminishes. In any case, the glorified militarism favored by producers like Jerry Bruckheimer *(Top Gun, Armageddon, Black Hawk Down, Pearl Harbor)* has surely been driven more by ideological than by technical priorities.

The war on terror reinvigorates an aggressive U.S. military strategy, the extension of an imperial agenda that long predates the current Bush presidency but which now has fewer limits of time and space—the best possible regimen for endless global struggle of good against evil, democracy against tyranny, civilization against barbarism. In a world of Hobbesian chaos where fanatical madmen and terrorists run wild, people are more easily mobilized to fight "good wars" for noble and patriotic ideals. Those same militaristic values that buttress the empire and its war machine intersect with the commercial and aesthetic priorities of a film industry long attached to battlefield epics featuring patriotic heroes pitted against despicable villains. Today this narrative defines not only the combat genre but also movie conventions like sci-fi, action-adventure pictures, historical dramas, and horror films. Hollywood can even transform romantic comedies into combat spectacles, as with *Mr. and Mrs. Smith* (2005), the story of a husband and wife, each working as a hired assassin and equipped with the latest automatic weapons, who set out to kill each other on assignment. Television has yet to match this cinematic wave, but Showtime's fall 2005 series *Sleeper Cell* follows the pattern laid down by the entertainment industry: a group of Islamic extremists plots to destroy an American city, inspired by nothing more than the desire to cause pure mayhem and destruction. The characters include an Arab thug posing as a member of a Jewish temple, showing again that terrorists can lead ordinary lives as they hatch barbaric schemes in the most unexpected places. Steven Bochco's *Over There,* an FX channel series inspired by the events of 9/11 and the Iraq war, dramatizes the travails of U.S. frontline troops and is advertised as a program that "supports the troops by humanizing them." As the motif of foreign terrorism feeds into right-wing agendas—aggressive foreign policy, technowar, expanded surveillance, lavish Pentagon spending, a harsher law-and-order regimen—the weight of such agendas is felt across the culture industry.

The familiar Hollywood obsession with monstrous enemies takes a predictable new turn in post–cold war media culture, with the casting of movie demons shifting from conventional Nazis, Japs, gooks, and redskins to a new lineup of modern-day evildoers: Arabs, Muslims, assorted terrorists, rogue tyrants, standard drug traffickers. Framed against the backdrop of U.S. global ambitions, such demons often represent racial stereotypes of the sort crudely recycled in hundreds of Hollywood Westerns.[2] Although white male heroes played by Sylvester Stallone, George Clooney, Arnold Schwarzenegger, Harrison Ford, and Steven Seagal have dominated the modern action-adventure genre, warrior-saviors now include minorities and women: *XXX* with Vin Diesel, *Under Siege* with Denzel Washington, *GI Jane* with Demi Moore, *Kill Bill* with Uma Thurman, *The Matrix Reloaded* with Carrie-Anne Moss, and *Mr. and Mrs. Smith* with Angelina Jolie. Of course such heroes (and heroines) equally rely on the marvels of technowar. Some within the new cycle of villains, moreover, might be expected to get hold of weapons of mass destruction—a motif exploited in such films as *True Lies, Under Siege, The Peacemaker,* and *Terminator 3,* in which last-minute heroics barely stave off nuclear catastrophe. Demons in popular culture, especially those with access to doomsday weapons, serve reactionary ends insofar as they provoke the wrathful vengeance of a power structure under siege. At the same time, dehumanized Others furnish easy psychological targets at moments of public fear and paranoia, which since 9/11 (and similar events in Europe) can be linked to public anxiety over possible new (Arab, Muslim) terrorist attacks.

As U.S. combat operations in Afghanistan and Iraq grow more destructive and costly—as the general contradictions of empire sharpen—the ideological functions of the military-entertainment complex take on new significance. The deadly effects of armed intervention include widespread human casualties, population displacements, a drain on material resources, and environmental ruin—not to mention the subversion of international law along with heightened attacks on domestic rights and freedoms. Among other things, propaganda distorts or conceals information regarding these and other costs. As the media become more structurally and ideologically concentrated to better fit elite agendas, propaganda aims are more readily achieved. One indication of this is the vanishing political differences between Republicans and Democrats, especially around foreign and military policy. The culture industry has for decades been a vital conduit of imperial agendas, and Hollywood studios (despite their reputed liberalism) have rarely departed from this norm. Motion pictures have the visual power to sway mass audiences interested mostly in simple diversion. While propaganda is usually viewed as a distinctly *state* function associated with dictatorial regimes, modern capitalism is more sophisticated in its hegemonic operations, relying on a labyrinthine network of corporate, media, government, and military structures that make even the most powerful ideological methods nearly invisible.

As high-tech information and control systems reshape U.S. military strategy, these same features of RMA also dominate media culture. Put differently, just as the Pentagon fixates on information technology and media power, the culture industry itself becomes increasingly fascinated with military imagery. There is a strong convergence as, during moments of buildup to armed intervention (Yugoslavia, Iraq), the media dutifully serve the Pentagon with continuous ideological framing operations: embedded reporting, hawkish "expert" commentary, right-wing talk shows, patriotic battlefield features. Since films take longer to produce and distribute than current-events TV and radio programs, Hollywood's impact on public opinion is inevitably more refracted, less direct and immediate. Yet, surveying dozens of mainstream films dealing with terrorism and war in the 1980s and 1990s, it is easy to see how the big screen has turned into a propaganda vehicle for every U.S. imperial gambit, usually without the need for drawn-out narratives or other verbal messages. In the theater, moreover, designated enemies can be graphically depicted in their full regalia, bigger than life, exaggerated in their diabolical features, and stereotyped, sooner or later to be destroyed by fearsome weaponry. Jack Shaheen documents how Arabs and Muslims have been targeted across many decades of American filmmaking, more flagrantly in the twenty years or so since Hollywood began dwelling on terrorism.[3] As portrayed in films like *Under Siege, The Sum of All Fears,* and even the otherwise enlightened *Three Kings* (1999), Arab and Muslim villains (typically thugs and terrorists) seem to fill an ideological void left by departing cold war enemies. Here the triumph of superior technology, namely, *military* technology, carries great narrative and political weight, endowing (usually patriotic, masculine) heroes with righteous virtues in their pursuit of exalted goals. In the instance of film, especially, media culture works more powerfully than cruder, more obvious forms of government indoctrination—and thus constitutes the ideal propaganda for empire.

## Hollywood and the Pentagon

The Pentagon has been increasingly sensitive about how the U.S. military presence around the world is depicted to mass publics. The film industry has a long partnership with the armed forces: military public-relations offices typically review movie scripts in exchange for access to bases, equipment, stock footage, and expert consultation, all needed for "authenticity." The deep patriotic and militaristic content of most combat pictures, however, is rarely determined by stringent Pentagon controls over the way producers, writers, and directors do their work; instead this content flows from the larger political and media culture that is the repository of imperialist ideology. So attached are many Hollywood filmmakers to the combat spectacle with its enduring assumptions of superpower benevolence that they rarely wander far from the "bipartisan" foreign-policy consensus.

Of course the Pentagon would prefer to transform Hollywood movies into simple infomercials for the military, but no filmmaker nowadays would be ready to follow such a diktat. Phil Strub, longtime chief of the Pentagon's liaison office, has said that "any film that portrays the military as negative is not realistic to us," adding that combat-themed movies ought to satisfy three criteria: depict military life as "realistically" as possible, inform the public about U.S. military prowess, and assist in recruitment.[4] Historically, this agenda has met with considerable success. As David Robb writes in *Operation Hollywood*: "Allowing the world's most powerful military to place propaganda into the world's most powerful medium—unchecked and unregulated—for over 50 years has certainly helped the Pentagon get more recruits for the armed forces and ever-increasing appropriations from Congress."[5] While there is a legacy of frequent, sometimes intense conflict over armed-forces guidelines, in fact Strub has been uniformly admired in Hollywood and few pictures have deviated much from the ideological consensus he fostered: patriotism, a virtuous U.S. military, glorification of battlefield exploits, masculine heroism.[6] Although the Pentagon has refused assistance to works like *Memphis Belle, Courage Under Fire, A Few Good Men*, and Oliver Stone's Vietnam trilogy—all savaged for their "negative" images of the military—the overall historical record is one of intimate collaboration serving both partners.

From its earliest days Hollywood promoted a culture of militarism, offering mass audiences a regular diet of combat and action movies replete with graphic scenes of death and destruction. At first this contribution was muted owing to the relatively small scale of U.S. military power. But the studios quickly became fascinated with the combat genre (the dominant form if combat Westerns are included) since it guaranteed huge box-office returns. The military brass naturally relished this kind of cinema too and worked diligently with filmmakers to glorify battlefield action and everything that surrounded it.

During and immediately after World War II, combat movies dwelled on noble American military triumphs over evil monsters like Hitler and Mussolini—propaganda for the ultimate good war, with no reservations or apologies. The famous Why We Fight series, organized by Howard Hawks and other studio luminaries including John Ford and Frank Capra, exemplified this close alignment of Hollywood and the War Department. With great war dramas fresh in mind, the public was drawn to battlefield stories made more authentic by extensive use of stock footage and technical advances over earlier renditions of combat. Films released over the next two decades fit this pattern, assisted by a swollen Pentagon public-relations apparatus. To win such assistance, studios had to follow strict guidelines: no "negative images" of military officers, no excessive foul language, no "sexual improprieties" like adultery, only moderate drinking, and so forth. Yet if filmmakers often argued with Pentagon censors over these strictures, the larger motifs of patriotism, male heroism, and the essential goodness of U.S. military action were taken for granted. Even those films that ran afoul of Pentagon censors, like *From Here to Eternity* and *The Caine Mutiny*, scarcely violated this ideological formula. The good-war narrative, de rigeur for sci-fi and horror as well as the combat genre, shaped the cold war era during which Hollywood gladly served as a cultural arm of U.S. global interests. The mixture of warfare and cinema was so explosive that it is easy to see how, across the decades, an actor like John Wayne could be so widely viewed as the ultimate icon of military courage and patriotism, the essence of a combat hero, dwarfing any real-life battlefield figure.[7]

In the aftermath of Vietnam, however, military portraits grew more complex and jaundiced at the hands of directors like Francis Ford Coppola, Oliver Stone, Stanley Kubrick, and Barry Levinson even as the cold war consensus remained intact. The Pentagon sought to counter film assaults on the military during the late 1970s and 1980s, but most "assaults," even when they were harsh in tone, rarely challenged the main premises of U.S. foreign and military policy. Any criticism would have meshed with what former secretary of defense Robert McNamara later conceded in his memoirs and in *The Fog of War*, namely, that certain "mistakes" and "miscalculations" were made in carrying out the Vietnam War: the problems were tactical, matters of implementation. Good-war pictures about humiliating U.S. defeat by a poor Third World country surely would have been difficult to make, even in Hollywood, but heralded antiwar messages of the "New Hollywood" directors were limited and inward, consumed mostly with home-front costs and traumas. At the same time, films of the period typically conveyed elements of the Vietnam syndrome tied to national failure and impotence, suggesting that Pentagon leverage over the film industry had at least temporarily waned. Where the military did assist in Vietnam War films (for example, the *Rambo* series), the idea was to convert painful defeat into miraculous victory, predictably with little success. Other reputedly antiwar films like *The Deer Hunter, Coming Home*, and *Casualties of War* portrayed the military debacle from a distinctly American standpoint.

Post-Vietnam erosion of the U.S. military image would soon be reversed by a new cycle of ultrapatriotic, militaristic films starting in the late 1980s, with Tony Scott's *Top Gun* (1986) a seminal turning point. More crucial yet was the first Gulf War, the first high-tech TV combat spectacle leading to a post–cold war revival of patriotism and militarism, with Desert Storm exposing viewers to all the flourishes of an action-adventure blockbuster.[8] Not coincidentally, it was the Gulf War that first enabled the U.S. military to unveil a truly integrated, networked communications system.[9] Throughout the 1990s the film industry rekindled its alliance with the Pentagon, while dazzling images of military prowess and battlefield heroism began to transcend the combat genre as such. Meanwhile, the refinement of digital technology meant that Hollywood no longer required military help to establish cinematic authenticity, which in any event mattered little to targeted youth audiences scarcely interested in the actual history of warfare. As high-tech spectacles reshaped both filmmaking and military action, themes of patriotism, technological wizardry, and combat heroism were more effectively conveyed to theater audiences. Profitable box-office returns of 1990s movies like *True Lies, Armageddon, Independence Day,* and *Black Hawk Down,* not to mention World War II epics like *Saving Private Ryan* and *Pearl Harbor,* fit this pattern. Those few pictures outside the dominant trend—for example, Ed Zwick's *Courage Under Fire* and Terrence Malick's *Thin Red Line*—would receive no Pentagon support and limited marketing resources.

As cinematic technology reshapes media culture, the appeal of martial narratives and images to males under thirty already steeped in video games inevitably spreads. Modern warfare builds on that same technology, visible not only in film but also in TV, the Internet, and popular magazines. The most successful recent Hollywood-Pentagon collaboration was the 2001 Bruckheimer–Michael Bay war epic, *Pearl Harbor,* with its sentimental love story, old-fashioned male heroism, glorification of aviation, drama of national revenge—and creative use of computer graphics, especially for the attack on battleship row. A $140 million film, *Pearl Harbor* was marketed heavily for its powerful historical symbolism, and the strategy worked despite the picture's lack of historical veracity. The military gave filmmakers full access to Pearl Harbor and Hickam Field, providing all the needed equipment, supports, and human resources. As before, public-relations officers were little concerned with factual authenticity, opting instead for a fairy-tale rendition of historical events, such as wildly overstating the efficacy of the U.S. aerial counterattack and devoting fully one-third of the movie to the ill-fated Doolittle raid on Tokyo in April 1942, falsely shown as a moment of triumphal revenge.

The much later "Pearl Harbor" turned out to be the terrorist attacks of 9/11—yet another case of an innocent nation under attack from sneaky evildoers, followed by an outpouring of vengeful patriotism. After 9/11 Bush emissary Karl Rove went to Hollywood seeking media help in the war on terror, but the response of industry leaders was decidedly cool; no studio or producer would commit to an ideological campaign along the lines of the Why We Fight series. Ironically, however, these same studios had been churning out films about the terrorist menace like the *Delta Force* and *Navy Seals* episodes,

*Executive Decision, The Peacemaker,* and *Under Siege* for nearly two decades—films that would safely have met the demands of Rove and the neocons.

## Technowar and Media Culture

By the 1990s the merging of technowar and media spectacle had become vital to the flexing of imperial power. Meanwhile, stepped-up U.S. efforts to colonize the Middle East, with Iraq as centerpiece, contributed further to the expanded military influence over public life. By mid-2002 the Bush-neocon drive toward war, in reality a bipartisan venture from the outset, was being expertly marketed by an ensemble of government, military, and corporate-media interests designed to forge popular consensus and marginalize dissent. Propaganda deftly tapped into public fears of a jihadic attack, of foreign madmen and terrorists gaining access to weapons of mass destruction. The phony rationale for war was dutifully repeated and sugarcoated by craven media, their jingoism fed by embedded journalism and the assurance of high ratings and profits.

The film industry was less directly engaged in the Iraq war, although dozens of movies glorifying high-tech combat against primitive foes of Western democracy had long ago made their imprint on the political culture. War and action-adventure movies of the 1990s seemed likely to bolster public readiness for U.S. military action against designated foreign threats. The warrior ethos was by no means limited to TV and cinema, having spread into a new wave of high-tech magazines and, above all, the lucrative video-game business, which by the late 1990s was offering a "full spectrum" of machines for both military training and entertainment geared to simulations of realistic battlefield action. In mid-2005 seven of the top ten best-selling games had combat motifs, which were increasingly in demand after the U.S. invasion of Iraq, popular among a young generation attuned to the ultraviolent virtual world of war. (Roughly 70 percent of all buyers are under twenty, despite legislative bans on sales to minors in several states.) War games are not only extremely bloody but also frequently contain racist and sexist targeting of enemies. Based on interactive battlefield scenes, the videos teach a simple lesson: violence is the preferred, usually the only, answer to human conflict, the more lethal the better. In the post-9/11 ambience many games, produced by corporate giants like Nintendo, Sony, and Microsoft, feature scenarios of payback through high-tech armed onslaught.

War games originated in the Vietnam era, but the main catalyst was the Pentagon embrace of RMA, which stresses high-tech weapons and communications systems, new surveillance devices, remote warfare, robotics, and the weaponization of space. The military is now the main designer of war games, developed through a working partnership with the entertainment industry, computer firms, and academia. At the University of Southern California, for example, the Institute for Creative Technologies (ICT) links these partners through a series of lucrative grants (including $100 million from the army in 2004) to manufacture sophisticated cycles of war games. The games replicate military field operations and present creative strategic and tactical options for players, focusing on unconventional or "asymmetric" warfare in mostly urban settings to fit counterinsurgency programs.

Simulated on large, high-resolution screens, the drama of war engulfs the total visual field, imbuing combat with elements of aesthetic beauty and playful excitement, what one game producer calls the "dopamine rush." Thanks to the wonders of digital imaging, techniques of video-game and film production have gradually merged since the mid-1990s, inspired by shared battlefield and action-adventure formats. Viewers see elements of technowar in such movies as the later *Star Wars* episodes, *Pearl Harbor, XXX, Windtalkers,* and *The Matrix* series. Related innovations have entered paid video programs linked to computers and portable devices, giving rise to a convergence of electronic products around film, video games, and the Internet, developments driven by tech firms like Microsoft, Intel, and IBM in collaboration with media giants like Disney, Time Warner, Sony, and NewsCorp.

With visual backdrops set in World War II, Vietnam, and Iraq, war games account for more than $28 billion in sales annually, a figure expected to rise dramatically. Their specialty is violent revenge fantasies like those in the Rambo series, many drawn from movies like *Delta Force, Black Hawk Down,* and *Batman Begins.* The games and movies are driven by the same digital technology, each influencing the other just as each embraces the military experience. In Full-Spectrum Warrior (2004), made by Microsoft and ICT and produced at the Army Infantry School in Fort Benning, Georgia, a realistic simulator allows participation in urban combat against guerrilla fighters. Atari's Act of War (2005), written by former army captain Dale Brown, features a group of military vets tracking down international terrorists who plan to destabilize the world economy. Produced at the same time, THQ's Destroy All Humans asks players in its marketing to take "One Giant Step *on* Mankind." At the 2005 Electronic Entertainment Expo in Los Angeles, the industry unveiled a new generation of video games and consoles, with giant screens marketing hundreds of commando adventures and warfare scenarios built around the latest interactive battlefield scenarios. Writing in a popular gaming magazine, Jack Thompson argues that when young players become absorbed in combat videos for hundreds or thousands of hours, they often wind up addicted to battlefield violence: "These games don't just teach skills—they break down the inhibition to kill. We've supposedly been trained by society and our parents not to kill another person, so the way to break that down is to put a soldier in a VR [virtual reality] setting, which will be far more effective in the long run."[10]

Pentagon strategists nowadays paradoxically mimic Hollywood, borrowing advanced technics of warfare created at the studios. One example is robotics, long a staple of the U.S. space program, which has come to play a vital role in both filmmaking and military planning. In 2004 the army created the SWORDS (Special Weapons Observation Reconnaissance Detection System) program, which features three-foot robotic fighters outfitted with tank tracks, night-vision devices, and mounted automatic weapons that can fire more than three hundred rounds per burst. In early 2005 the army deployed eighteen SWORDS units to Iraq for the first-ever sustained use of remote-control ground warfare, and more units have been ordered. The system recalls images of killer droids in earlier sci-fi movies, renegade cyborgs in *Blade Runner,* and robotic armies facing off in different *Star Wars* episodes (although some contain distinctly anti-imperialist narratives). The Pentagon also built an unmanned "trauma pod" that deploys robots for surgeries and other medical procedures in combat situations, part of its move to automate diverse sectors of the battlefield, both ground and air; at least one-third of all military vehicles are expected to be unmanned by 2015. In spring 2006 the unmanned ground vehicle R-Gator, built by John Deere and iRobot, is scheduled to be deployed, one of a new cycle of "smart" vehicles built to perform a series of combat missions. Added to these inventions will be refined microwave-beam weapons that can be deployed for "crowd control" in urban warfare.

In 2003 producers of the Schwarzenegger vehicle *Terminator 3* created a spectrum of high-tech weapons and vehicles specifically for that picture, a film tribute to robotic combat. Marketed through its own "official" magazine, the movie introduces a "new universe of machines" powerful enough to vanquish any imaginable foe. The magazine describes Schwarzenegger as an "unstoppable cyborg" fresh off the assembly line, equipped with an arsenal of devastating "T3" products. For the movie Honda built the most advanced humanoid robot ever, said to profoundly influence the conduct of battlefield action in both cinema and real warfare, using remote systems driven by molecular and cellular devices made possible by nanotechnology. According to one writer, stressing the connection between film and combat videos, "one of the most important things to note with remote warfare is that it distances soldiers from death . . . and [they] find it easier to kill. A generation of children raised on violent video games could therefore be excellent future soldiers."[11] Technowar allows for a safe psychological distancing from the horrors of combat, something intrinsic to aerial warfare and now extended to ground action. The killing process has grown more technically ritualized: targets on a screen are identified and then blown away by pressing buttons or deploying robots to unleash deadly missile and bomb attacks.

The Pentagon's own Defense Advanced Research Projects Agency (DARPA) closely follows these cinematic innovations—a staple of recent combat, action-adventure, and sci-fi movies—as it sharpens new battlefield technology along the lines of SWORDS. Robotics, information technology, militarization of space, combat video games, high-tech and unmanned planes, and precision-guided weapons reconfigure modern warfare as embraced by both Hollywood and the Pentagon. The military openly solicits technological assistance from the film industry, video-game business, and academic centers like ICT. A vast extension of George Lucas's *Star Wars* empire, recently installed at the San Francisco's Presidio, formerly a U.S. Army post, is equally rich in cinematic and military potential. The Letterman Digital Arts Center cost $350 million and employs 1,500 people who work to create a universe of epic clashes between good and evil, where warrior cultures and superweaponry take center stage in the drama of superhero myths drawn from the work of Joseph Campbell and others.[12] And like other studios always looking to create more spectacular warfare imagery, the sprawling Lucas facilities hire scores of retired military officers as technical consultants.

As a linchpin of U.S. global power, technowar strengthens the military component of imperialism at a time when Washington understandably prefers to downplay its unsurpassed arsenal of weapons of mass destruction. The 2005 round of new Pentagon reductions, including dozens of base closings across the country and in Europe, is best seen within Secretary of Defense Donald Rumsfeld's modernization scheme to make combat forces lighter, more flexible, more high-tech, and more lethal—a project encoded in the 2005 Quadrennial Defense Review. (The calculated savings are paltry—probably no more than $5 billion yearly.) A redesigned military is supposed to augment U.S. capacity to control the planet at a time when explosive turbulence (social, environmental, military) is expected to increase throughout the twenty-first century.

The neocons have always viewed the militarization of space as basic to solidifying U.S. command and control systems over the planet, as it permits a more efficient worldwide attack capacity. The Bush administration, working to revamp the National Space Policy, has pushed hard for a more aggressive space program. General Lance Lord, head of the Air Force Space Command, has said that the United States must seek absolute military domination of space—a goal seen as both easily reachable and nonnegotiable, and one that means eventual deployment of sophisticated weapons in space (including nuclear devices). The United States now has roughly seventy satellites in orbit. These are vital to such military purposes as navigation, communications, and intelligence; without them the launch of unmanned Predator drone planes and other high-tech devices used in Afghanistan and Iraq would be impossible. Surveillance mechanisms are crucial: the Pentagon is now developing a new generation of spy satellites as part of the classified Future Imagery Architecture program. Based on the Hubble Space Telescope, except that they face the earth, these satellites will be equipped with optical lenses that can take detailed photos of even the smallest human earthly movements. Assisted by space technology, the Pentagon already possesses a hypersonic glider with global strike capability; it can strike any target in the world within ninety minutes. The misnamed Strategic Defense Initiative, primarily an *offensive* weapons scheme, is central to a full-spectrum strategy that would enable the United States to counter Russian and Chinese military power.[13] The militarization of space aggravates the threat of a new arms race likely to pose the question of planetary survival, but, as Noam Chomsky points out, "the basic [U.S.] principle is that hegemony is more important than survival."[14] Now roughly $20 billion a year, the space budget is expected to skyrocket to $50 billion by 2007.

Technowar further emboldens a reckless militarism and messianic exceptionalism that concede few limits to American power. Moreover, technological superiority has come to signify, and justify, a moral and political supremacy that is often invoked to rationalize any U.S. imperial aggression, helping legitimate "preemptive" military action and justify outright contempt for troublesome international rules and agreements. High-tech warfare ultimately reduces curbs on U.S. militarism and helps fuel the crude turn toward *Machtpolitik* by elites of both parties. The United States has violated or refused to endorse several international treaties and laws, ignored the UN Charter's prohibition of military aggression, flouted the Geneva Accord in its systematic mistreatment of prisoners, and carried out deliberate assaults on civilian populations (as during 2004 in Fallujah, where an entire city was destroyed to suit counterinsurgency goals). While such criminal behavior has deep roots in American history, new refinements of technowar give U.S. leaders yet another powerful weapon—both materially and ideologically—in their pursuit of a new Manifest Destiny.

## The Limits of Technowar

Since high-tech militarism does so much to revitalize the warfare system, its capacity to strengthen U.S. imperial power ought to be substantial. The evidence so far, however, suggests what logic might reveal: technowar is riddled with its own illusions and contradictions. What saturates movies and video games is not always so easily translated into real life. While the purely *informational* element of military operations has been augmented, not to mention the sheer firepower and accuracy of modern weaponry, the U.S. drive toward world supremacy—aligned with its push for neoliberal globalization—gives rise to problems that technowar itself cannot possibly solve. Some of these problems are visible in escalating blowback, notably in militant forms of resistance produced by the invasion and occupation of Iraq.

While technowar broadly understood promises all the spectacular combat achievements of a blockbuster film or video game, replete with fascinating "shock and awe" battlefield scenarios, its success has fallen well short of what Pentagon strategists clearly expected. The Iraq calamity reveals both strengths and weaknesses of a high-tech military—rapid battlefield victories followed by a protracted, bloody occupation that American planners surely never anticipated and probably cannot defeat short of nuclear war. Since mid-2003, moreover, public support for this failed venture has steadily waned as costs mount and resistance intensifies, sinking to Vietnam War levels of under 35 percent by early 2006 and producing the first signs of Congressional opposition. Meanwhile, recruitment quotas for all service branches were well off target, a predicament deepening with each, almost daily, horror story out of Afghanistan and Iraq. The army was lagging 25 percent behind its 2005 quota with no turnaround in sight, even as recruiters aggressively solicited teenagers with offers of bonuses up to $35,000 and promises of exciting jobs. The Iraq disaster alone has taxed Pentagon human resources well beyond capacity: of some 140,000 troops in the field, more than 60,000 were drawn from National Guard units, with additional tens of thousands returning for a second tour of duty. The nightmare of fending off tenacious, skilled, dispersed insurgents fighting on their own turf, in often brutal weather conditions, has taken a severe toll on U.S. morale and combat efficiency. Young field-grade officers, many recently graduated from West Point, are reportedly leaving the army in record numbers. After long months in the field, moreover, troops can look forward to possible home-front ordeals including bleak job prospects and various post-traumatic stress disorders leading to high incidence of mental breakdowns, substance abuse, and suicide.

As recruitment and retention problems worsen, the Pentagon brass becomes more desperate. The capacity to sustain imperial hegemony, which Rumsfeld and the neocons naively believed could be solidified by means of technowar, now seems well beyond the resources of an all-volunteer force. The army spends $1.5 billion yearly on recruitment, with six thousand operatives sent around the nation to cajole mostly poor youth with inducements of jobs training, good pay, and exotic assignments, although what the armed forces really want is a steady influx of frontline warriors for long tours of duty in life-threatening battle zones. High-school students encounter zealous recruiters in hallways, at home, in shopping malls, and on their computers. Bush's 2002 No Child Left Behind Act grants recruiters access to students' private information and allows unsolicited visits to homes. So anxious is the army for recruits that criminal records, drug problems, and lack of diplomas are increasingly overlooked. Junior ROTC programs have been established nationwide, as the Pentagon moves to build a corps of "teen cadets" in high schools and even middle schools.[15] The U.S. military has grown so desperate that it has poured considerable resources into a media campaign *within Iraq* to smooth over the inevitable horrific images of occupation.

But recruiting campaigns have mostly stalled, torpedoed mostly by the Iraq disaster—a point conceded by General John P. Abizaid, chief of the U.S. Central Command, who in spring 2005 said the military reports from Iraq create new obstacles for recruiters, suggesting that a youth regimen of action-adventure blockbusters and combat video games has failed to produce the expected ideological results. Nor has a majority of Americans bought ridiculous Bush-neocon attempts to frame Iraq as a World War II–style good war, or even as a heroic front in the antiterror crusade. In fact the psychological outcome of such cultural products as films and games cannot be assumed: violent combat on screen might well end up as little more than fantasy, only rarely translated into real-life situations. Aside from PlayStation 2 and Xbox, it is true that young people have always played games, some rather violent—and indeed there is no evidence proving that kids have become more violent over the past two decades. In the case of movies, the blockbuster phenomenon apparently is of less import to a young generation concerned less with movie *content* than with the high-tech thrills, celebrity tales, and incessant tabloid gossip that surrounds it.

In early 2005 the Pentagon hired an outside marketing firm, BeNow, Inc., to carry out direct advertising, hoping to reach a targeted youth population where a militarized popular culture had so far failed. Set up by the Joint Advertising, Marketing, Research, and Studies Office of the Pentagon, the program is designed to compile databases on teenagers and college students, including academic, banking, and motor-vehicle records. Noncitizens are targeted as part of the Development, Relief, and Education for Minors Act, directed at children of undocumented workers residing in the United States for at least five years and entitling them to citizenship after serving a full military term. Still, the Army Recruiting Command head, General Michael D. Rochelle, predicted that recruiting difficulties would continue and likely worsen through at least 2006, with the army needing yet another eighty thousand *combat* soldiers just to maintain its 2005 Iraq occupation strength. (The army can be expected to focus recruiting efforts on the tens of thousands of evacuees produced by Hurricane Katrina, many of whom could be homeless and/or jobless well into the future.)

The crisis of an all-volunteer military illustrates a flawed premise of technowar and RMA: that a smaller, flexible, more high-tech armed forces can serve U.S. imperialism better at a time when conventional ground warfare has largely exhausted its potential. The present volunteer model goes back to 1973, when forty years of conscription was finally scrapped, an inevitable outcome of the Vietnam War. The difficulty facing war planners today is that global domination requires far more than superior technology and firepower, especially when ground troops are needed in large numbers to fight counterinsurgency, a lesson U.S. elites seemingly never absorbed from Vietnam. The United States presently has 1.4 million troops in uniform, but fewer than one-third are available for field operations and fewer yet serve as frontline troops. In Iraq and Afghanistan, the military presence includes not only large infantry, armor, and airborne deployments but also forces for intelligence, security, logistics, and ongoing infrastructural tasks. Despite privatization of certain support activities, such undertakings cannot be sustained for long without reimposing some version of the draft, an option fraught with new and likely unacceptable political costs.

Technowar is laden with other problems: refined data-gathering methods can heighten combat efficiency, but their value ultimately depends on how that data is filtered, interpreted, and acted upon, that is, on *human* intelligence with its peculiar frailties and biases. Machines at the disposal of the Pentagon and agencies like the CIA, the FBI, and the National Security Agency (NSA) do not function autonomously but rather work through a series of institutional and ideological mediations. There is nothing shocking about the fact that repeated warnings of impending major terrorist attacks, furnished by U.S. intelligence in the months leading up to 9/11, were ignored or downplayed because the Bush administration had fixed its gaze on entirely different horizons, mainly regime change in Iraq. In the case of the Iraq war, it has become clear that intelligence was wildly distorted and even manufactured to suit White House plans for remapping the Middle East. As James Bamford shows in *A Pretext for War*, U.S. intelligence operations have often morphed into sheer propaganda thinly disguised as data gathering, then used indiscriminately by journalists like Judith Miller of the *New York Times* to support Pentagon military objectives.[16] As for high-tech surveillance, NSA eavesdropping devices that rely on spy satellites orbiting some twenty-two thousand miles above Earth can transmit only so much useful intelligence—and virtually nothing about elusive insurgent or terrorist operations. (Whether the touted new Future Imagery Architecture system will transcend such limits is doubtful.) Reports from the field in Afghanistan and Iraq indicate that patrols rarely have adequate knowledge of imminent attacks despite access to the most advanced electronic communications. Two murky "battlefields" confronting the U.S. military today—jihadic violence and insurgency—have no identifiable fronts or fixed targets that fit conventional models. Pentagon strategy is confounded by a world of dispersed, ever-shifting networks that are extremely difficult to locate, much less destroy, by means of standard or high-tech military action. Moreover, new global communications systems (not only encryption but also fiber optics and the Internet) process literally billions of electronic transmissions daily, further complicating the task of processing and interpreting what is received.

U.S. military strategy persists in the illusion that challenges to American global power can be isolated and zapped by overwhelming force—an arrogant, militaristic outlook that technowar with its fixation on supposedly fail-proof information systems only reinforces. The Iraq venture magnifies this illusion, at the cost of tens of thousands of lives and yet another devastated country, as the Pentagon faces growing insurgencies and jihadic forces that it has no viable military doctrine to fight. One intractable problem is that the very power and scope of U.S. armed might, a surface advantage, dictates that many antisystem forces will adopt "asymmetric warfare," designed to neutralize that very advantage. It might be that technowar, despite its capacity to destroy the planet many times over, rests upon crumbling strategic foundations, exacerbated by the chauvinistic belief that American "values" (i.e., imperial domination) are so righteous, so inseparable from universal goals of peace, democracy, and human rights, that they will be eagerly welcomed by everyone outside a few small enclaves of evildoers. The idea that resistance to U.S. global hegemony is confined to tiny pockets of anti-Western fanatics bereft of motive, logic, or political aims, a plague to be eradicated by maximum force—something technowar should easily achieve given enough time—turns on itself. Such an illusion ensures new cycles of blowback along with a strengthening of the warfare and security-state systems at the heart of a ruthless—but increasingly vulnerable—imperial order.

# Notes

## Introduction

1. Norman Denzin, *The Cinematic Society* (London: Sage, 1991).

2. See George Ritzer, *Enchanting a Disenchanted World* (Thousand Oaks, CA: Pine Forge, 1999); and Guy Debord, *The Society of the Spectacle* (New York: Zone Books, 1995).

3. Denzin, *Cinematic Society,* 14.

4. Denzin, *Cinematic Society,* 15.

5. Denzin, *Cinematic Society,* 24.

6. Denzin, *Cinematic Society,* 36.

7. Earlier seminal works on the popular media and culture industry include Max Horkheimer, *Critical Theory* (New York: Seabury, 1972), esp. 273–90; Marshall McLuhan, *Understanding Media* (New York: McGraw-Hill, 1964); Debord, *Society of the Spectacle;* Edward Herman and Noam Chomsky, *Manufacturing Consent* (New York: Pantheon, 1988); Jean Baudrillard, *Simulations* (New York: Semiotext(e), 1983) and *Fatal Strategies* (New York: Semiotext(e), 1990); Douglas Kellner, *Media Culture* (New York: Routledge, 1995); Robert McChesney, *Rich Media, Poor Democracy* (New York: New Press, 1999).

8. On the profound rightward shift of the mass media, see David Brock, *The Republican Noise Machine* (New York: Crown, 2004), chap. 1.

9. McChesney, *Rich Media, Poor Democracy,* 77.

10. See Thomas Schatz, "The Return of the Hollywood Studio System," in *Conglomerates and the Media,* ed. Erik Barnouw et al. (New York: New Press, 1997), 83.

11. Neal Gabler, *An Empire of Their Own* (New York: Crown, 1988), 431–32.

12. See "Monster Budgets," *Entertainment,* December 9, 2005.

13. Lawrence Suid, *Guts and Glory* (Lexington: University Press of Kentucky, 2002), 2.

14. For a historical overview of U.S. imperialism, see Carl Boggs, *Imperial Delusions: American Militarism and Endless War* (Lanham, MD: Rowman & Littlefield, 2005), chap. 1.

15. T. D. Allman, *Rogue State* (New York: Nation Books, 2004), 366, 369.

16, Floyd Rumin, *CounterPunch,* January 1–15, 2006, 5.

17. See Noam Chomsky, *Rogue States* (Boston: South End Press, 2000), 124–55.

18. Robert D. Kaplan, *Warrior Politics* (New York: Vintage, 2002), 77.

19. Kaplan, *Warrior Politics,* 146–47; emphasis in original.

20. Robert Kaplan, *Imperial Grunts* (New York: Vintage, 2005), 99.

21. Robert Kagan, *Of Paradise and Power* (New York: Alfred Knopf, 2003), 86.

22. Kagan, *Of Paradise and Power,* 57.

23. Christopher Hitchens, *A Long Short War* (New York: Penguin, 2003), 48.

24. Cited in Bruce Miroff, *Pragmatic Illusions* (New York: David McKay, 1976), 55.

25. Neal Wood, *Tyranny in America* (London: Verso, 2004), 141.

26. Wood, *Tyranny in America,* 123–24.

27. Kellner, *Media Culture,* 2.

28. On the decline of the liberal tradition, see H. W. Brands, *The Strange Death of American Liberalism* (New Haven: Yale University Press, 2001).

29. On negative images of Arabs in Hollywood cinema, see Jack G. Shaheen, *Reel Bad Arabs* (New York: Olive Branch Press, 2001).

30. On racist depictions of Japanese in the Pacific theater, see John Dower, *War without Mercy* (New York: Pantheon, 1986).

31. Chris Hedges, *War Is a Force That Gives Us Meaning* (New York: Public Affairs, 2002).

32. David L. Robb, *Operation Hollywood* (Amherst, NY: Prometheus Books, 2004), 365.

33. Nafeez Mosaddeq Ahmed, *The War on Truth* (Northhampton, MA: Olive Branch Press, 2005), 364–65.

34. Brock, *The Republican Noise Machine,* chaps. 2, 7.

35. James Bamford, in *Rolling Stone,* December 1, 2005, 61.

36. *Los Angeles Times,* December 18, 2005.

# Chapter 1:  Militarism in American Popular Culture

1. Mary Edwards Wertsch, *Military Brats* (New York: Random House, 1991), 381.

2. Barbara Ehrenreich, *Blood Rites: Origins and History of the Passions of War,* chap. 10.

3. Ward Churchill, *Fantasies of the Master Race* (San Francisco: City Lights, 1998), 25.

4. Hedges, *War Is a Force,* 3.

5. Hedges, *War Is a Force,* 103.

6 See Bob Woodward, *Bush at War* (New York: Simon & Schuster, 2002).

7 Hedges, *War Is a Force,* 150.

8. *Los Angeles Times,* April 19, 2003.

9. Joel Andreas, *Addicted to War* (Oakland, CA: AK Press, 2002).

10. Richard Rhodes, *Why They Kill* (New York: Vintage, 1999), 290–93.

11. Rhodes, *Why They Kill,* 296.

12. Rhodes, *Why They Kill,* 304.

13. James William Gibson, *Warrior Dreams* (New York: Hill & Wang, 1994).

14. Gibson, *Warrior Dreams,* introduction.

15. Gibson, *Warrior Dreams,* 11.

16. See William W. Zellner, *Countercultures* (New York: St. Martin's, 1995), 52.

17. On the growth of paranoid images in American popular culture, see Ray Pratt, *Projecting Paranoia* (Lawrence: University of Kansas Press, 2001), chap. 1.

18. Quoted in Gore Vidal, *Perpetual War for Perpetual Peace* (New York: Nation Books, 2001), 117.

19. Joel Dyer, *Harvest of Rage* (Boulder, CO: Westview Press, 1997), 216.

20. Dyer, *Harvest of Rage,* 107.

21. Vidal, *Perpetual War,* 109–10.

22. Vidal, *Perpetual War,*107.

23. See Zellner, *Countercultures,* chap. 1.

24. Darrell Y. Hamamoto, "Empire of Death and the Plague of Civic Violence," in *Masters of War,* ed. Carl Boggs (New York: Routledge, 2003), 277–92.

25. See Philip Carlo, *The Night Stalker* (New York: Pinnacle Books, 1997), 160.

26. James B. Stewart, *Blind Eye* (New York: Touchstone, 1999), 290.

27. Stewart, *Blind Eye,* 291.

28. See Hamamoto, "Empire of Death," 286.

29. Sheldon Rampton and John Stauber, *Weapons of Mass Deception* (New York: Tarcher, 2003), 139.

30. Zygmunt Bauman, "The Uniqueness and Normality of the Holocaust," in*Violence: A Reader,* ed. Catherine Besteman (New York: New York University Press, 2002), 173.

31. Bauman, "Uniqueness and Normality of the Holocaust," 83.

32. Wertsch, *Military Brats,* 375–76.

33. Wertsch, *Military Brats,* 94.

34. Wertsch, *Military Brats,* 119.

35. Wertsch, *Military Brats,* 196.

36. R. Claire Snyder, "Patriarchal Militarism," in Boggs, *Masters of War,* 264–68.

37. See Joshua Goldstein, *War and Gender* (New York: Cambridge University Press, 2001).

38. Catherine Lutz and John Elliston, "Domestic Terror," *Nation,* October 14, 2002.

39. *Los Angeles Times,* March 15, 2003.

40. McChesney, *Rich Media, Poor Democracy,* xvii, xviii.

41 David Brock, *The Republican Noise Machine* (New York: Crown Publishers, 2004), 11.

42 Brock, *Republican Noise Machine,* chap. 2.

43. On the neoconservative influence on Bush's foreign policy, see Rahul Mahajan, *Full Spectrum Dominance* (New York: Seven Stories Press, 2003), chap. 2.

44. See Robert McChesney, *Corporate Media and the Threat to Democracy* (New York: Seven Stories Press, 1997), 7.

45. See David Croteau and William Hoynes, *By Invitation Only* (Monroe, ME: Common Courage, 1994), chap. 3.

46. Norman Solomon and Reese Erlich, *Target Iraq* (New York: Context Books, 2003), 31.

47. Scott Ritter, quoted in *Extra!* August 2002.

48. Douglas Kellner, *The Persian Gulf TV War* (Boulder, CO: Westview, 1992), esp. 400–26.

49. Kellner, *Persian Gulf TV War,* 420–26.

50. Kellner, *Persian Gulf TV War*, 420.

51. Kathleen Hall Jamieson and Paul Waldman, *The Press Effect* (New York: Oxford University Press, 2003), 152.

52. See the commentary by Michael Massing in the *Nation,* November 11, 2002.

53. Ziauddin Sardar and Merryl Wyn Davies, *Why Do People Hate America?* (New York: Disinformation, 2002).

54. Rampton and Stauber, *Weapons of Mass Deception,* chap. 3.

## Chapter 2: War and Cinema

1. Lawrence H. Suid, *Guts and Glory: The Making of the American Military Image in Film* (Lexington: University Press of Kentucky, 2002), 13.

2. Lewis Jacobs, "Movies in the World War," in *The Movies in Our Midst,* ed. Gerald Mast (reprint, Chicago: University of Chicago Press, 1983), 164–65.

3. Cited in Suid, *Guts and Glory,* 21.

4. Suid, *Guts and Glory,* 39.

5. Churchill, *Fantasies of the Master Race,* 177.

6. Thomas Schatz, *Hollywood Genres* (New York: McGraw-Hill, 1981), 45.

7. See Robin Wood, "Drums along the Mohawk," in *The Book of Westerns,* ed. Ian Cameron and Douglas Pye (New York: Continuum, 1996), 180.

8. Wood, "Drums along the Mohawk," 176.

9. Andre Bazin, "Evolution of the Western," in *What Is Cinema?* ed. Hugh Gray (Berkeley and Los Angeles: University of California Press, 1971), 2:149.

10. Andrew Sinclair, *John Ford: A Biography* (New York: Lorimer, 1984), 85.

11. Richard Maltby, "A Better Sense of History: John Ford and the Indians," in Cameron and Pye, *The Book of Westerns,* p. 35.

12. Tag Gallagher, *John Ford: The Man and His Films* (Berkeley and Los Angeles: University of California Press, 1986), 341.

13. See Howard Zinn, *Howard Zinn on War* (New York: Seven Stories, 2001), 101.

14. Michael Shull and David Edward Wilt, *Hollywood War Films 1937–1945* (Jefferson, NC: McFarland Press, 1996), 16.

14. Dan Auler, *Hitchcock's Notebooks* (New York: Harper Entertainment, 1999), 128.

15. Shull and Wilt, *Hollywood War Films,* 16.

16. Robin Wood, *Hitchcock's Films Revisited* (New York: Columbia University Press, 1989), 76.

17. Wood, *Hitchcock's Films Revisited,* 77.

18. Suid, *Guts and Glory,* 129.

19. Cited in John Dower, *War without Mercy: Race and War in the Pacific* (New York: Pantheon, 1986), 79.

20. Dower, *War Without Mercy,* 91.

21. Sven Lindqvist, *A History of Bombing* (New York: New Press, 2001), 105.

22. See Thomas Doherty, *Projections of War* (New York: Columbia University Press, 1993), 5.

23. Doherty, *Projections of War,* 5.

24. See Howard Zinn, *A People's History of the United States* (New York: New Press, 2003), chap. 16.

25. Zinn, *People's History,* 404.

26. Nicholas Christopher, *Somewhere in the Night* (New York: Henry Holt, 1997), 42.

27. David N. Meyer, *A Girl and a Gun* (New York: Avon Books, 1998), 153.

28. Meyer, *A Girl and a Gun,* 261.

29. Jim Kitses, *Gun Crazy* (London: British Film Institute, 1996), 34.

30. See Ray Pratt, *Projecting Paranoia* (Lawrence: University Press of Kansas, 2001), 7–14.

31. Christopher, *Somewhere in the Night,* 49.

32. Suid, *Guts and Glory,* 218.

# Chapter 3: The Vietnam Syndrome

1. David Desser, "Charlie Don't Surf," in *Inventing Vietnam,* ed. Michael Anderegg (Philadelphia: Temple University Press, 1991), 97.

2. Leonard Quart and Albert Auster, *American Film and Society since 1945* (New York: Praeger, 2002), 122.

3. Suid, *Guts and Glory,* 336.

4. Quart and Auster, *American Film and Society,* 124.

5. Suid, *Guts and Glory,* 537.

6. Suid, *Guts and Glory,* 479.

7. Suid, *Guts and Glory,* 541.

8. Suid, *Guts and Glory,* 457.

9. Suid, *Guts and Glory,* 549.

10. See *California Monthly,* April 2004, 28–29.

11. *Pentagon Papers,* ed. George C. Herring (New York: McGraw-Hill, 1993), p. 198; emphasis added.

12. Robert S. McNamara, *In Retrospect: The Tragedy and Lessons of Vietnam* (New York: Vintage, 1995), 320 (emphases added).

13. McNamara, *In Retrospect,* xv.

14. Cited in Bruce Miroff, *Pragmatic Illusions* (New York: David McKay, 1976), 146.

15. *Pentagon Papers,* 58.

16. *Pentagon Papers,*130.

17. McNamara, *In Retrospect,* p. xx.

18. James William Gibson, *The Perfect War* (New York: Atlantic Monthly, 1986), p. 242.

19. *Pentagon Papers,* 159.

20. *Pentagon Papers,* 123.

21. Cited in Marilyn Young, *The Vietnam Wars, 1945–1990* (New York: Harper Perennial, 1991), 178 (emphases in original).

22. Lindqvist, *A History of Bombing,* 157.

23. *California Monthly,* 30.

24. *California Monthly,* 30.

25. See Christopher Hitchens, *The Trial of Henry Kissinger* (London: Verso, 2001).

26. Joseph Persico, *Nuremberg* (New York: Penguin, 1994), 261.

27. See Telford Taylor, *Nuremberg and Vietnam* (Chicago: Quadrangle Books, 1970), 8.

28. Taylor, *Nuremberg and Vietnam*, 440.

29. Cited in Taylor, *Nuremberg and Vietnam,* 176–77.

## Chapter 4: Recycling the Good War

1. Hedges, *War Is a Force*, 25.

2. Suid, *Guts and Glory,* 640.

3. Robert B. Stinnett, *Day of Deceit: The Truth about FDR and Pearl Harbor* (New York: Free Press, 2000).

4. Dower, *War without Mercy.*

5. Quoted in Frank Sanello, *Spielberg: The Man, the Movies, the Mythology* (Lanham, MD: Taylor, 2002), 180.

6. Hannah Arendt, *Eichmann in Jerusalem* (New York: Penguin, 1963).

7. Douglas Brode, *The Films of Steven Spielberg* (New York: Citadel, 1995), 84.

8. Brode, *Films of Steven Spielberg,* 166.

9. Tim Cole, *Selling the Holocaust* (New York: Routledge, 2000), 78.

10. Peter Biskind, "Blockbuster: The Last Crusade," in *Seeing through Movies,* ed. Mark Crispin-Miller (New York: Pantheon, 1990).

11. Brode, *Films of Steven Spielberg,* 193.

12. Susan Mackey-Kallis, *Oliver Stone's America* (Boulder, CO: Westview Press, 1996), 79.

13. Quoted in Brode, *Films of Steven Spielberg,* 269.

14. Tom Doherty, *Projections of War,* 306.

15. Suid, *Guts and Glory,* 151.

16. *Tribute,* 21.

17. Suid, *Guts and Glory,* 655.

18. Theodore C. Mason, *Battleship Sailor* (Annapolis: Naval Institute Press, 1982), 68.

19. Mason, *Battleship Sailor,* 249.

20. Mason, *Battleship Sailor,* 268–69.

21. See Michael Slackman, *Target: Pearl Harbor* (Honolulu: University of Hawaii Press, 1990), 8.

22. Stinnett, *Day of Deceit,* chap. 1.

23. Dower, *War without Mercy,* 33.

24. Dower, *War without Mercy,* 37.

25. Stinnett, *Day of Deceit,* xiv.

26. Stinnett, *Day of Deceit,* 137–38.

## Chapter 5: Cinematic Warfare in the New World Order

1. See Kellner, *Persian Gulf TV War.*

2. Neal Gabler, *Life: The Movie* (New York: Knopf, 1999).

3. Pratt, *Projecting Paranoia,* 236.

4. Pratt, *Projecting Paranoia,* 237.

5. Diana Johnstone, *Fool's Crusade* (New York: Monthly Review, 2002), 1.

6. Jack Shaheen, *Reel Bad Arabs,* 404–6.

7. Donald G. McNeil Jr., "For the Somalis, a Manhunt Movie to Muse Over," *New York Times,* January 22, 2002.

8. Dana Calvo and Rachel Abramowitz, "Uncle Sam Wants Hollywood but Hollywood Has Qualms," *Los Angeles Times,* November 19, 2001.

9. *9/11 Commission Report* (Washington D.C., 2004), 421.

10. Cited in Shaheen, *Reel Bad Arabs,* 158.

11. Kellner, *Media Culture,* 86.

12. Shaheen, *Reel Bad Arabs,* 189.

13. See Doug Lummis, "Terrorism as New Human Type," *CounterPunch,* December 1–15, 2002.

14. Pratt, *Projecting Paranoia,* 13.

15. Sardar and Davies, *Why Do People Hate America?* 13.

16. Walter Lacqueur, *The New Terrorism* (New York: Oxford University Press, 1999), 5.

17. Neal Gabler, "An Eternal War of Mind-Sets," *Los Angeles Times,* October 7, 2001.

18. Jean Baudrillard, *The Transformation of Evil* (London: Verso, 1993), 75–76.

# Chapter 6: Pentagon Strategy, Technowar, and Media Culture

1. *Creative Screenwriting,* vol. 12, no. 3 (2005): 52.

2. Churchill, *Fantasies of the Master Race,* 167–224. Churchill refers to this as the "cinematic colonization of American Indians."

3. Shaheen, *Reel Bad Arabs.*

4. Robb, *Operation Hollywood,* 143.

5. Robb, *Operation Hollywood,* 365.

6. The Pentagon is hardly alone in this practice: taxpayers help fund the propaganda efforts of other government interests, including the FBI, CIA, Secret Service, State Department, and even the White House.

7. Suid, *Guts and Glory,* 135.

8. Kellner, *Persian Gulf TV War,* chap. 10.

9. See Bruce Berkowitz, *The New Face of War* (New York: Free Press, 2003), 71.

10. *Electronic Gaming Monthly,* June 2005, 32.

11. *Terminator* magazine, 2003, 52–53.

12. "Life after Death," *Wired,* May 2005.

13. Karl Grossman, *Weapons in Space* (New York: Seven Stories Press, 2001), 9–18.

14. Noam Chomsky, *Hegemony or Survival* (New York: Holt, 2003), 231.

15. See Karen Houppert, "Military Recruiters Are Now Targeting Sixth Graders. Who's Next?" *Nation,* September 12, 2005.

16. James Bamford, *A Pretext for War* (New York: Anchor Books, 2004), 294.

# Filmography

***Air Force* (1943).** Howard Hawks's World War II film was one of the first to feature military action in the Pacific enhanced with actual air force combat footage. The action takes place in a bomber that happened to be approaching Honolulu just as the Japanese attacked the military bases. From that point onward, the crew find themselves in the thick of the action, presented on screen as some of the best in combat film history.

***Air Force One* (1997).** Wolfgang Peterson cast Harrison Ford as U.S. President James Marshall, a former Vietnam War hero, who regains control of *Air Force One* after it has been seized by terrorists from Kazakhstan. Marshall displays James Bond–like martial arts skills and manages to regain control of the aircraft and defeat the villains, who are depicted as ruthless but unimaginative.

***The Alamo* (1960).** John Wayne not only starred in but also directed this combat Western, presented here as the War for Texas Independence (instead of as the theft of Mexican territory). Wayne filmed this costumer in Bracketville, Texas, using an all-star cast of Western actors (Richard Widmark, Lawrence Harvey, Richard Boone) along with some more recent actors like Frankie Avalon. Wayne filled his film with distorted views of historical events culminating in the 1836 siege of the Alamo, perpetuating a series of myths about American heroes fighting against daunting odds and eventually being overwhelmed by Mexican forces.

***The Alamo* (2004).** John Lee Hancock's postmodern version of the venerable Alamo saga features Billy Bob Thornton, Dennis Quaid, and Emilio Echeverria and achieves greater historical accuracy than Wayne's earlier effort, but at a cost. Thornton's Davy Crockett is more realistic than Wayne's, but Hancock's attempt to demystify Crockett drew hot rebukes from champions of the Crockett legend.

***All Quiet on the Western Front* (1930).** Lewis Milestone's great antiwar epic has chauvinistic Germans enticing high-school boys into the army with patriotic lures of fame and glory, only to learn too late about war's true nature. Lew Ayres stars as a schoolboy caught up in patriotic hysteria. He enlists in the army but realizes war's futility and destructiveness and tries to warn other young schoolboys not to enlist; his efforts are of no avail, and he dies from a sniper's bullet while attempting to catch a beautiful butterfly. This film still deserves its ranking among the best combat films of any era.

*Apocalypse Now* **(1979).** Francis Ford Coppola's Vietnam War–era adaptation of Joseph Conrad's *Heart of Darkness* continues to win critical acclaim. Coppola's film features Martin Sheen as a Special-Ops captain on a secret mission to "terminate" a rogue officer, Colonel Kurtz (Marlon Brando), who has effectively seceded from the army and become a private warlord. Coppola's film is a surrealistic masterpiece that makes a powerful if at times refracted antiwar statement.

*Bataan* **(1943).** Tay Garnett's early World War II film chronicles the doomed efforts of American forces to hold a bridge long enough to allow General Douglas MacArthur to evacuate U.S. forces from the Philippines ahead of an inevitable Japanese victory. Garnett turns this episode into a tale of heroism and duty at a time when U.S. forces lacked victories to celebrate.

*Behind Enemy Lines* **(2001).** John Moore's action-adventure film takes place in Bosnia during the late 1990s. American airman Chris Burnett (Owen Wilson) is shot down behind enemy lines during the Bosnian war. His commander, Admiral Reigert (Gene Hackman), launches a rogue rescue mission even though his orders from NATO forbid it. Burnett must go it alone, and he rises to the occasion by performing virtually impossible physical feats, dodging machine-gun fire and turning the tables on his maddened Bosnian pursuers. This film invokes the rationale that antidemocratic regimes were engaging in genocide, thereby justifying U.S. military intervention.

*The Best Years of Our Lives* **(1946).** William Wyler crafted this classic "home front" film about returning soldiers experiencing class conflict, adulterous wives, disabilities, and other conditions brought about indirectly by World War II. Wyler's film chronicles the lives of several returning GIs, played by Frederic March, Dana Andrews, and Harold Russell, and their women, played by Myrna Loy, Theresa Wright, and Virginia Mayo. Each must make painful adjustments to civilian life. Wyler's film was one of the first to suggest that, despite Allied victory, challenging social problems remained.

*The Big Parade* **(1925).** King Vidor's antiwar epic focuses on World War I and the barrage of lies, deceits, and tragedies that surround it. Vidor cast John Gilbert as a naive youth swept up in pro-war hysteria who enlists in the army, only to discover that the real war is far more brutal and deadly than he had thought, after he loses a leg in the ferocious Battle of Belleau Woods.

*The Big Red One* **(1980).** Director Samuel Fuller's autobiographical account of the First Infantry Division during World War II features Lee Marvin as a tough, cigar-chomping sergeant who keeps his squad going through the war despite horrific battles and other misadventures of combat. Later, after his troops become prisoners of war, he helps them stay together until the Allies liberate their concentration camp.

*The Birth of a Nation* **(1915).** D. W. Griffith's landmark film became the first "blockbuster," creating long lines of people eager to view this sensational Civil War drama. Griffith's film follows the fortunes of two Civil War families. Its battlefield scenes were the most realistic to date and involved thousands of troops as extras as well as the loan of Civil War–era weaponry. Griffith's decision to cast the Ku Klux Klan as the film's courageous heroes makes his film very difficult for today's audiences to view, though it has long been revered by the Klan. At 186 minutes, this was the first feature-length film, and it is certainly the most controversial of all pre–World War I pictures.

***Black Hawk Down* (2001).** Ridley Scott directed this film depicting tragic events during the 1993 U.S. mission to Somalia. U.S. forces pursue a powerful warlord with Black Hawk helicopters and armed convoys in Mogadishu, where they encounter stiff armed opposition. Somalian fighters down two helicopters, killing eighteen soldiers and airmen, and capture one airman alive, who ultimately is released through political negotiations. Though sanitized somewhat (Scott was given access to military hardware), the film remains a stark reminder that U.S. military interventions are destined to encounter fierce opposition.

***Blade Runner* (1982).** Ridley Scott's dark, dystopic neo-noir movie pits Deckard (Harrison Ford), a futuristic former Los Angeles cop against a dangerous group of "replicants," superhuman androids, who have mutinied against their former controllers and invaded Earth. Deckard, who may himself be a replicant, relies on his own superhuman skills as he tracks and eventually apprehends these dangerous villains. With its constant guerilla-like clashes between replicants and humans, this sci-fi film functions much like a combat picture.

***The Blue Max* (1966).** John Guillermin's often trite World War I film features George Peppard and James Mason as German fliers who engage in exciting dogfights in Europe. Peppard's ambitious Bruno Stechel sets out to shoot down twenty enemy planes, even taking credit for one he did not down, thereby winning the coveted Blue Max award.

***Born on the Fourth of July* (1989).** Oliver Stone's great antiwar epic, the second of his Vietnam trilogy, stars Tom Cruise as Vietnam veteran Ron Kovic, who begins as a gung-ho warrior and ends up as a paraplegic from his wartime injuries. He eventually becomes a strong antiwar voice and helps organize Vietnam Veterans Against the War, reminiscent of the early efforts of John Kerry. Stone's film is one of the most well crafted of the antiwar epics that appeared in the post-Vietnam period.

***The Bridges at Toko-Ri* (1955).** Mark Robson created this Korean War film about Lieutenant Harry Brubaker's (William Holden) experiences flying jet fighter missions off the Korean coast. His boss, Rear Admiral Tarrant (Fredric March), explains that "if we don't stop the Koreans here, they'll be in Japan, Indochina, and the Philippines," and then on to Missouri. Eventually, Brubaker pays the ultimate price after his plane is shot down by enemy forces.

***The Caine Mutiny* (1954).** Edward Dmytryk cast Humphrey Bogart as Captain Queeg, a cowardly navy commander who mentally unravels during a heavy storm and is replaced by his executive officer, played by Van Johnson. Later, the mutineers go on trial and Queeg breaks down under withering cross-examination to reveal a frightened, insecure, petty man. Dmytryk's film, especially Bogart's performance, remains memorable.

***Casualties of War* (1989).** Brian De Palma directed Michael J. Fox, Sean Penn, and John C. Riley in a somewhat confusing antiwar drama set in the Vietnam War. Penn plays an over-the-top sergeant who captures and abuses a teenage Vietnamese girl (Thuy Thu Le). Fox acts as the platoon's conscience and attempts to assist her, but his efforts ultimately fail. Critics have noted an emotionally detached style that, along with some confusing plot points, weakens De Palma's film.

***Catch-22* (1970).** Mike Nichols's antiwar classic is set on an Italian island during World War II, but its real subject is the increasingly unpopular Vietnam War. Based on Joseph Heller's popular novel, Nichols's film explores the war with surreal absurdism through the eyes of bombardier Yossarian (Alan Arkin), who goes mad with overwork as his commanders continue raising the number of missions airmen must fly before being sent back to the United States.

***Cheyenne Autumn* (1964).** John Ford's last cavalry epic also represents a significant change from the director's earlier Westerns. In this one Ford abandoned his previous anti-Indian stance and depicted Cheyenne Indians on a challenging journey from their government reservation back to their ancestral homeland. Richard Widmark plays a cavalry officer who becomes alienated from anti-Indian racism and increasingly sympathetic to the Cheyenne. Carroll Baker plays a white schoolteacher who decides to join the Cheyenne on their long-distance march. This influenced later films that feature white characters saving Indians (*Little Big Man*, *Dances with Wolves*).

***Civilization* (1916).** William Ince's classic film features two fictitious countries at war with each other. Both sides suffer massive casualties until finally Jesus Christ returns to earth and orders the two sides to make peace. This deus ex machina plot device was borrowed often by sci-fi films. Ince's antiwar message was intended to boost Woodrow Wilson's 1916 presidential campaign (he ran on a peace platform), and it was credited with swinging the election to Wilson. Ironically, Wilson declared war a few weeks after inauguration.

***Coming Home* (1978).** Hal Ashby's anti–Vietnam War epic joins paraplegic soldier Luke Martin (Jon Voight) and Sally Hyde (Jane Fonda), the wife of an army captain played by Bruce Dern. Sally and Luke form a romantic relationship while Sally's husband serves in Vietnam, but when Captain Dern returns from duty, confused and disillusioned, Luke and Sally's illicit relationship comes into the open. It proves to be the final straw that finally cracks the husband's sanity. This film is one of the most strongly antiwar films ever made.

***Courage Under Fire* (1996).** Edward Zwick's film chronicles events during Operation Desert Storm. Lieutenant Colonel Nathan Sterling (Denzel Washington), himself under investigation for a friendly-fire accident during his watch, leads an investigation to determine if a helicopter pilot, Captain Karen Walden (Meg Ryan), should receive a Medal of Honor for her courage while providing cover for another downed helicopter under intense fire from Iraqi units. Sterling's investigation reveals multiple versions of the event, each related by one of the participants and each significantly different from the others. Zwick's film raises thorny issues about individual responsibility and courage.

***Crash Drive (1943).*** Archie Mayo's submarine movie was one of the early World War II films, a thriller featuring a romantic triangle between the two leads, Tyrone Power and Dana Andrews, and schoolteacher Jean Hewlett (Anne Baxter). Mayo's film contains action-packed scenes in which their submarine plays cat-and-mouse with German U-boats, but it is also memorable for its major African American supporting character, Oliver Cromwell Jones (Ben Carter).

***Dawn Patrol* (1930).** Howard Hawks's World War I epic stars Richard Barthelmess and Douglas Fairbanks Jr. as pilots in France battling German planes in 1915. The film features dramatic aerial dogfights amid a human drama pitting pilots against their commanding officer. This film was remade in 1938 by Edmund Goulding.

***D-Day, the Sixth of June* (1956).** Henry Koster directed this extravaganza showcasing the Allied invasion of Europe told from the perspective of an American officer, played by Robert Taylor, and a British officer, played by Richard Todd. Koster showers audiences with spectacular scenes depicting the dramatic events at Normandy. The film is a prime example of the good-war motif celebrating American military victories.

***The Deer Hunter* (1978).** Michael Cimino's film was Hollywood's first major motion picture set during the Vietnam War. The film follows the military careers of three friends, Steven (John Savage), Michael (Robert De Niro), and Nick (Christopher Walken), who decide to join the army and ship out to Vietnam. Once there, they undergo horrendous experiences, including being held captive in a Vietcong prison. Their jailers engage in mind-shattering games of Russian roulette with the captives. Later, after the war, Nick continues playing this dangerous game in Saigon.

***The Delta Force* (1986).** Menahem Golan cast Chuck Norris and Lee Marvin in this Special Ops spectacle involving a terrorist plane hijacking in the Middle East. Tensions mount between hostages and terrorists until American special forces agents arrive and, in a series of comic-book adventures, maim and kill the terrorists and free the hostages.

***Die Hard* (1988).** John McTiernan directed this terrorist thriller starring Bruce Willis as New York police officer John McClane, who witnesses an attempted takeover of a Los Angeles high-rise office building and the taking hostage of a large group of people by a gang of German terrorists headed by Hans Gruger (Alan Rickman). McClane displays remarkable ingenuity and courage as he singlehandedly kills or captures the entire gang and frees the hostages. Typical of Hollywood films, American skill and ingenuity overwhelm the shady foreign terrorists.

***Die Hard 2* (1990).** Renny Harlin directed this sequel in which John McClane (Bruce Willis) happens to learn of a terrorist plot involving Dulles International Airport in Washington, D.C. This film follows the familiar pattern of an innocent bystander, McClane, becoming aware of a terrorist plot and taking action to prevent it. In a sense, the government hopes that ordinary citizens will become involved once they uncover a terrorist plot, although they discourage ordinary citizens from tackling the terrorists directly as McClane does time after time.

*Die Hard with a Vengeance* (1995). John McTiernan returned to the genre with this sequel, also featuring John McClane, although this time he has been ousted from the New York Police Department. He teams up with a Harlem store owner (Samuel L. Jackson) to defeat a terrorist (Jeremy Irons) threatening to bomb New York City. (New York also is the setting for Edward Zwick's 1998 thriller, *The Siege*.)

*The Dirty Dozen* (1967). Robert Aldrich provides one of the most memorable World War II films, featuring Lee Marvin as Major John Reisman, who forges a commando unit from misfits and convicts played by Charles Bronson, Jim Brown, George Kennedy, John Cassavetes, Clint Walker, and Donald Sutherland, among others. Their mission is to assassinate high-ranking Nazis at a resort. Aldrich's film borrows escapist action and ironic attitudes from the popular James Bond series.

*Dive Bomber* (1941). Michael Curtiz's first World War II film predates his more famous *Casablanca* by one year, and it too deserves viewing. Curtiz's film derives its central tensions from the dynamics between the characters, Lieutenant Doug Lee (Errol Flynn), a research-oriented navy doctor who decides to become a pilot, and Commander Joe Blake (Fred MacMurray), an overconfident career pilot, as much as from its battle scenes. Curtiz's film was in production before the Japanese attack on Pearl Harbor, and it capitalized on the sudden interest in war subjects after the attack. It avoids the more strident propagandistic tone of most war films that followed.

*Dr. No* (1962). Terrance Young directed Sean Connery as the first James Bond on screen. Bond investigates some weird events near Jamaica and discovers Dr. No, a master terrorist working for the world Communist conspiracy, who is easily vanquished by Bond, armed with British mechanical ingenuity.

*Dr. Strangelove, or: How I Learned to Stop Worrying and Love the Bomb* (1964). Stanley Kubrick's black comedy brilliantly satirizes cold war paranoia with the considerable assistance of Peter Sellers's comic portrayal of three characters, including the title figure, reputed to have been modeled after Henry Kissinger. Kubrick populated his film with offbeat characters like General "Buck" Turgidson (George C. Scott), General Jack D. Ripper (Sterling Hayden), Colonel "Bat" Guano (Keenan Wynn), Major T. J. "King" Kong (Slim Pickins), and, of course, Strangelove himself. Sellers also plays Group Captain Lionel Mandrake and President Merkin Muffley. The plot involves a doomsday device, a rogue officer attempting to incite a war with the USSR, and the Nazi-like Strangelove as presidential adviser.

*Drums Along the Mohawk* (1939). John Ford directed this combat film, one of the rare ones set during the Revolutionary War. A colonist, played by Henry Fonda, and his wife, played by Claudette Colbert, combat pro-British elements, led by a villainous character played by John Carradine. Change the costumes and the time period and you get *Fort Apache* or *She Wore a Yellow Ribbon*.

*Executive Decision* (1996). Stuart Baird directed this terrorist thriller starring Kurt Russell and Steven Seagal as two Special Ops agents who intercept and board a 747 in flight that has been taken over by Arab terrorists, aiming to wrest control of the aircraft. The situation proves tense for the Americans, who, of course, manage to accomplish their mission and prevent the terrorists from detonating a deadly nerve gas weapon that could wipe out Washington, D.C.

***Fat Man and Little Boy*** **(1989).** Roland Joffe cast Paul Newman as General Leslie Groves, the army officer given the task of creating the first atomic bomb, and Dwight Schultz as Dr. Robert Oppenheimer, the scientist who organized the Manhattan Project, which ultimately built two atomic bombs, a larger version and a smaller one, nicknamed "Fat Man" and "Little Boy." Joffe's film provides a fascinating behind-the-scenes glimpse of the top-secret project that unleashed a weapon that would ultimately threaten the entire planet. The drama is marred somewhat by a flawed script.

***Fighting Seabees*** **(1944).** Edward Ludwig directed this propagandistic combat film starring John Wayne as "Wedge" Donovan, hotheaded boss of a construction gang that gets recruited into the navy as "Seabees," armed navy construction engineers. The men see plenty of battlefield action against the Japanese after they deploy to the South Pacific. This film served as a model for many other John Wayne combat films that followed.

***First Blood*** **(1982).** Ted Wotcheff cast Sylvester Stallone as John Rambo, ex–Green Beret Vietnam veteran who runs afoul of local law enforcement near the small town of Hope, British Columbia, while searching for a former member of his unit. Rambo escapes the local sheriff after suffering mistreatment and moves into the forest, where he creates booby-traps and hideouts reminiscent of Kit's (Martin Sheen) and Holly's (Sissy Spacek) South Dakota defenses in Terrence Malick's *Badlands*. *First Blood* exudes a sense of paranoia and celebrates an individualistic, antigovernment ethos that militia members would find appealing. General audiences found this film laughable in its comic-book simplicity.

***Flying Leathernecks*** **(1951).** Nicholas Ray's flyboy epic features John Wayne as Major Kirby, a hard-as-nails flight commander pitted against not only the Japanese but also one of his own men, Captain Griffin (Robert Ryan), who empathizes with the plight of the pilots. The resulting dynamics between contrasting personalities and values provided a model for later combat films.

***The Fog of War*** **(2003).** Errol Morris's documentary chronicles the Vietnam War through the eyes of Robert S. McNamara, secretary of defense during the war. Morris interviews the eighty-five-year-old McNamara, who presents his side of the events he helped shape. The former secretary's comments are often insightful, but the tragic events he describes and helped to create are never satisfactorily explained.

***Fort Apache*** **(1948).** One of John Ford's celebrated U.S. Cavalry films, this one featuring a Custer-like army officer, Colonel Thursby (Henry Fonda), pitted against an independent-minded subordinate officer, Captain York (John Wayne). Thursby lays a trap for a large force of hostile Indians, led by Apache chief Geronimo, and decides to move his own forces close to the Indian lines. When York protests, Thursby denounces him as a coward, but soon Thursby's own forces are picked off by Indians and he too is eventually killed.

***From Here to Eternity* (1953).** Fred Zinnemann's classic postwar film depicts peacetime army life in Hawaii with unusual realism, including a strictly taboo relationship between an enlisted man, Sergeant Warden (Burt Lancaster), and his commanding officer's wife, Karen Holmes (Deborah Kerr). Zinnemann also presents large doses of sadism, prostitution, and alcoholism. No wonder the navy banned this film from all its ships.

***From Russia with Love* (1963).** Terence Young directed this James Bond cold war thriller starring Sean Connery. Bond is his usual witty and deadly self. Here he is pitted against mysterious agents and a virtual army of enemies. The fight scenes in this film are the longest of any in the Bond series, and, with the usual emphasis on high-tech weaponry, this film exudes a strongly militaristic ethos.

***Full Metal Jacket* (1987).** Stanley Kubrick's trenchant critique of the Vietnam War could not be more direct. His villain, an insane drill sergeant named Hartman (R. Lee Ermey), epitomizes the war's failures. He is cruel, sadistic, and completely domineering, yet also effective in transforming naive young men into professional killing machines. Kubrick's film identifies many factors contributing to the U.S. failure in Vietnam, including misdirected policies, naive soldiers, and sociopathic officers. A colonel explains the purpose of the U.S. mission: "We are here to help the Vietnamese, because inside every gook there is an American trying to get out. It's a hardball world, son. We've got to try and keep our heads until this peace craze blows over."

***Gardens of Stone* (1987).** Francis Ford Coppola's anti–Vietnam War narrative features James Caan as a soldier assigned to Arlington National Cemetery who yearns to see action in the Vietnam War.

***A Gathering of Eagles* (1963).** Delbert Mann directed this Strategic Air Command film set in peacetime. Rock Hudson plays an unlikable colonel whose wife (Mary Peach) has difficulty adjusting to military life. Despite its peaceful setting, this film was made at the height of the cold war and reflects mounting tensions between civilians and the military. Its message is that the air force has been relying too much on nuclear weapons, whereas individuals, with their courage and training, are the real key to victory.

***G.I. Jane* (1997).** Ridley Scott cast Demi Moore as a test case for determining women's fitness for military combat. GI Jane trains hard and pumps iron to assert herself against a variety of challenges, including her "Master Chief" trainer played by Viggo Mortensen. Scott's film provides a good example of a recent cycle of Hollywood films glorifying combat.

***Good Morning, Vietnam* (1987).** Barry Levinson directs Robin Williams in a virtual one-man show as an army disc jockey assigned to Saigon who specializes in maniacal, irreverent, yet always witty and insightful monologues that radically transform radio journalism in the field. Levinson, true to form, allows Williams great latitude in developing his character, and the results are predictably good.

**The Great Santini (1979).** Louis John Carlino's film features fighter pilot Lieutenant Colonel "Bull" Meecham (Robert Duvall), who wields strict military discipline over his reluctant family as a substitute for armed combat. Meecham terrorizes his family, especially his teenage son, played by Michael O'Keefe. Meecham appears even more villainous when he demands that his son engage in dirty tricks and personal fouls during a basketball game, but at the end of the drama he decides to crash his fighter plane rather than bail out over a city and risk civilian casualties. He thereby turns into the film's hero instead of its villain.

**The Green Berets (1968).** John Wayne codirected (with Roy Kellogg) this Vietnam War film starring himself as a Special Ops colonel fighting the Vietcong while also educating an embedded journalist, played by David Janssen, about the necessity of fighting the Communist enemy. Wayne's film is filled with clichés and clumsiness: for example, in the final scene Wayne and a young Vietnamese boy are depicted gazing at the setting sun, which sinks slowly in the ocean, an impossibility in Vietnam, which has no western ocean. This film, not surprisingly, appealed to the Vietnam War hawks.

**Hamburger Hill (1987).** John Irwin directed this war-is-hell Vietnam War epic featuring soldiers from the 101st Airborne Division who encounter well-entrenched Vietnamese forces. The two sides attack and destroy each other with monotonous regularity, hence the title. Irvin owes a debt to Louis Milestone's Korean War drama *Pork Chop Hill.*

**Hart's War (2002).** Gregory Hoblit cast Bruce Willis as Colonel McNamara, an American soldier held captive in a Nazi prison camp during World War II. As the highest-ranking prisoner, McNamara represents the other prisoners of war. He is assisted by a young lieutenant (Colin Farrell). Issues become murky after two African American airmen join the other prisoners and discover racism among the American prisoners. Hoblit's film loses focus at times, but it still evokes powerful elements of the good-war film.

**Heaven and Earth (1993).** This film, the third part of Oliver Stone's Vietnam trilogy, begins in a Vietnamese village with a young girl (Hiep Thu Le) getting caught between two sides in the civil war. She also is caught between her traditional, rural values and the new urban values she encounters. Still in the throes of transition, she finally journeys to the United States. Stone's film is based on the real-life experiences of Le Ly Hayslip.

**Home of the Brave (1949).** Mark Robson's film is one of the few to expose World War II racism. An amnesiac African American soldier, Peter Moss (James Edwards), experiences a mysterious paralysis of his entire lower body after a dangerous reconnaissance mission on a Pacific island. His army psychologist (played by Jeff Corey), seeks the cause of the illness by interviewing Moss's fellow soldiers. They gradually recall the mission's details, revealing racial tensions between Moss and another soldier. Although the film fails to probe the depths of racism, Robson deserves some credit for being one of the first filmmakers to even approach the issue.

***The Hunt for Red October*** (**1990**). John McTiernan adapted this Tom Clancy cold war novel about a Soviet submarine captain who appears to be on the verge of defecting to the West, taking with him his supersecret sub armed with nuclear weapons. Alec Baldwin plays CIA agent Jack Ryan, who is assigned to monitor the submarine and its commander. A great cat-and-mouse thriller with some unexpected plot twists sums up this cold war narrative.

***The Invaders*** (**1941**). Michael Powell directed this early British World War II film about Nazis whose U-boat sinks along the Canadian coast. Powell's cast includes Anton Walbrook, Leslie Howard, and Lawrence Olivier. This film is an early entry into the good-war genre of World War II films, and viewers should still find it entertaining because of fine acting and a good script.

***Invasion of the Body Snatchers*** (**1956**). Don Siegel's classic sci-fi film pits earthlings, played by Kevin McCarthy, Dana Winter, and Larry Gates, against extraterrestrial "pod people," aliens who are exact duplicates of the humans around them. The pod people seem to lack feelings and emotions and to embrace a frighteningly dystopian vision of the future. They bear an uncanny resemblance to popular conceptions of soulless Communists during the cold war, and Siegel's film is, in fact, a disguised cold war combat film.

***Key Largo*** (**1948**). John Huston introduced a number of combat film elements into this classic film noir starring Humphrey Bogart, Edward G. Robinson, and Lauren Bacall. Gangster Johnny Rocco (Robinson) and his gang take over a Florida vacation lodge, holding its residents hostage, including Frank McLeod (Humphrey Bogart), a decorated World War II veteran who is visiting the family of his dead comrade from the war. With the help of other hostages, Frank overthrows the gangsters, concluding with a final battle with Rocco. Here again, the forces of good overcome the forces of evil in this thinly disguised combat film.

***Kill Bill: Vol. 1*** (**2003**). Tarantino's thriller is part samurai, part spaghetti Western. It features Uma Thurman as the Bride, a former member of a yakuza-like assassination squad, who has barely survived their attack. Healed and deadlier than ever, the Bride returns to avenge herself against her attackers and their leader, Bill (David Carradine). Although the characters in this film prefer samurai swords to assault rifles and handguns, they engage in nearly continuous combat as the Bride, though vastly outnumbered, emerges victorious. Tarantino's film certainly deserves to be called a disguised combat film.

***Kill Bill: Vol. 2*** (**2004**). Quentin Tarantino's sequel is just as violently dramatic as the original. In this version the Bride (Uma Thurman) must destroy two superhuman rivals in order to confront her onetime mentor and current nemesis, Bill (David Carradine). Her battle against Bill is the film's climax, the sign of another thinly disguised combat film.

***Lifeboat*** (**1944**). Alfred Hitchcock's irreverent depiction of the survivors of a Nazi U-boat attack on a freighter bound for England met with howls of disapproval upon release. Hitchcock presents a nuanced portrait of a group of Allied survivors imbued with every human weakness, including lust, prejudice, greed, hubris, and aggression. Great drama occurs when the survivors murder a German named Willy (Walter Slezak). Hitchcock refused to take sides in this film, castigating both the Nazi "superman" fantasies and the comforting Allied belief in moral superiority.

**The Longest Day (1962).** Darryl F. Zanuck's D-Day chronicle features the work of four other directors. It chronicles the twenty-four-hour period during the Allied invasion of Normandy through the eyes of characters drawn from both enlisted ranks and the officer corps. As soon as General Eisenhower (David Grace) signals the attack, events move in a chaotic direction as Private Schultz (Richard Beymen) becomes separated from his unit; Private Steele (Red Buttons) parachutes into a church as Major Pluskat (Hans Christian Blech) becomes the first German officer to realize that the invasion is under way. After the two armies clash, the mood shifts into a celebration of Allied (especially American) courage and valor in fighting the good war.

**The Lost Patrol (1934).** John Ford's World War I thriller bears more than a faint resemblance to his early Westerns, including his decision to shoot the film on location in Arizona. The shadowy Arabs who attack a patrol in North Africa could easily be Indians attacking U.S. Cavalry outposts. The adventure begins after the lieutenant is killed, leaving the command in the hands of the sergeant (Victor McLaglen), who does not know the objective or the destination of the unit. A nightmarish scenario plays out slowly as members of the unit are picked off one by one. Ford's film served as a model for later war-is-hell films like *Sahara* and *Platoon*.

**The Manchurian Candidate (1962).** John Frankenheimer is credited with inventing the post–World War II thriller with his formalist adaptation of Richard Condon's popular cold war novel. A brainwashed killer named Raymond Shaw (Lawrence Harvey) receives a bogus citation for bravery as part of a shadowy plot to overthrow the U.S. government. Weak-minded, McCarthy-like Senator Iseland (James Gregory) is being groomed for the presidency. This film is dripping in cold war paranoia made more poignant by the assassination of John F. Kennedy, which occurred just after release. Frank Sinatra, who costarred as Major Bennet Marco, owned a controlling interest in the production and decided to pull it out of release because of Shaw's attempt to assassinate Iseland. The film was not rereleased until decades later, but it remains a powerful if at times surrealistic antiwar and even antipolitical film.

**M*A*S*H (1970).** Robert Altman's comedic portrait of a Korean War medical team resonates strongly with Vietnam War motifs, mostly concerning the increasing unpopularity of the war at the time. Donald Sutherland and Elliott Gould play army surgeons attempting to heal broken, wounded bodies, the chief reference to war's carnage. Such graphic portrayal of the wounded and dying in Vietnam would have seemed unpatriotic while Americans in large numbers were losing their lives in the war. Altman manages to throw ironic barbs at military leaders while indirectly satirizing the Vietnam War, making *M*A*S*H* one of the first anti–Vietnam War films.

***The Matrix* (1999).** Andy and Larry Wachowski directed this cyber-thriller in which the world of ordinary reality is exposed as an illusion created by computers that have taken over the earth. Keanu Reeves plays Neo, a computer hacker who "accidentally" discovers the sham and also learns that he is "the chosen one" destined to save humanity. This film is not only a disguised combat film but also an example of what might be called a technowar film.

***The Matrix Reloaded* (2003).** The Wachowski brothers directed the sequel to their popular 1999 cyber-thriller in which a vast army of machines attempts to annihilate the last outpost of humanity hunkered down in the city of Zion. Keanu Reeves again plays Neo, a computer hacker who battles humanity's machine and computer foes. This film, like its predecessor, contains strong elements of New Age philosophy about mind over body and the illusionary nature of ordinary reality.

***Memphis Belle* (1990).** Michael Colin-Jones directs this British war movie based on William Wyler's documentary about the final European mission of a B-17 Flying Fortress bomber crew. Starring Mathew Modine and Eric Stoltz, the film contains some realistic aerial combat scenes in its second half. The first half is more confusing and seems much slower paced.

***Memphis Belle: A Story of the Flying Fortress* (1944).** William Wyler's documentary showcases the mighty B-17 Flying Fortress bomber and its dedicated crew. The film begins with bombs being loaded on to the *Memphis Belle,* which is scheduled to bomb a German submarine base. Wyler, who enlisted in World War II at the age of forty, insisted on filming every aspect of the bomber, including a landing from the dangerous ball turret. The picture still seems fresh and exciting due to the artistry of Wyler and his talented crew.

***Midway* (1976).** Jack Smight crafted this realistically filmed World War II drama starring Charlton Heston as a senior naval officer who sees lots of action in the Pacific. Smight used actual combat footage to add realism to his depiction of this seminal battle, but he saddled the film with a silly subplot involving Heston's young son falling in love with a beautiful Japanese woman. This film is best viewed as an action-adventure combat film, with the plot regarded as largely irrelevant.

***Mr. and Mrs. Smith* (2005).** Doug Limon directed this modern thriller, which owes a debt to Alfred Hitchcock's 1941 comedy of the same name starring Carol Lombard and Robert Montgomery. Limon's film stars Brad Pitt and Angelina Jolie as John and Jane Smith, a couple experiencing marital problems because the fire has gone out of their relationship. Incredibly, the Smiths are both professional assassins, and neither realizes that the other is so employed. Things come to a head after they receive assignments to eliminate each other. Limon's film revels in gratuitous violence and is a prime example of technowar cinema.

***Mrs. Miniver* (1942).** William Wyler's propagandistic World War II home-front thriller focused attention on the Battle of Britain, not Pearl Harbor (the Japanese attack came while this film was under production). Mr. Miniver (Walter Pidgeon) joins Churchill's evacuation of Dunkirk, while Mrs. Miniver (Greer Garson) copes with a downed German paratrooper. Released after the Japanese attack on Pearl Harbor, Wyler's film became one of the first to tap rising American patriotism. It proved immensely popular with audiences and critics alike, garnering six Academy Awards, including Best Picture.

***Navy Blue and Gold* (1937).** Sam Wood directed this propagandistic saga starring Robert Young and James Stewart as Annapolis midshipmen. The film suffers from a hackneyed plot, although Wood's directing skills provide some enjoyable scenes, including the exciting but predictable football-game climax.

***Navy Seals* (1990).** Lewis Teague cast Charlie Sheen as a member of the Seals, the U.S. Navy's elite Special Ops unit (Sea, Air, Land). Sheen and his fellow commandos do battle with Middle Eastern terrorists, their victory proving once again the superiority of U.S. military forces.

***1941* (1979).** Steven Spielberg's first World War II film is a far cry from *Saving Private Ryan*, yet this zany comedy contains some brilliant satire. The scenes involve bumbling Japanese submariners who attempt to destroy Hollywood but are unable even to locate Los Angeles. General Stilwell (Robert Stack) watches cartoons on television while his aide attempts to seduce the general's secretary. Meanwhile, Captain Wild Bill Kelso (John Belushi) flies sorties against nonexistent Japanese Zero fighters, while Captain Maddox (Warren Oates) imagines Japanese airstrips hidden in Pomona alfalfa fields. The result of all of this chaos and mayhem is a fairly good comedy. This film proved that Hollywood can spoof World War II, as in *Catch-22*, but nowhere does Spielberg engage in a serious critique of the war.

***Night of the Living Dead* (1968).** George Romero's low-budget horror film features zombies attacking and devouring humans. Virtually the entire film consists of violent battles involving two humans, played by Duane Jones and Judith O'Dea, battling hordes of crazed zombies trying to kill them. With its emphasis on violent clashes between the two groups, this film can be considered a disguised combat film.

***Only Angels Have Wings* (1938).** Howard Hawks's proto–combat film involves mail fliers in South America instead of fighter pilots in wartime, but it was the closest Hawks could come to combat on the eve of World War II. Instead of dogfights with German fighters, these pilots, played by Cary Grant and Richard Barthelmess, battle myriad elements as they conduct dangerous flights over the Andes in vulnerable small aircraft. As in many films, the pilots wind up falling in love with the same woman. Robert Ray suggests that Hawks's film served as a model for real combat films that followed after World War II commenced.

***Paths of Glory* (1957).** Stanley Kubrick's first combat film is an antiwar drama set during World War I. Like *All Quiet on the Western Front* and *The Blue Max*, Kubrick's effort here features European soldiers rather than Americans. French general Mireau (George Macready) orders Colonel Dax (Kirk Douglas) to storm "the Anthill," a strategic outcropping heavily defended by German forces. Dax leads the doomed attack, and after the defeat he is ordered to execute three soldiers selected at random as a response to their "cowardice." Kubrick's irony rises to a fever pitch as the blundering French staff make scapegoats out of innocent soldiers. This film, like most World War I films, makes an antiwar statement revolving around the insanity of warfare.

*Patton* **(1970).** Franklin Schaffner's paean to World War II general George Patton (George C. Scott) ranks among the foremost good-war films glorifying U.S. military actions. American commanders like Patton and General Omar Bradley (Karl Malden) appear highly intelligent and competent while foreign commanders do not fare as well. Field Marshal Montgomery (Michael Bates) comes off as a hotheaded prima donna, while the German High Command appears inept and unimaginative. Schaffner's extremely well-crafted film still evokes patriotism (it was reputed to be Richard Nixon's favorite film). *Patton* swept the Academy Awards with Scott as Best Actor, Schaffner as Best Director, and the film receiving Best Picture.

*The Peacemaker* **(1997).** Mimi Leder directed this terrorist thriller starring George Clooney and Nicole Kidman as two U.S. intelligence agents assigned to investigate a mysterious nuclear explosion in Russia. "The Peacemaker" is a nuclear-tipped guided missile capable of mass destruction. Its loss and recapture provide the rationale for action in this compelling thriller, which despite being entertaining, reinforces the familiar stereotypes of foreign terrorist zealots pitted against heroic American officers.

*Pearl Harbor* **(2001).** Michael Bay's blockbuster hit manages to alter significantly military history and showcase two American pilots, played by Ben Affleck and Josh Hartnett, courageously defending military bases in Hawaii and shooting down a large number of Japanese Zeroes. Bay depicts Colonel Jimmy Doolittle's raid on Tokyo as a stunning retaliation for the attack on Pearl Harbor, even though the American raid did little damage to Japan, whereas the Japanese attack severely damaged the American fleet. Bay's film serves to vindicate American defense of Pearl Harbor while making the Doolittle raid appear far more important and decisive than it actually was. The basic plot involving a romantic triangle between the two airmen and a nurse (Kate Beckinsale) was lifted nearly intact from William Wellman's *Wings* (1927).

*Platoon* **(1986).** Oliver Stone's combat epic showcases the intense culture clashes surrounding the Vietnam War. Sergeant Barnes (Tom Berenger) represents the redneck war hawk of the period, complete with Confederate flag, plenty of Jack Daniels, and Merle Haggard on the stereo. He adopts a harsh "take no prisoners" attitude toward Vietnamese villagers suspected of assisting the Vietcong, and he appears more than willing to execute a few in order to gain their respect. Sergeant Elias (Willem Dafoe) serves as Barnes's nemesis, saving villagers from Barnes and befriending the troops. He instinctively seeks the company of the "heads," who smoke pot underneath a portrait of Ho Chi Minh and listen to rock and roll. Eventually, these two clash, with Barnes proving the stronger force as he cold-bloodedly murders Elias. This film not only serves as an anti–Vietnam War polemic but also carries a profoundly pessimistic message about the defeat of reason and human compassion.

***Pork Chop Hill*** **(1959).** Lewis Milestone makes a strong antiwar statement in this film, a companion piece to his earlier antiwar epic *All Quiet on the Western Front*. Gregory Peck stars as Lieutenant Joe Clemons, who is considerably older than the other lieutenants. He is ordered to lead 135 soldiers of King Company on a night attack to capture a strategic hill. Clemons agrees, with the understanding that his superiors will send troops to assist. Reinforcements fail to arrive, however, because the commanding officers mistakenly believe Clemons is having no difficulty in taking the hill. As the carnage mounts, the film grows increasingly somber and pessimistic. In the end, the engagement seems ill conceived, undermanned, and murderous to large numbers of troops.

***Rambo: First Blood Part II*** **(1985).** George Cosmanos directed this sequel to the first Rambo film, *First Blood* (1982). It also stars Sylvester Stallone as John Rambo, a former Green Beret who still relies on his survival gear, including his trademark large knife. In this iteration Rambo journeys to Cambodia in search of MIAs, only to discover that he has been tricked by the U.S. government. Like its predecessor, *First Blood*, Cosmanos's film pits rugged individualism against a corrupt, untrustworthy U.S. government, a plot that appeals to right-wing militia members and their supporters.

***Rio Bravo*** **(1959).** Howard Hawks's great combat Western stars John Wayne, Dean Martin, Ricky Nelson, Angie Dickinson, and Walter Brennan. Wayne plays a tough sheriff determined to thwart the escape of a jailed killer with powerful connections, with only a drunken deputy, played by Martin, to assist him. Gradually, he acquires a few more allies, who engage in a guerilla street war against a ruthless, powerful gang.

***Rio Grande*** **(1950).** This was to be the final film in John Ford's Cavalry trilogy (following *Fort Apache* and *She Wore a Yellow Ribbon*). Like the others, it stars John Wayne, although this time the tough frontiersman has been promoted to become Colonel Kirby York. It focuses more on the father-son relationship between York and his son, a new recruit played by Claude Jarman Jr., than on the threat posed by hostile Indians.

***Rules of Engagement*** **(2000).** William Friedkin directed this thriller about an attempted takeover by Islamic militants of a U.S. Embassy in the Middle East. After the demonstrators appear to be turning to violence, Colonel Terry Childress (Samuel L. Jackson) orders his men, who are providing security for the evacuation of U.S. personnel, to open fire. The resulting firefight kills or wounds nearly two hundred foreigners. Put on trial for the incident, Childress asks a close friend, Colonel Hayes Hodges (Tommy Lee Jones), to serve as his lawyer. Friedkin's film faults the national security adviser for attempting to railroad Childress for crude political reasons.

***Saboteur*** **(1942).** Alfred Hitchcock's comic thriller is an updated American version of *The 39 Steps* (1935). It stars Robert Cummings as Barry Kane, an aircraft factory worker who becomes a suspect in a terrorist bombing of the factory. He eludes capture while attempting to locate the real culprits, led by wealthy fascist Charles Tobin (Otto Kruger). Kane's journey brings him face to face with a cell of Nazi fifth columnists who hope to gain power by crippling the United States.

***Sahara* (1943).** Zoltan Korda cast Humphrey Bogart as tank commander Sergeant Joe Gunn, on temporary loan, along with his tank, to the British in North Africa. Gunn receives orders to retreat from advancing Germans, but before he reaches his distant objective, he picks up several stragglers of different nationalities to add to his already full tank. Korda modeled his film after John Ford's *Lost Patrol*, which also features a group of soldiers picked off by unseen enemies along a desert march. Like many combat films, Korda's features the interactions of a large ensemble cast.

***Sands of Iwo Jima* (1949).** Allan Dwan cast John Wayne as Sergeant John Stryker, the quintessential tough leatherneck. Stryker first sees action in Guadalcanal, later fights in Tarawa, and eventually takes part in the hugely symbolic capture of Iwo Jima from Japanese forces. Stryker keeps the troops in line and generally takes care of business in this classic good-war epic.

***Saving Private Ryan* (1998).** One of Steven Spielberg's ambitious good-war films, *Saving Private Ryan* features abundant combat realism. Tom Hanks stars as Captain Miller, a battle-hardened veteran who receives an unexpected assignment: locate and retrieve Private Ryan (Matt Damon), a paratrooper trapped behind German lines. Ryan's three older brothers have just been killed, and General George C. Marshall (Harve Presnell) is determined that no family be completely wiped out in the war. As the mission progresses, Miller and his men engage in traditional combat-film male bonding. Once they locate Ryan, they are faced with a decision: whether to assist in a fight over a contested bridge or return to their own lines and "follow orders." Ultimately, of course, they choose to ignore their orders and fight. Spielberg naturally depicts Normandy and World War II as the ultimate good war, but the stark realism he presents in battle scenes creates a subtle war-is-hell undercurrent.

***Schindler's List* (1993).** Steven Spielberg's big Holocaust epic showcases the adventures of German businessman Oskar Schindler (Liam Neeson), who managed German factories during World War II. Schindler relied on skilled Jewish workers under the direction of Itzhak Stern (Ben Kingsley). The Jews were not permitted to own or operate factories in Germany or German-occupied territories, and Schindler, valuing their high productivity, encouraged them to work in his factories under Stern's expert direction. While shielding his men from concentration camps, Schindler ended up saving the lives of many of them. By focusing on a sympathetic German, Spielberg goes against the stereotype of racist, cold, greedy Germans. By depicting the brutality of German policies and the monstrous insensitivity of a concentration camp commander, Spielberg in effect celebrates the Allied war efforts and, by extension, U.S. military actions.

***The Searchers* (1956).** John Ford's classic Western depicts episodes in the Indian Wars of the nineteenth century. A few years after the Civil War, Ethan Edwards (John Wayne) returns to his family homestead to visit his brother and sister-in-law and their three children. Soon, Ethan is drawn away from the homestead to investigate a dead settler, only to discover upon his return that Indians have massacred his entire family, except Debbie (Natalie Wood), his teenage niece. Ethan sets out on a quest to recover his niece, who has been taken by the Indians. He is accompanied by a young family friend Martin Pauley (Jeffrey Hunter), and the two men spend years tracking a band of renegade Indians. Fine acting and fine directing combine to make this film one of the most well-crafted examples of the combat Western genre.

**Sergeant York (1941).** Howard Hawks's stunningly effective propaganda piece was set not in World War II but in World War I, a far less popular conflict. Hawks cast Gary Cooper as Sergeant York, a hillbilly sharpshooter who charms and wows his army commanders after enlistment. A famous marksman back home in Kentucky, York distinguishes himself in the military both on the firing range and on the battlefield. Hawks's film may be set in World War I, but its actual focus was the later war in Europe. This is one of a few early combat films with a patriotic message just before the United States entered World War II.

**She Wore a Yellow Ribbon (1948).** John Ford's combat Western, the second in his famous Cavalry trilogy, features John Wayne as Captain Nathan Brittles, a tough cavalry officer leading a hundred troops on a reconnaissance mission deep into Indian Territory. He is also charged with escorting Olivia Dandridge (Joanne Dru), daughter of the camp commander, out of the territory in anticipation of an Indian attack on the fort. With the help of Sergeant Tyree (Ben Johnson), Brittles defeats the evil white traders selling whiskey and guns to the Indians and restores order to the frontier. Ford eulogizes cavalry officers stationed at remote forts as "men in dirty-shirt blue. . . . [O]nly a cold page in the history books mark[s] their passing. But wherever they rode and whatever they fought for, that place became the United States."

**The Siege (1998).** Edward Zwick pits two U.S. intelligence agents, FBI operative Anthony Hubbard (Denzel Washington) and CIA operative Elise Kraft (Annette Benning) against a jihadist cell that has been setting off bombs in New York City. The government declares martial law and sends in troops with General Devereau (Bruce Willis) in charge. Devereau escalates tensions by placing hundreds of people of Middle Eastern origin in a makeshift concentration camp. Ultimately, Kraft and Hubbard outmaneuver Devereau and force him to stand down. This film includes scenes of military officers torturing a suspected Islamic terrorist by, among other things, having him strip down in front of a woman in a manner that seems all too prescient today.

**Star Wars (1977).** George Lucas gave birth to an entire global industry when he produced and directed this sci-fi classic. The original film in the series stars Mark Hamill, Harrison Ford, and Carrie Fisher as intergalactic travelers in conflict with an evil, totalitarian empire supported by Darth Vader. Lucas fashioned his space epic around the old Flash Gordon comics, and this film exudes comic-book qualities, including a simplistic good-versus-evil morality. Intergenerational conflicts between the son, Luke Skywalker (Hamill), and the father (ultimately Vader) provide opportunity for character development. As the final space battles occur around the Death Star, Lucas's epic reveals itself as a powerful combat film.

**Star Wars Episode I: The Phantom Menace (1999).** George Lucas cast Jake Lloyd as the young Luke Skywalker. He joins a space war after being contacted by Obi-Wan Kanobi (Ewan McGregor) and Oui-Gon Jinn (Liam Neeson). Lucas's film follows the pattern of the original and the two sequels that followed by adopting the familiar combat pattern in which a small group of comrades bond together to defeat a stronger enemy.

***The Steel Helmet* (1951).** Legendary director Sam Fuller presents a sharply dystopic Korean War film featuring the semiautobiographical, cigar-chewing Sergeant Zack (Gene Evans), who leads a group through a nightmarish "lost patrol" world that may bear a resemblance to battlefields in North Africa and Europe where Fuller served during World War II. This picture is an excellent example of the war-is-hell combat genre emphasizing the more destructive features of warfare. It is highly regarded today in part because of its gritty, realistic portrait of combat and for its antiwar message.

***The Sum of All Fears* (2002).** Phil Alden Robinson adapted the Tom Clancy novel about CIA agent Jack Ryan (Ben Affleck), who fails to prevent a nuclear terrorist attack on the United States. This time the villains improbably are Nazis plotting to manipulate the new, largely unknown president of Russia into launching a nuclear attack on the United States, hoping to provoke a devastating counterattack. Once Russia and the United States are destroyed, the neo-Nazis will be able to unify Europe and rule the world. The most frightening part of this film is not the Nazi villains but the scene in which the terrorists detonate a nuclear bomb at the Super Bowl in Baltimore. The U.S. president (James Cromwell) and his security chief (Morgan Freeman) escape the blast in a helicopter, and Ryan is left to solve the crime and neutralize the perpetrators, which he ultimately does.

***Taxi Driver* (1976).** Martin Scorsese's neo-noir features Travis Bickel (Robert De Niro), a Vietnam War veteran insomniac who drives taxis for long hours, occasionally driving "off the meter" as his own agent. He suffers from a stress-related psychosis that prompts him to violence. First he thinks about assassinating a political candidate, then kills a pimp named Sport (Harvey Keitel) because he believes Sport is keeping a young woman in white slavery as a prostitute. Scorsese's dystopic depictions of characters exploding into violence speaks to some of the indirect costs of the Vietnam War.

***The Terminator* (1984).** James Cameron's futuristic sci-fi adventure film stars Arnold Schwarzenegger as the Terminator, a superhuman android or "cyborg" from the future on a terrorist mission to assassinate a seemingly innocent girl to prevent a future event from occurring. The Terminator, with his advanced weaponry, represents a sophisticated war machine, while the armed forces arrayed against him make *The Terminator* a disguised combat film.

***Terminator 2: Judgment Day* (1991).** James Cameron's sequel to his earlier film also stars Arnold Schwarzenegger, but this time the Terminator is benign. Instead of an attempt to assassinate a young woman, his mission is to protect a woman from a rival cyborg bent on her assassination. Despite this transformation from villain to hero, Cameron's film, like the earlier version, features much violent conflict between superhuman war machines. It too is a thinly disguised combat film.

***Terminator 3: Rise of the Machines* (2003).** Jonathan Mostrow directed the second sequel to the 1984 blockbuster. This one also features Arnold Schwarzenegger as a cyborg pitted against other cyborgs, including a sleek, sexy female played by Kristianna Loken. The clashes of the increasingly sophisticated killing machines evoke both the substance and the spirit of conventional combat films.

***The Thin Red Line* (1998).** Terrence Malick's brilliant, idiosyncratic portrait of the Battle of Guadalcanal earned him few accolades. This was supposed to be Malick's new *Days of Heaven* (1974), which had proved a box-office disaster despite wide critical acclaim. However, Malick's combat film, a war-is-hell epic modeled in part on films like *Pork Chop Hill* and *Hamburger Hill*, seems a disjointed series of episodes featuring strong actors (Sean Penn, John Cusack, and Woody Harrelson among them). He no doubt intended a strong antiwar statement, but the film contains enough battlefield excitement to undermine much of that message.

***Thirty Seconds over Tokyo* (1944).** Mervyn Leroy cast Van Johnson and Robert Walker as bomber pilots involved in a secret mission to bomb Tokyo. Spencer Tracy plays General James Doolittle, commander and mastermind of the famous raid. This film is a perfect example of "good war" motifs glorifying U.S. military victories. In reality the Doolittle raid contributed little to the war effort.

***Three Kings* (1999).** David O. Russell's satiric Gulf War film stars George Clooney as Special Ops Captain Archie Gates. He, along with three other Gulf War enlisted men (Mark Wahlberg, Ice Cube, Spike Jonze), embarks on an adventurous trek across Iraq in search of stolen Kuwaiti gold bullion. Along the way they become involved with refugees who are the target of troops loyal to Saddam Hussein. The renegade U.S. troops end up saving the refugees' lives. This fantasy may help to assuage ill feelings about U.S. military forces pulling out and leaving Iraqi civilians defenseless at the close of the Gulf War.

***Topaz* (1969).** Alfred Hitchcock's cold war thriller is reminiscent of the Cuban missile crisis. Hitchcock cast John Forsythe as Michael Nordstrom, an American intelligence agent stationed in Copenhagen, who assists Boris Kusenov (Per-Axel Arosenius), a Russian double agent, to defect to the United States. French Embassy official André Devereaux (Frederick Stafford) is dispatched to Cuba to uncover evidence of nuclear weapons. The plot twists leave this film less than realistic, and it lacks Hitchcock's usual wit and genius.

***Top Gun* (1986).** Tony Scott cast Tom Cruise as a young naval pilot in training at the elite "Top Gun" air base in San Diego in this classic cinematic embrace of U.S. militarism. There he falls in love with one of his instructors, played by Kelly McGillis. Scott embellished his film with video-game-like qualities (as in the dogfight scenes) and focused too much attention on sexy shots and dialogue and not enough on character and plot development.

***Tora! Tora! Tora!* (1970).** Richard Fleischer served as lead director for this docudrama of the Japanese attack on Pearl Harbor; he included the work of two Japanese directors, Toshio Masuda and Kinji Fukasaku, in the ensemble. Perhaps for that reason he was criticized for what some observers believed was an overly positive treatment of the

Japanese role in the attack. Fleisher's film lays much of the blame for the stunning lack of readiness of U.S. forces on Lieutenant General Walter Short (Jason Robards Jr.), a favorite choice for scapegoat. Superb aerial photography renders the battle believable and realistic, perhaps even enough to inspire the sympathies of American audiences for the Japanese. Tatsuya Mihashi plays Commander Genda; other Japanese cast members also deliver skillful renditions. This film, though slow moving in many sections, is still one of the best depictions of the December 7 attack and stands the test of time much better than Michael Bay's *Pearl Harbor*.

***Torn Curtain* (1966).** Alfred Hitchcock's cold war movie stars Paul Newman as American astrophysicist Michael Armstrong, who journeys to East Germany seeking technical assistance on his top-secret antimissile system. As a cover, he pretends to defect to the East. He is pursued by his girlfriend, fellow astrophysicist Sarah Sherman (Julie Andrews). After Armstrong learns the missile secrets, the two go undercover and elude capture with the help of local CIA operatives. This film received a lukewarm reception upon release, but critics now admire it much more than they did at the time. It is an excellent example of a cold war film.

***True Lies* (1994).** James Cameron cast Arnold Schwarzenegger in a superman-like role as a master sleuth working for a top-secret government intelligence agency. His wife, played by Jamie Lee Curtis, believes the cover story that he is a nerdy computer sales-man completely lacking in machismo. Schwarzenegger's real occupation provides for a multitude of thrilling stunts and hand-to-hand combat, in which he displays superhu-man skills. His home life, on the other hand, resembles Clark Kent's and Lois Lane's relationship. In the end, the wife learns the truth, but by that time the audience has enjoyed an action-adventure combat film exuding more than a faint trace of militarism.

***Twelve O'Clock High* (1949).** Henry King crafted this classic World War II flier film, one of the most memorable of the period. Gregory Peck stars as air force general Savage. Savage shapes up a beleaguered flight group that has been suffering catastroph-ic losses during "precision" daylight bombing runs over Germany, after concluding that Colonel Davenport (Gary Merrill), the group leader, "overidentifies" with the pilots under his command. Although King's film now appears rather dated, the acting in it is superb, and it is well worth viewing as an intermediate stage between the military glorification of *Sands of Iwo Jima* and the more dystopic images of films like *The Best Years of Their Lives*.

***U-571* (2000).** Jonathan Mostow rewrites history in this World War II drama set in the Atlantic in which an American submarine crew unexpectedly encounters an abandoned German U-boat. On board is a transmitter of the top-secret Enigma Code, which gar-bled German radio transmission and rendered it unintelligible to Allied intelligence. Eventually, the crew masters the workings of the U-boat and retrieves the code machine, thereby cracking the German secret code. The only problem is that, historically, British intelligence agents, not American seamen, cracked the Enigma Code. In effect, Mostow steals from the British and falsely bestows accolades on the United States.

***Ulzana's Raid*** **(1972).** Robert Aldrich cast Burt Lancaster as a gritty, direct Indian scout assigned to a green lieutenant (Bruce Davison) in pursuit of a rogue Apache chief, Ulzana (Joaquin Martinez). The clash between whites and Apaches and the tensions between the experienced scout and the green officer qualify this film as a combat Western.

***Uncommon Valor*** **(1983).** Ted Kotcheff cast Gene Hackman as a retired army officer who assembles a band of marginalized men to rescue his son from a Vietnamese prison. This action-adventure film features jungle combat scenes and several plot twists. It turns out that the officer's son is being held not in Vietnam but in Laos. Kotcheff's film lays the blame for the confusion over prisoners of war at the feet of the U.S. government.

***Under Siege*** **(1992).** Andrew Davis cast Stephen Seagal as a Special Ops agent assigned as a cook aboard a huge battleship. Terrorists seize the ship and attempt to steal its cargo of nuclear arms, but Seagal picks them off one by one, with the help of one of the crew. This film has been described as *Die Hard* at sea.

***Under Siege 2: Dark Territory*** **(1995).** Geoff Murphy directed the sequel to *Under Siege,* also starring Stephen Seagal. In this terrorist thriller villains commandeer a cross-country train and seize a secret weapon, a satellite particle beam that can destroy warships, high-rise buildings, and even aircraft in flight. The villains did not realize, however, that Casey the cook is also a highly trained Special Ops agent, who thwarts their plot (with the help of a young, frightened porter). Like its predecessor, *Under Siege 2* is a contrived, stylized, almost surrealistic thriller with a simplistic plot.

***Union Pacific*** **(1939).** Cecil B. DeMille directed this classic Western chronicling the struggle to create the first transcontinental railroad. At one point Indian warriors attack the train, only to be driven away by the U.S. Cavalry, qualifying it as a combat Western featuring armed conflict between Indians and cavalry.

***Wag the Dog*** **(1997).** Barry Levinson's political drama satirizes the sexual misdeeds of a Bill Clinton–style U.S. president as well as the questionable ethics of media moguls. The film stars Robert De Niro as Conrad Brean, a manipulative, cynical political spin master, and Dustin Hoffman as Stanley Motss, an over-the-top Hollywood producer. They conspire to launch a phony media "war" with Albania to distract the public from rumors of sexual misconduct by the president. Today, Levinson's satire of the Clinton administration seems almost trivial in light of subsequent events.

***War of the Worlds*** **(2005).** Steven Spielberg's quasi-combat film is also a sci-fi feature, an adaptation of H. G. Wells's 1898 novel about a Martian invasion, transferred from nineteenth-century England to twenty-first-century America. His aliens are flat characters who seem to exist only for killing and conquest, reminiscent of the pod people of *Invasion of the Body Snatchers* and the reptilians who attack humans in *Alien* and *Aliens.* Unfortunately, even a director with Spielberg's talents appears reluctant to create complex, fully developed extraterrestrials.

***What Price Glory*** **(1926).** Raoul Walsh directed this classic silent film set during World War I, depicting a rivalry between Captain Flagg (Victor McLaglen) and

Sergeant Quirt (Edmund Lowe) over the affections of the beautiful Charmaine (Dolores Del Rio). It vacillates between depicting war as glorious and, to a lesser degree, as a hellish nightmare.

***The Wild Bunch*** **(1969).** Sam Peckinpah directed this classic revisionist Western featuring a gang of outlaws, the Wild Bunch, headed by Pike Bishop (William Holden). The gang robs a train carrying explosives and attempts to sell the explosives to Pancho Villa and his Mexican revolutionaries. Before they do so, however, they encounter a large contingent of Mexican soldiers. The two sides engage in a pitched battle, with the results a foregone conclusion because of the overwhelming superiority in numbers of the Mexican forces. Although this film is classified formally as a Western, it possesses all of the elements of a combat film.

***Windtalkers*** **(2002).** John Woo's World War II tale of Navajo "code talkers" who translated radio messages into the Navajo language to confuse the Japanese becomes instead a confusing psychological drama surrounding, not the Navajos, but a white soldier played by Nicolas Cage, who is assigned to protect the Navajos. Woo's decision to relegate the Navajos to the background and to focus instead on Cage's character appears to be a mistake, since the film seems to lose its sense of purpose once Cage takes over.

***Wings*** **(1927).** William Wellman's World War I dogfight epic stars Clara Bow as Mary Preston, a small-town girl who, in 1917, inspires the love of two local youths, played by Charles "Buddy" Rodgers and Richard Arlen. After war breaks out, the two go to flight school and become best friends. This familiar plot can be found in Howard Hawks's *Dawn Patrol,* Michael Bay's *Pearl Harbor*, and several other films.

***XXX*** **(2002).** Rob Cohen's action thriller stars Vin Diesel as a sports maniac recruited by an NSA agent (Samuel L. Jackson) to work undercover in Prague to monitor a rogue Russian. Once there, the agent engages in improbable stunts on foot, on a motorcycle, and on virtually every other means of transportation to prevail over a shadowy, improbable army. This film is long on stunts and short on substance and entertainment.

# Index

# About the Authors

**CARL BOGGS** is the author of numerous books in the fields of contemporary social and political theory, European politics, American politics, U.S. foreign and military policy, and film studies, including *The Impasse of European Communism* (1982), *The Two Revolutions: Gramsci and the Dilemmas of Western Marxism* (1984), *Social Movements and Political Power* (1986), *Intellectuals and the Crisis of Modernity* (1993), *The Socialist Tradition* (1996), *The End of Politics: Corporate Power and the Decline of the Public Sphere* (2000), *Imperial Delusions: American Militarism and Endless War* (2005). With Tom Pollard, he authored *A World in Chaos: Social Crisis and the Rise of Postmodern Cinema* (2003). He edited an anthology, *Masters of War: Militarism and Blowback in an Era of American Empire* (2003). He is on the editorial board of several journals, including *Theory and Society* (where he is book-review editor) and *New Political Science*. For two years (1999–2000) he was chair of the Caucus for a New Political Science, a section within the American Political Science Association. He has written more than two hundred articles along with scores of book and film reviews, has had three radio programs at KPFK in Los Angeles, and was a political columnist for the *L.A. Village View* during the 1990s. After receiving his PhD in political science at the University of California, Berkeley, he taught at Washington University in St. Louis, the University of California, Los Angeles; the University of Southern California; the University of California, Irvine; and Carleton University in Ottawa. For the past eighteen years he has been professor of social sciences at National University in Los Angeles and more recently has been an adjunct professor at Antioch University in Los Angeles.

**TOM POLLARD** is currently professor of social sciences at National University in San Jose, having taught in higher education for thirty years after receiving his PhD in American studies at the University of Kansas. His most recent book (coauthored with Carl Boggs) is *A World in Chaos: Social Crisis and the Rise of Postmodern Cinema* (2003). He has published more than twenty articles, essays, and reviews in several academic journals, most of them in the area of film and popular culture. He has been involved for more than ten years in the making of documentary films, the most recent being a work that chronicles the sixtieth anniversary of World War II in the Battle of Peleliu, titled *Once We Were Enemies*. His most recent documentary is *Crystal Fear / Crystal Clear*, a collaborative work involving Canadian filmmakers. His documentaries have appeared on BBC, Discovery Channel, the Life Network, the Canadian Broadcasting System, and various PBS channels. His other documentaries include *Paradise Bent: Boys Will Be Girls in Samoa*, *The Maya Pompeii*, and *Weird Homes of North America*, all shown at major film festivals worldwide.